Understanding Chess Move by Move

John Nunn

First published in the UK by Gambit Publications Ltd 2001

ISBN-13: 978-1-901983-41-8
ISBN-10: 1-901983-41-2

DISTRIBUTION:
Worldwide (except USA): Central Books Ltd, 99 Wallis Rd, London E9 5LN, England.
Tel +44 (0)20 8986 4854 Fax +44 (0)20 8533 5821. E-mail: orders@Centralbooks.com

Gambit Publications Ltd, 99 Wallis Rd, London E9 5LN, England.
E-mail: info@gambitbooks.com
Website (regularly updated): www.gambitbooks.com

Edited by Graham Burgess
Typeset by John Nunn
Printed in Great Britain by The Cromwell Press, Trowbridge, Wilts.

10 9 8 7

Gambit Publications Ltd
Managing Director: GM Murray Chandler
Chess Director: GM John Nunn
Editorial Director: FM Graham Burgess
German Editor: WFM Petra Nunn
Webmaster: Dr Helen Milligan WFM

Contents

3 Endgame Themes   215

Symbols

+	check
++	double check
#	checkmate
!!	brilliant move
!	good move
!?	interesting move
?!	dubious move
?	bad move
??	blunder
1-0	the game ends in a win for White
½-½	the game ends in a draw
0-1	the game ends in a win for Black

Introduction

The basic intention of this book is to explain some of the most important chess themes in a modern context. The most significant word in this description is 'modern'. There are plenty of other general chess books, but in my view many of these have failed to keep pace with developments in the game. Chess knowledge and understanding have increased enormously in the past half-century, but the textbooks have, by and large, not kept pace with the flow of new ideas. Chess at the start of the 21st century is far more dynamic than the chess of the past, and many of the old established principles are now recognized to be at best half-truths.

Here are a few examples of this new approach. Everybody knows that you shouldn't move the same piece twice in the opening, should castle early and should then bring your rooks to the central files. Everybody, that is, except possibly Khalifman (1999-2000 FIDE World Champion) and Kasparov (currently ranked No. 1 in the world). In Game 13 Khalifman, playing Black, sacrifices his queen as early as move 15 and wins the game without ever moving his king, king's bishop or king's rook. His pieces were able to leap straight into the attack from their original squares without the usual stepping-stone of 'development'. In Game 20, Kasparov moves his knights seven times in the first thirteen moves, develops his queen's rook to a4 and b4, and only castles on move 25. Such games are impossible to explain using the time-honoured general principles formulated in many textbooks. Of course, the old rules are not totally invalid – there are still more games in which rooks are developed centrally than to a4 and b4 – but it is clear that the number of exceptions is much greater than formerly thought.

The modern outlook on the game is far more flexible than that which persisted for the bulk of the 20th century. General principles are seen to have a place, but their limitations are now more clearly recognized. Much greater emphasis is placed on the concrete requirements of a given position than on obeying abstract principles. If a leading grandmaster of today thinks that the position requires a particular plan, he will embark on it even if in doing so he flouts much of the dogma of the past.

Unfortunately, these new dynamic ideas have, by and large, not found their way into textbooks. Instead, one finds treatments that differ little from those by Euwe in the 1950s. Euwe was an influential writer of his day, and his books were excellent summaries of chess knowledge as it stood at that time, but chess has moved on since then. Just as one would not like to submit to the ministrations of a surgeon using a 50-year-old instruction manual, those relying on outdated ideas will not perform as well as those who have grasped the new developments in chess.

In this book, I hope to explain this new attitude to chess in a way that is comprehensible to a wide audience. To this end I have chosen thirty key themes and found one game to illustrate each theme.

When writing a general book such as this, the author has two options. He can either choose excerpts from a large number of games, or he can give a smaller number of complete games. Each method has advantages and disadvantages. The use of excerpts means that a wider range can be covered, but it cannot show how each theme fits into the overall context of a game. In view of the wide-ranging nature of this book, I decided on the use of complete games. Even though some parts of each game are not strictly relevant to the intended theme, they can be used to reinforce ideas mentioned in other parts of the book.

The selection of games was based on the following main criteria:
1) They should be clear demonstrations of the intended theme;
2) They should be top-level, evenly matched struggles;
3) They should preferably be recent;
4) They should be as sound as possible.

Criterion 1 is clear enough, but perhaps some comments are appropriate regarding Criterion 2. It is quite easy to find a one-sided game illustrating a particular theme, but this can be deceptive. There are many games, often between players of disparate strength, in which the loser puts up no real resistance and the winner can do very much as he pleases. Of course, a clear-cut demonstration has its advantages, but it can also create a false impression. If one chooses a particular theme, say the weakness of the isolated d-pawn, and then gives several examples in which the hapless owner of the pawn is roundly crushed, then the reader may easily draw the conclusion that such positions are virtually lost. Then he gets such a position in one of his own games. Suddenly things are not as easy as he thought; his opponent finds all sorts of counter-chances and annoying tactical threats, and suddenly the game goes downhill and he loses. Thus it is important to present each theme in a balanced way, and a good way to do this is to choose hard-fought games between strong grandmasters, in which both sides skilfully try to exploit the assets of their position. Criterion 3 is also clear, given the book's intention to present a modern perspective; 27 of the 30 games in this book were played in or after 1990. Criterion 4 is desirable but, as we shall see, the target of soundness is not so easy to achieve.

The selection and annotation of these games proved to be a time-consuming task. There are many people who believe that the use of computers makes it easy to write a chess book – you just turn on the machine, it checks all the analysis, and you have a book with hardly more effort than pressing a few keys. Nothing could be further from the truth. As the power of computers grows, they become more and more adept at finding holes in games formerly thought to be sound. My new 950 MHz machine is a monster in this respect, and after it had torn many of my intended games to analytical shreds I had to go back to my database to look for further examples, only to have the process repeated.

Readers may be quite surprised to see the number of question marks that adorn the games in this book. Surely, you might think, with just thirty games to select, it should have been easy to find some sound games. However, I can assure you that it was not. I feel that with the computing power available today, it is possible to find fault with virtually any complex, hard-fought game (and even more so with annotations published in magazines or *Informator*). Whether one finds this disturbing depends on one's attitude to the game. I have never felt that my play was anywhere near completely accurate, so I personally don't find these revelations distressing. However, some may find it hard to admit that chess as played by human beings is less accurate than previously thought.

My annotations strongly emphasize understanding and general principles, and readers will find a higher percentage of words than in my previous books. Despite this, there are many positions that can only be understood in terms of concrete variations. If the evaluation of the position depends on a tactical finesse eight moves deep, then it is misleading to pretend that the position can be assessed using general principles. However, I have made an effort only to descend into concrete variations where it is really necessary. The vast majority of moves have a comment of some sort. Exceptions are opening moves that are repeated from earlier games, forced moves such as recaptures and some moves at the end of the game when the struggle has already been decided.

I would like to acknowledge the influence that John Watson's book *Secrets of Modern Chess Strategy* (Gambit Publications, 1998) has had on me. While there are many differences between his book and mine, both in terms of content and approach, the core philosophy is somewhat similar.

I hope that readers will find these games both instructive and entertaining, and that by the end of the book they will have gained a greater insight into contemporary chess thinking.

John Nunn
Chertsey, September 2000

1 Opening Themes

I will start, as is only natural, with the opening. There are a huge number of books dealing with the details of this or that opening, but here I am only concerned with the general principles governing opening play. Each player has three main objectives in the opening:

1) To develop the pieces;
2) To safeguard the king (usually by castling);
3) To exert control over the centre.

The first of these is critical. Pieces sitting on their original squares are not really taking part in the battle. They need to be brought out as quickly as possible, so time is of the essence. Normally the minor pieces are developed first, castling takes place, and then the rooks can be brought into play. However, one of the themes of this book is that all these basic principles have many exceptions, and you have to take the specifics of each position into account. We shall see several games in which this standard pattern of development does not occur, because the particular position demands a different plan. However, a couple of general principles are valid in the majority of cases:

a) Don't make repeated moves with the same piece in the opening. It is better to spend three moves developing three different pieces than to move the same piece three times. There are both obvious and subtle exceptions to this. An obvious exception is if a piece is attacked and you have to move it again to avoid losing it. More subtle exceptions arise when the repeated moves of the same piece have in mind a concrete aim that outweighs the time lost. Game 20 is an example, with White moving his knights around to induce a weakness in the enemy pawn-structure.

b) Don't develop pieces to squares where they can be chased away by the opponent with gain of time. This applies especially to early queen development.

Questions of development are dealt with in Game 1.

The king is quite exposed in the centre of the board. One or more of the central pawns will normally be advanced during the opening in order to let the pieces out and this removes some or all of the pawn-cover in front of the king. Thus in most cases the king will need to be castled to one side or the other, where there are still unmoved pawns, in order to be reasonably safe. Early castling is desirable, not only for reasons of king safety, but also because it allows the rooks to come into play more easily.

Once again, there are exceptions and we shall see some later in the book. If the opponent is not in any position to exploit the king in the centre, then castling can be delayed while some other, more important, operation takes place. However, one should *always* take great care when leaving the king uncastled and should only do so after careful consideration of the risks.

In the vast majority of cases, however, early castling does take place. The dangers of leaving the king in the centre are discussed in Game 2.

The first two of the three main objectives in the opening can usually be achieved without much interference from the opponent. However, this is not the case with central control because both sides are battling for the same part of the board. Thus, while it is desirable to control the centre, one is unlikely to achieve anything more than partial control.

The question of central control is quite a complex one because there are various methods of trying to achieve it. The most common is to occupy the centre with pawns. However, there are dangers with this. Each tempo spent moving a pawn is a tempo not spent developing a piece, so if you have played c4, d4, e4 and f4 you are likely to fall behind in piece development. A large pawn-centre insufficiently supported by pieces is a rickety structure that is likely to collapse at the opponent's first prod. Thus a pawn-centre well supported by pieces is desirable, whereas one that is over-extended and vulnerable is not. The dividing line between these two cases is often quite fine, and may depend on tactical nuances specific to the given position. In Game 3 we examine a well-constructed and formidable pawn-centre, while in Game 4 we see one that is weak and vulnerable.

I cannot leave the subject of opening play without discussing gambits. The mere mention of the word brings to mind those classic 19th century games played with the Evans Gambit and the King's Gambit. However, defensive technique has improved a great deal since then and the wild sacrificial attacks that characterized mid-19th century chess would not succeed in today's world. The Evans Gambit has more or less disappeared, and while the King's Gambit is still played from time to time, today's handling has a distinctly positional flavour. Despite this, gambit play is alive and well, but today's gambits are very different from those of 150 years ago. They tend to be positionally oriented and often aim more for long-term compensation than for a quick attack. Contemporary attitudes to gambit play are considered in Game 5.

Get the Pieces Out!

One of the main objectives in the opening is to bring the pieces into play. In the initial position, all the pieces are on the back rank, far from contact with the enemy. The knights, being short-range pieces, are particularly ineffective and one of the main priorities is to advance them into better positions. Early piece development is so crucial that failure to handle it effectively can result in the battle being lost while most of the army is still in bed. This is Black's fate in the following game. All the decisive action takes place while his queenside pieces stand unmoved and unable to participate in the struggle.

Game 1

A. Chernin – J. van der Wiel

European Clubs Cup, Slough 1997

English Opening

1 ♘f3

Many decades ago, virtually all games started with 1 e4 or 1 d4. Today, most games still start with one of these two moves, but the contemporary attitude to opening play is more flexible and open-minded. One often sees 1 c4 and 1 ♘f3, and occasionally other moves such as 1 b3 and 1 g3.

The advantage of 1 ♘f3 is its flexibility. White retains various options, and waits to see Black's reply before deciding the type of structure to adopt. A later c4 may lead to the English Opening (as in this game), while a later d4 may transpose into a Queen's Pawn opening. If Black plays 1...c5, White might even transpose into a Sicilian by 2 e4.

1 ... d6

White's first move prevented Black from playing 1...e5, so if Black wants to occupy e5 with a pawn, then he must prepare it. It is also perfectly reasonable to play 1...d5 or 1...c5, while 1...♘f6 would show that Black, too, can aim for flexibility.

2 g3

The development of a bishop at g2 (or the corresponding squares b2, b7 and g7) is called a *fianchetto*. At one time, this type of bishop development was frowned upon, but these days it is commonplace in a wide range of openings. While the fianchetto is not always appropriate, it has the advantage of moving the bishop to one of the longest diagonals on the board, where it may later exert a great deal of influence. The disadvantages are that it takes two moves to get the bishop out, and if the bishop is later exchanged, the kingside pawn-structure will have been weakened by the advance g3.

2 ... e5

This is the natural follow-up to Black's previous move. Although he now has a pawn in the centre while White does not, this does not mean that Black has won the battle for control of the centre.

3   ♗g2

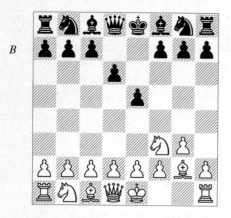

White's bishop on g2 will exert pressure on the light squares e4 and d5, and this enables White to conduct the central struggle on at least equal terms.

3   ...   f5

Black's third pawn move in a row. Because piece development is so important, it is risky to play too many pawn moves right at the start of the game – the more pawn moves you play, the fewer moves are available for developing pieces. A few pawn moves are essential, as otherwise only the knights could be developed, but it can be risky to play extra pawn moves that are not strictly necessary. A good rule of thumb is that you should not make more than three pawn moves in the first eight moves. As with all chess principles, there will inevitably be many exceptions, but if you violate a principle such as this, you should at least be clear in your mind exactly why you are violating it. Here Black's move is not a mistake; the pawn on f5 improves Black's central influence and, by attacking e4, helps to combat White's plan to dominate the central light squares.

4   c4

White is not only bringing his pieces out, but he is also doing so with a concrete plan in mind: to control the central light squares, especially d5, and to exert pressure against Black's queenside with the bishop on g2. His pawns and pieces must cooperate in executing this plan. The text-move stakes a claim to the d5-square; White will follow up with ♘c3 to increase his control. Note that it would have been wrong to play 4 ♘c3 first, as this would block the c-pawn and prevent c4.

4   ...   ♘f6

This natural move develops a piece and contests White's control of d5.

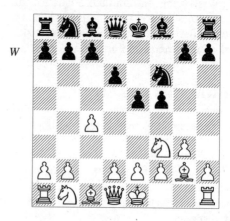

5   b4!?

This is an ambitious and slightly provocative move. It fits it with White's plan of exerting pressure against Black's queenside, because it helps to gain space on that part of the board, but was it really more important to do this than to develop a piece? Most players have thought otherwise, since 5 ♘c3 is the most common move in the diagram position, but Chernin's idea has a good deal of logic. After 5 ♘c3 ♘c6, White would at some stage like to play b4, but now this requires further preparation by a3 or ♖b1. By playing b4 at once, White may be able to manage without one of these preparatory moves and thereby save a tempo. In addition, a psychological element was probably involved; Van der Wiel is a direct attacking player and Chernin may have guessed that Black would try to 'refute' White's early pawn advance and thereby indulge in premature aggression.

5   ...   e4?!

Van der Wiel is duly provoked and lunges forward in the centre. Such central advances have pros and cons. Here Black gains space and the e4-pawn blocks out the bishop on g2; the drawback is that the white bishop may be released by a later d3, and that the a1-h8 diagonal is weakened, which White can easily exploit by developing his other bishop to b2. My view is that this last factor outweighs the others. Moreover, to play 5...e4 is inconsistent in that Black has spent two moves occupying e5 (...d6 and ...e5) and to give this up just to give White's knight a harmless prod seems a poor bargain. Black should have completed his kingside development by either 5...♗e7 or 5...g6 and 6...♗g7, followed by castling.

6 ♘d4 d5

This active move is the idea behind the previous advance, but it is already Black's fifth pawn move, so the warning lights should have been flashing. Black could have developed his kingside by 6...c5 7 bxc5 dxc5 8 ♘b3 ♗d6 9 ♘c3 0-0, although after 10 0-0 ♘c6 11 d3 Black cannot maintain his pawn on e4 and so faces the problem of the activity of the g2-bishop, while his own light-squared bishop is restricted by the f5-pawn.

7 cxd5 ♘xd5

After 7...♕xd5, White has a choice of promising lines. The simple 8 ♘c2 ♗d6 9 ♘c3 ♕f7 10 0-0 0-0 11 d3 again activates the g2-bishop, while the more complicated 8 ♗b2 ♗xb4 9 ♕a4+ ♗d7 10 ♕xb4 c5 11 ♘c3! cxb4 12 ♘xd5 ♘xd5 13 f3 gives White a very promising ending. Black cannot keep his extra pawn and after 13...♘f6 14 fxe4 fxe4 (14...♘xe4 15 g4 is very awkward) 15 ♘c2 ♗c6 16 ♗xf6 gxf6 17 ♘xb4, for example, Black's pawn-structure is seriously inferior.

8 b5

Now White had to do something about the doubly attacked b-pawn; this advance makes it harder for Black to develop the b8-knight.

8 ... ♘f4

Black goes in for a little piece of tactics that gives White doubled f-pawns. As we shall see, this does not help Black, but there was nothing better; for example, 8...♗c5 9 ♗b2 ♕f6 10 e3 ♘b4 11 0-0 ♘d3 (this looks good, but without any supporting pieces, the knight is not doing much on d3) 12 ♗c3 0-0 13 f3! exf3 14 ♗xf3 and Black is in trouble. His queen and d3-knight are exposed to attack, and while Black is rescuing these White will amass a large lead in development.

9 gxf4

Forced.

9 ... ♕xd4
10 ♘c3

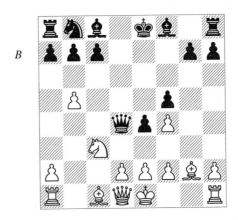

B

White meets the attack on his rook with a useful developing move.

10 ... ♗c5?

Black threatens mate in one, but White can meet this with gain of tempo, whereupon the bishop proves to be tactically vulnerable on c5 (after a later ♖c1 and ♕c2). 10...♘d7 would have been a better chance, heading for b6. This would prevent the ♗f1-c4 manoeuvre which is so important in the game.

11 e3

White notices.

11 ... ♕c4?!

This is designed to prevent castling, but once again the queen is exposed and will have to move again after a later ♖c1. It is usually unwise to play aggressively with the queen early on, because the queen is subject to the attack of the enemy's lesser pieces, and can easily be chased around with loss of time. Another consequence of the 'rapid development' principle is that one should not repeatedly move the same piece in the opening, thereby losing time for the development of the remaining pieces. In eleven moves, Black has so far played a bishop move, five pawn moves, three queen moves and two knight moves; moreover, this knight has now vanished from the board, so Black did not really obtain any benefit from these two moves. In other words, Black has obtained very little in terms of development for his eleven moves and is now in serious trouble. Whereas most of Black's pieces are on their original squares, White has two pieces out and the others can move directly to active squares (by ♖c1 and ♕c2 or ♕b3), gaining tempi in the process. Black's central pawn advance has gained some space, but at the cost of leaving a huge vacuum behind; the a1-h8 and a2-g8 diagonals are especially weak. White, it is true, has doubled pawns, but if anything this helps him. The assessment of doubled pawns depends very much on the position. Sometimes they can be a serious weakness; in other cases they can be an asset. In this position the following factors operate in White's favour:

1) The f4-pawn actually serves to increase White's central control by covering e5. This is especially relevant as White is set to dominate the a1-h8 diagonal. Doubled pawns resulting from a capture towards the centre are usually much better than doubled pawns resulting from a capture away from the centre – the former increase central control, whereas the latter decrease it.

2) The creation of the doubled pawn has opened the g-file. Is this open file useful? Definitely, yes! After White plays ♖g1, the rook will work in tandem with the dark-squared bishop on b2 to exert terrible pressure against g7. In view of Black's unmoved queenside, castling there is a distant dream, so Black will probably castle kingside, but then the pressure on g7 will be especially dangerous. Of course, playing ♖g1 means that White's king will stay in the centre. Haven't I said that king safety is one of the objects of opening play? Doesn't this mean that White has sinned just as much as Black? Not at all. White's play in this game is a good example of the way old principles are flexibly interpreted in contemporary practice. White's centralized king would only be a weakness if Black could somehow mount an attack against it. However, the game will be speedily decided by White's lead in development and ferocious piece activity. Black is never in a position to mount any kind of attack – it is all downhill from now on.

Black could have resisted slightly more by 11...♕d6, but after 12 ♗b2 0-0 13 ♖g1 his position is unenviable.

12   ♗b2

White's bishop occupies the weakened diagonal.

12   ...   0-0

It is too late for 12...♘d7, as 13 ♖c1 is very strong; for example, 13...0-0 14 ♘a4! ♕d5 (14...♕xb5 15 ♗f1 ♕c6 16 ♖g1 and 14...♕b4 15 a3 ♕xb5 16 ♗f1 are also hopeless for Black) 15 ♗f1 (threatening 16 ♗c4) 15...♔h8 16 ♖g1 and Black cannot defend g7 without allowing ♗c4 or leaving c5 *en prise*.

13   ♖g1!

The pressure against g7 is especially dangerous in that White can uncover the rook with gain of tempo by playing ♗f1.

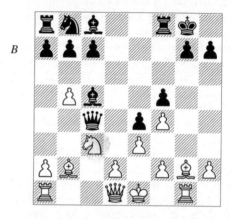

B

13   ...   ♖f7

Attempting to defend g7, but the line-up of pieces on the a2-g8 diagonal can be exploited by the manoeuvre ♗f1-c4. Two other lines show how White might break through sacrificially:

1) 13...♕f7 14 ♗xe4! fxe4 15 ♘xe4 ♗e7 16 ♕b3! ♔h8 (16...♕xb3 loses to 17 ♖xg7+ ♔h8 18 axb3) 17 ♗xg7+ ♕xg7 18 ♖xg7 ♔xg7 19 ♔e2, followed by ♖g1+, and Black's king has no chance with most of his pieces still at home.

2) 13...♘d7 14 ♗f1 ♕f7 15 ♘xe4! fxe4 16 ♗c4! ♕xc4 17 ♖xg7+ ♔h8 18 ♖xh7+ ♔xh7 19 ♕h5+ ♔g8 20 ♕g6#.

14   ♖c1!

White conducts the attack accurately. The lurking threat against the insecure c5-bishop restricts Black's options. By contrast, 14 ♗f1 would allow Black to limp on by 14...♕e6 15 ♕a4 ♕d6.

14   ...   ♕b4

Or 14...♗f8 (14...♕e6 loses after 15 ♘xe4 fxe4 16 ♖xc5) 15 ♘xe4 ♕xb5 16 ♘g5 ♖d7 (16...♕xb2 17 ♗d5) 17 ♗e5, and Black cannot meet the threat of 18 ♗f1 and 19 ♗c4+, coupled with ♕h5 if necessary.

15   ♕c2

White defends the attacked bishop with gain of tempo, as Black must meet the threat to win a piece by 16 ♘d5 ♕xb5 17 ♗f1, followed by 18 ♕xc5.

15   ...   ♗d6

After 15...♗b6, the simplest win is by 16 ♘d5 (16 ♘xe4 fxe4 17 ♗xe4 is also very good) 16...♕d6 17 ♗f1 ♔h8 (17...♗e6 loses to 18 ♘f6+ ♔h8 19 ♘e8) 18 ♗c4 ♗e6 19 ♗xg7+ ♖xg7 20 ♕b2 ♕f8 21 ♘xb6 axb6 22 ♗xe6 with a comical situation in which Black can hardly move a piece.

16   ♘d5!

The final attack begins.

16   ...   ♕xb5

16...♕a5 17 ♗f1 is also decisive.

17   ♘f6+

The immediate 17 ♗f1 is also very good.

17   ...   ♔h8

Forced.

18   ♗f1

This long-awaited blow is decisive. After ♗c4, the two bishops, operating against Black's king on parallel diagonals, will prove too much.

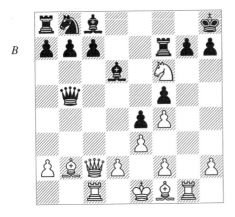

18   ...   ♕xb2

In desperation, Black surrenders his queen. There is nothing better; for example, 18...♕c6 19 ♕d1 ♕b6 20 ♕h5, 18...♕b6 (18...♕b4 19 ♗c4 is the same) 19 ♗c4 ♖e7 20 ♘d5 (or 20 ♘h5), or 18...♕a5 19 ♕b3, with even greater material loss in every case.

19   ♕xb2   ♖xf6

Black has two minor pieces and a pawn in return for the queen, which might allow him to prolong the game for a while, except for one

thing: he is still catastrophically behind in development.

20   ♕xf6!

White finds the simplest solution to the technical task by liquidating to an ending in which he is the exchange up for nothing.

20   ...   gxf6

21   ♗c4

Now Black must surrender a piece.

21   ...   ♗e6

After 21...h6 22 ♖g8+ ♔h7 23 ♖xc8 Black is not only the exchange down, but also hopelessly pinned on the eighth rank.

22   ♗xe6   ♘a6

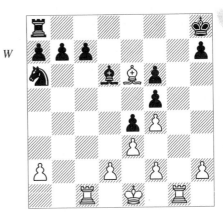

Black has avoided mate on g8, but the situation is hopeless. He is material down, White's pieces are very active and the pawns on f5 and e4 are sitting ducks.

23   ♔e2

Black cannot save the f5-pawn.

23   ...   ♘c5

Trying at least to defend the e4-pawn.

24   ♗xf5   ♖d8

25   ♖g3   1-0

White threatens 26 ♖h3, and after 25...♖g8 26 ♖xg8+ ♔xg8 27 ♖g1+ ♔h8, the simplest win is by 28 f3 exf3+ 29 ♔xf3, followed by d4 and e4-e5, when the pawns march through.

This was a powerful display by Chernin. Admittedly, Van der Wiel was not on his best form, but the way in which Black's position was torn to shreds was impressive. Note in particular how White was not hamstrung by traditional ideas. When it was best to abandon the idea of castling, White did so without hesitation, knowing that his centralized king would never be a factor in the struggle. Similarly, White managed to dominate the central squares almost without using his pawns at all. Remember the bishops on the a1-h8 and a2-g8 diagonals, spearing Black's kingside through the centre; this activity was only possible because of Black's poor development and concessions in the centre (mainly 5...e4?!).

The lessons here are:

1) Do not make too many pawn moves in the opening.

2) Do not expose your queen to harassment by enemy pieces in the opening.

3) Do not repeatedly move the same piece in the opening.

4) Weaknesses are only relevant if they can be exploited.

King in the Centre

Another of the main objectives of opening play is to safeguard the king. In most openings, the players advance one or more central pawns in order to develop the pieces. This has the side-effect of exposing the king and in the great majority of cases it is necessary to castle in order to avoid an early attack on the king. Castling has the beneficial side-effect of making way for the rooks to occupy the central files, which are the most likely to become open during the middlegame.

Just as with any chess guideline, there will always be exceptions to this advice. If the centre becomes blocked with pawns, so there is no easy way for the enemy to attack through the centre, then it may be possible for the king to stay in the centre. Grandmasters sometimes prepare for castling, but then delay the actual castling move, safe in the knowledge that the king can be whisked away at a moment's notice if danger should threaten in the centre. However, it must be emphasized that these cases are very much the exception; in most cases, early castling is advisable. The following game is a drastic example of what may happen, even to a grandmaster, if castling is too long delayed.

Game 2

A. Khalifman – E. Sveshnikov
Russian Championship, Elista 1996
Queen's Gambit Declined

1   d4

This is one of the two most common first moves, the other being 1 e4. The view is sometimes expressed that 1 d4 is a more positional move than 1 e4. Actually, I can't see much difference. There are many sharp openings after 1 d4, just as there are many quiet openings resulting from 1 e4.

1   ...   d5

This symmetrical reply is one of the most popular responses.

2   c4

This is the characteristic move of the Queen's Gambit. White intends to exchange Black's central d-pawn for the non-central c-pawn. Then White will have two central pawns to Black's one, which gives him chances to exercise greater control of the centre (another of the key objectives of opening play).

2   ...   e6

Although this opening is called the Queen's Gambit, it isn't really a gambit at all because if Black accepts it by 2...dxc4, then he cannot maintain his extra pawn. For example, after 3 e3 b5? (3...♗e6 4 ♘a3 regains the pawn with advantage) 4 a4 Black's pawn-chain disintegrates and not only must he give back the pawn, but also his position is shattered. Note that 4...c6 is impossible due to 5 axb5 cxb5 6 ♕f3 trapping the rook on a8. As a matter of fact, White can also regain the pawn with 3 e4 or 3 ♘f3.

Rather than take on c4, it is most common to support the d5-pawn with either 2...c6 or 2...e6.

Then if White plays cxd5, Black is ready with take back with a pawn, retaining a central pawn on d5.

3   ♘f3

3 ♘c3 is also played frequently. In many cases the two moves lead to the same position, but there are some differences since each cuts out certain options. In chess, it is desirable to remain flexible, but committal decisions are inevitable.

3   ...   c6

Black sets up a pawn-structure typical of the so-called 'Semi-Slav'. This name arises because the structure with pawns on d5 and c6 is the Slav, while that with d5 and e6 is characteristic of the Orthodox Queen's Gambit. When Black plays both ...c6 and ...e6, it is a kind of mixture of the two, which lends some logic to the name 'Semi-Slav'. This pawn-structure is very popular in modern grandmaster chess. It is solid, since the important central d5-pawn is reinforced, while at the same time Black can often develop his pieces comfortably by ...♘f6, ...♘bd7, ...♗d6 and ...0-0. That only leaves his c8-bishop to be deployed, but Black hopes to solve this by either ...dxc4, followed by ...b5 and ...♗b7, or by ...b6.

4   g3

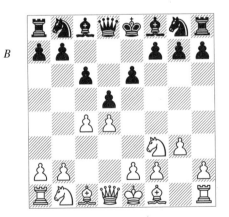

4 ♘c3 would lead into the main lines of the Semi-Slav. Khalifman's interesting idea is based on the point that Black often plays ...dxc4 followed by ...b5 in the Semi-Slav. By placing his bishop on the long diagonal, he is ready to exploit the weakening of that diagonal resulting from ...dxc4. The risk is that this is a genuine gambit. We saw above that White can regain the

pawn after 2...dxc4, because the bishop on f1 helps White break up Black's b5-c4 pawn-chain. However, when the bishop is on g2, White cannot regain the pawn by force.

4   ...   ♘f6

Black could have taken the pawn at once by 4...dxc4 5 ♗g2 b5, but he decides to develop a piece first.

5   ♗g2

Some players have chosen to defend the c4-pawn by 5 ♘bd2 or 5 ♕c2, but Khalifman persists with offering a gambit.

5   ...   dxc4

Sveshnikov takes up the challenge. The alternative was to continue his development without accepting the sacrifice (for example by 5...♘bd7). While Sveshnikov understandably wants to exploit the negative side of White's plan, he now comes under a dangerous attack and it would have been more prudent to decline the offer.

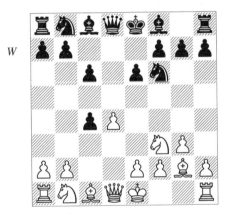

6   0-0

The immediate 6 ♘e5 is also possible. It is true that Black then has the disruptive 6...♗b4+, but after 7 ♘c3 (not 7 ♗d2? in view of 7...♕xd4, however) 7...♘d5 8 ♗d2 White again has good compensation for the pawn.

6   ...   b5

Black has no hope of retaining the pawn on c4 without this move and if he is forced to play it, then it is most flexible to play it straight away. After 6...♘bd7 7 a4 b5, for example, 8 axb5 cxb5 9 ♘g5! ♘d5 10 e4 ♘c7 11 e5 ♖b8 12 ♕h5 g6 13 ♕f3 gives White a near-decisive attack. If Black simply allows White to regain the pawn on c4 then he will stand at a disadvantage.

The whole point of his opening play was to offer the d5-pawn firm support. To give up the strong point at d5 without the compensation of an extra pawn would be totally inconsistent and would allow White a free hand in the centre.

7 a4

Threatening 8 axb5 followed by a discovered attack on the long diagonal, much as in the line given in the previous note.

7 ... ♗b7

Black counters the threat by reinforcing the long diagonal.

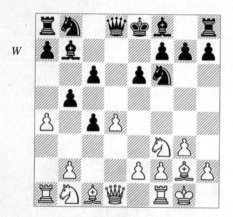

This is a good moment to stop and assess the situation. Positionally speaking, White has a good game since he has an extra central pawn and a lead in development. Black, on the other hand, has a pawn more. Judging the relative merits of material and positional advantages is always difficult, and this is not a clear-cut case. However, one important point is clear: one of the main elements of White's compensation is the fact that Black is still two moves away from castling. It follows that White must operate with direct threats so far as possible, to keep Black off-balance and deny him the two tempi he needs to safeguard his king. Moreover, White must try to open lines. At present, there is quite a lot of wood between White's forces and the enemy king; as lines are opened, White's attacking possibilities will increase.

8 ♘e5

Creating the direct threat of 9 axb5, and bringing two pieces to bear on the weak c6-pawn. If at any stage Black shields this pawn by ...♘d5, then White will gain the free tempo e4 for his attack.

8 ... ♕b6

Black defends his bishop, so as to answer axb5 by ...cxb5. 8...a6 is another idea, but after 9 axb5 axb5 10 ♖xa8 ♗xa8 11 ♘c3, White brings out a piece while at the same time threatening 12 ♘xb5, so once again Black is unable to develop his kingside.

9 b3!

This very strong move was played for the first time in the current game. Hitherto, White had preferred 9 e4, but the text-move keeps Black more off-balance, as he must counter the threat of 10 bxc4.

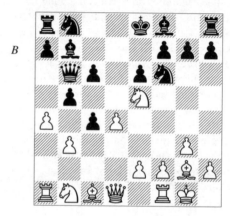

9 ... cxb3

Forced, as otherwise White regains his pawn while keeping his attack.

10 ♕xb3

Now White has no immediately devastating threat, but Black will have to be ready to answer White's attack on the b5-pawn after 11 ♘a3.

10 ... ♘bd7?

Black decides that the priority is to get rid of the dominating knight on e5, but he cannot afford to waste any time in preparing kingside castling. A better line was 10...♗e7 11 ♘a3 0-0 (returning the extra pawn is best; after 11...b4 12 ♘ac4 ♕xd4 13 ♗b2 White has an enormous attack for the two pawns) 12 axb5 cxb5 13 ♗xb7 ♕xb7 14 ♕xb5. Here White still has a slight advantage, since his e5-knight is active while Black has yet to move his b8-knight. It is possible that Sveshnikov rejected 10...♗e7 because he did not relish the prospect of defending this inferior position, but if so he made a common chess mistake: in attempting to avoid a small disadvantage, he ends up with a large one!

The greedy 10...♕xd4 is probably also better than the text-move, even though Black's position hangs on a knife-edge. After 11 ♗b2 ♕b6 12 axb5 cxb5 13 ♗d4! ♕xd4 (13...♗d5 loses material to 14 ♕xd5!) 14 ♗xb7 ♖xa1 (14...♕xe5 15 ♖a5 a6 16 ♗xa8 ♗d6 17 ♗f3 is good for White; the open files are ideal for the rooks and Black cannot develop his b8-knight) 15 ♕xb5+ ♘bd7 16 ♘xd7 ♘xd7 17 ♗xa8 ♕e5 18 ♕a4 ♕c7 Black can just about keep his position intact thanks to a neat tactical point: 19 ♖d1 ♗d6 20 ♘a3 0-0! (20...♔e7 21 ♘b5 ♕c5 22 ♘xd6 ♖xa8 23 ♘e4 ♕c7 24 ♕a3+ ♔e8 25 ♘d6+ wins) 21 ♘b5 ♕b8 22 ♖xd6 a6! 23 ♘c7 (23 ♖xa6? ♘c5) 23...♘b6! and Black is able to defend.

11   ♗e3!

Now White's attack really starts to gather momentum. The immediate threat is the central breakthrough 12 d5.

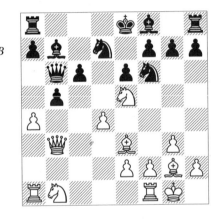

11   ...   c5?!

Opening the position usually plays into the hands of the better-developed player. Black could have tried 11...♘d5 12 ♘xd7 ♔xd7, attempting to set up some sort of blockade in the centre; for example, 13 a5 ♕a6 14 ♗d2 f5 and White cannot easily force through e4. However, there cannot be many players who would like to take on a position like this, extra pawn or no extra pawn. Black's queen is sidelined on a6, and his king is floating around in the centre.

12   ♘xd7

This exchange is the preliminary to a central breakthrough.

12   ...   ♘xd7

13   d5!

An excellent move based on an accurate assessment of the position. White could have achieved a safe advantage by 13 dxc5 ♗xc5 14 a5 ♕c7 15 ♗xb7 ♕xb7 16 ♗xc5 ♘xc5 17 ♕c3, followed by ♕xg7, but in this case Black would still have defensive chances. Khalifman, however, perceives that his position is so strong that he should not be content with a modest advantage, but should be playing for more. By opening lines in the centre, he creates avenues of attack against the black king. Moreover, by threatening 14 dxe6, he once again gives Black no time to bring his f8-bishop out. The fact that this move costs White a second pawn is of little relevance.

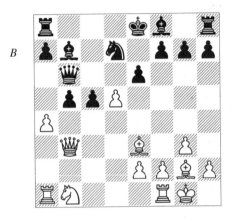

13   ...   bxa4

White wins after 13...exd5 14 ♘c3! d4 15 a5! ♕e6 (15...♕a6 loses to 16 ♘xb5) 16 ♕xe6+ fxe6 17 ♗xb7 ♖b8 18 ♗c6; for example, 18...dxe3 19 ♖fd1 ♖d8 20 ♖xd7 ♖xd7 21 ♖d1. Nor is 13...c4 satisfactory in view of 14 ♕xb5 ♕xb5 15 axb5 ♗xd5 16 ♗xd5 exd5 17 ♘c3 ♘f6 18 b6 with a large advantage for White.

14   ♕xa4

Black has solved the problem of White's threats to his b5-pawn, but at the cost of setting up a pin along the a4-e8 diagonal, which will in the end prove decisive. Moreover, the opening of the b-file will inevitably present White with a free tempo when he plays a rook to b1.

14   ...   exd5

14...♗xd5 fails to help Black. After 15 ♘c3! ♗xg2 16 ♔xg2 ♕b7+ (if Black omits this check, then he will have to answer ♖ab1 by ...♕c7, giving White another free tempo after ♗f4) 17 ♔g1 ♖d8 18 ♖ab1 ♕c7 (after 18...♕c8

19 ♗f4, followed by ♖b8, Black has to part with his queen and, ironically, he will still be unable to castle) 19 ♖fd1 ♖c8 (19...♗e7 20 ♗f4 e5 21 ♘d5 ♕d6 22 ♖b7! is decisive) 20 ♘b5 ♕c6 21 ♕a5 ♕b6 22 ♕a1 White has a winning position.

15   ♘c3

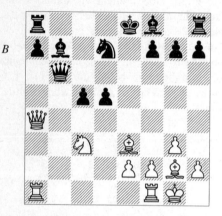

B

White is now two pawns down, but his lead in development has increased. All his pieces are now in play, whereas Black is still two moves away from castling kingside. In addition, White has opened various lines: the b-file and a4-e8 diagonal are already open, and if the d5-pawn falls then the d-file will also be open. These lines provide ample opportunity for White's pieces to converge on Black's helpless king, which is held in the centre by a combination of poor development and the pinned d7-knight.

15   ...   d4

There is no defence. 15...♗c6 16 ♘xd5! ♗xa4 17 ♘xb6 axb6 18 ♗xa8 gives White a material advantage and a large lead in development, while 15...♕c6 (15...♕b4 is also met by 16 ♗xd5) 16 ♗xd5 ♕xa4 17 ♖xa4 ♗xd5 18 ♘xd5 ♗d6 19 ♖a6! ♗b8 20 ♖d1 completely ties Black up (20...0-0? 21 ♘e7+).

Perhaps 15...♕e6 is the only real alternative to the text-move. Then White wins by thematically smashing open lines: 16 ♘xd5! ♗xd5 (or 16...♗d6 17 ♘c7+ ♗xc7 18 ♗xb7 and now after 18...♖b8 19 ♗c6 or 18...♖d8 19 ♗xc5 Black is again prevented from castling) 17 ♗xd5 ♕xd5 18 ♖fd1 ♕e6 19 ♖xd7! (the various open lines all come into play in this combination – the d-file, the e-file and the various diagonals) 19...♕xd7 20 ♕e4+ ♗e7 21 ♕xa8+ ♕d8 (or

21...♗d8 22 ♗xc5 and – dare I say it again? – Black cannot castle!) 22 ♖xa7 ♕xa8 (22...0-0 loses to 23 ♕xd8 ♗xd8 24 ♗xc5 ♖e8 25 ♖a8 followed by ♗b6) 23 ♖xa8+ ♗d8 24 ♗xc5, followed by ♗b6, and White wins the pawn ending after exchanging off all the pieces on d8 (in ♔+♙ endings with all the pawns on the same side, an extra pawn is usually enough to win with 2 vs 1, and almost always wins with 3 vs 2 or 4 vs 3).

16   ♘d5!

Not the careless 16 ♖fb1?, when 16...♗xg2! 17 ♖xb6 axb6 18 ♕d1 ♖xa1 19 ♕xa1 ♗c6 turns the tables.

16   ...   ♗xd5

White also wins after 16...♕c6 17 ♕xc6 ♗xc6 18 ♘c7+ ♔d8 19 ♘xa8 ♗xg2 20 ♔xg2 dxe3 21 ♖fd1 or 16...♕d8 17 ♗f4 ♖c8 18 ♘f6+ ♕xf6 19 ♗xb7 ♖d8 20 ♗c7.

17   ♗xd5

White's bishop exercises unopposed control over the light squares.

17   ...   ♖d8

Black supports his pinned knight, but he will never have time for ...♗e7 and ...0-0.

18   ♗f4

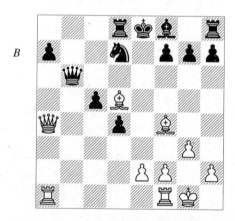

B

18   ...   ♕f6

After 18...♗d6 (or 18...♕b4 19 ♕a2! and f7 collapses, while if 18...♗e7, then 19 ♗c6 ♕b4 20 ♕xa7 and Black is doomed by his pinned knight) 19 ♖fb1 ♕c7 20 ♗g5 f6 (20...♖b8 21 ♖xb8+ ♕xb8 22 ♗xf7+ ♔xf7 23 ♕xd7+ ♔f8 24 ♖xa7 is winning for White) 21 ♖b7 ♕xb7 (21...♕c8 22 ♗d2, followed by ♗a5, is painful) 22 ♗xb7 fxg5 Black has a miscellaneous collection of bits and pieces for the queen, but

White's powerful initiative decides the game quickly: 23 ♕c6 ♔e7 (23...♗e7 24 ♖xa7) 24 ♖xa7 ♗b8 25 ♕e4+ and Black collapses.

| | 19 | ♕b5 |

The simplest. White clears the way for the a1-rook to penetrate to a6 or a7.

| | 19 | ... | ♗d6 |

The bishop finally moves, only to land immediately in a fatal pin. However, 19...♗e7 20 ♖xa7 ♕b6 21 ♕xb6 ♘xb6 22 ♗c6+ ♔f8 23 ♗c7 results in heavy loss of material, while 19...♕b6 20 ♕c4 ♕g6 21 ♖xa7 ♗e7 22 ♕b5 puts Black's position under intolerable pressure.

| | 20 | ♖a6 |

This second pin decides the game at once.

| | 20 | ... | ♖b8 |

As good or bad as any other move.

| | 21 | ♗b7 |

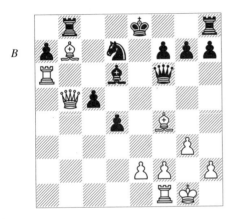

B

White maintains both pins.

| | 21 | ... | ♗xf4 |

Giving up the queen for only a rook is equivalent to resignation.

| | 22 | ♖xf6 | gxf6 |
| | 23 | gxf4 | f5 |

Black is still gripped by the pin on his knight.

| | 24 | ♕c6 |

Threatening 25 ♗c8.

| | 24 | ... | ♔d8 |

Unpinning the knight.

| | 25 | ♕d5 |

Pinning it again. Now 26 ♗c6 is the threat.

| | 25 | ... | ♔c7 |
| | 26 | ♗c6 | 1-0 |

The c5-pawn falls, and mate is not far off.

This was a very dynamic win by Khalifman. After offering a pawn, he kept Sveshnikov under pressure with a constant barrage of threats. When Black turned down the last chance to bring his king into safety (as early as move 10) he was immediately in considerable difficulties. Khalifman realized the importance of opening lines and was prepared to offer further material to strengthen his attack. In the later stages, Black's problems were compounded by a crippling weakness on the light squares.

The lessons here are:
1) Castling is desirable in the large majority of games.
2) A king left in the centre can easily become the target of an attack.
3) When pursuing such an attack, keep the defender off-balance.
4) The key to many attacks is the opening of lines towards the enemy king.

Successful Control of the Centre

The third main objective of opening play is to gain control of the centre. The centre of the board is particularly important for two reasons. First of all, most pieces display greater activity when in the centre of the board; this is particularly pronounced in the case of the knight, but it affects all the pieces except the rook to a greater or lesser extent. Thus if one can control the centre, one's pieces will almost automatically be more effective than the opponent's. The second great advantage of central control is flexibility. If your pieces are positioned on the kingside, they will have little influence on the queenside. This may not be a problem if you are conducting a kingside attack against the enemy king, for example, because the kingside is where the action is and that's where you want your pieces. However, if it is as yet unclear where your pieces will be needed, then it may be too committal to feed your pieces to the kingside. Your opponent may arrange things so that they are ineffective, for example by castling queenside, and then it may turn out that they would be better placed elsewhere. If your pieces are near the centre, they can easily be switched to the kingside or queenside at short notice. This gives you additional flexibility in deciding where to attack, and makes it easier to counter your opponent's plans, no matter which side of the board he decides to take action.

However, control of the centre is not easy to define. It's more a case of recognizing it when you see it, rather than applying a formula. It may be that it involves occupying the centre with pawns (as in the following game), but we already saw in Game 1 that this need not be the case. In that game White controlled the centre with pieces from a distance, but the result was no less effective. As a general rule, whether or not the centre is occupied by pawns, the action of the pieces is critical. A pawn-centre that is not properly supported by pieces will probably collapse (see Game 4). So the general principle is that **you should develop your pieces so as to exert the greatest influence on the centre**.

Game 3

K. Aseev – N. Rashkovsky

Russian Championship, St Petersburg 1998
Modern Defence, Austrian Attack

1   e4

Along with 1 d4, this is one of the two most popular opening moves. White frees his queen and bishop, and at once plants a pawn in the centre.

1   ...   g6

Alekhine, commenting on the game Edward Lasker-Capablanca, New York 1924, wrote about 1...g6: "From the present-day theoretical standpoint this move cannot be regarded as wholly valid, because Black commits himself to a certain position without being able to influence in any way his adversary's development in the centre." However, this didn't stop Capablanca from winning the game, and these days the move 1...g6 (called the 'Modern Defence') is regarded as a wholly acceptable opening. By playing 1...g6 Black does not, as Alekhine supposed, forfeit the possibility of central play; instead, he delays it until White has committed himself in the centre. Usually, Black's counter-action involves either ...c5 or ...e5, although there are a few lines in which Black plays ...d5.

Here it is worth giving one word of warning regarding the Modern Defence. In many Classical openings, such as the French (1 e4 e6 2 d4 d5), Black's central play is inherent in his choice of opening, whereas with the Modern Defence Black has more choice. With this additional freedom comes an extra responsibility to ensure that Black's central action, when it

comes, is both timely and appropriate. If Black delays too long, and allows White to consolidate his grip on the centre, then Black will run into the difficulty mentioned by Alekhine, that of not being able to challenge White in the centre at all.

2   d4

Forming an ideal pawn-centre, but will White be able to maintain it?

2   ...   ♗g7

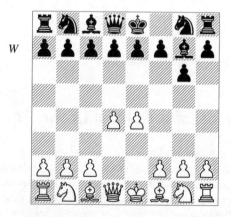

W

Already exerting some pressure against d4. In most cases Black will seek to enhance this pressure by further play on the dark squares.

3   ♘c3

White must choose whether to occupy c3 with his c-pawn or his knight. Playing 3 c3 reinforces the d4-square and reduces the activity of the g7-bishop, but it takes away the most active square from the b1-knight, so most players prefer the natural text-move.

3   ...   d6

Once again a 'dark-square move'. This is good preparation for an eventual ...c5 or ...e5.

4   f4

This represents White's most aggressive system against the Modern Defence. He forms a broad pawn-centre, aiming to develop his pieces behind it by ♘f3, ♗d3 (or ♗e2) and 0-0. If White is allowed to complete his development with his pawn-centre unchallenged, then Black will face difficulties. Accordingly, quick action by Black is essential. There are a number of alternatives to the text-move. 4 ♘f3 is the positional approach, intending simple development by ♗e2 and 0-0. White can also adopt a 'halfway house' system such as 4 ♗e3 and 4 ♗g5, which can be handled either positionally or aggressively, depending on how Black reacts.

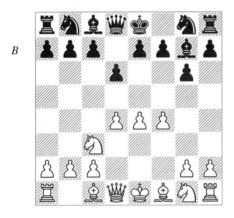

4   ...   a6?!

Black decides to fianchetto his other bishop, but this process takes three moves and gives White time to support his centre. Black does, it is true, gain some space on the queenside, but this is not sufficient compensation for the time lost. In club games, players often get away with such eccentric moves because their opponents do not try to exploit them, or do not know how to take advantage of their weaknesses. In this game Aseev reacts correctly: he develops as rapidly as possible, while putting as many stumbling blocks as possible in the way of Black's development. This one slip is not enough for

Black to lose, but he must be very careful from now on, especially as he is still two moves away from castling.

Black has a number of acceptable options. 4...♘f6 would transpose into a closely related opening called the Pirc Defence (1 e4 d6 2 d4 ♘f6 3 ♘c3 g6 4 f4 ♗g7 would be the Pirc move-order). If Black wants to adopt a pure Modern Defence system, then he could try 4...♘c6 or 4...c6. All these moves are targeted at the centre, while 4...a6 is not.

5   ♘f3

Developing a piece and supporting d4.

5   ...   b5

Black continues with his plan of developing his bishop at b7.

6   ♗d3

This is the best square for the bishop, since e4 will require support after Black plays ...♗b7, especially bearing in mind that Black can drive the c3-knight away by ...b4.

6   ...   ♗b7

Black's intention is to nibble away at White's centre by ...♘d7 and ...c5, perhaps eventually reaching a position similar to the Sicilian after the exchange ...cxd4 (or, equivalently, dxc5).

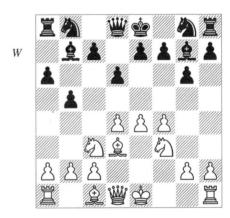

7   e5

White handles the opening in a very aggressive fashion. This pawn advance has several advantages:

1) It prevents Black from developing his g8-knight to the natural square f6.

2) If Black plays ...b4, then the knight can move to e4 rather than retreating.

3) It introduces the possibility of playing the pawn sacrifice e6.

White has to take care not to over-extend himself, but in view of Black's slow play this is not yet a danger.

Players with a more positional disposition might have preferred a second promising line: 7 0-0 ♘d7 8 ♘e2. The idea is that White is ready to meet ...c5 by c3, keeping his pawn-centre intact. After 8...c5 9 c3 ♘gf6 10 ♘g3, for example, Black has still not made any real inroads into White's central control, while White's pieces are massing ominously for a later kingside attack.

7 ... e6?

Black is worried about the possibility of e6 by White, and so spends a move preventing it, but this move is simply too slow. Black should have continued with his plan by 7...♘d7. Then the key line is 8 0-0 c5 9 ♗e4 (9 exd6 cxd4 is unclear) 9...♗xe4 10 ♘xe4 cxd4 11 e6 (11 exd6 ♕b6 offers Black counter-chances) 11...fxe6 12 ♘eg5 ♘f8 (Black cannot allow the knight to leap in to e6 and 12...♘c5 is not possible because of 13 b4) 13 ♘xd4, leading to an intriguing position in which Black is a pawn up, but his arrangement of pieces on the kingside is almost comical. I would prefer to be White since it is not clear how the knight will ever get away from f8, but it is true that Black's position is relatively solid.

8 a4!

A good move. White's basic plan involves a kingside attack based on 0-0, ♘e4 and ♕e1-h4. However, first of all White induces Black to push his pawn to b4. Then a later ♕e1 will gain a tempo by attacking the b4-pawn. While this might not seem too significant, finesses such as this are very important. The tempo White will gain accelerates his attack, and there is no downside at all – it's just an extra move for free.

8 ... b4

More or less forced. Black cannot continue 8...c6, because after 9 ♘e4 the knight would hop into d6, while 8...bxa4 would shatter Black's queenside pawns and bring White's a1-rook into play.

9 ♘e4 ♘e7

Black wisely takes the chance to remove his king from the centre.

10 0-0 0-0

Both sides castle, but there the similarity ends. White's king is indeed safe on g1, but

Black's king will still be exposed to danger on the kingside. The reason is that Black has just two minor pieces on the kingside, while White already has a bishop and two knights ready for action. Once the white queen joins in, Black's defenders will have their work cut out.

11 ♕e1

White duly cashes in the tempo he reserved earlier.

11 ... a5

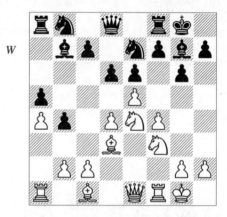

12 c3!

This is a very instructive and strong move. White obviously has the makings of a dangerous kingside attack, but he is still quite a long way from a forced mate, so he cannot afford to ignore the rest of the board. Leaping in immediately with 12 ♕h4 would be counter-productive. Black would reply 12...♘f5 and White would have to retreat with 13 ♕h3 if he wanted to carry on with his attack. However, the queen is offside on h3 and it is much better to leave the queen where it is until the switch to the kingside produces a more concrete result.

The text-move places Black in an awkward situation. On the one hand White stabilizes his centre and supports it against a possible attack by ...c5 at a later stage (for example, Black might play ...♗xe4, followed by ...d5, ...♘d7 and ...c5). On the other hand, it immediately threatens to win a pawn by 13 cxb4, against which Black has no natural defence. If he plays 12...bxc3, then 13 bxc3 opens the way for a later ♗a3. This would force Black to move his d6-pawn, thereby both increasing the scope of the a3-bishop and freeing the c5-square for White's knight on e4. These advantages would give White virtually a winning game on the *queenside*, and there might never be a kingside attack at all. One possible continuation runs 13...♗xe4 14 ♗xe4 d5 15 ♗d3 c5 16 ♗a3 ♘d7 17 ♗b5 cxd4 18 cxd4 with crushing queenside pressure. Black could play 12...♘bc6, but now that d4 is secure, White could continue his attack by 13 ♘fg5, much as in the game.

12   ...   ♗a6

Black plays for exchanges, which is a standard ploy to reduce the force of an attack. Although Black manages to swap the bishops, he is left with an offside knight on a6 which plays little further part in the game.

13   ♗xa6   ♘xa6

Black would prefer to play 13...♖xa6, but he cannot as he must defend b4. Note how White's queenside diversion with c3 has forced Black to make a further positional concession, which in turn improves the prospects for White's attack.

14   ♘fg5

Things start to look ominous for Black. White has various threats, but one of the simplest is 15 g4, keeping Black's knight out of f5, and then either 16 ♕h4 or 16 ♘f6+. Thanks to White's central domination, Black finds it impossible to feed any of his queenside pieces across to the defence.

14   ...   h6

14...dxe5 15 fxe5 doesn't help at all and only serves to introduce the c1-bishop into the attack. Black therefore tries to repel White's knight.

15   ♘f6+!

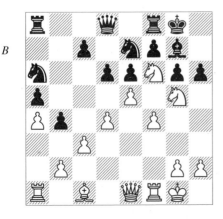

It is sometimes possible to conduct an attack that demands little calculation, but this is rare

against determined opposition. More often, there comes a critical moment when precise analysis is required if the attack is to succeed. This moment has arrived, and Aseev proves he is up to the challenge.

15   ...   ♔h8

Rashkovsky declines the offer, but the knight on f6 proves too strong. The critical continuation is 15...♗xf6 16 exf6 and now:

1) 16...♘c8 17 ♘xe6 fxe6 18 ♕e4 wins by attacking both g6 and a8.

2) 16...♘d5 17 ♘xe6! fxe6 18 ♕xe6+ ♔h7 19 ♕xd5 ♕xf6 20 ♕xa5 and Black has little to show for the two pawns.

3) 16...♘f5 (16...hxg5 17 fxg5 ♘f5 18 g4 transposes) 17 g4 hxg5 (after 17...♕xf6 18 ♘e4 White wins a piece) 18 fxg5 ♖e8 19 gxf5 exf5 20 ♕h4 ♖e4 21 ♗f4, followed by ♖f3-h3, wins.

4) 16...♘c6 17 ♘e4! d5 18 f5! (the most vigorous continuation, opening up the kingside and simultaneously activating the c1-bishop) 18...dxe4 (18...exf5 19 ♕h4 dxe4 20 ♗xh6, followed by ♗g7, mates) 19 fxg6 fxg6 (19...♕d5 20 ♕g3 ♕d6 21 ♕g4, followed by ♗xh6, gives White a winning attack) 20 ♕xe4 ♖xf6 21 ♖xf6 ♕xf6 22 ♕xc6 is the most instructive variation. Material is equal, but Black is doomed by his positional weakness on the queenside, especially the badly-placed knight on a6. After 22...♖f8 23 ♗e3 e5 24 ♕d5+ White wins easily since Black's pawns are dropping off.

16   ♘gh7

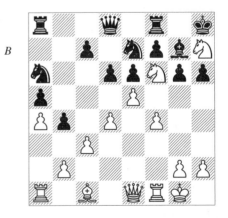

White's knights present a pretty picture. In order to avoid losing the exchange, Black must surrender his important defensive bishop.

16   ...   ♗xf6

17 ♘xf6

White has a winning position. There is no way to remove the knight from f6, and while this knight remains Black has no hope of defending his kingside.

17 ... ♔g7

There is little Black can do to prevent White bringing the reserves into the attack by playing f5. After 17...♘g8 18 ♕h4 ♔g7, for example, White wins by 19 f5! exf5 20 ♗g5 ♕c8 21 ♖f3 ♖d8 (21...h5 22 ♘xh5+ gxh5 23 ♗f6+ mates) 22 ♘xg8 hxg5 23 ♕h6+ ♔xg8 24 ♖h3, mating.

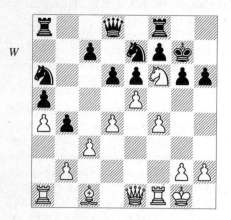

W

18 f5!

The thematic blow, threatening to force mate by 19 ♗xh6+ ♔xh6 20 ♕h4+, a motif that recurs in the subsequent play.

18 ... ♖h8

18...♘xf5 19 ♖xf5 exf5 20 ♗xh6+ mates, so Black defends h6.

19 fxe6

Now that Black's rook has been forced to abandon the f-file, it is to White's advantage to open it up.

19 ... fxe6

20 ♕f2!

White threatens mate in two by 21 ♘h5+.

20 ... ♕f8

20...♖f8 allows 21 ♗xh6+.

21 ♗f4?

White retains a winning position even after this move, but by blocking the f-file White makes the win more difficult. It is a pity that Aseev did not spot the forcing line 21 ♘h5+ gxh5 (21...♔g8 22 ♕g3 ♕d8 23 ♖f6 ♖h7 24 ♖xe6 is catastrophic) 22 ♕g3+ ♘g6 23 ♖xf8, followed by exd6, with an easy win on material.

The text-move threatens 22 exd6 cxd6 23 ♗xd6, followed by ♗e5.

21 ... d5

Forced, as 21...♖d8 loses to 22 ♕e2 (that a6-knight again!) 22...♘b8 23 exd6 cxd6 24 ♗xd6! ♖xd6 25 ♘h5+ gxh5 26 ♕e5+, followed by taking the queen and then the rook.

22 ♖ac1

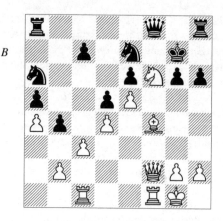

B

A typical idea. White cannot make any immediate progress on the kingside, so he worries Black on another part of the board. Now Black has to take into account the possibility of White opening the c-file, by either cxb4 or c4. There is no harm in making such useful preparatory moves, since Black is unable to improve his position.

22 ... c5

Black decides he cannot sit passively by any longer, and lashes out. 22...bxc3 23 ♖xc3 is bad for Black because the rook will switch to the kingside, so the only alternative was to wait, for example by 22...c6. In that case White would win by 23 cxb4 axb4 (or 23...♘xb4 24 ♖c3, followed by ♖h3) 24 ♗d2, when there is no reasonable way to prevent 25 ♘h5+ ♔g8 (25...gxh5 26 ♕g3+) 26 ♕g3.

23 dxc5

White takes and keeps the pawn.

23 ... ♘f5

After 23...♘c6 24 ♗e3, followed by ♗d4, White cements his dark-squared grip on both sides of the board (24...♘xe5 loses at once to 25 ♗d4).

24 g4

Back again!

24 ... ♘e7

By inducing g4, Black has at least prevented the ♘h5+ and ♕g3+ trick, but his position is beyond hope in any case.

25   ♗d2

Threatening to exchange on b4 and then push the c-pawn.

25   ...   ♘c6

Blocking the c-pawn, but now Black misses the knight on the kingside.

26   cxb4   ♘axb4

White also wins after 26...axb4 27 ♕g3 ♕e7 28 ♘h5+! ♔h7 29 ♖f6 ♖af8 30 ♕e3, when h6 collapses.

27   ♖c3

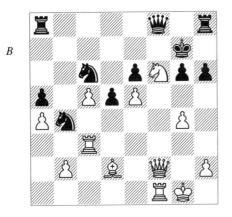

Now that c3 is free, White's rook can switch to the kingside for the *coup de grâce*.

27   ...   ♕e7

27...♘xe5 28 ♕g3 leaves Black defenceless; for example, 28...♘bc6 29 ♘d7 ♘xd7 30 ♖xf8 ♖hxf8 31 ♕c7 ♘ce5 32 c6 or 28...♕b8 29 ♗f4 ♘bc6 30 ♘d7.

28   ♖h3

Threatening the old 29 ♗xh6+ trick.

28   ...   g5

Meeting the threat, but conceding the h5-square and opening the b1-h7 diagonal.

29   ♘h5+   ♔g8
30   ♘f6+   ♔g7
31   ♘h5+   ♔g8

Presumably White was in time-trouble, and repeats moves so as to approach the time-control at move 40 (currently the standard time-limit in international play is 2 hours per player for the first 40 moves).

32   ♗xb4

Closing in for the kill.

32   ...   axb4

32...♘xb4 33 ♖f3 ♖a7 34 c6 ♖c7 (34...♘xc6 35 ♖f8+ ♔h7 36 ♕c2#) 35 ♖f8+ ♔h7 36 ♖f7+ ♕xf7 37 ♕xf7+ ♖xf7 38 ♖xf7+ ♔g8 39 ♖g7+ ♔f8 40 c7 leads to mate.

33   ♕c2

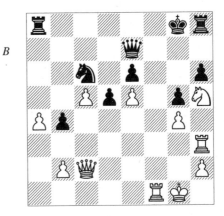

White threatens 34 ♕g6+, exploiting the weak b1-h7 diagonal.

33   ...   ♘xe5

A last meal.

34   ♘f6+   ♔g7
35   ♘h5+   ♔g8
36   ♖e3

The knight cannot move as it must cover g6, so Black has come to the end of the road.

36   ...   b3

36...♕c7 loses to 37 ♖xe5.

37   ♕c3

Not 37 ♕b1? ♕xc5, when Black is off the hook.

37   ...   ♘xg4
38   ♖xe6   1-0

After 38...♕h7 (to cover g6) 39 ♕f3, threatening 40 ♕xg4, 40 ♕xd5 and 40 ♖e8+ ♖xe8 41 ♕xd5+, it will be mate in a few moves.

In this game Aseev punished Black severely for his liberties in the opening (4...a6?! and especially 7...e6?). The way White built up his attack was noteworthy. He first established a well-supported pawn-wedge in the centre (c3-d4-e5-f4) and then started to feed his pieces across to the kingside. At the same time, he kept his eyes open for any chance to inconvenience Black on the other side of the board (for example, by playing ♗a3 or by exploiting the a6-knight). When Black was forced to exchange off his dark-squared bishop, the end was already in sight in view of his crippling dark-square weaknesses. Even though Aseev missed the quickest win, it was only a matter of time before he found a way to break open Black's position and finish the game off.

The lessons here are:

1) Control of the centre is an important objective of opening play.

2) It is unwise to allow your opponent too free a hand in the centre.

3) A well-supported centre is often the springboard for a flank attack against the king.

4) A firmly-entrenched knight on the sixth rank usually exerts a paralysing effect on the enemy forces.

An Over-Extended Pawn-Centre

If a player occupies the centre with pawns during the opening, he is taking on a significant responsibility. If he can maintain the pawn-centre intact, and support it adequately with pieces, then he is likely to gain the advantage. If, however, the support is inadequate, then, like any rickety construction, the pawn-centre is likely to collapse if given a good shove. The most common reason for poor piece support is lack of development. Erecting a pawn-centre consumes a certain number of tempi, which cannot also be used for developing pieces. Thus it is only natural that a large pawn-centre and a lack of development go hand-in-hand. The big question is whether the opponent has a way of exploiting the lack of development quickly, since otherwise the occupier of the centre will catch up with his development and gain the advantage. It is often extremely difficult to judge what the end result of such a contest will be. Indeed, there are whole opening systems that are based on allowing the opponent to construct a large pawn-centre; even after decades of analysis, nobody knows whether some of these systems are correct. In the following game Black adopts precisely such an opening. White duly builds up his centre, and battle is joined.

Game 4
J. van der Wiel – R. Vaganian
Ter Apel 1993
Alekhine Defence, Four Pawns Attack

1   e4

See Game 3 for comments on this move.

1   ...   ♘f6

This is one of the most forthright defences to 1 e4 in that Black's plan is plain from the very first move. By attacking the e-pawn, he restricts White's options. The only two natural moves are 2 ♘c3 and 2 e5. However, at the very least 2 ♘c3 allows Black's to transpose into an innocuous King's Pawn Opening by playing 2...e5 (this opening, called the Vienna Game, usually arises after 1 e4 e5 2 ♘c3 ♘f6). Therefore, the only real test of Black's first move is 2 e5. At first sight White should display no hesitation in advancing his pawn, because he not only gains space in the centre, but he also apparently gains time, since Black must move his knight again.

However, the basis of Black's idea is that in order to support the advanced pawn on e5, White will have to play further pawn moves – d4 at the very least. In this game White decides to go the whole way and plays c4 and f4 as well. This gives White a broad centre, but in the meantime he falls behind in development. As mentioned in the introduction to this game, it is very hard to tell whether the centre will prove strong or just collapse – indeed, Alekhine's Defence has been the subject of theoretical debate for around 80 years, with no clear conclusions being reached.

2   e5   ♘d5

The best square. 2...♘e4 really would be too provocative; after 3 d4 the knight is stranded on e4.

3   d4

White supports his advanced pawn, while reserving the option of chasing the knight further by c4.

3   ...   d6

As always, you should not allow your opponent to erect a broad centre unchallenged. Here Black already starts to exert pressure on the e5-pawn.

4   c4

White decides to push another pawn. Black again has to move his knight, so this isn't really a loss of time by White. However, White has taken on the additional responsibility of defending the c4-pawn. The feeling today is that these further pawn advances do not benefit White a great deal, and currently the favoured strategy is for White to content himself with the two pawns he has also already advanced and concentrate on supporting those. The best way to achieve this is by 4 ♘f3, followed by ♗e2 and 0-0.

4   ...   ♘b6

Exerting pressure on the c4-pawn and thereby limiting the activity of White's light-squared bishop.

5   f4

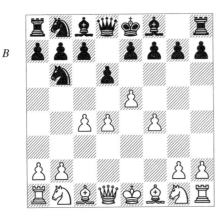

B

We met John van der Wiel in Game 1 and are familiar with his direct and aggressive style. Here he adopts the most ambitious, but also one of the most risky, lines against the Alekhine Defence. This so-called Four Pawns Attack is based on staking out a massive swathe of territory in the centre, in the hope of developing the pieces behind it by ♘c3, ♘f3, ♗e3 and so on.

5   ...   dxe5

This exchange opens up the d-file for Black's queen and prepares to exert pressure against the d4-pawn.

6   fxe5

After 6 dxe5 ♕xd1+ 7 ♔xd1 ♘c6 Black's lead in development will become serious, as White must lose further time with his king. In any case, it makes no sense to play an aggressive line such as the Four Pawns Attack and then offer the exchange of queens.

6   ...   ♘c6

Attacking d4.

7   ♗e3

White makes his first piece move. Had Black not wasted some time himself, the luxury of six consecutive pawn moves would surely have been fatal for White. However, Black has spent three moves having his knight chased to b6, so White's lag in development, while real enough, is not so serious as to cause an immediate disaster.

7 ♘f3 is a mistake because after 7...♗g4 8 ♗e3 e6 Black effectively gains a tempo over the game continuation. It is more accurate to wait until Black plays ...♗f5 before continuing ♘f3, since then Black will have to spend an extra tempo if he wants to pin the knight.

7   ...   ♗f5

Preparing to free his last minor piece by ...e6. At this stage it is not clear whether Black will aim for kingside castling or play for quick pressure against d4 by means of ...♕d7 followed by ...0-0-0.

8   ♘c3

White is eager to make up for his deficit in development.

8   ...   e6

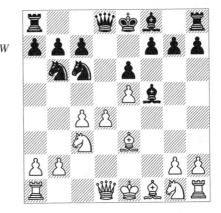

W

The f8-bishop can be developed to e7 or b4, according to circumstances.

9   ♘f3

Both sides have spent the past few moves concentrating on piece development, but now Black must decide how to step up the pressure against White's pawns before White develops his remaining pieces and castles. One idea is 9...♗e7, aiming to play ...0-0 and ...f6. This plan is quite effective, so White usually meets 9...♗e7 by 10 d5, aiming to rip open Black's position before he can castle. This book is not the place for a detailed discussion of opening theory; suffice to say that 10 d5, although very complicated, is considered satisfactory for Black. However, Vaganian decides to adopt another plan, which also appears to give Black a comfortable game. The fact that Black has a range of satisfactory options is the main reason why the Four Pawns Attack is rarely seen in contemporary grandmaster play.

9   ...   ♗g4

Yes, Black has voluntarily moved the same piece twice, but with a definite purpose in mind. The elimination of the f3-knight will weaken White's defence of d4, and after ...♕d7 and ...0-0-0 White may have real trouble defending it.

10   ♗e2

10 ♕d2 is another idea, intending to defend the d4-pawn by 0-0-0. One possible line is 10...♕d7 (10...♗b4!? 11 a3 ♗e7 is interesting; after White plays 0-0-0, the reply ...♘a5 will not only attack c4, but also threaten a fork at b3) 11 ♗e2 0-0-0 12 0-0-0 ♘a5, when White can no longer maintain his pawn-centre intact and must attempt to escape tactically by 13 ♗g5, with unclear complications.

10   ...   ♗xf3

Thanks to the pressure against c4, White has to recapture with the pawn, which breaks up his pawns and exposes his king. 10...♕d7 11 ♕d2 would transpose to the previous note.

11   gxf3   ♕d7!?

This move appears slightly odd in conjunction with the exchange on f3, although in view of its success in this game it is hard to criticize it. Black normally prefers 11...♕h4+ 12 ♗f2 ♕f4 13 c5 ♘d7 14 ♗b5 ♗e7, a theoretical line usually given the verdict 'unclear'. Indeed, the motivation for exchanging on f3 is precisely

with the idea of checking on h4. The text-move leads to positions similar to those arising in the note to White's 10th move, but where Black has voluntarily exchanged on f3 (i.e. without being forced to by White playing h3).

12   f4?!

White seeks to exploit the early exchange on f3 by reinforcing the e5-pawn, and thereby setting up a possible thrust d4-d5. However, this plan is too ambitious given that White's king is still in the centre and his development is rather poor. The result is that he soon ends up in trouble.

12 ♕d2, followed by 0-0-0, is better. Then White's king is relatively safe and he has reinforced d4. In that case the position would be roughly equal.

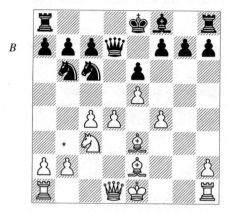

12   ...   ♖d8!

Van der Wiel may well have overlooked this unexpected move. At first sight 12...0-0-0 seems more natural, but this allows White to play 13 c5! ♘d5 14 ♘xd5 ♕xd5 15 ♗f3 ♕d7 16 d5, when he has achieved his central breakthrough. Black cannot play 16...exd5 because of the pin 17 ♗g4, while otherwise White plays d6, driving a massive wedge into Black's position and holding up the development of Black's kingside. By playing ...♖d8 rather than ...0-0-0, Vaganian cunningly side-steps the pin ♗g4, and now this line, on which White had been pinning his hopes, no longer works. This is an interesting example of how, when making chess decisions, the specific should always override the general. In principle, Black would rather castle than not, but when concrete analysis shows the latter to be superior, Vaganian shows no hesitation in abandoning the general principles.

13   d5

The attack on the d4-pawn is not easy to meet. After 13 c5 ♘d5 14 ♘xd5 ♕xd5 15 ♗f3 ♕d7 White has nothing better than 16 ♖c1 (16 ♖g1 ♘xd4 17 ♗xd4 ♕xd4 18 ♕xd4 ♖xd4 19 ♗xb7 ♗xc5 picks up a pawn) 16...♘xd4 17 ♗xb7 ♕b5 18 ♗xd4 ♕xb7 19 ♕a4+ c6 20 0-0 ♗e7. This position is very unpleasant for White. His bishop is bad, and after Black plays ...0-0, ...♖d5 and ...♖fd8 White will face increasing problems along the d-file.

Van der Wiel plays the only alternative, namely to lunge forwards with the d-pawn. If a broad pawn-centre starts to come under intolerable pressure, a critical moment often arises when the only alternative to simply losing the pawns is to use them as a battering-ram to open up the enemy position. Whether this succeeds obviously depends on specific features of the position, but here one can say straight away that it doesn't look good for White – his rooks are not yet in play and his king is exposed.

13   ...   ♗b4!

This is stronger than the alternative 13...exd5 14 cxd5 (14 ♗g4 ♕e7 15 cxd5 is tempting, but 15...♕b4! is awkward for White) 14...♗b4 (14...♘xd5?! 15 ♗g4 forces Black into a dubious queen sacrifice by 15...♕xg4 16 ♕xg4 ♘xe3) 15 ♔f2! ♕h3 (the key tactical point is that 15...♗xc3 16 dxc6 ♕xc6 17 ♕b3 threatens both the bishop and ♗b5, and so wins a piece) 16 ♕b3 ♗xc3 17 dxc6 with a very unclear position.

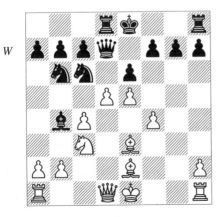

14   ♗xb6?

In this critical position White makes a serious error. The alternatives were:

1) 14 dxc6? ♕xc6 attacks both d1 and h1, winning for Black.

2) 14 ♗f3? exd5 15 ♗xb6 transposes to the game.

3) 14 ♖g1 exd5 15 ♗xb6 axb6 16 cxd5 ♕h3! is very good for Black after 17 ♖xg7 ♕h4+ 18 ♖g3 ♕xh2 or 17 ♕d3 ♕xh2 18 ♖xg7 ♕h1+ 19 ♗f1 ♖xd5.

4) 14 ♔f2! is the most resilient defence. After 14...♗xc3 (14...exd5?! 15 cxd5 transposes to the previous note) 15 dxc6 ♕xc6 16 ♕g1! (here 16 ♕b3 doesn't work, because there is no threat of ♗b5; the move ♕g1 is the reason why 14 ♔f2! is better than 14 0-0 – another example of the specific overriding the general) 16...♗d4 17 ♕xg7 ♖f8 Black has some advantage because White's king is the more exposed, but the battle is far from over.

The text-move is wrong since White's dark-squared bishop is a key defensive piece. Without it, the dark squares in White's position are horribly weak. It is true that the elimination of the b6-knight means that White can maintain his wobbly pawn-centre a bit longer, but the new weaknesses enable Black to exploit White's problems in another way. The advancing pawns have left a huge vacuum behind them; with the disappearance of the last remnants of White's dark-square control, Black's pieces (in particular his queen) can funnel in through the gaping fissures.

14   ...   axb6
15   ♗f3

Necessary if White is to avoid losing the d5-pawn. 15 ♖g1 exd5 transposes into line '3' of the preceding note.

15   ...   exd5

Now this exchange serves a useful purpose – it allows Black's queen to penetrate.

16   cxd5

16 ♗xd5 ♕h3 17 ♕f3 ♕xf3 18 ♗xf3 ♖d4 is no improvement, as White will lose at least one pawn.

16   ...   ♕h3

White is struggling to meet the immediate threat 17...♕h4+.

17   ♔e2

The only defence.

17   ...   0-0

Rubbing salt in the wound. White's king is now floundering helplessly in the middle of the board, while Black's is perfectly safe. The idea is ...♖fe8, when a piece sacrifice on e5 would be just around the corner.

18   ♕d3

After 18 ♘b5 (18 ♘e4 ♗c5!, followed by ...♘d4+, wins for Black) 18...♖fe8! (18...♕h4 19 ♕c1 ♗c5 is also winning) 19 ♕b3 the sacrifice is deadly: 19...♘xe5 20 fxe5 ♖xe5+ 21 ♔d1 ♖de8 (threatening 22...♖e3) 22 ♘d4 ♗c5 and everything collapses.

18   ...   ♘e7?!

Black is winning even after this, but it would have been simpler to put White out of his misery by 18...♕h4 19 ♕e4 ♗c5 20 ♖af1 f5! 21 ♕a4 ♘d4+, etc.

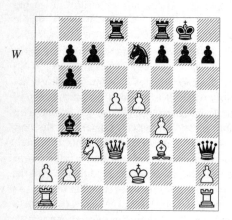

19   ♕c4?!

Now Black is once again comfortably winning. 19 ♖ad1 is a tougher defence, when Black should continue 19...♕h4 20 ♕e4 ♗xc3 (the alternative 20...♗c5 21 ♖df1 ♘g6 22 f5 is less clear) 21 bxc3 ♘g6 22 ♖d4 c5! 23 dxc6 ♖xd4 24 cxd4 bxc6 25 f5 ♘f4+ 26 ♔d1 ♖d8 and White's exposed king must succumb.

19   ...   ♗xc3

20   bxc3   b5!

Vaganian finishes with great energy. He only needs to open the d-file to complete the encirclement of the white king.

21   ♕xb5

Or 21 ♕d4 ♘g6 22 a4 (22 ♖ag1 ♖a8 and 22 ♖ab1 ♖a8 are hopeless, because the threats of 23...♖xa2+ and 23...♖a4 cannot be met) 22...c5 23 ♕e3 ♕f5 and f4 falls.

21   ...   c6!

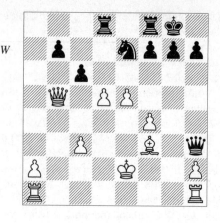

This is the point behind the previous move. Now the d5-pawn disappears and White's king is attacked from all sides.

22   dxc6

22 ♕xb7 ♘xd5 is hopeless for White.

22   ...   bxc6

23   ♕c4

Defending f4, but not for long.

23   ...   ♘g6

Threatening 23...♕h4 or 23...♕f5.

24   ♖ag1

After 24 ♕e4 (24 ♖ad1 ♕h4 attacks both f4 and e5) 24...♕h6 25 ♔e3 ♘xf4 26 ♕xf4 ♖d3+ 27 ♔e4 ♕g6+ 28 ♕f5 ♖e3+ White loses his queen.

24   ...   ♕f5

Threatening both 25...♘xf4+ and 25...♕c2+.

25   ♖g4

White cannot meet both threats.

25   ...   ♕c2+

The queen penetrates decisively.

26   ♔e3

26 ♔f1 loses to 26...♖d1+ 27 ♗xd1 ♕xd1+ and 28...♕xg4.

26   ...   ♕d2+

The king-hunt will not last long.

27   ♔e4   ♖d5

0-1

A nice finish, unpinning the f7-pawn and threatening 28...f5+ 29 exf6 ♖e8#. 28 ♗e2 is the only defence, but then Black can choose between the simple 28...f5+ 29 exf6 ♖e8+ 30 ♔f3 ♕e3+ and the computer's 28...♖c5 29 ♕d3 f5+ 30 exf6 ♖e8+ 31 ♔f3 ♖xc3.

The difference between a strong and a weak pawn-centre can be very fine. When one player adopts the ambitious plan of forming a large pawn-centre, a small slip can often prove fatal. Here, Van der Wiel made the slip as early as move 12, when he played one pawn move too many and fell seriously behind in development. Had Vaganian responded in stereotyped fashion, then Van der Wiel might have got away with it, but Black produced a series of very accurate moves to put White in trouble. When White missed a chance to stay in the game at move 14, it was effectively all over. A combination of dark-squared weaknesses, a king stuck in the centre and a huge vacuum behind his over-extended pawn-centre led to a rapid collapse.

The lessons here are:

1) Forming a large pawn-centre is often double-edged. If the pawn-centre can be maintained and supported by pieces then it will be strong, but there is a danger that it might collapse.

2) Once you have built a large pawn-centre, you must hurry with your development; further time-wasting can be fatal.

3) The exchange of a bishop for a knight may leave weaknesses on the squares that were controlled by the bishop.

4) In deciding on a move, general considerations may be useful, but concrete analysis always takes precedence.

Modern Gambit Play

Back in the mid-19th century, gambits were commonplace. The King's Gambit was one of the most popular openings, and led to many beautiful wins for White, especially when the defender greedily took all the material on offer (the 'Immortal Game' is an example). Since then, the play of both defenders and gambiteers has been considerably refined. First of all, the defenders strengthened their hand by taking a certain amount of material and then refusing the later offerings. Sometimes they would even return all the sacrificed material in order to obtain a positional advantage. When these advances in defensive technique were applied in practice, it soon became clear that many of the gambits that had been popular weren't really sound, and these gradually disappeared. However, this does not mean that gambit play has been entirely sidelined. On the contrary, the realization that compensation can be at least partly positional has led to the development of many new gambit ideas. For example, two of Frank Marshall's inventions, the Marshall Attack in the Ruy Lopez (1 e4 e5 2 ♘f3 ♘c6 3 ♗b5 a6 4 ♗a4 ♘f6 5 0-0 ♗e7 6 ♖e1 b5 7 ♗b3 0-0 8 c3 d5!?) and the Marshall Gambit in the Semi-Slav (1 d4 d5 2 c4 e6 3 ♘c3 c6 4 e4!?) are regularly seen in top-class grandmaster play. These modern gambits typically involve the sacrifice of a limited amount of material (usually a pawn, or occasionally two), for which the attacker obtains both positional compensation and some attacking chances.

Game 5

T. Markowski – A. Onishchuk

Rubinstein Memorial, Polanica Zdroj 1999

Catalan Opening

1   ♘f3

See Game 1 for comments on this move.

1   ...   d5

A no-nonsense reply. Black simply occupies the centre.

2   g3

If White plays d4 at some stage, the game normally transposes into a standard Queen's Pawn opening. That is what eventually happens in the current game, but for the moment White keeps his options open regarding his d-pawn. The text-move aims, just as in Game 1, to exert pressure against Black's centre using the fianchettoed bishop on g2. However, in Game 1 Black arranged his central pawns on dark squares, which gave him a measure of central control at the cost of ceding the light squares to White. Here Black aims to play on the light squares himself; in particular he would like to maintain a central pawn on d5 to restrict the g2-bishop. This is a less ambitious plan, but it also gives White less leeway.

2   ...   ♘f6

The most natural square for the g8-knight is f6, and from here it supports the d5-pawn.

3   ♗g2

This is the obvious follow-up to White's previous move.

3   ...   e6

Black plays consistently to reinforce his d5-pawn. This move also enables him to develop the rest of his kingside without difficulty. The only fly in the ointment is the c8-bishop, which is now blocked in by the e6-pawn. In some lines Black will solve this problem by ...b6 and ...♗b7, but as we shall see, in this game Black opts for a more dramatic solution.

4   c4

The battle for the d5-square intensifies. This move does not constitute a gambit because after 4...dxc4 White can easily regain the pawn by 5 ♕a4+.

4   ...   ♗e7

For the moment Black is content to continue his kingside development.

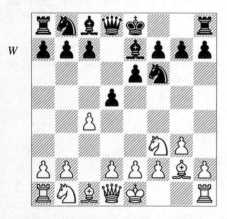

5   d4

White finally decides to play d4 and thereby transpose into an opening called the Catalan. This system is based on exploiting the power of the fianchettoed bishop on g2. If Black retains his pawn on d5, then the bishop will exert pressure on it, but if Black plays ...dxc4 the bishop's range of action will be extended towards Black's queenside.

5   ...   0-0

It is usually better to play necessary developing moves before optional ones, in order to keep the maximum flexibility. Black's main decision in the Catalan is whether to play ...dxc4. This move has the advantage that White may have to waste time regaining the pawn on c4, but the disadvantage is that the pressure of the g2-bishop against the b7-pawn may make the development of Black's c8-bishop even more difficult.

6   ♘c3

A rather unusual move, perhaps because it does not fit in with the 'necessary moves before optional ones' principle. The most common continuation is 6 0-0. If Black then plays 6...dxc4 (maintaining the d5-pawn by 6...c6 followed by ...♘bd7 is also popular), White has the choice between various methods of regaining the c4-pawn: 7 ♕c2 (most common), 7 ♕a4 and 7 ♘e5. This last possibility can transpose into the game after the further moves 7...♘c6 8 ♗xc6 bxc6 9 ♘xc6 ♕e8 10 ♘xe7+ ♕xe7 11 ♕a4 c5 12 ♕xc4 cxd4 13 ♕xd4 e5 14 ♕h4 ♖b8 15 ♘c3.

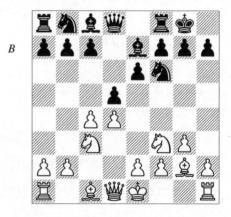

6   ...   dxc4

This capture looks especially logical in view of White's unusual move-order. By playing ♘c3 first, White has voluntarily ruled out one of the plans mentioned above (that based on ♕c2).

7   ♘e5

White is now virtually committed to this plan, since 7 ♕a4 allows Black easy equality by

7...a6 8 ♕xc4 b5 9 ♕b3 ♗b7, followed by ...c5, while after 7 0-0?! ♘c6 the pressure against d4 makes it a real challenge to regain the c4-pawn.

After the text-move, White threatens to regain the pawn by ♘xc4, and then quietly complete his development. This would give him an advantage, as he has an extra central pawn and his g2-bishop is far more active than its counterpart on c8. Thus Black must act quickly.

7   ...   ♘c6!

Here is the gambit. The choice was between this move and 7...c5, and the reasons for preferring the text-move are typical for the modern, dynamic approach to the openings. 7...c5 aims for an exchange of the pawns on c5 and d4, thereby creating a symmetrical pawn-structure, which would give Black equalizing chances. The problem is that White would retain the pressure against Black's queenside, which might make it hard for Black to equalize completely. Moreover, this is a negative strategy – even if all goes well, the maximum Black can hope for is a draw. After 7...c5 8 dxc5, White retains an edge after both 8...♕xd1+ 9 ♘xd1 ♗xc5 10 ♗d2 ♘d5 11 ♘xc4 and 8...♕c7 9 ♘xc4.

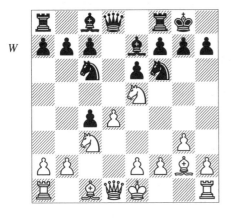

The text-move is far more combative in that Black offers a pawn in order to activate his pieces, especially the c8-bishop. White has the choice between allowing easy equality, or accepting the pawn. In the latter case he faces a long period of careful defence in a very sharp position. After 7...c5 White could play for a win without risk, because it would be hard to lose in the resulting placid positions, but 7...♘c6 raises the stakes: at the cost of some risk, Black acquires winning chances.

8   ♗xc6

White accepts the challenge and plays to win a pawn. After 8 ♘xc6 bxc6 9 ♗xc6 ♖b8 10 0-0 ♘d5 Black has no problems. His pieces are active and White's bishop is stranded on c6.

8   ...   bxc6

9   ♘xc6

After 9 ♘xc4 c5 Black liquidates his doubled pawns, when his two bishops and active pieces are more important than his slightly broken queenside pawn-structure.

9   ...   ♕e8

This is probably more accurate than 9...♕d6, because then 10 ♕a4 ♗b7 11 ♘xe7+ ♕xe7 12 0-0 leads to a position similar to the game, but with the important difference that Black's bishop is already committed to b7. As we shall see, this blocks the b-file and prevents Black attacking the b2-pawn with ...♖ab8.

10   ♘xe7+

Although this move is universally adopted, it is also possible to play 10 ♕a4 here. After 10...♗d6 11 ♘e5 ♕xa4 12 ♘xa4 ♘e4 13 ♘xc4 ♗b4+ Black should have enough for the pawn; for example, 14 ♗d2 ♘xd2 15 ♘xd2 ♖d8 16 e3 e5 or 14 ♔f1 ♖d8 15 ♗e3 ♗d7 16 a3 ♗e7 17 ♘c5 ♘xc5 18 dxc5 a5. However, in view of the fact that the game continuation appears entirely satisfactory for Black, those who wish to play this line with White need to investigate possible alternatives.

10   ...   ♕xe7

The liquidation that has occurred strongly favours Black. All his pieces can now enter the game freely, the rooks by ...♖b8 and ...♖d8, and the bishop by ...♗b7 or ...e5. Moreover, the disappearance of White's light-squared bishop has left his kingside light squares weak. Black's own light-squared bishop is the ideal piece to exploit these weaknesses, and while there are no serious threats as yet, White might run into long-term problems on the kingside.

11   ♕a4

White needs to have something to compensate for all these factors favouring Black, and so he is essentially committed to the capture of the c4-pawn, in order to have material solace for his positional shortcomings.

11   ...   c5

It would be quite wrong for Black to try to hold the c4-pawn by 11...♗b7 12 0-0 ♗d5. This costs time and so loses the initiative, while the bishop cannot be maintained at d5 in any case. After 13 ♗g5 c5 14 ♗xf6 gxf6 15 ♕a3 ♖ac8 16 e4 ♗a8 17 d5, for example, Black has a miserable position with pawn weaknesses on both wings.

The text-move systematically opens up the position, while at the same time liquidating Black's only pawn weakness – the isolated c-pawn.

12   ♕xc4

Not 12 ♕a3? ♕b7, followed by ...cxd4, when Black wins.

12   ...   cxd4

13   ♕xd4

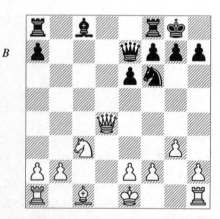

B

It is time to take a look at the position and assess what Black has achieved with his gambit. First of all, Black has a lead in development, which one may judge to be approximately two tempi: he has castled while White has not, and Black will gain at least one tempo thanks to the

exposed position of White's queen. Secondly, White has been deprived of his light-squared bishop, which in so many lines of the Catalan exerts unwelcome pressure against Black's queenside. Indeed, here it is the other way round – it is more likely to be Black's light-squared bishop that will exert unwelcome pressure against White's kingside. Note that we are not talking about anything so crude as a queen and bishop mate along the long diagonal. It is easy enough for White to prevent any such attack by a combination of f3 and/or e4. It is more that White constantly has to worry about the weaknesses near his king and this is just one of many small factors which individually are not too troublesome, but which together add up to a considerable defensive burden. Finally, Black's position is entirely without weaknesses. This means that if White employs the time-honoured anti-gambit measure of returning the sacrificed material, then he is unlikely to gain any advantage.

White, on the other hand, does have his extra pawn. His position is fairly solid, with the notable exception of his kingside light squares. If he had time to play f3 and e4 to shield the long diagonal, and then develop the c1-bishop, then he could look forward to good winning chances. Black, therefore, must try to complete his development while restricting White's.

Practical experience from this position suggests that Black's compensation just about balances White's extra pawn. White can, if he wishes, return the pawn with an equal position, but if he tries to hang on to it then he runs considerable risks.

13   ...   e5

A good move which forces White's queen to declare its intentions. Moreover, White now has to worry that his king will be trapped in the centre by ...♗h3.

14   ♕h4

This prevents ...♗h3 and puts the queen on a square where it is not easy to attack, but the queen is offside on h4 and reactivating it will not be straightforward. 14 ♕a4 ♗h3 15 ♕h4 ♗g2 16 ♖g1 ♗c6 also does not solve White's problems, since although he can develop his queenside more easily, his king will be stuck in the centre.

14   ...   ♖b8!

In order to make the most of his lead in development, Black must play accurately. This move has two functions. Firstly, it prevents, at least for the moment, the development of the c1-bishop; secondly, it prepares ...♖b4 to inconvenience White's queen. If White meets this by e4, the e4-pawn will be weak and subject to attack.

Note that 14...♗b7 is much less accurate, since after 15 0-0 White is already threatening to bring his bishop out.

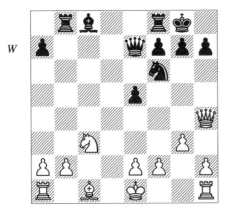

15   0-0
White plays to keep the extra pawn. After 15 ♗g5 ♖xb2 16 0-0 (after 16 ♘d5 Black should be satisfied with a draw by 16...♕b7 17 ♘xf6+ gxf6 18 0-0 fxg5 19 ♕xg5+, since 16...♕d6 17 ♘xf6+ gxf6 18 ♗h6 followed by 19 0-0 can only be better for White) 16...♕e6 17 ♗xf6 ♕xf6 18 ♕xf6 gxf6 19 ♖ab1 ♖xb1 20 ♖xb1 the game reduces to a drawn ending.

15   ...   ♖b4
Now White is more or less forced to push his e-pawn.

16   e4
After 16 f4 ♕c5+ 17 e3 ♕c6, followed by ...♗b7, White can no longer use his kingside pawns to block the long diagonal, and the threat to penetrate to g2 or h1 with the queen is very dangerous.

16   ...   h6!?
The first point behind this move is simply to make it harder for White to develop his c1-bishop, since now ♗g5 is prevented. It also introduces a new element into the position – the possibility of trapping the white queen by ...g5. This is not an immediate threat because the

h6-pawn is hanging, and even ...♔h7 does not threaten ...g5, since then the h-pawn is pinned. However, it acts as a restraining influence on White. For example, there is a tempting line-up of black pieces on the a3-f8 diagonal, which might be exploited by b3 and ♗a3. It is harder for White's bishop to quit the c1-h6 diagonal when there is ...g5 in the air.

As a matter of fact, this position is very comfortable for Black, and while the text-move is perhaps the most awkward for White, there are alternatives which are good enough to hold the balance; for example, 16...♗b7 17 f3 ♕c5+ 18 ♔g2 ♖d8 19 ♖f2 ♖d3 20 ♗g5 ♕b6, when White cannot avoid the loss of the b2-pawn.

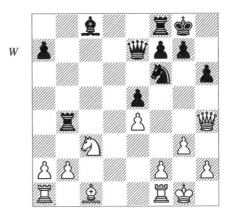

17   ♖e1?
White does not face any instant threats and so has a move or two to improve his position. The priorities are:

1) to support the weak light squares and vulnerable e4-pawn;

2) to bring the queen back into the game;

3) if possible, to develop the c1-bishop.

There will probably not be time for all of these, but the first two are more important than the third, and so White should concentrate on those. The move that helps towards both the first two objectives is 17 f3, aiming to play g4 and ♕f2. Then, with the b2-pawn covered, White can set about the third objective. The text-move is inferior because, although it supports e4, it does nothing for the queen, a factor which Black is quick to exploit. After 17 f3 ♖d8 18 g4 ♖d3 19 ♕f2 ♕b7 (again tying down the c1-bishop) the position is roughly equal, with Black's pressure providing compensation for the pawn but no more. However, there is no doubt that White has to take great care and in practice it is easier to play Black's side. For example, the obvious 20 ♖d1? runs into the reply 20...♖xd1+ 21 ♘xd1 ♘xe4! 22 fxe4 ♕xe4, followed by 22...♗b7, with a decisive attack. 20 ♖e1 is better, intending 21 ♖e3.

17 ...　　　　♖d8

Threatening 18...♖d3, preventing f3, when White will be virtually paralysed.

18 f3

White ends up playing this move in any case, which only emphasizes that 17 ♖e1 was a waste of time. However, there was nothing better; for example, 18 b3 ♖d3 19 ♘a4 (19 ♗b2? ♔h7, threatening 20...g5, is one line in which Black exploits the bad position of the white queen) 19...♖xe4! 20 ♖xe4 ♖d1+ 21 ♔g2 ♗b7 22 ♘c3 (22 f3 loses to 22...♗xe4 23 fxe4 ♕b4) 22...♕d7 23 ♘xd1 (after 23 f3 ♘xe4 24 fxe4 ♖e1 25 ♔f2 ♕d4+ 26 ♔xe1 ♕xc3+ 27 ♔f2 ♕xa1 28 ♕d8+ ♔h7 29 ♕d2 ♕b1 Black wins a pawn while retaining attacking chances against White's king) 23...♘xe4! (23...♕xd1 24 ♗g5! and 23...♗xe4+ 24 f3 ♗xf3+ 25 ♔xf3 ♕xd1+ 26 ♔g2 ♕e2+ 27 ♔g1 are less clear) 24 ♘e3 (24 ♗e3 ♘g5+ 25 f3 ♕f5 26 ♘f2 ♕xf3+ 27 ♔f1 ♕g2+ 28 ♔e2 ♗a6+ 29 ♔d1 ♕f3+ 30 ♔c2 ♕xe3 31 ♘d1 ♕e2+ wins for Black) 24...♘g5+ 25 f3 ♕c6 26 ♕h5 (26 ♕g4 ♗c8 27 ♕h5 g6 is the same) 26...g6 27 ♕g4 ♗c8 and Black wins.

18 ...　　　　♖d3

Now the f3-pawn is weak.

19 ♔g2

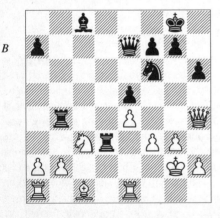

An unfortunate necessity; White is not yet ready to play ♕f2, and the b2-pawn is hanging

so White cannot play a piece to e3. The textmove is undesirable for two reasons: firstly, if Black does eventually capture on b2, it will be with check, and secondly the king is placed on the long diagonal, which increases the chances of a sacrificial breakthrough on e4.

19 ...　　　　♕b7!

Black immediately exploits both defects of ♔g2. The immediate threat of 20...♖xb2+ 21 ♗xb2 ♕xb2+ 22 ♘e2 ♖d2 23 ♔f2 ♗a6 utilizes the first, while the game continuation takes advantage of the second.

Curiously, Markowski had reached this position in an earlier game (Markowski-S.Ivanov, Polish Team Championship, Krynica 1997) and had lost after 19...♕e6. It is quite hard to see the attraction of this dismal position – presumably Markowski had prepared an improvement over his earlier game, but Onishchuk finds an even more effective move for Black than 19...♕e6 and puts paid to this position once and for all.

20 ♖e2

Defending b2. 20 ♔f2 loses to 20...♕b6+ 21 ♔g2 ♖xb2+, etc., while 20 g4 is blown apart by 20...♗xg4! 21 fxg4 ♘xe4 22 ♘xe4 ♖xe4 23 ♔g1 ♕b6+ 24 ♔g2 ♕b4!.

20 ...　　　　♗g4!

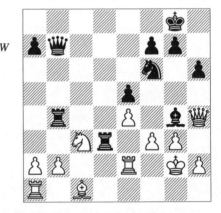

It looked as if any explosion on e4 would occur via ...♘xe4, but Black finds another way to eliminate the f3-pawn. This beautiful move forces open the long diagonal and exposes the white king to the combined fire of Black's major pieces.

21 fxg4

21 ♖f2 loses to 21...♗xf3+ 22 ♖xf3 ♘xe4 23 ♖xd3 (23 ♘xe4 ♖xe4 24 ♖xd3 ♖xh4+)

23...♘xc3+ 24 ♔f2 (24 ♖f3 ♖xh4 25 gxh4 ♘e2 leads to further material loss) 24...♖xh4 25 gxh4 ♕b6+ 26 ♔e1 (or else the d3-rook falls) 26...♕g1+ 27 ♔d2 ♘e4+ 28 ♔c2 ♕xh2+ 29 ♗d2 ♕xh4 and the four(!) connected passed pawns are overwhelming.

21 ... ♘xe4

With two of White's most important pieces, the queen and a1-rook, playing no part at all in the defence, Black's attack is irresistible.

22 ♖xe4

Or:

1) After 22 ♔h3 ♘f6! there is no defence to the numerous threats, which include 23...♖xg4 and 23...♕f3.

2) 22 ♔g1 ♘xc3 23 bxc3 ♖d1+ 24 ♔f2 ♕h1 and Black wins since 25 cxb4 allows 25...♕g1+ 26 ♔f3 ♖f1+ 27 ♔e4 ♕d4#.

22 ... ♖xe4

23 ♔h3

After 23 ♘xe4 ♕xe4+ 24 ♔h3 ♕e1 25 ♗xh6 (25 ♕e7 ♖xg3+! 26 hxg3 ♕h1#) 25...♕xa1 26 ♕g5 ♕f1+ 27 ♔h4 there are many ways to win. 27...♕f6 28 ♕xf6 gxf6 29 ♔h3 ♖d1 is one of the simplest, since Black wins a queenside pawn immediately.

23 ... ♖e1

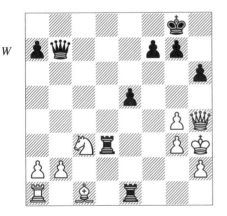

Threatening 24...♕h1 or 24...♖g1.

24 ♗xh6

Spinning the game out by a few moves.

24 ... ♖xa1

Black sees no reason to turn down a free rook.

25 ♕g5

At least White gets to threaten mate before he resigns.

25 ... f6

Stopping the mate with gain of tempo.

26 ♕g6 ♖xc3

0-1

After 27 bxc3 ♖g1 28 ♔h4 ♖g2 29 h3 (29 ♔h3 ♖e2), one win is 29...♕f7 30 ♕e4 (30 ♕xf7+ ♔xf7 31 ♗c1 g5+ 32 ♔h5 ♖xg3 33 h4 ♖h3 wins the bishop) 30...♖h2, followed by ...gxh6 or ...g5+, when White will be a whole rook down.

Gambit play is still common today, but the emphasis is rather different from that in the 19th century. Instead of aiming for a do-or-die attack on the enemy king, modern gambits are often based at least as much on positional considerations as on immediate attacking chances. In this game Onishchuk offered a pawn as early as move seven in order to free his position and wrest the initiative from White. In return for the pawn, he obtained a whole range of small positional advantages. Of these, the most significant were his light-squared pressure and the ability to use his lead in development to prevent White completing his own development (mainly by means of pressure against b2 and later e4). Markowski could have returned the pawn to equalize, but he chose the risky path of holding on to his extra material. It only required one error, at move 17, and Black's attack was already unstoppable. Onishchuk pressed his attack home with a powerful and attractive piece sacrifice to gain control of the light squares White had weakened in the act of accepting the gambit.

The lessons here are:

1) Gambits are part and parcel of opening play. In this game a gambit proved the best answer to White's plan of exerting positional pressure.

2) A lead in development and some positional advantages may be enough compensation for a pawn.

3) Restraining the opponent's development often gives time to build up a powerful attack.

4) Pressing home an attack may require imagination and the willingness to sacrifice.

2 Middlegame Themes

The middlegame is to some extent *terra incognita* for chess literature. There are a huge number of opening books, but relatively few about the middlegame – even though most games are decided in the middlegame. Perhaps the problem is that the structure of opening books is quite standard, the author knows what he is supposed to do and the reader knows what to expect. The middlegame, on the other hand, is a large, amorphous subject which resists a case-by-case approach. Most authors who have tackled the middlegame have narrowed their field and dealt with just one specialized aspect (such as the attack on the king, or pawn-structures).

One side-effect of the relative dearth of middlegame literature is that recent developments in the handling of middlegame issues have not been reflected in chess literature. One notable exception, which I have already mentioned in the Introduction, is John Watson's *Secrets of Modern Chess Strategy*. My aim is to partially remedy the lack of up-to-date middlegame literature by covering a wide range of middlegame topics from a contemporary viewpoint.

I have divided this lengthy chapter into three sections, dealing respectively with attacking play, defensive play and positional play. As I have already mentioned, the middlegame is a huge subject and the choice of topics must inevitably be limited, but I have made an effort to focus on those areas which are of greatest practical importance.

2.1 Attacking Play

Chess nomenclature is a tricky subject, because there are many terms for which there is no generally accepted definition. 'Attack' is one of these. If White moves all his pieces towards the enemy king and mates Black, then probably we would all agree that this was an attack, but there are many less clear-cut cases. For example, there is a strategic concept involving the advance of a smaller number of pawns against a larger number. This is called a 'minority attack' (see Game 21), but it does not bear much resemblance to the attack on the king mentioned above. In this section on attacking play we will deal with attack in the sense of 'aggressive action with concrete objectives, usually based on short-term threats'. Note that it is not necessarily directed against the king, although in practice the king will often be the target. Later on in the book we will cover more positional forms of attack, such as the minority attack mentioned above.

Game 6 deals with the basic attacking ideas and in Game 7 we consider the importance of having sufficient forces in the attack to finish the job off.

There are a number of standard sacrifices which can be used in an attack, such as the Greek Gift (♗xh7+) and the double bishop sacrifice (♗xh7+ followed by a later ♗xg7). In Game 8 we look at just one of these, the Greek Gift, and show how the standard pattern may have to be modified according to the demands of a particular position.

Once the attack has started, the attacker has to be unwavering in his determination to see the attack through, even if it means sacrificing almost all his pieces. Game 9 is an excellent example.

A typical situation which leads naturally to attacks is that of opposite-side castling; in this case the opponent usually has a counter-attack, and the interplay of attack and counter-attack can lead to very complex play. This situation is discussed in Game 10.

Finally, with many dynamic openings being based on fianchettoed bishops (such as the Sicilian Dragon and the King's Indian), attacking play on the long diagonals has become a common feature of contemporary chess. This situation is covered in Game 11.

Basic Attacking Ideas

Our coverage of attacking play starts with some of the fundamental attacking ideas. In order for an attack to be launched with any hope of success, at least some elements of the position must already favour the attacker. The nature of these preconditions can vary quite a lot, but typical examples are more active pieces, better central control, a lead in development, weaknesses in the opponent's position and an exposed enemy king. Not all of these need be in place, but an attack is unlikely to succeed unless at least some of them are present. Once the attack has started, the attacker must bear in mind the following important attacking ideas:

1) Momentum: it is important to keep the impetus of the attack going, in order to give the defender no chance to organize his position and beat off the attacking forces. Thus attacks often operate with direct threats.

2) Opening lines: the attacking forces must be able to get to grips with the enemy, and this is easier if there are several open lines leading into the enemy position. If these open lines do not exist to begin with, it may be possible to force them open by appropriate pawn moves or, in extreme cases, by a sacrifice.

3) Remove defenders: the exchange of a key defensive piece may make the difference between success and failure.

4) Force weaknesses: if the opponent's position is initially without weaknesses, you may have to induce some before the attack can really get under way. This applies particularly in the case of a direct attack on the king.

The following game is an excellent example of the first three attacking ideas mentioned above.

Game 6
G. Kasparov – N. Short
VSB tournament, Amsterdam 1994
French Defence, Classical Variation

1   e4

For comments on this move, see Game 3.

1   ...   e6

This modest pawn advance, called the French Defence, plans to challenge the e4-pawn by ...d5 without having to recapture with the queen after exd5. In this respect it is quite similar to the Caro-Kann Defence 1...c6 (see Game 25), but in other ways it is quite different. The main defect of the French Defence is that Black, with his very first move, blocks the most natural diagonal for developing the c8-bishop. Many games in the French revolve around this bishop; if Black can activate it, then he often gets a good game, but if it ends up permanently imprisoned behind Black's central pawns, then he may well be in trouble.

Both the Caro-Kann and the French are safe and solid methods of meeting 1 e4. The slightly passive positions Black obtains may not suit the style of every player, but there is no question that White has a great deal of work ahead to make any real inroads into Black's position.

2   d4

White takes the chance to form a 'two-abreast' pawn-centre...

2   ...   d5

...which Black immediately challenges.

3   ♘c3

Kasparov once described 3 ♘c3 as 'the strongest move in this position' and most players would agree with him. The main alternatives are:

1) 3 ♘d2, which avoids a possible pin with ...♗b4 (since White could reply c3), but accepts a less active position for the queen's knight.

2) 3 e5, closing the centre straight away. This tips White's hand rather early and does not cause Black any serious problems.

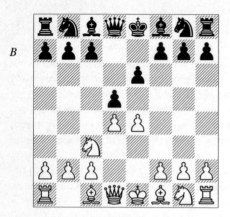

B

3 ... ♘f6

One of two equally popular moves. The other is 3...♗b4, which, by pinning the knight, attacks e4 and so virtually forces White's hand in the centre. After the sequence 4 e5 c5 5 a3 ♗xc3+ 6 bxc3 a complex and double-edged position arises. Black has exchanged off his 'good' bishop (the one not impeded by his central pawns) and is now somewhat weak on the dark squares. On the other hand, he has shattered White's queenside pawns. The struggle between these advantages and disadvantages usually leads to sharp play.

The text-move, by contrast, is more conservative. Black again forces White to commit the e4-pawn by exerting pressure on e4, but without conceding his dark-squared bishop in the process. Of course, the disadvantage is that Black also doesn't double White's c-pawns.

4 e5

This is one of two main options, the other being 4 ♗g5. Note that defending the e4-pawn by 4 ♗d3 would be a mistake since the d4-pawn is then undefended. Black would reply 4...c5, breaking up White's centre and solving all his problems.

4 ... ♘fd7

4...♘e4 is a risky move. After 5 ♘xe4 dxe4 White can gain the advantage by either 6 ♗c4 or 6 ♗e3, since the protruding pawn on e4 can easily become weak.

After the text-move we have a typical position with a blocked pawn-centre. White controls more space, but his pawn-centre can easily be attacked by ...c5. The exchange of the d4-pawn might very well leave the e5-pawn weak, so White hastens to offer it extra support.

5 f4

Now that the e5-pawn is secure, White can develop his pieces by ♘f3, etc.

5 ... c5

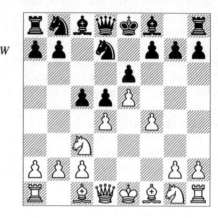

W

White's pawn-centre certainly looks strong, and if he is allowed to develop in peace behind it, then Black will soon start feeling cramped. Therefore Black must strike straight away, before White has a chance to consolidate. When battling against a pawn-chain such as that on d4 and e5, there is usually a choice between attacking the base of the chain (here d4) or its head (here e5). Most textbooks will tell you that it is right to attack the base of the pawn-chain, but the truth of the matter is that it all depends on the precise position. Here White's e5-pawn has the extra support of the pawn on f4, so ...f6 is ineffective – White can maintain the pawn on e5 without difficulty. Thus the attack by ...c5 is indicated. However, once the d4-pawn has been exchanged, Black may later on consider an attack by ...f6, since the e5-pawn will have less support. We will return to the subject of pawn-chains in Game 24.

6 ♘f3

If White's knight weren't on c3, then he would probably support his d4-pawn by playing c3, but as it is, the best he can do is to offer piece support.

6 ... ♘c6

Black steps up the pressure on d4 with this natural developing move.

7 ♗e3

It is essential to lend further support to the key square d4. Here is what might happen if White casually starts to develop his kingside: 7

♗e2? cxd4 8 ♘b5 (8 ♘xd4 loses a pawn to 8...♘dxe5! 9 fxe5 ♕h4+) 8...♗c5 9 ♘bxd4 ♘dxe5! and again Black wins a pawn.

7 ... cxd4

Black has quite a wide range of plans here. One is to step up the pressure on d4, by 7...♕b6 or 7...cxd4 8 ♘xd4 ♕b6. Alternatively, he can just continue his development, when he must decide whether to give priority to the queenside (by 7...a6 8 ♕d2 b5) or, as in this game, to the kingside.

8 ♘xd4 ♗c5

Short plays to complete his kingside development.

9 ♕d2

White still cannot simply continue his kingside development, since 9 ♗e2 0-0 10 0-0 runs into 10...♕b6 11 ♘a4 ♗xd4! 12 ♘xb6 ♗xe3+ 13 ♔h1 ♗xb6 with an excellent position for Black. Although three minor pieces have the same 'point value' as a queen, in most middlegame positions they are far superior.

Therefore White prepares to castle queenside, when d4 will have plenty of support. With the players castling on opposite sides, sharp play can be expected.

9 ... 0-0

Now that Black's king is in safety, he can consider starting an attack by means of a gradual advance of his queenside pawns.

9...♗xd4 10 ♗xd4 ♘xd4 11 ♕xd4 ♕b6 is an alternative, but the resulting endgame slightly favours White for two reasons; firstly, White controls more space and secondly his bishop is more active than Black's.

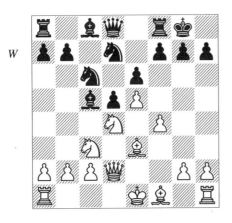

10 0-0-0

The general structure of the position indicates that White will play for a kingside attack and Black will aim for a queenside counterattack. At first sight White's attacking chances look rather good; Black's kingside is devoid of defensive minor pieces and the e5-pawn prevents Black from easily switching defensive units to the kingside. However, two factors mean that White's attack is far from straightforward:

1) Black's kingside pawns are unweakened, so there is no obvious target on the kingside. In order to force such a weakness, White must either manoeuvre with his pieces or play h4-h5-h6, but both these plans require considerable time.

2) The pressure against d4 restricts White's freedom of movement. For example, the f1-bishop is currently playing no part in the attack, but it cannot move to d3 without interrupting the queen's guard of d4.

10 ... a6

Black's counterplay inches forwards.

11 h4

This is a good move which serves a dual purpose. As mentioned above, the pawn might go all the way to h6, in order to force a weakness in Black's kingside pawn defences. However, White might prefer to conduct the attack using pieces, and now the manoeuvre ♖h3-g3 is available. The rook is quite well placed on the third rank, since it can also perform a defensive function by operating sideways. This slightly unusual method of developing the rook is here quite logical. Not only does it fit in best with White's kingside ambitions, but also the only other option would involve developing the f1-bishop, which could only go to the relatively useless square e2. White still hopes to play the bishop to d3 in one move, so at present the bishop should stay on f1 if it is at all possible.

11 ... ♘xd4

This exchange is a necessary preliminary to playing ...b5.

12 ♗xd4 b5

13 ♖h3

This is a more flexible move than 13 h5. White develops his rook, but is not yet committed to a particular plan of attack.

13 ... b4

The most direct response, which forces White to decide on the destination for his knight.

However, 13...♛b6 and 13...♝b7 are playable alternatives.

14   ♘a4

If White plays 14 ♘e2, then 14...a5 is a good reply since Black makes progress with his queenside action and permits the inactive c8-bishop to be developed at a6.

14   ...   ♝xd4

The attack on c5 forces Black to exchange on d4.

15   ♛xd4

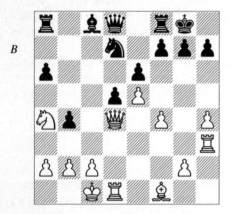

B

Now White is able to develop his bishop at d3, but on the other hand the a4-knight looks somewhat offside.

15   ...   f6?!

Black seeks to attack the e5-pawn and so further reduce White's central control. If the exchange of pawns ...fxe5, fxe5 occurs, then the e5-pawn will be weak and exposed to attack. However, the move has a serious defect: Black opens the position up while he is behind in development. The newly-opened lines permit White to launch an attack which would not otherwise have been possible. In other words, there is nothing wrong with Black's basic idea (to undermine e5) but in the given position it doesn't work for concrete tactical reasons. While strategic planning is an important component of chess thinking, it is always necessary to take the specifics of a position into account. Having said that, Short's idea only fails because of very accurate and dynamic play by Kasparov – a half-hearted response by White would have given Black good chances.

It is worth nothing that had White played 13 h5 instead of 13 ♖h3, then the move ...f6 in the

analogous position would have good chances of success – as we shall see, the activity of White's rook along the third rank is an important factor.

15...a5 is best, threatening 16...♝a6. After 16 ♝b5 ♖b8 (16...♝a6?? loses the exchange to 17 ♝xd7 ♛xd7 18 ♘b6) 17 ♝d3 Black, it is true, can no longer play ...♝a6, but he has gained time and by continuing 17...♛c7 can reach a reasonable position.

16   ♛xb4!

Better than 16 exf6 ♛xf6 17 ♛xf6 ♖xf6 18 ♖f3, which promises White only a slight endgame advantage.

16   ...   fxe5

Thus Black completes the demolition of White's centre. However, in return White has gained a dangerous initiative.

17   ♛d6

Attacking both the e6- and e5-pawns.

17   ...   ♛f6

The only move to avoid losing a pawn, since 17...♖xf4 fails to 18 ♛xe6+ ♔h8 19 ♛xd5 ♖b8 20 ♘c5. However, after the text-move everything appears fine for Black. The pawn on f4 is attacked, and the obvious 18 fxe5 loses a piece after 18...♛f4+ 19 ♔b1 ♛xf1!.

18   f5!!

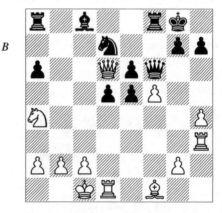

B

This pawn sacrifice is a brilliant solution to White's problem. In the introduction to the game, I mentioned two key aspects of attacking play: the opening of lines, and the elimination of defensive pieces. Kasparov's move combines both these themes in one move. If Black takes this pawn, the f-file is opened; this allows White's rook to switch to f3, where it is able to eliminate Black's defensive rook on the f-file. The exchange of this rook would be a serious blow to Black, since his three queenside pieces are poorly placed to help with the defence of the kingside.

18   ...   ♕h6+

The only move. 18...♕xf5 loses to 19 ♖f3 ♕g4 20 ♖xf8+ ♘xf8 21 ♘b6, when White wins a piece.

19   ♔b1   ♖xf5?!

Black decides to accept the pawn, but rapidly runs into serious trouble. 19...♘f6 was a better defence, when Kasparov gave the line 20 fxe6 ♘e4 21 ♕xd5 ♘d2+ 22 ♖xd2 ♖xf1+ 23 ♖d1 ♖xd1+ 24 ♕xd1 ♗xe6 25 ♘c5 as very good for White. However, in the middle of this variation Black can play 22...♗xe6! 23 ♕d6 ♕xd2! 24 ♕xd2 ♖xf1+ 25 ♔c1 ♗xa2+ 26 ♔xa2 ♖xc1, when it is not White but Black who wins. 20 ♗d3 also fails to achieve much: after 20...exf5 (20...♕h5 21 ♖e1 e4 22 ♗e2 ♕f7 23 ♘b6 ♖a7 24 ♖c3 is slightly better for White) 21 ♕xe5 f4 22 ♖hh1 ♗g4 23 ♖df1 ♖ae8 Black has active piece-play to compensate for his somewhat weakened pawns. White therefore does best to settle for the modest 20 ♕xe5 ♘e4 21 ♕d4 (21 g4 ♘f2 22 ♘b6 ♘xd1 23 ♘xa8 ♘f2 24 g5 ♕h5 25 ♗e2 ♖xf5 26 ♖c3 ♖xe5 27 ♖xc8+ ♕e8 28 ♖xe8+ ♔f7 leads to an unclear ending) 21...♖xf5 22 ♖f3, when he retains some positional advantage thanks to his more active bishop; for example, 22...♖f4 23 ♘b6 ♖b8 24 ♕e5 ♖xf3 25 gxf3 ♘d2+ 26 ♔a1 ♖xb6 27 ♕c7 ♕e3 28 ♕xc8+ ♔f7 29 ♗d3 with a dangerous attack for White.

White steadfastly aims to swap the important rook. Black's queenside pieces are virtually paralysed: his bishop cannot move, a knight move allows ♘b6 and ...♖b8 is liable to run into ♘c5. Thus, once the f5-rook has gone, Black will be playing with only his queen.

Note how Kasparov works with a succession of direct threats. Black never gets a chance to repair the defects of his position because he is constantly having to deal with the immediate danger.

20   ...   ♖xf3

After 20...♕f6 21 ♖xf5! ♕xf5 22 ♗e2 White makes use of the open f-file, which he created with his pawn sacrifice. In order to meet the threat of 23 ♖f1, Black must play 22...♕f7 but then 23 ♗g4 ♘f6 24 ♘b6 wins the exchange for inadequate compensation.

By exchanging on f3, Black blocks the dangerous f-file, but opening the f1-h3 diagonal allows White's bishop to occupy a very active post on h3.

21   gxf3

With the deadly threat of 22 ♗h3 (22 ♕e7 is also very strong) 22...♔f7 23 f4! exf4 (23...e4 24 f5) 24 ♖e1 and Black's position collapses.

21   ...   ♕f6

The only move. 21...♔f7 loses to 22 ♕c6 ♖b8 23 ♗xa6! ♗xa6 24 ♕xd7+ ♔g8 25 ♕a7.

22   ♗h3   ♔f7

Once again Black has no choice, because 22...♘f8 23 ♘b6 ♕xf3 24 ♖f1 and 22...♔h8 23 ♗xe6 ♕xf3 24 ♘c3 d4 25 ♗d5 are both winning for White.

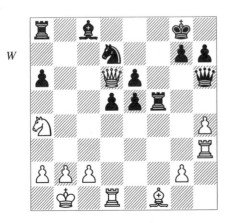

20   ♖f3!

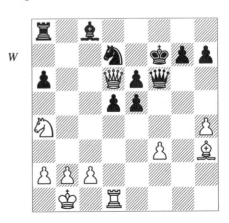

After the text-move Black has temporarily met the enemy threats and so White must come up with a method of reinforcing his attack. Once again the key is to open lines.

23   c4!

The next wave of the attack strikes Black's position. White even had a second very promising continuation, also based on the theme of line-opening: 23 f4!. Then 23...exf4 24 ♖e1 wins for White, so 23...♕e7 24 fxe5 ♕xd6 25 exd6 is forced. This ending is extremely unpleasant for Black, since his pieces are still tied up. The continuation might be 25...♖a7 26 ♖f1+ ♘f6 27 ♘c5 h6 28 b3, when Black is virtually paralysed.

23   ...   dxc4

23...d4 is met by 24 f4 (24 c5 is less convincing after 24...♕e7 25 ♕c7 ♘f8 26 ♕xe5 ♕xh4 27 ♘b6 ♕xh3 28 ♘xa8 ♕xf3 29 ♕xd4 e5! with counterplay, e.g. 30 ♕c4+ ♔f6 31 ♖d6+ ♔e7! or 30 ♕d8 ♘e6) 24...♕e7 25 fxe5 ♕xd6 26 exd6 e5 27 c5 (27 ♖e1 is also good) 27...♘xc5 28 ♗xc8 ♖xc8 29 ♖c1 ♘xa4 30 ♖xc8 ♔e6 31 ♖a8 and White should win the ending.

23...♕g6+ 24 ♔a1 d4 is no better: 25 f4! (line-opening again!) 25...exf4 26 ♕xf4+ ♔g8 27 ♕xd4 ♘f8 28 ♘b6 ♖b8 29 ♕d6 and wins.

24   ♘c3!

A cruel move. White returns his knight to the centre to exploit the newly-available square e4. Maintaining the pressure is much stronger than cashing in immediately by 24 ♕c6 ♖b8 25 ♖xd7+ ♗xd7 26 ♕xd7+ ♔g6, when Black has some counter-chances.

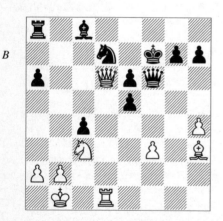

The immediate threat behind the text-move is 25 ♘e4 ♕e7 and now either 26 ♗xe6+ or 26 ♕c6 followed by ♘d6+.

24   ...   ♕e7

Black puts up the maximum resistance, but the position is beyond hope. 24...♘f8? loses to 25 ♕c6 ♖b8 26 ♕c7+.

25   ♕c6   ♖b8
26   ♘e4

White closes in for the kill.

26   ...   ♘b6

Once again Black keeps the game going as best he can. After 26...♔f8 27 ♗xe6 ♕b4 28 ♖d2 White wins a piece, while 26...♘f8 27 ♘d6+ ♔g8 28 ♘xc8 ♕b4 is beautifully met by 29 ♕xe6+! ♘xe6 (29...♔h8 loses to 30 ♕xe5) 30 ♗xe6+ ♔f8 31 ♖d8#.

27   ♘g5+   ♔g8

27...♔f8 is only marginally better. After 28 ♘xh7+ ♔g8 29 ♘g5 ♗b7 30 ♗xe6+ ♔h8 31 ♕d6! ♕xd6 32 ♖xd6 ♗a8 33 ♔c2 Black is totally tied up and must soon start shedding pawns.

28   ♕e4

The simplest. White centralizes his queen with gain of tempo.

28   ...   g6
29   ♕xe5

Again gaining time, this time by attacking Black's rook.

29   ...   ♖b7
30   ♖d6!

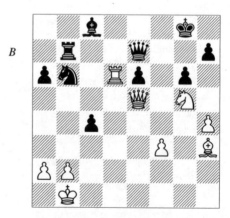

All White's pieces occupy excellent positions; Black cannot avoid heavy material loss.

30   ...   c3

30...♘a4 is decisively met by 31 ♗xe6+ ♗xe6 32 ♖xe6 ♖xb2+ 33 ♕xb2.

31   ♗xe6+

31 ♖xe6 also wins.

31   ...   ♗xe6

32   Rxe6   1-0

After 32...♘c4 the simplest win is 33 ♕xc3! ♘a3+ 34 ♔c1 ♕d8 35 bxa3.

In this game, White's space advantage and active pieces hinted at a possible attack, but it couldn't actually be launched until Black unwisely opened up the position with 15...f6?!. Kasparov responded powerfully, forcing open the f-file with 18 f5!! and thereby compelling Black to exchange his defensive rook. Short never had a chance to get back into the game, as his time was occupied responding to White's

threats. Further line-opening with 23 c4! sealed Black's fate. All in all, a textbook attacking performance by Kasparov.

The lessons here are:
1) An attack should not be launched without at least some pre-existing advantages.
2) Open lines favour the attacker.
3) The attacker should try to identify and eliminate key defensive pieces.
4) Keeping the defender off-balance with a stream of threats greatly improves the chance of the attack succeeding.

Bring Up the Reserves

In the case of an attack on the king, the two main factors determining the success of an attack are the balance of forces in the vicinity of the king, and the state of the king's defences. If the king is severely exposed and lacking defenders, even a relatively modest attacking force (such as a queen and a knight) may be enough to decide the game. However, it is more common for the king to have some defensive pieces and shielding pawns. In this case the attacker needs a considerable local superiority of force in order to break through. It follows that the more pieces take part in the attack, the more likely it is to succeed.

One of the most common attacking errors is to start an attack with insufficient force to drive the attack home. By the time this becomes obvious, it is too late to bring up the reserves. It is therefore a good idea to bring as many pieces as possible into aggressive positions before making an irrevocable commitment to the attack. It may not be possible to do this with every piece, but make whatever preparations you can. It is better to bring a piece into the attack before, rather than after, sacrificing a piece!

The following game is a good example of this principle in action.

Game 7

G. Kasparov – A. Karpov

World Championship match (game 20), New York/Lyons 1990
Ruy Lopez, Flohr-Zaitsev Variation

1   e4

For comments on this move, see Game 3.

1   ...   e5

This symmetrical response is the traditional answer to White's 1 e4. Although to some extent it has been overshadowed by the immense popularity of the Sicilian Defence (1...c5 – see Game 8, amongst others), it remains a very common and reliable reply. By controlling d4, Black tries to stop White forming a two-abreast pawn-centre.

2   ♘f3

Overwhelmingly the most popular move, attacking the e5-pawn. If White is obstinate and plays 2 d4 in any case, then after 2...exd4 3 ♕xd4 ♘c6 White has to lose time with his queen. That is not to say that this line is unplayable – indeed, such strong players as Adams and Morozevich have experimented with it – but the prevailing view is that having to move the queen twice in the first four moves gives Black a relatively easy time. Other second moves, such as 2 f4 (King's Gambit), 2 ♘c3 (Vienna Opening) and 2 ♗c4 (Bishop's Opening) are also relatively rare in contemporary tournament play.

2 ... ♞c6

Again the most common move, although the counter-attacking 2...♞f6 (Petroff's Defence) is running it a close second at the higher levels of grandmaster chess. With 2...♞f6, Black is aiming to neutralize White's advantage by an early liquidation in the centre, and so this move tends to lead to less exciting positions than 2...♞c6, which maintains the tension in the centre for longer. Whether this is an advantage or a defect depends on your point of view. In top-class grandmaster chess, a draw with Black is generally regarded as a desirable objective, hence the popularity of 2...♞f6 at this level. In recent times White has certainly found it hard to prove any real advantage against it.

For players lower down the ranking list, whether to play 2...♞f6 or 2...♞c6 depends much more on personal style. Minute differences in theoretical opinion are much less important than reaching a position of a type that you play well. For top GMs, who can normally play all types of position well, such subjective factors are less important.

3 ♗b5

This opening, the Ruy Lopez (or Spanish, as it is called in many countries) has been regarded as a sound system for the past 100 years, and this opinion is unlikely to change in the next 100 years. Such classic openings are perennially popular, largely because they are not really a single opening. The Ruy Lopez, for example, consists of a whole complex of different systems; if one falls out of favour, there are plenty of others to provide a viable replacement. The text-move prepares a possible exchange of the c6-knight, thereby removing the only defender of the e5-pawn. White is not immediately threatening to win a pawn (see the note to White's fourth move), but this possibility is a constant cause of concern for Black.

The main alternative is 3 d4, the Scotch Opening (see Game 16), which is similar to 2 d4 except that White avoids the problems associated with an early queen development (after 3...exd4 4 ♞xd4 ♞xd4 5 ♕xd4 it is not easy for Black to harass the queen). While Kasparov has had some success with the Scotch, other players do not seem able to emulate his results.

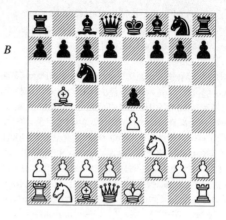

B

3 ... a6

This is the most popular reply. At this moment White cannot win a pawn by taking on c6, so Black takes the opportunity to kick the bishop back to a4. Then Black will have the option of removing the attack against c6 by playing ...b5. Another sound system is 3...♞f6 (the Berlin Defence) although, like 2...♞f6, this line often leads to rather dull positions.

4 ♗a4

4 ♗xc6 dxc6 5 0-0 (after 5 ♞xe5, Black regains the pawn by 5...♕d4) genuinely threatens the e5-pawn, but Black has various possible counters: 5...f6, 5...♗g4, 5...♕d6 and 5...♗d6 are all reasonable replies. This so-called Exchange Variation suits white-players who like quiet positions and endgame play.

4 ... ♞f6

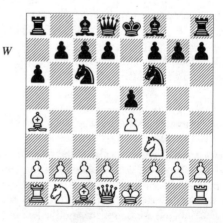

W

Black develops his knight to the most natural square, at the same time attacking White's e4-pawn.

5 0-0

White is able to ignore the attack and continue his development, because if Black takes on e4, White can regain his pawn by force.

5   ...   ♗e7

This move leads to the Closed Variation of the Ruy Lopez. The main alternative is 5...♘xe4, the Open Variation. Although the Open Variation is not especially popular, there is nothing really wrong with it; after 6 d4 b5 (6...exd4 is dubious since after 7 ♖e1 d5 8 ♘xd4 both black knights are awkwardly pinned) 7 ♗b3 the greedy 7...exd4? 8 ♖e1 d5 favours White since 9 ♘c3! ♗e6 (9...dxc3?! 10 ♗xd5 is even worse for Black, while 9...♗e7? loses a piece to 10 ♗xd5) 10 ♘xe4 dxe4 11 ♖xe4 ♗e7 12 ♗xe6 fxe6 13 ♘xd4 gives Black nothing to show for his extremely weak e-pawn. Therefore Black does best to give the pawn back by 7...d5 8 dxe5 ♗e6, when an interesting position arises in which Black's main asset is his active knight on e4. Despite many decades of analysis, the best continuation for White is far from clear, although most grandmasters seem to think that White can retain an edge.

6   ♖e1

White defends the e4-pawn and does not allow Black a second chance to take on e4. This move is stronger than the obvious 6 ♘c3, because White still aims to set up a two-abreast pawn-centre with c3 and d4, and so he should avoid blocking the c-pawn. This plan is time-consuming, but if White succeeds in establishing and maintaining his pawn-centre, then he will have promising long-term chances.

6   ...   b5

White was really threatening to win a pawn by 7 ♗xc6 dxc6 8 ♘xe5, so this is the appropriate moment to drive the bishop away.

7   ♗b3   d6

Round about here Black must decide how he is going to counter White's plan. The text-move indicates that Black intends to respond by reinforcing his grip on e5, to make sure that it can resist the pressure White will exert on that square when he plays d4.

The main alternative is 7...0-0 8 c3 d5, the famous Marshall Attack, whereby Black offers a pawn in return for a lead in development and kingside pressure. These days the Marshall Attack is still played occasionally, but is not regarded as especially fearsome. Not only is it

possible (albeit double-edged) to accept the pawn, but also White can avoid the Marshall entirely by playing 8 a4 instead of 8 c3.

8   c3

This not only prepares d4, but also gives the bishop a chance to slip back to c2 in case it is attacked by ...♘a5.

8   ...   0-0

Black proceeds with his development and brings his king into safety.

9   h3

White continues his preparation for d4. If he plays 9 d4 at once, Black replies 9...♗g4 and White must make some concession. Black's threat is to double White's pawns by ...♗xf3 (since the reply ♕xf3 would cost White his d-pawn). There are then two main possibilities for White. The first is 10 d5, but this gives up one of the main benefits of a two-abreast pawn-centre – its flexibility. The second is 10 ♗e3 but the bishop is not ideally placed here since it blocks the e-file. After 10...exd4 11 cxd4 ♘a5 12 ♗c2 c5 Black's lead in development compensates for White's slightly superior central control.

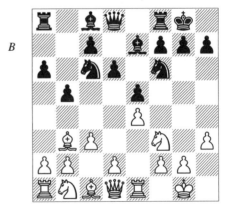

9   ...   ♗b7

This is a key decision-point for Black. He cannot hold up White's d4 advance any longer, so he has to start thinking about the post-d4 world. Although Black has to face the fact that White will be better placed in the centre, Black has a lead in development as compensation. He must put this to good use, because given time White will catch up in development, when Black will simply be worse because of the situation in the centre, which inherently favours

White. There are two main plans Black can adopt:

1) To attack White's centre using his pawns. Since ...d5 is unlikely to be playable owing to the weakness of e5, this means using ...c5 to put pressure on White's d4-pawn, hoping to force a clarification of the central pawn-structure. There are two ways to implement this plan:

1a) 9...♘a5 10 ♗c2 c5 11 d4 ♕c7 is the first. Black has already played ...c5, and he will quickly develop his remaining pieces by ...♗d7 and ...♖ac8 (possibly with ...cxd4 thrown in). The pressure against d4 and along the c-file is quite awkward for White. As usual in the Closed Ruy Lopez, the question is whether White can withstand the temporary pressure and complete his development with his centre intact, or whether he has to play d5 or dxe5 under unfavourable circumstances.

1b) The other way is 9...♘b8 10 d4 ♘bd7, the Breyer Defence. This line may look odd but it is actually quite logical. Black manoeuvres his knight to defend e5 from a square that does not block the thematic ...c5. After 11 ♘bd2 ♗b7 another benefit of Black's knight manoeuvre is revealed: on d7, the knight does not block the long diagonal and therefore White's e-pawn comes under unwelcome pressure. In order for White to complete his queenside development, he must move his d2-knight to f1, but at the moment this is impossible. Therefore White usually plays 12 ♗c2, followed by ♘f1-g3, but of course this represents a loss of time and gives Black the opportunity to strike out with a timely ...c5.

2) Black's second plan is to interfere with White's development using piece pressure against White's centre. This means mounting a rapid attack against e4, so as to prevent the important ♘bd2-f1 manoeuvre (rather as in the Breyer Defence above). Thus the bishop should move to b7; the attack against e4 is currently masked by the c6-knight, but White must still bear it in mind.

10   d4

White has succeeded in building a good pawn-centre, but the cost is a lag in development.

10   ...   ♖e8

Black intends ...♗f8 to step up the pressure against e4. At first sight the text-move looks wrong, because White can play 11 ♘g5, forcing Black to return his rook to f8. However, White cannot make any use of the knight on g5, and has nothing better than to return it to f3. This means that a draw by repetition is in White's hands, if he wants it. Many games have finished like this, but most players are unwilling to concede the advantage of the white pieces so easily!

11   ♘bd2

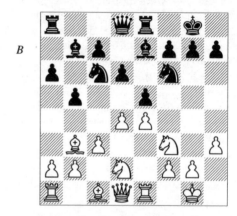

The pawn on c3 means that d2 is the best square available for the knight, despite the obvious defect of blocking in the c1-bishop and thus the a1-rook. If White could complete the manoeuvre ♘f1-g3, then he would be able to support the e4-pawn without blocking in the bishop, so Black should try to prevent this.

11   ...   ♗f8

Black is just in time to set up an attack on e4.

12   a4

12 ♘f1 is bad because of 12...exd4 13 cxd4 ♘a5, when White has no good reply to the triple attack on e4 (not, however, 13...♘xe4? due to 14 ♖xe4! ♖xe4 15 ♘g5 ♖e7 16 ♕h5 with a very strong attack). 12 ♘g5 is again ineffective, this time because of 12...♖e7. 12 ♗c2 appears logical, the aim being to free the d2-knight to move to f1 and g3. However, 13 ♘f1 isn't really a threat, because after 13...exd4 14 cxd4 ♘b4 Black threatens both the e-pawn and 15...♘xc2, eliminating a useful bishop.

Therefore, White switches to a different plan; he intends to develop queenside play while leaving the knight on d2. The text-move is useful because White's rook may have to stay at a1 for a considerable time while he is sorting out the development of the c1-bishop. Playing a4 introduces the possibility that the rook may enter play along the a-file. Moreover, White may be able to step up the pressure against the b5-pawn and force Black to clarify the queenside pawn-structure.

> **12**   **...**   **h6**

Observing that White has few useful moves, Black decides to spend a tempo preventing ♘g5. However, this move is by no means forced and both 12...g6 and 12...♕d7 are playable.

> **13**   **♗c2**

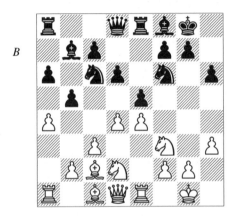

White has indeed run out of useful moves and must now concede this voluntary retreat. The intention is 14 ♗d3, forcing Black to make an awkward decision regarding the attack on the b5-pawn.

> **13**   **...**   **exd4**

This move is clearly very double-edged, because Black surrenders his central strongpoint on e5. On the other hand, it opens various possibilities for active piece-play. The e8-rook is now directly attacking the e4-pawn, and Black will be able to step up his pressure on White's centre with gain of tempo. 13...♖b8 and 13...♘b8 are playable alternatives, although both have a slightly passive appearance.

> **14**   **cxd4**

A hidden benefit of this capture is that it opens the third rank, increasing White's chances of activating the a1-rook via a3.

> **14**   **...**   **♘b4**

Black clears the way for ...c5, to try to break up White's centre. Unlike the lines 9...♘a5 and 9...♘b8 discussed in the note to Black's 9th move, in this case Black frees the c-pawn with

gain of tempo and occupies an excellent outpost with his knight.

> **15**   **♗b1**

White must keep his bishop, since it is currently one of his few active pieces.

> **15**   **...**   **c5**

It is perfectly natural for Black to strike at White's centre like this, but the move has both good and bad features. On the minus side, after White's reply the b7-bishop will be shut out of play. On the plus side, Black gains space and stabilizes the central pawn-structure.

> **16**   **d5**

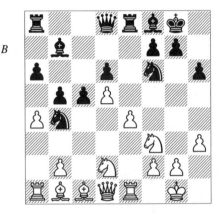

The only challenging move, maintaining a 2-1 central pawn-majority. The central pawn-structure now resembles one arising from a Benoni (1 d4 ♘f6 2 c4 c5 3 d5 e6 4 ♘c3 exd5 5 cxd5 d6) rather than a Ruy Lopez. However, the arrangement of pieces is not typical for a Benoni so we cannot transplant typical ideas and plans from the Benoni into the current situation.

In the diagram position, White's ambitions lie mainly on the kingside. Although currently White's pieces are not menacing Black's kingside, it only requires a few moves – ♖a3, ♘h2 and ♖g3 – and the threats already look quite serious. Black, for his part, will aim to make use of his queenside majority, for example by ...♘d7, ...c4 and ...♘c5 (aiming for d3), possibly coupled with ...g6 and ...♗g7. The arrival of a knight on d3 is a key feature of this system, not only because it is an excellent outpost in itself, but also because it would block the activity of the b1-bishop and so reduce the force of White's attack.

16   ...   ♘d7

A flexible move. The first idea is ...c4 and ...♘c5, as mentioned previously; the second idea is revealed with Black's next move.

17   ♖a3

White makes the first ominous move towards Black's kingside.

17   ...   f5!?

Black ups the stakes with this double-edged move. One of the main principles of defending against an attack on the king is not to create unnecessary weaknesses, yet here is a top-class player lunging forwards in contravention of precisely this rule. In view of the battering Black receives in this game, it might seem that justice was indeed dispensed, yet in fact this move is not at all bad. Certainly, it is very risky, yet it has many positive features. It is quite likely that the e4-pawn will disappear (either through exf5 or ...fxe4), but then the d5-pawn will be weak. If Black can take it, then his formerly inactive b7-bishop will suddenly become very powerful. If White plays exf5, then an exchange of rooks will tend to reduce the force of White's attack.

It is true that if White's attack were further advanced, Black could not get away with a move such as ...f5, but White's threats are as yet quite far away and so Black still has time to break up White's centre. Indeed, ...f5 can be seen as a pre-emptive strike to fight for activity before White's attack becomes too strong.

The alternative is 17...c4, aiming to play ...♘c5. This is perfectly playable and possibly safer than the text-move, although it does have the defect of allowing the f3-knight to occupy d4.

18   ♖ae3

Even today, nobody knows whether this is the strongest move. In addition to the text-move, 18 g4, 18 exf5, 18 e5 and (most recently) 18 ♘h2 have all been tried with varying degrees of success. Perhaps this last move is most logical as White does not yet commit his rook to a particular square; it might move to e3, f3 or g3 according to circumstances. In any case, White's main aim is to bring his remaining pieces into the attack without allowing too many exchanges. When attacking, it is essential to have enough firepower available to finish the job. What constitutes 'enough firepower' varies

a lot from position to position. If the enemy kingside is weakened and lacks defensive pieces, then even a small attacking force may be enough. However, in practice it often happens that the attack is being conducted against a relatively solid kingside, and in this case more pieces must be brought to bear to ensure success.

White's main problem is to coordinate his forces for the attack. The c1-bishop in particular is quite inactive, and is likely to remain so because the knight must stay on d2 to be ready to recapture on e4. Kasparov therefore moves his a3-rook to a more active position, preparing to activate the bishop by b3 and ♗b2.

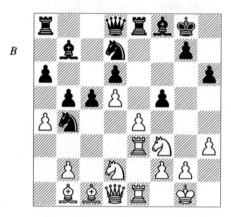

18   ...   ♘f6

The situation in the centre remains fluid for a number of moves, the reason being that neither player wishes to resolve the e4-f5 tension. Black, it is true, can win the d5-pawn by playing ...fxe4, but this capture brings the d2-knight to an aggressive position with gain of tempo. It also gives both white bishops an obstructed view of Black's kingside. In the end, Black may be forced to make this capture, but he intends to make as many constructive moves as he can first. Likewise, the move exf5 would be a concession by White. True, this avoids losing a pawn, but more importantly it loses time, since the knight stays on d2, and the pawn on f5 can actually obstruct White's attack. Thus White also would prefer to find constructive moves that do not involve resolving the central tension.

The alternatives to the text-move are:

1) 18...f4!? attempts to block the position. After 19 ♖3e2 ♘e5 20 ♘f1 ♘xf3+ 21 gxf3

♕h4 a very unclear position arises. If Black can cement his hold on e5 then he will stand well, but there is a danger that White will unleash all the energy in his position by playing e5 himself.

2) 18...fxe4?! is a concession since after 19 ♖xe4 (19 ♗xe4 is doubtful because of 19...♘f6, while 19 ♘xe4 ♘xd5 20 ♖3e2 ♘7f6 is unclear) 19...♖xe4 20 ♘xe4 ♘xd5 21 ♕e2 White's c1-bishop has entered the attack. The fact that Black has won a pawn is less important. White now threatens 22 ♘xd6, and Black has defensive difficulties; for example, after 21...♘7f6 22 ♘xf6+ ♕xf6 (22...♘xf6 23 ♕e6+ ♔h8 24 ♘h4 is crushing) 23 ♕e4 Black can hardly prevent White's queen landing on h7 (23...g6 is met by 24 ♘h4!).

19   ♘h2

White decides to clear the third rank after all, and introduces the possibility of a later ♘g4 (after the f5-pawn has disappeared) to eliminate a kingside defender. If this is really White's best move, then it was surely better to play ♘h2 last move, as the rook might want to move from a3 to g3 in one go.

19 exf5?! is wrong; after 19...♖xe3 20 ♖xe3 ♘bxd5 Black gains time and the f5-pawn blocks White's attack.

the tempo is not especially significant. Here, with a violent storm about to break over Black's kingside, it looks very risky to spend a tempo on this move, which actually has little clear benefit. If White is going to hack his way into the kingside sacrificially, it probably isn't going to make much difference whether the king is on g8 or h8. After the text-move, Black must proceed with extreme accuracy in order not to be wiped out by White's attack.

19...fxe4 is again wrong. After 20 ♘xe4 ♘bxd5 (20...♘fxd5 21 ♖g3 is extremely dangerous for Black; for example, 21...♔h8 22 ♗xh6 gxh6 23 ♕g4 ♘e7 24 ♘f6 with a quick mate) 21 ♘xf6+ ♘xf6 22 ♖xe8 ♘xe8 23 ♕d3 ♘f6 24 ♘g4 White has an extremely strong attack.

Black should have played 19...♕d7 connecting the rooks, supporting the b5-pawn and offering some lateral defence along the second rank. I do not want to go into a deep discussion of what is still opening theory; suffice it to say that White has not been able to prove any advantage after 19...♕d7. This move was played in a later Kasparov-Karpov game (Euwe Memorial, Amsterdam 1991) and on that occasion Black equalized and the game ended in a draw.

20   b3!

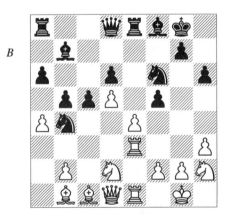

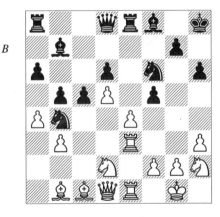

19   ...   ♔h8?!

Only here does Black commit a perceptible inaccuracy. Tidying-up moves such as ♔g1-h1 and ♔c1-b1 (or ...♔g8-h8 and ...♔c8-b8 by Black) are of course common enough, but one must be sure that the gain is worth the tempo spent on the move. This is more likely to be the case when the position is relatively quiet and

In order for White's attack to stand a chance of success, he needs to have as many pieces as possible participating. Leaving the situation in the centre to look after itself, Kasparov simply deploys his dark-squared bishop on the long diagonal. This is an especially tempting prospect with the enemy king sitting at the end of the diagonal.

20   ...   bxa4!

Karpov correctly decides to play for an outpost at d3, so that he can block the b1-h7 diagonal at a moment of his choosing. Although this is a good plan, the long dark-square diagonal remains open, so the black king remains in danger even if White has to surrender his light-squared bishop.

Playing for the win of a pawn by 20...fxe4 is critical, but gives White a dangerous attack after 21 ♘xe4. Then:

1) 21...♘bxd5 22 ♘xf6 ♖xe3 (22...♘xf6 23 ♖xe8 ♘xe8 24 ♕d3 ♘f6 25 ♘g4 and 22...♘xe3 23 ♕d3 win for White) 23 ♖xe3 ♘xf6 (23...♕xf6 24 ♕c2 and 23...gxf6 24 ♖g3 give White a decisive attack) 24 ♘g4 and the weakness of the b1-h7 diagonal gives White a very strong attack (in this line the move ...♔h8 proves especially unfortunate as the king will have to return to g8 to avoid mate).

2) 21...♘xd5 22 ♘xf6 ♖xe3 23 ♖xe3 ♕xf6 24 ♘g4 (24 ♗d2 is less effective in view of 24...♗g8!) 24...♕d4 25 ♗d2 (threatening 26 ♘xh6) 25...♔g8 26 ♕c1 with many threats, including 27 ♗xb4 followed by 28 ♕c2.

3) 21...♘fxd5 and now:

3a) 22 ♘xd6 is wrong because of 22...♘xe3 23 ♘f7+ ♔g8 24 ♘xd8 ♘xd1 25 ♖xe8 ♗c6.

3b) 22 ♖f3 (intending ♘g4 coupled with ♗b2) 22...♘f6 23 ♖xf6!? gxf6 24 ♘g4 is perhaps not entirely clear after 24...♗xe4 (24...♖e6 25 ♗b2 ♗g7 26 ♘exf6 is very bad for Black; for example, 26...♕e7 27 ♖xe6 ♕xe6 28 ♕d2 {threatening 29 ♘h5} 28...♕xb3 29 ♘xh6 with a winning attack for White) 25 ♖xe4 ♖xe4 26 ♗xe4 d5! (26...♖a7? 27 ♗b2 ♗g7 28 ♕d2 ♕f8 29 ♕f4 looks very dangerous for Black). One line is 27 ♗g6 d4 28 ♘xh6 ♗xh6 29 ♕h5 ♕e7 and now 30 ♗xh6 can be met by 30...♕e1+ 31 ♔h2 ♕e5+.

3c) 22 ♖g3!? ♘f6 23 ♘xf6 ♖xe1+ (after 23...♕xf6 24 ♘g4 ♕d4 25 ♗d2 ♖xe1+ 26 ♕xe1 ♘d5 27 ♘xh6!, 27...gxh6 28 ♕e6 wins for White, while 27...♘f6 28 ♗c3 ♕f4 29 ♘f7+ ♔g8 30 ♗g6 gives White a very strong attack for no material sacrifice) 24 ♕xe1 ♕xf6 25 ♗d2 followed by ♘g4 looks dangerous for Black.

Thus, winning the d5-pawn immediately would not have been better than the text-move.

21   bxa4   c4

Now Black is ready to play ...♘d3 when necessary. However, as this move inevitably costs a pawn, Black won't play it until he has already taken the d5-pawn or White has sacrificed something on the kingside.

22   ♗b2

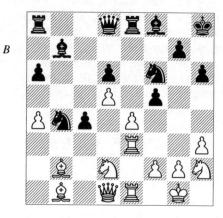

B

22   ...   fxe4

Having done all he can to improve his position, Black now goes for the d5-pawn. There is no better move. For example:

1) 22...♘d3 23 ♗xd3 cxd3 24 ♗xf6 (24 ♕b3 ♘xe4 25 ♕xb7 ♖b8 is unclear) 24...♕xf6 25 ♕b3 and White wins a pawn.

2) 22...♖c8 23 ♕f3! (after 23 ♗c3 a5 White has dangerous attacking chances, but Black would still be in the game) 23...fxe4 (23...♕d7 24 ♗xf6 gxf6 25 ♖c1 favours White on account of Black's many weak pawns) 24 ♘xe4 and now:

2a) 24...♗xd5 25 ♘xf6 ♗xf3 26 ♖xe8 ♕xe8 (26...♕c7 loses to 27 ♗f5! ♖xe8 28 ♖xe8 ♕f7 29 ♗g6) 27 ♖xe8 ♖xe8 28 ♘xe8 ♗c6 29 ♘c7 ♗xa4 30 ♘g4 and the extra piece should be enough to win.

2b) 24...♘fxd5 25 ♘xd6! and now:

2b1) 25...♘xe3 26 ♘f7+ ♔g8 27 ♘xh6+ ♔h8 (after 27...gxh6, 28 ♗h7+! ♔xh7 29 ♕f7+ mates) 28 ♘f7+ ♔g8 29 ♗h7+ ♔xh7 30 ♕h5+ ♔g8 31 ♘xd8 ♖cxd8 32 fxe3 and White should win.

2b2) 25...♖xe3 26 ♘f7+ ♔g8 27 ♘xh6+ ♔h8 (27...gxh6 28 ♗h7+) 28 fxe3 and White is a pawn up with a dangerous attack.

23   ♘xe4   ♘fxd5

The only possible way to take the d5-pawn. The alternatives fail as follows:

1) 23...♗xd5? 24 ♘xf6 ♖xe3 25 ♘xd5 ♖xe1+ 26 ♕xe1 ♘xd5 27 ♕e4 with a winning position for White.

2) 23...♘bxd5?! 24 ♘xf6 ♖xe3 (24...♘xe3 25 ♕h5 leaves Black defenceless against the threat of 26 ♕g6; for example, 25...gxf6 26 ♕g6 ♗e4 27 ♗xe4 ♖xe4 28 ♗xf6+ ♕xf6 29 ♕xf6+ ♗g7 30 ♕g6 wins) 25 ♖xe3 gxf6 (25...♘xe3 loses to 26 ♕h5 as before; 25...♘xf6 26 ♕c2 c3 27 ♘g4 and White wins) 26 ♕g4 ♗g7 27 ♖g3 ♕g8 (27...♕e7 28 ♕f5 gives White a winning attack) 28 ♕xc4 and White has a large positional advantage in addition to a very strong attack.

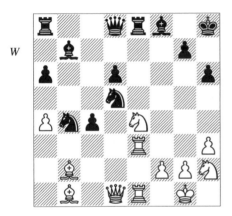

W

24 ♖g3

The correct method to continue to attack is to move White's pieces quietly into attacking positions, rather than to go for an immediate knockout. For example, 24 ♘xd6 fails to 24...♘xe3 25 ♘f7+ ♔g8 26 ♘xd8 ♘xd1 27 ♖xe8 ♘xb2, when Black wins, while after 24 ♕h5 Black can continue 24...c3! 25 ♗xc3 ♘xc3 26 ♘xc3 ♖xe3 27 ♖xe3 ♕g5, escaping to an ending in which he is only slightly worse.

24 ... ♖e6!

This is the best defence. Black supports the third rank in anticipation of the coming ♘g4, which will attack the h6-pawn. In some lines the black queen can move behind the rook, setting up an awkward pin along the e-file. Instead, 24...♘d3 forces a liquidation, but does not solve Black's problems, as after 25 ♗xd3 cxd3 26 ♕h5 ♖e6 27 ♖g6 ♖xg6 28 ♕xg6 ♕e8 29 ♕xh6+ ♔g8 30 ♕g5 d2 31 ♖xd2 ♕xa4 32 ♕g5 ♕b4 33 ♖e2 White retains a strong attack for no material compensation.

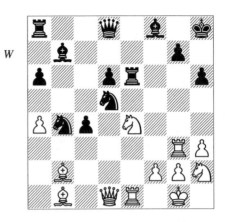

W

25 ♘g4

25 ♘f3 is tempting, heading for d4, but after 25...♘f4 26 ♘d4 ♖e5 the position is not clear.

After the text-move, every single one of White's pieces occupies an aggressive position. With so many attacking pieces, Black will be hard pressed to prevent some sort of sacrificial breakthrough on the kingside.

25 ... ♕e8?

Up to here, Black has defended very well in a dangerous situation, but the strain of finding the correct move time after time finally tells on him. Karpov tries to defend by pinning the e4-knight against the rook, but it turns out that White can break through despite the pin. The alternatives are:

1) 25...♕h4? loses to 26 ♘c5! ♖xe1+ 27 ♕xe1 dxc5 28 ♕e4 ♘d3 29 ♖xd3.

2) 25...♕d7? 26 ♕c1! (26 ♘ef6? ♘xf6) and now:

2a) 26...♘d3?! 27 ♗xd3 cxd3 28 ♘xh6 ♖ae8 29 ♘f5 ♘f6 (29...♖xe4 30 ♖xe4 ♖xe4 31 ♕h6+ ♔g8 32 ♗xg7 and White wins) 30 ♗xf6 gxf6 31 ♘xf6! ♖xf6 (31...♖xe1+ 32 ♔h2 ♕h7 33 ♕b2 wins) 32 ♖xe8 ♕xe8 33 ♕g5 ♕e6 34 ♕h5+ ♖h6 (34...♗h6 loses to 35 ♘xh6 ♖xh6 36 ♕g5) 35 ♘xh6 ♗xh6 36 ♖g6 is decisive.

2b) 26...♖ae8 27 ♕xc4 (27 ♘xh6 c3!) 27...a5 28 ♕d4 looks good for White. For the moment White is rather tied down by the e-file pin, but he still has an impressive array of pieces pointing at Black's kingside. In return Black has no material compensation.

3) 25...♘f4? and now:

3a) 26 ♘xh6? ♖xh6 27 ♘g5 is tempting, but fails if Black finds the correct defence. The main lines are:

3a1) 27...♕d7? 28 ♕g4! ♕xg4 29 ♘f7+
♔g8 30 ♘xh6+ gxh6 31 ♖xg4+ and White
wins.

3a2) 27...♖f6? 28 ♗xf6 ♕xf6 29 ♖e6 also
wins for White.

3a3) 27...♕c7? 28 ♖e6! (after 28 ♘e6 ♖xe6
29 ♖xe6 ♘bd3 30 ♖h6+ ♔g8 Black defends)
28...♘xe6 (28...♖h4 29 ♔g4 ♖h5 30 ♖xf4 ♖xg5
31 ♖h6+ ♔g8 32 ♗h7+ ♔h8 33 ♗f5+ ♔g8 34
♗e6+ and White wins) 29 ♘xe6 ♕f7 30 ♘xg7
♗xg7 31 ♖xg7 ♕xg7 32 ♗xg7+ ♔xg7 33
♕g4+ ♔h8 34 ♕g5 is good for White; for example, 34...♖e6 35 ♕h4+ ♔g7 36 ♕h7+ ♔f6
37 ♕g6+ ♔e7 38 ♕g7+ ♔d8 39 ♕f8+ ♔d7 40
♕f7+ winning the rook.

3a4) 27...♔g8! is the only move, but it is a
good one. After 28 ♕g4 ♘bd5 29 ♗xg7 (29
♕f5 ♕c7 is also unsatisfactory for White)
29...♗xg7 (29...♗c8? loses to 30 ♘e6) 30 ♘f7
♕f6 31 ♘xh6+ ♕xh6 32 ♕d7 ♖f8 33 ♕xb7
♘c3 Black is better.

3b) 26 ♘ef6! is the spectacular key to success: 26...♖xe1+ (26...♕e7 27 ♖xe6 ♕xe6 28
♖e3 ♕f7 29 ♘xh6 gxh6 30 ♘e8+ ♔g8 31
♕g4+ is winning for White) 27 ♕xe1 ♘bd3
(27...♕e7 loses to 28 ♖e3 ♕f7 29 ♘xh6) 28
♗xd3 cxd3 (after 28...♘xd3, 29 ♕e6 is decisive) 29 ♘xh6 ♘e2+ 30 ♕xe2 ♕xf6 31 ♕d2
♕e6 32 ♕g5 and the attack is decisive.

4) 25...♘d3! is the correct defence; Black
must eliminate one of the dangerous white bishops without delay. After 26 ♗xd3 (26 ♘xh6
♖xh6 27 ♘g5 ♕d7 is unsound for White, while
26 ♖xd3 cxd3 27 ♕xd3 ♘b4 is at best unclear)
26...cxd3 27 ♖xd3 ♕e8! (27...♕a5 28 ♖d4 offers White more chances) the e-file pin gives
Black counterplay. A likely continuation is 28
f3 ♘b6 29 ♖b3 ♗xe4 (29...d5 30 ♕d4 ♘xa4 31
♖xb7 dxe4 32 ♖xg7 ♗c5 is riskier but is probably also a draw after 33 ♖g5+ ♗d4+ 34
♗xd4+ ♔h7 35 ♖g7+ ♔h8 36 ♖xe4 ♖xe4 37
fxe4 ♕d8 38 ♗e5 ♕b6+ 39 ♔h2 ♖f8, when it
is time for perpetual check) 30 ♖xb6 ♗xf3 31
♖xe6 ♗xd1 32 ♖xe8 ♖xe8 33 ♘xh6 with a
drawn ending.

I have given this analysis in detail because it
might seem a serious error to miss 25...♘d3! –
after all, playing the knight to d3 was one of the
key elements of Black's defensive plan. However, when you see the maze of complex variations, the error is not so surprising.

26   ♘xh6!

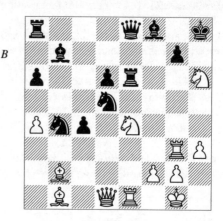

After this spectacular sacrifice Black is in serious trouble. His problem is that he can shut
out the dark-squared bishop with ...c3 or the
light-squared bishop with ...♘d3, but he cannot
do both.

26   ...   c3

There is nothing better:

1) 26...♖xh6 27 ♘xd6 wins for White in all
variations:

1a) 27...♖xd6 loses to 28 ♖xe8 ♖xe8 29
♕h5+.

1b) 27...♕xe1+ 28 ♕xe1 ♖xd6 29 ♕e4 wins
for White after 29...♘d3 30 ♕h4+ ♔g8 31
♗xg7 ♗xg7 32 ♕g4 or 29...♖h6 30 ♗c1 ♖h5
31 ♖g5 ♖h6 32 ♖f5.

1c) 27...♕d7 28 ♕g4 ♕xg4 29 ♘f7+ ♔g8
30 ♘xh6+ gxh6 31 ♖xg4+ ♔f7 32 ♗g6+ ♔g8
33 ♗f5+ ♔f7 34 ♗e6+ and White wins.

1d) 27...♕h5 28 ♖g5! ♕xd1 29 ♘f7+ ♔g8
30 ♘xh6+ ♔h8 31 ♖xd1 c3 32 ♘f7+ ♔g8 33
♗g6 ♘f4 (33...cxb2 34 ♖h5 mates) 34 ♗xc3
♘xg6 35 ♗xb4 ♔xf7 36 ♖d7+ ♔f6 37 ♖xg6+
♔xg6 38 ♖xb7 with two clear extra pawns.

2) After 26...♖c8, we see a key tactical element which arises in several variations. White
would like to use the e4-knight in the attack, but
moving it drops the e1-rook with check. However, the preliminary 27 ♔h2!, threatening 28
♘g5, creates decisive threats. One variation is
27...♖xh6 28 ♘xd6 ♕d7 29 ♕g4! ♕xg4 30
♘f7+ ♔g8 31 ♘xh6+ ♔h8 32 ♖xg4 c3 33
♘f7+ ♔g8 34 ♗g6 (with the idea of mating on
h8) 34...♖c7 35 ♗xc3 ♘xc3 36 ♖h4 ♖xf7 37
♗xf7+ ♔xf7 38 ♖f4+ ♔g6 39 ♖e6+ ♔h7 40
♖xf8 and White wins.

The text-move leaves White's b1-bishop in a dominant position.

27   ♘f5!

Absolutely correct. White can jettison the b2-bishop in the interest of furthering his attack.

27   ...   cxb2

27...♖c8 28 ♕g4 cxb2 transposes to line '4' in the note to Black's 28th move.

28   ♕g4!

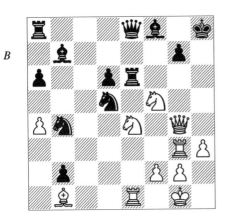

Once again Kasparov demonstrates the important principle of having all the pieces participating in the attack. White aims to overwhelm Black's kingside by sheer weight of attacking force.

28   ...   ♗c8

There is no defence:

1) 28...♘c3 29 ♘f6 ♖xe1+ 30 ♔h2 mates in a few moves.

2) 28...♕d7 29 ♕h5+ ♔g8 30 ♖g6 ♖xe4 (30...♖xg6 loses to 31 ♕xg6 ♔h8 32 ♘g5) 31 ♖xe4 ♕c7 (31...♖c8 32 ♖h4) 32 ♖h4 ♕c3 33 ♘h6+ ♔h8 34 ♘g4+ ♔g8 35 ♖f6! mating.

3) 28...g6 29 ♔h2 ♕d7 (29...♗e7 30 ♘xe7 ♕xe7 31 ♘xd6 ♖xe1 32 ♕xg6 and 29...♔g8 30 ♘exd6 are hopeless for Black) 30 ♘h4! ♗c8 (30...♘e7 loses to 31 ♘f6) 31 ♘xg6+ ♖xg6 32 ♕xg6 ♕g7 33 ♕h5+ ♕h6 34 ♕f7 and White wins.

4) 28...♖c8 (aiming to block out the light-squared bishop with ...♘c2) 29 ♔h2! (again this key move, so that White can move the e4-knight without dropping the rook with check) 29...♘c2 (29...♖c4 30 ♘xg7 ♖g6 31 ♕h5+ ♔xg7 32 ♘f6! forces a quick mate) 30 ♕h4+ ♖h6 (30...♔g8 loses to 31 ♘g5) 31 ♘xh6 gxh6

32 ♗xc2 ♖xc2 33 ♘xd6 with a decisive attack; for example, 33...♕d7 34 ♕d4+ ♔h7 35 ♕d3+ ♔h8 36 ♕g6 ♕g7 37 ♘f7+ ♔g8 38 ♕xc2.

29   ♕h4+

29 ♘xg7? ♖g6! allows Black to fight on.

29   ...   ♖h6

Or 29...♔g8 30 ♔h2! and there is no defence to the threat of 31 ♘g5.

30   ♘xh6   gxh6

31   ♔h2!

Once again this key move, which carries the deadly threats of 32 ♘xd6 and 32 ♘f6, proves decisive. Even here White could still go wrong; for example, 31 ♘f6? ♕xe1+ 32 ♔h2 ♗e6 leads to nothing, while 31 ♘xd6? ♕xe1+ 32 ♔h2 ♕e6 defends.

31   ...   ♕e5

Black cannot avoid a disaster; for example, 31...♖a7 32 ♘f6 ♕f7 33 ♖e8 leads to a quick mate.

32   ♘g5

Threatening the queen and mate in one.

32   ...   ♕f6

33   ♖e8!

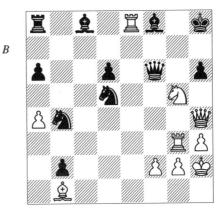

The diagram presents a perfect attacking picture. White's whole army is swarming around the enemy king.

33   ...   ♗f5

34   ♕xh6+

The only small slip in an excellent attacking game by Kasparov. 34 ♘f7+! ♕xf7 (34...♔h7 35 ♕xf6 ♘xf6 36 ♗xf5#) 35 ♕xh6+ ♗h7 36 ♖xa8 would have forced mate in a few moves.

34   ...   ♕xh6

35   ♘f7+   ♔h7

36   ♗xf5+   ♕g6

37   &xg6+

37 &xg6! would have been even more crushing since 37...&e7 38 &g5+ &h8 39 &xe7 mates quickly, but of course it makes no difference to the result.

37   ...   &g7

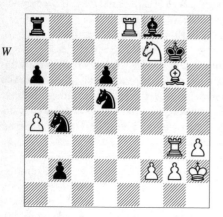

W

38   &xa8

Black could have given up here in view of White's enormous material advantage.

38	...	&e7
39	&b8	a5
40	&e4+	&xf7
41	&xd5+	1-0

This game reflects credit on both players. Kasparov's attack would have blown away a lesser opponent, but Karpov put up an excellent fight. The important point to note is how methodically Kasparov built up his attack, swinging his queen's rook across to the kingside and repositioning his f3-knight to g4. Up to 25 &g4, White's commitment to the attack had been relatively modest (the sacrifice of his d-pawn), but in return he had been able to position every single piece on an attacking square. This was necessary because Black's kingside was fairly secure, so White needed a considerable superiority of force on the kingside in order to break through. At just this moment Karpov made the decisive error, and Kasparov won brilliantly.

The lessons here are:

1) Bring as many pieces into aggressive positions as you can, before committing yourself irrevocably to the attack.

2) In practice, it is usually more difficult to defend than to attack.

3) A pin against any piece other than the king is not absolute. The 'pinned' piece might suddenly move, wreaking havoc.

4) The final breakthrough often requires a sacrifice.

Standard Sacrifices

In textbooks of attacking play, one can find all sorts of standard combinations: the 'Greek gift' sacrifice (&xh7+ followed by &g5+), the double bishop sacrifice on h7 and g7, etc. There are also many typical mating formations, such as Anastasia's Mate (with a knight on e7, a sacrifice on h7 followed by mate along the h-file) and Boden's Mate (against a king castled queenside, &xc6+ followed by &a6#). You probably won't be a successful attacking player unless you are familiar with all these standard ideas – they are, as it were, the basic vocabulary of attack. I will not be presenting a list of attacking formations in this book, as my purpose is to show how the fundamental chess ideas fit into the overall strategy of a game.

If you are lucky, an opponent will allow one these familiar ideas in an absolutely clear-cut form. Then you need only check that everything works as it should, and you will have a point in the bag. Unfortunately, opponents are rarely so cooperative. Thus, when one of these standard ideas actually arises in practice, it is often in a rather unclear form. Considerable work may be required to determine whether the sacrifice is correct. It may even be the case that it is too complex for definite analysis, and then you must rely on your judgement. If your style inclines towards attacking play, then you may be prepared to take on the risk of an unclear sacrifice, whereas another player with a more positional outlook might make the opposite choice. Thus personal style influences the equation.

In the following game, it could not have been a surprise to anybody when, presented with a possible 'Greek gift' sacrifice, Alexei Shirov snapped off the h7-pawn without hesitation.

Game 8
A. Shirov – D. Reinderman
Wijk aan Zee 1999
Sicilian Defence, Taimanov Variation

1 e4

See Game 3 for comments on this move.

1 ... c5

This move is the Sicilian Defence, one of the most common present-day openings. The reason for this popularity is its combative nature; in many lines Black is playing not just for equality, but for the advantage. The drawback is that White often obtains an early initiative, so Black has to take care not to fall victim to a quick attack.

2 ♘f3

White would like to play d4, but the immediate 2 d4 cxd4 3 ♕xd4 is bad in view of 3...♘c6, gaining time. Thus White makes ready to recapture on d4 with his knight. Another popular line is 2 c3 (see Game 30), again preparing d4 but this time with the idea of recapturing with a pawn on d4.

2 ... ♘c6

Black has a wide range of moves here: 2...d6 (Game 10) and 2...e6 (Game 20) are also very popular.

W

3 ♘c3

Although there is nothing wrong with 3 d4, White sometimes plays 3 ♘c3 so as to avoid certain lines for Black. For example, after 3 d4, Black can enter the popular Sveshnikov system via 3...cxd4 4 ♘xd4 ♘f6 5 ♘c3 e5. If White

does not care to face this system, then he can make it more difficult for Black to reach it with 3 ♘c3. If Black then plays 3...♘f6, White can continue 4 ♗b5 and we have reached a Rossolimo Sicilian (2 ♘f3 ♘c6 3 ♗b5) in which Black can no longer play certain lines. In textbooks on the Sicilian, you will find that the main variations are always given with a standardized move-order. Unfortunately, this obscures subtleties of move-order that can be quite important in practice.

3 ... e6

Black continues with a flexible move, which still leaves open the possibility of entering a range of systems.

4 d4

White decides to transpose into a standard Open Sicilian, although here too he could have reached a line of the Rossolimo by playing 4 ♗b5.

4 ... cxd4

5 ♘xd4

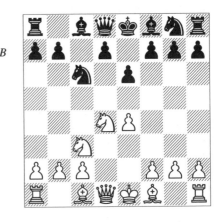

B

The exchange of Black's c-pawn for White's d-pawn is characteristic of the Sicilian, and this change in pawn-structure forms the basis of future strategy for both sides. Black has an extra central pawn, which represents a small but significant positional asset. White, on the other hand, can easily bring all his minor pieces into play and therefore is likely to complete his development before Black. Thus the battle-lines are drawn: White's lead in development and greater space in the centre against Black's longer-term positional assets.

5   ...   a6

With this move Black indicates that he will probably be heading for the Taimanov system, a line which is based on delaying the move ...d6 so as to leave open the option of developing the dark-squared bishop actively to c5 or b4. Had Black played 5...d6, we would have been heading for a Scheveningen system (which is based on pawns at d6 and e6), while after 5...♘f6 there would still have been various options open (see Game 20).

6   ♗e2

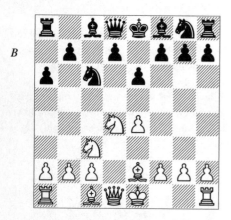

B

White has many possible moves, but Shirov opts simply to complete his kingside development and castle quickly.

6   ...   ♘ge7

Now we are definitely in the Taimanov system. The idea behind the text-move is to continue with ...♘xd4 followed by ...♘c6, gaining time by attacking the white queen. The defect is that Black's remaining pieces are not well posted to defend the kingside.

7   f4

White has tried several moves in this position, but Shirov's is one of the most logical. The reason is that, now that the f2-square is cleared, the manoeuvre ...♘xd4 and ...♘c6 can be met by ♕f2. The queen is very well posted on f2, partly because after a subsequent ♗e3 White is able to exert considerable pressure on Black's queenside dark squares. Moreover, from f2 the

queen is able to participate in a possible kingside attack, for example after f5.

7   ...   ♘xd4

Black can delay this exchange, but he will have to play it sooner or later, since otherwise the e7-knight will prevent the development of his kingside pieces.

8   ♕xd4   b5

If 8...♘c6, then of course 9 ♕f2, so Black delays ...♘c6 in the hope that White will make the mistake of playing ♗e3, preventing the retreat to f2.

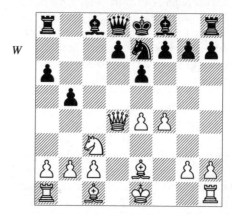

W

9   0-0

For the moment White need not commit his queen.

9   ...   ♕c7

Black continues to develop his queenside, and now that c5 is covered by the queen, there are some tricky ideas such as 10...♘f5 in the air.

10   ♕f2

In view of the danger along the a7-g1 diagonal, White decides to pull his queen back voluntarily. It turns out that Black has nothing better than to reply ...♘c6, since otherwise he cannot develop his kingside, so in fact Black has gained nothing by delaying ...♘c6.

10   ...   ♘c6

Compared to a normal Sicilian position, one pair of knights has disappeared. White is missing a knight on d4, and Black on f6. The exchange of one pair of knights has reduced White's attacking power, but two other factors work slightly in White's favour. Firstly, Black has no defensive knight on the kingside, so despite the reduced forces available White might still be able to mount a successful attack, and secondly Black has no pressure against e4, so White has greater freedom than normal to manoeuvre his pieces. Nevertheless, this system is perfectly playable for Black and White cannot count on anything more than a slight edge.

11 &e3

The natural move, sending a probing glance towards the squares c5 and b6.

11 ... &e7

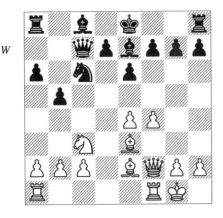

The bishop is best placed here, in order to provide some defence for Black's vulnerable kingside.

12 a4!?

Shirov could, of course, have continued to develop with 12 &ad1, but White should be thinking about what his plan will be after he has brought out all his pieces. A direct kingside attack is not yet likely to succeed, as White's pieces are not aimed at Black's kingside. White's main idea must be to improve the conditions for a possible kingside attack. One plan is 12 e5, intending moves such as &e4, &ad1, &d3, etc. However, this might not lead to anything if Black replies 12...d6 or 12...d5.

Shirov decides instead on a slower approach. The text-move more or less forces ...b4, when White can reposition his knight by &b1-d2. Now that Black no longer has ...&b4, White can play &d3, lining up against Black's king position. Depending on circumstances, the knight can move to f3 to help with the attack, or to c4 to probe Black's queenside, especially the b6-square. If White is going to adopt this plan, he should do so before moving the rook from a1 as otherwise Black is not forced to reply ...b4.

12 ... b4

With the rook on a1, 12...bxa4 can be met by 13 &xa4, when the a6-pawn is very weak.

13 &b1

White starts his knight manoeuvre.

13 ... &b8

Preventing an annoying &b6.

14 &d2

The knight returns to active play.

14 ... 0-0

Black finally castles. In this case there was no particular risk involved in leaving the king in the centre for so long, as White's pieces were not active enough to pose any real danger.

15 &d3

The first overt sign of aggressive intent on the kingside.

15 ... d6

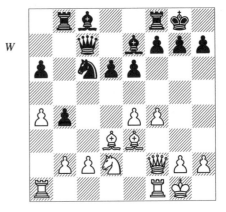

Black would like to play his dark-squared bishop to f6, but first of all he must prevent the reply e5.

16 &ad1

In fact, this is the first new move of the game. In Van der Wiel-Andersson, Wijk aan Zee 1987 White played more directly for an attack with 16 &g3 (intending f5), but Black countered by 16...f5! 17 exf5 exf5 18 &f3 &f6 19 &ab1 &e7 20 &fe1 &b7 with approximately equal play. Black has an isolated d-pawn, but this slight weakness is compensated for by the active position of his bishops on the long diagonals. Shirov's move prepares the attack more gradually.

16 ... b3?

This imaginative and ambitious move turns out badly, since Black's position isn't strong enough to support such an aggressive idea. The plan with ...f5 is not so effective with the rook on d1, since after 16...f5 17 exf5 exf5 18 ♖fe1 Black cannot easily reposition his pieces as in the Van der Wiel-Andersson game given above. The reason is that after 18...♗f6? 19 ♘c4!, there is already a threat of 20 ♘xd6 ♕xd6 21 ♗c4+, and 19...d5 20 ♗c5! is a neat tactical point giving White a clear advantage. However, Black should have continued with his basic plan by 16...♗f6, when White would have to decide how to meet the attack on the b2-pawn.

17   cxb3

After 17 ♘xb3 ♗f6 18 ♗c1 ♖b4 Black regains the pawn with an equal position; for example, 19 a5 ♘xa5 20 ♘xa5 ♗d4 21 ♗e3 ♗xe3 22 ♕xe3 ♕xa5.

17   ...   ♗f6

After 17...♘b4 18 ♗e2! ♗f6 19 ♖c1, followed by ♘c4, Black doesn't have much to show for the pawn.

18   ♖c1!

Shirov finds the best reply; he returns the pawn in order to denude Black's kingside of defenders. White could have kept the extra pawn by 18 ♗b1, since then 18...♗xb2 is bad because of 19 ♘c4. However, by 18...a5, intending ...♗a6 and ...♘b4, Black could have obtained considerable piece activity in compensation. 18 ♖b1 is also playable, but again Black has some play after 18...♘b4 19 ♗e2 ♗b7. In all probability, neither of these lines gives Black fully adequate compensation for the pawn, but in general it is better to have equal material with a strong initiative than to be a pawn up but have to grovel in defence.

18   ...   ♗xb2

Otherwise Black will be a pawn down for nothing; for example, 18...♗b7 19 ♘f3.

19   ♖c2

Now Black faces a dangerous pin along the c-file.

19   ...   ♗a3

Black must retain control of c1 as 19...♗f6 loses to 20 ♖fc1 ♗b7 21 e5! ♗e7 (21...dxe5 22 ♗e4) 22 ♗xa6 ♗xa6 23 ♖xc6 ♕b7 24 exd6. Thanks to Black's misguided 16th move, the conditions for a kingside attack by White have significantly improved. Black has no defensive minor pieces at all on the kingside, and he has to deal with the c-file pin.

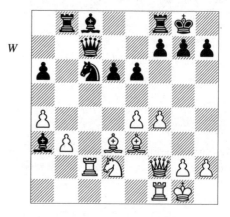

20   e5!

White opens up the diagonal for his light-squared bishop with gain of time, since Black must counter the threat of 21 exd6 ♕xd6 22 ♗e4 followed by ♘c4.

20   ...   d5

20...dxe5 fails to 21 ♗e4 ♗b7 22 ♖a1 ♗b4 23 ♗xc6 ♗xc6 24 ♖ac1, when White wins material.

21   ♘f3

This move introduces two unpleasant possibilities. The first is simply 22 ♘d4 ♗b7 23 ♖a1, followed by ♖ac1 winning material, and the second is the 'Greek gift' sacrifice ♗xh7+.

21   ...   ♕d7?!

After this the sacrifice on h7 is correct, although it demands very high-quality play by the attacker. Moving the other way by 21...♕b7 is not much help. Then 22 ♗xh7+ ♔xh7 23 ♕h4+ ♔g8 24 ♘g5 ♖e8 25 ♕h7+ ♔f8 gives White an enormous attack after 26 ♖fc1! ♗d7

27 f5!; for example, 27...exf5 28 Qh8+ Ke7 29 Qxg7 Kd8 30 Nxf7+ Kc8 31 Bc5 Bxc5+ 32 Rxc5 and the defence crumbles.

Black's only chance was to be brave and play 21...Rxb3. Now the best line is 22 Bxh7+! Kxh7 23 Nd4 (23 Qh4+ Kg8 24 Ng5 is probably not correct as White has the additional worry that his e3-bishop is hanging), aiming to regain the piece while keeping good attacking chances on the kingside. The variations are worth looking at in detail because they reveal how, when conducting a 'kingside' attack, one must be aware of tactical possibilities over the whole board:

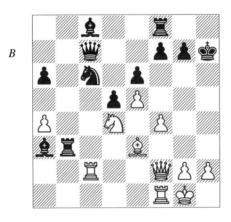

1) 23...Rb6 24 Nb5! (this is a case in point!) 24...axb5 25 Bxb6 Qb7 26 axb5 Ne7 27 Rc3 Bb4 28 Rb3 with an easy win for White.

2) 23...Rb2 24 Bc1! Rxc2 (after 24...Nxd4 25 Qh4+ Kg8 26 Rxc7 Ne2+ 27 Kh1 Black has only two minor pieces for the queen) 25 Qxc2+ Kg8 26 Bxa3 Qb6 27 Bxf8 and White wins.

3) 23...Rb4! 24 Rxc6 Qb7 25 Rc3! (25 f5 exf5 26 Rf6!? is an imaginative idea, but after 26...Bb2! White has no clear way to continue) 25...Bb2 26 Qc2+ Kg8 27 Rc7 Bxd4 (Black should eliminate this knight before it reaches g5; after 27...Qb8 28 Nf3 Rc4 29 Rxc4 dxc4 30 Ng5 g6 31 Qxc4 White is a pawn up and Black's kingside is very weak) 28 Bxd4 Qa8 (28...Qb8 29 Ba7 Qa8 30 Rb1 Rxb1+ 31 Qxb1 paralyses Black) 29 Qc3 is awkward for Black. Material is equal, but White's pieces occupy active positions and Black's kingside remains weak due to the missing h-pawn. After 29...Rb7, for example, the breakthrough 30 f5

exf5 31 e6 fxe6 32 Rxg7+ Rxg7 33 Bxg7 Re8 34 Be5 gives White a crushing attack on the dark squares; 29...Rxa4 is also met by 30 f5. Thus Black's best chance is probably 29...Rc4 30 Rxc4 dxc4 31 Qxc4, hoping to grovel to a draw a pawn down.

This analysis shows how finely balanced the position is. In one line, White follows up his sacrifice on h7 not by a direct attack on the king, but by play on the queenside (although with frequent glances to the other flank). After the text-move, however, the balance is tipped in favour of the direct kingside assault.

22 Bxh7+!

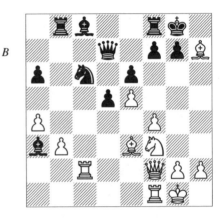

The 'Greek gift' sacrifice is a familiar idea, which can be found in all books on attacking play. In favourable circumstances it can be immediately decisive: White follows up with Ng5+, meeting ...Kg8 with Qh5 and ...Kg6 with either h4, Qg4 or Qd3+ according to the precise position. Here, however, it is far less clear-cut. Black is immediately mated if he plays ...Kg6, but the ...Kg8 defence proves a tough nut to crack. Where White is able to play Ng5+ and Qh5, a move by the f8-rook can often be met by a crushing Qxf7+, but here the queen is on h4 rather than h5, so there is no attack on f7 (it is not important that the black queen defends f7, as it can be deflected by Rxc6). In fact White is able to win, but he must display considerable creativity to do so. Even within the general framework of a familiar idea, chess offers scope to the imagination.

22 ... Kxh7
23 Qh4+

23 Ng5+ amounts to the same thing.

23	...	♔g8

Not 23...♔g6? 24 g4 mating in a few moves.

24	♘g5	♜e8

24...♜d8?! is inferior because Black's king may need d8 to escape: after 25 ♕h7+ ♔f8 26 ♕h8+ ♔e7 27 ♕xg7 ♜f8 (27...♜e8 28 ♕f6+ ♔f8 29 ♘h7+ ♔g8 30 ♕g5+ ♔xh7 31 ♜f3 mates) 28 ♘h7 ♗b7 29 f5 White has a crushing attack.

25	♜f3!

White finds an original concept that you won't find in any textbook of attacking play. The classical examples of the 'Greek gift' almost always involve chasing the king with 25 ♕h7+ ♔f8 26 ♕h8+ ♔e7 27 ♕xg7, but here Black continues 27...♔d8, escaping the immediate threats. Shirov realizes that he must reinforce his attack without allowing Black's king to escape via e7 and d8. The threat is simply 26 ♜h3.

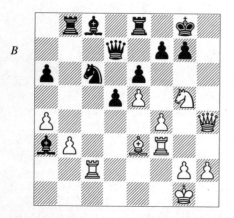

25	...	♘e7

The key point is that 25...♔f8? loses: 26 ♘h7+ ♔g8 27 ♘f6+! gxf6 28 ♜g3+ ♔f8 29 exf6 mating. As Black's king cannot run, he must try to provide a defence on the kingside; a quick look shows that the text-move is the only one to avoid an immediate disaster.

26	♕h7+

Now the checks are appropriate, as 26 ♜h3?? ♘g6 allows Black to defend.

26	...	♔f8
27	♕h8+	♘g8

White's finesse has allowed him to bring his queen to h8 while Black's king is still on f8. Once again, chasing the king by 28 ♘h7+ ♔e7 29 ♕xg7 ♔d8 would only ease Black's task.

Instead, White must stir up trouble for the king before it can escape.

28	f5!

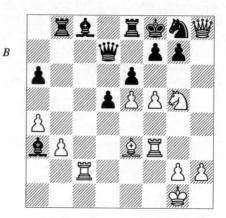

A successful attack often requires the participation of all, or almost all, the attacker's pieces. At the moment, White's queen and knight are in active positions, while the c2-rook looks well-placed to cut off a fleeing black king. However, the bishop and f3-rook are not doing very much. White finds a way to bring these into the attack and at the same time he bears in mind a second general principle: open lines generally favour the attacker. The text-move is the start of a breakthrough that fulfils both objectives: lines are opened and the two inactive pieces can use these same lines to join the attack.

28	...	exf5

Forced, as otherwise Black could not meet the multiple threats of 29 fxe6 ♜xe6 30 ♘h7+, 29 ♘h7+ ♔e7 30 ♗g5+ and 29 f6.

29	e6!

Opening more lines. 29 ♘h7+ ♔e7 30 ♕xg7 is far less clear.

29	...	fxe6

Once again forced, as 29...♜xe6 loses to 30 ♘h7+ ♔e7 31 ♗g5+ f6 (31...♔d6 32 ♗f4+) 32 ♕xg8, threatening mate on f8.

30	♜g3

The rook starts to play its part. Now that the seventh rank is opened, White has the deadly threat of 31 ♘h7+ followed by 32 ♜xg7+.

30	...	g6

Black cannot even try surrendering the queen by 30...e5 31 ♘h7+ ♔e7 32 ♜xg7+ ♔d6, as the finesse 33 ♜g6+! (33 ♜xd7+ is of course not bad) 33...♜e6 (33...♕e6 34 ♕g7! threatens mate at c7 and leads to even greater material gains, while 33...♔e7 runs into 34 ♗g5+ ♔f7 35 ♕g7#) 34 ♖xg8 is crushing: Black cannot meet the threats of 35 ♖gxc8, 35 ♖d8, 35 ♘f6 and 35 ♘f8, to name but a few.

31   ♘h7+   ♔f7

Or 31...♔e7 32 ♗g5+ ♔d6 (32...♔f7 transposes to the game) 33 ♗f4+ e5 (33...♔e7 34 ♕g7+ ♔d8 35 ♗c7+) 34 ♖xg6+ ♖e6 35 ♗xe5+ ♔e7 36 ♕g7+ with a quick mate.

32   ♗h6

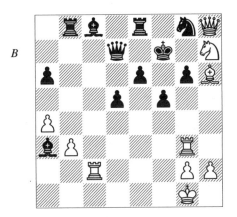

A beautiful and thematic finishing blow, threatening mate in one. White's bishop utilizes the open lines created by the f5 breakthrough to join the attack.

32   ...   ♔e7

Both 32...♘xh6 33 ♕f6+ ♔g8 34 ♖xg6+ ♔xh7 35 ♖xh6+ ♔g8 36 ♖h8# and 32...♗f8 33 ♘xf8 ♘xh6 34 ♖xg6 ♖xf8 35 ♖f6+ ♔e7 36 ♕xf8# lead to mate.

33   ♗g5+   ♔f7

The king cannot escape: 33...♔d6 34 ♗f4+ ♔e7 (34...e5 35 ♖xg6+ also leads to mate) 35 ♕g7+ ♔d8 36 ♗c7+ mates next move.

34   ♗f6

34 ♘f6 was a simpler win, but it would be churlish to criticize Shirov after such a wonderful attack.

34   ...   ♖f8

34...♕a7+ 35 ♔h1 doesn't help Black, while 34...e5 35 ♖c7 ♕xc7 36 ♕g7+ wins the queen.

35   ♖c7!

Here, too, this move wins the black queen.

35   ...   ♘xf6

35...♕xc7 36 ♕g7+ ♔e8 37 ♕xc7 is equally hopeless for Black.

36   ♕xf6+   ♔e8

Or 36...♔g8 37 ♖xg6+ ♔xh7 38 ♖h6+ ♔g8 39 ♖h8#.

37   ♕xg6+

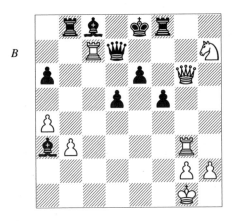

36   ...   ♔d8

37...♖f7 38 ♘f6+ is even worse.

38   ♖xd7+

White cashes in.

38   ...   ♗xd7

39   ♘xf8   ♗xf8

Black has no hope with only two bishops for the queen.

40   ♕f6+   ♗e7

40...♔e8 loses to 41 ♖g8.

41   ♖g8+

Forcing the exchange of rooks. The rest is easy.

41   ...   ♔c7

42   ♕c3+   ♔b7

43   ♖xb8+   ♔xb8

44   h4   1-0

44...♗xh4 is met by 45 ♕h8+ while otherwise the h-pawn runs through.

The 'Greek gift' sacrifice goes back at least 400 years, but it is still relevant today. Like the other standard attacking ideas, it claims victims somewhere in the world every day. These days, however, defenders are more aware of such possibilities and are unlikely to allow them in a clear-cut form.

In this game the preconditions for the sacrifice arose as a result of play on the other side of the board, where an unwise operation by Black (16...b3?) led to his dark-squared bishop being deflected from the defence of the kingside.

When the possibility to play ♗xh7+ arose, Shirov went in for it even though he could not have worked out every variation. He undoubtedly calculated several lines, and from these judged that the weight of attacking force would be too great for Black to resist. The key idea was to combine the sacrifice with a central breakthrough by f5 and e6, thereby opening up more lines and allowing his entire army to participate in the attack. An attractive finish rounded off an excellent attacking game by Shirov.

The lessons here are:

1) A good grasp of the standard attacking ideas and sacrifices is essential if you want to be a successful attacker.

2) Typical ideas provide useful guidance, but you may have to adapt them to the specific requirements of the position in front of you.

3) When conducting a kingside attack, keep your eye open for tactical possibilities on other parts of the board.

4) The more open lines there are, the better it is for the attacker.

The All-Out Sacrificial Onslaught

Every chess player dreams of conducting a brilliant attack, with multiple sacrifices leading up to a spectacular mate. It doesn't happen very often. The two main reasons are, firstly, that the circumstances for such an attack don't arise very often, and secondly that even when they do arise, the player lacks the courage to go in for the sacrifice, or mishandles the later play.

As regards the circumstances, this depends to a large extent on one's style of play. Those who like exploiting tiny positional advantages are unlikely to reach a situation in which they can make a cascade of sacrifices. Even if you have the right style, reaching a promising attacking position often involves taking a certain amount of risk, for example by playing a gambit.

Lacking the courage to make the sacrifice even when you have seen it is often the result of a lack of confidence in one's own calculating ability. Faced with a sacrifice which depends on calculating a variation ten moves deep, with no way out if something goes wrong, many players will back down. This problem can be solved by suitable tactical training, testing yourself with tricky positions and afterwards checking your analysis with a computer (dare I suggest *John Nunn's Chess Puzzle Book* as a suitable source of examples...). Assuming the sacrifice is correct, mishandling it at a later stage may well be the result of over-excitement or other psychological factors. It is probably impossible to stay completely calm when faced with a maelstrom on the board, but one should at least try!

Game 9
J. Nunn – I. Nataf
French Team Championship 1998/9
Sicilian Defence, Kalashnikov Variation

1	e4	c5
2	♘f3	♘c6

For comments on the moves up to here, see Game 8.

3 d4

As explained in Game 8, White sometimes plays 3 ♘c3 to try to restrict Black's options. However, the most common choice is the straightforward text-move. White at once opens the game and secures free development for his pieces, at the cost of allowing Black a 2 vs 1 majority in the centre.

3 ... cxd4

Black is happy to remove White's centre pawn.

4 ♘xd4 e5

This slightly unusual move introduces the Kalashnikov Variation. The basic idea is the same as that of the more popular Sveshnikov Variation (which may arise after 4...♘f6 5 ♘c3 e5 – see Games 20 and 23), namely that Black gains time by chasing the white knight around. The penalty is the weakening of the d5-square and the backwardness of Black's d-pawn. In the early decades of this century, great emphasis was laid on the importance of static pawn weaknesses such as backward pawns. Many textbooks still reflect this viewpoint, but chess as played by leading grandmasters has moved a long way forward since the days of Tarrasch. These days there is much more emphasis on dynamic possibilities, and it is recognized that it may be well worthwhile accepting a pawn weakness if compensation can be found in the form of active pieces or a lead in development.

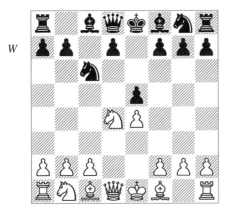

W

5   ᐂb5

This is the only real test of Black's last move. White threatens to jump into d6.

5   ...   d6

In fact, 4...e5 is far from being a completely new idea. It was played occasionally in the 19th century (including three outings in the famous McDonnell-Labourdonnais matches of 1834) and experienced a brief surge of popularity just after the Second World War. However, these earlier appearances were largely based on the idea of playing 5...a6 6 ᐂd6+ ♗xd6 7 ♕xd6 ♕f6, by which Black surrenders the two bishops in the hope of achieving a lead in development. These days, this strategy is regarded with deep suspicion and when 4...e5 appears in contemporary play, it is almost always with the idea of following up with 5...d6. It may seem a paradox that while today's grandmasters are quite happy to accept a weak pawn in return for better development, they won't give up the two

bishops for the same end! However, in the 5...a6 line the two bishops really are a significant factor, since the position is fairly open, while Black's lead in development isn't especially important because White can bring his own pieces into play quite easily.

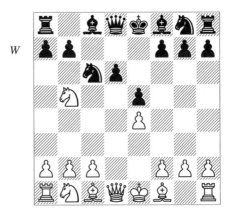

W

6   c4

There are several differences between the position after 5...d6 and the more familiar Sveshnikov position arising after 4...ᐂf6 5 ᐂc3 e5 6 ᐂdb5 d6. The most obvious is that the c2- and f7-pawns are not blocked, which gives extra options to both players. Secondly, Black is not obliged to play ...ᐂf6. He may play this knight to e7, or he may delay its development for some time in order to try exchanging his dark-squared bishop with ...♗e7 and ...♗g5 (after ...a6, of course). White has two main options. The first is simply to continue 6 ᐂ1c3. If Black plays ...ᐂf6 at some stage we will be back in a normal Sveshnikov, but more likely Black would continue 6...a6 7 ᐂa3 b5 8 ᐂd5 ᐂge7, when White's standard Sveshnikov move ♗g5 no longer has the same effect. In particular, Black avoids the doubled f-pawns that are a hallmark of many Sveshnikov positions.

Thus the text-move is most common in practice. White consolidates his grip on d5, dooming the d6-pawn to permanent backwardness. Moreover, when the b5-knight is chased back by ...a6, Black will not have the option of queenside expansion by ...b5, as in the Sveshnikov. On the other hand, playing c4 costs a development tempo and slightly weakens the d4-square.

6   ...   ♗e7

This is by far the most popular move. Black keeps as many options open as possible; he may still play ...♘f6, he may aim for ...♗g5 (perhaps supported by ...h6) or he may play ...f5. White is kept guessing.

7   ♘1c3

White has a problem with his knights, because both of them would like to be on c3. There is no perfect solution to this problem. If the b5-knight voluntarily retreats to c3, then not only does White lack a good square for the b1-knight, but Black might also be able to save a tempo by missing out ...a6. The text-move means that the b5-knight will have to retreat to the inferior square a3, but at least Black is obliged to spend a tempo on ...a6.

7   ...   a6

Forced, as White was threatening 8 ♘d5.

8   ♘a3

B

Of course, a3 is not an ideal square for the knight, so White aims to play ♘c2 and possibly ♘e3.

8   ...   f5

The most common line is 8...♗e6, which again aims to keep Black's options open. The text-move is distinctly unusual. The exchange of White's e-pawn for Black's f-pawn further weakens Black's pawn-structure, and it is easy to imagine how White might eventually establish a dominating grip on the e4- and d5-squares. However, in the meantime Black has active pieces, so it is not clear if White can realize his dream.

9   ♗d3

It may well be that this ambitious move is not best. The alternative is 9 exf5 ♗xf5 10 ♗d3

♗e6 11 0-0 ♘f6 12 ♘c2 0-0. In this case Black still has his weak pawns, but his pieces are active and he has some pressure down the half-open f-file. Perhaps White has some advantage, but it cannot be all that great. The text-move aims to induce Black to take on e4 himself, which would effectively give White an extra tempo.

9   ...   f4!

Black stakes out an ambitious claim of his own. The f4-pawn makes it awkward for White to develop his dark-squared bishop, and cuts across White's planned manoeuvre ♘c2-e3.

10   g3

I decided to remove the restrictive pawn, and at this stage I felt quite confident about my position. White can, of course, simply develop by b3 and ♗b2, followed by queenside castling, but then what is his long-term plan? With his king on the queenside it will be risky to take action there and once Black has completed his development it will be hard to challenge the f4-pawn.

10   ...   ♘f6!

A surprising reply, offering the f4-pawn. I had expected 10...fxg3 11 hxg3 ♘f6, but then White has a definite edge. After 12 ♘c2 0-0 13 f3 followed by ♗e3, ♕d2 (or ♕e2) and 0-0-0, White would have a ready-made attack on the kingside thanks to the open h-file and possibility of g4-g5.

After the text-move, White has to accept the sacrifice or his last move has no point.

11   gxf4   exf4
12   ♗xf4   0-0

Black has some play for the pawn since White's kingside is shattered, which makes 0-0 uninviting, and it will take a couple of moves before he can organize queenside castling. However, I wasn't especially worried as White is not behind in development – indeed, Black's queenside pieces are mostly still on their original squares. In this respect my opponent showed better judgement than I did. The two moves it takes for White to castle turn out to be one too many. An additional problem for White is his out-of-play knight on a3. When the hand-to-hand battle starts, White will sorely miss this knight. Again, it takes two moves to bring the knight back into play, time that White cannot afford.

As we saw in Game 2, when your opponent's king is stuck in the centre, quick action is essential (an exception may arise if the king has permanently lost the right to castle). Maintaining the momentum of the attack, and keeping the opponent off-balance with threats, are essential elements of the attack. If further material needs to be invested, then so be it.

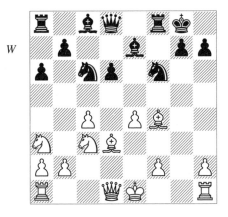

13   ♗g3

This is the most natural move. The bishop was vulnerable on f4 and would have to move sooner or later in any case, so moving it now preserves the greatest flexibility. The position after 13 ♕d2 ♘g4! already reveals how dangerous Black's threats can become; for example, 14 ♗g3 ♘xf2! 15 ♗xf2 ♖xf2 16 ♔xf2 ♗g5 wins for Black, as White has no reasonable square for the queen (17 ♕e2 ♗h4+ forces mate in a few moves). Since 14 0-0-0? is impossible due to 14...♖xf4, White would probably have to play 14 ♘d5, but even then 14...♗h4 is awkward for White.

13   ...   ♘g4!

Black focuses on the traditional weak spot in the case of an uncastled king – the f2-square (f7 for Black). Beginners are warned of the potential danger of an attack on this square, and it is worth being reminded that this danger applies not only to beginners. Black is preparing to start an all-out sacrificial attack on f2 and despite White's free move it is very difficult to stop it.

14   ♗e2?

This seemed like the saving move, because White now has a check on d5 to activate his queen with gain of tempo, but in fact the sacrifice still works. 14 ♕d2? loses to 14...♘xf2!, as

in the previous note, while 14 h3? ♘xf2! 15 ♗xf2 ♖xf2 16 ♔xf2 ♗h4+ 17 ♔e2 (other moves also lead to mate) 17...♘d4+ 18 ♔d2 ♕g5# is a nice mate. In fact, the only reasonable moves to prevent the sacrifice are 14 ♖f1 and 14 0-0. After 14 ♖f1 ♘d4 15 ♗e2 ♘xe2 16 ♕xe2 ♘e5 Black has good compensation for the pawn, so White should have tried 14 0-0, with unclear play.

14   ...   ♘xf2!

I think this is one of those combinations where one cannot give any kind of justification based on general principles. Indeed, given that relatively few of Black's pieces are in active attacking positions, it is hard to imagine that it is correct. Yet when it comes down to concrete lines, Black's command of the dark squares, White's offside a3-knight, and the possibility for Black's pieces to come into play with gain of tempo tip the balance in his favour. Other moves give White the advantage; for example, 14...♘ge5 15 ♕d5+ followed by 16 0-0-0, bringing the king into safety, or 14...♘ce5 15 f4 ♘e3 16 ♕d2 ♘g2+ 17 ♔d1 ♘g6 18 ♘d5 and Black doesn't have much for the pawn.

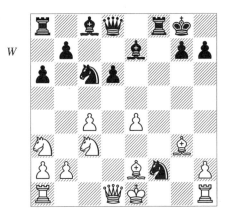

15   ♕d5+

White cannot do without this check, as 15 ♗xf2 ♖xf2 16 ♔xf2 ♗h4+ 17 ♔g2 (17 ♔e3 ♕g5+ 18 ♔d3 ♘b4+ 19 ♔d4 ♕c5#) 17...♕g5+ 18 ♗g4 ♘e5 (18...♗xg4? 19 ♕d5+) 19 h3 h5 wins back a piece, while retaining an enormous attack. With the queen on d5, Black no longer has a check on g5, so the sacrifice is much less clear-cut.

15   ...   ♔h8
16   ♗xf2?

In fact White should continue 16 ♖f1, when 16...♘g4 is just slightly better for Black. However, I had missed Black's 24th move and so accepted the sacrifice, believing that it would lead only to perpetual check. After the game Nataf said that at this stage he had also not seen his 24th move, but he was encouraged by the strength of his attack, and reassured by the presence of a safety-net in the form of a forced perpetual check (by 24...♕xf3+).

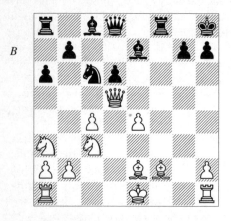

B

16 ... ♘b4

White's ♕d5+ was designed to deprive Black of a queen check on g5; this move is designed to reclaim g5 for Black's queen. Black should not play 16...♗h4?, when 17 ♗g3 wins, but he could also have inverted his moves by 16...♖xf2 17 ♔xf2 ♘b4, since the only additional possibility 18 ♕f7 ♗h4+ 19 ♔f3 fails to the neat switchback 19...♘c6! 20 ♕f4 g5 21 ♕e3 ♗h3!, when the king is trapped.

17 ♕h5

White strives to retain control of g5. Other moves lose more quickly:

1) 17 ♕d1 ♖xf2! 18 ♔xf2 ♗h4+ 19 ♔g2 ♕g5+ 20 ♗g4 ♗xg4 and Black wins.

2) 17 ♕d4 ♖xf2! 18 ♔xf2 ♗h4+ 19 ♔f3 ♗h3! 20 ♘d5 (there is nothing better) 20...♕g5 21 ♘f4 ♖f8! (21...♕xf4+ 22 ♔xf4 ♖f8+ is wrong because of 23 ♕f6) 22 ♕xd6 ♗g4+ 23 ♔e3 ♖xf4 24 ♕xf4 ♗f2+ 25 ♔xf2 ♕xf4+ with further massive loss of material to come.

3) 17 ♕d2 ♖xf2! 18 ♔xf2 ♗g5! 19 ♕d4 ♗h4+ transposes to line '2'.

17 ... ♖xf2!

Another hammer-blow on f2; acceptance is forced.

18 ♔xf2 ♗h4+

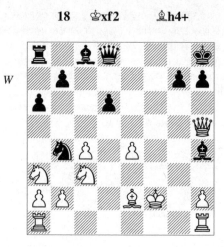

W

Conducting such a sacrificial attack obviously places a premium on pure calculating ability, but it is also useful to look at the position from a general point of view. Here, although the sacrifice looks a bit unlikely, there are some points operating in Black's favour, the main one being that his domination of the dark squares is more or less complete. White's knights both stand on dark squares and so control only light squares, White no longer has his dark-squared bishop, and both rooks are still on their original squares and can play no immediate part in the battle. Thus it is left to White's queen to fight for some control of the dark squares. Since the queen and to some extent the light-squared bishop are White's only defenders, the fact that not all Black's pieces are yet in play becomes less relevant, because in the area around White's king he has at least a chance of a numerical superiority – it all depends on whether his queen can join the attack with gain of tempo. Such a general assessment can at least point one's calculations in the right direction and Black can conclude that:

1) He need only look at very forcing lines; if White is given a chance to bring a rook into play, or control some dark squares with a knight, then the attack is unlikely to succeed.

2) Bringing his queen into the attack with gain of tempo is a key factor.

Having such pointers in mind can be a great time-saver when it comes to precise calculation. However, this method does have many limitations; for example, I don't think there is any way in which a spectacular move such as

Black's 24th can be anticipated on general principles – you just have to see it – and some players are better than others at spotting tactical opportunities.

19 ♔g2

The alternatives are no better. 19 ♔g1 g6 20 ♕f3 ♕g5+ 21 ♔f1 transposes to the game, while 19 ♔e3 g6 20 ♕f3 ♕g5+ 21 ♕f4 ♕c5+ 22 ♔d2 ♗g5 picks up the queen.

19 ... g6

The key point is that 20 ♕h6 loses after 20...♗g5, so White has to give up control of g5.

20 ♕f3 ♕g5+

Now Black's pieces start to enter the attack with gain of tempo.

21 ♔f1

Just looking at the board, Black's sacrifice still appears far from convincing. White is a whole rook up, and Black's queenside pieces have yet to join the attack.

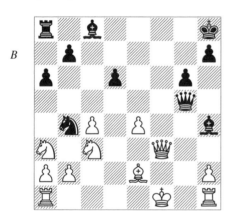

B

21 ... ♗h3+!

Another sacrifice. It is worth investing a further piece in order to activate the rook with gain of tempo.

22 ♕xh3

I didn't have much to think about during this phase of the game, as all White's moves are forced.

22 ... ♖f8+

23 ♗f3

White cannot even escape by giving up his queen with 23 ♕f3 ♖xf3+ 24 ♗xf3 owing to 24...♕e3 25 ♔g2 ♕f2+ 26 ♔h3 ♕xf3+ 27 ♔xh4 h6 28 ♖hg1 g5+ 29 ♖xg5 hxg5+ 30 ♔xg5 ♕g2+ followed by ...♕xb2, with a further harvest on the queenside.

23 ... ♕e3

24 ♕xh4

24 ♘d1 ♖xf3+ 25 ♕xf3 ♕xf3+ 26 ♔g1 ♘d3 forces mate in a few moves.

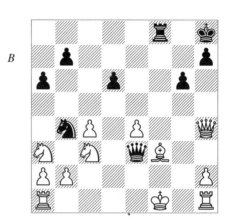

B

24 ... ♘d3!

This is a remarkably quiet move considering that Black is a rook and two pieces down. Neither capture on f3 wins, but this move, bringing the last reserves into the attack, decides the game in Black's favour. Instead, 24...♕xf3+ 25 ♔g1 ♕e3+ 26 ♔g2 is only perpetual check, while 24...♖xf3+? 25 ♔g2 would even lose for Black. The text-move threatens mate in three by 25...♖xf3+ 26 ♔g2 ♘f4+ 27 ♕xf4 ♕f2#.

25 ♘d5

After 25 ♔g2 ♕xf3+ 26 ♔g1 ♘f4, Black mates in a few moves, and 25 ♕g3 doesn't stop the threat: 25...♖xf3+ 26 ♔g2 ♘f4+.

25 ... ♕xf3+

It doesn't make any difference to the result of the game, but Black could have forced mate in seven starting with 25...♖xf3+! 26 ♔g2 ♕e2+ 27 ♔g1 g5. This seems to be the only (very minor) slip by Black in an exceptionally well-played game.

26 ♔g1 ♘f2

27 ♔f1

27 ♘f6 was the only way to play on, but it's quite hopeless after 27...♘h3+ (27...♖xf6 28 ♕xf6+ ♕xf6 29 ♖f1 is less clear) 28 ♕xh3 ♕xh3 29 ♖f1 ♕e3+ 30 ♔g2 ♕g5+ 31 ♔h3 ♖xf6 32 ♖xf6 ♕xf6, when White loses at least two pawns on the queenside.

27 ... ♕xh1+

28 ♔e2 ♕xa1

0-1

Nataf's combination deservedly won him the prize for the best game in *Informator 75*.

Nataf's greatest strength is his tactical ability and his opening was well-chosen to exploit this. By playing sharply and ambitiously at an early stage, he threw down the gauntlet to White: back down and accept little or no advantage from the opening, or accept the challenge. I accepted (by playing 9 ♗d3), but an error at move 14 allowed Black to start an imaginative attack against White's centralized king. Then it was all downhill, as White's position reeled from one sledgehammer blow after another.

The lessons here are:

1) When White's king has not castled, f2 is a vulnerable square, even for an experienced grandmaster.

2) After the first sacrifice, the attack must be pursued with maximum energy so as not to allow the defender a breathing space.

3) It is useful to have a *safety-net*, i.e. a possible reserve continuation (perhaps leading to a draw), in case the main attacking line proves less favourable than expected.

4) You probably shouldn't try to play like this unless you have a fair degree of tactical ability!

Opposite-Side Castling

It is often hard to decide whether to attack with pieces or pawns, since each method has its advantages and disadvantages. A piece attack can often be mounted quickly, but unless there are already weaknesses in the enemy castled position, it may be hard to break through with pieces alone. A pawn attack, on the other hand, is much slower, but once it does arrive it is often irresistible. The advancing pawns tear holes in the enemy castled position, which the attacker's pieces can then exploit. Another point is that while the pawns are unmoved, it is hard for the attacker to bring his rooks to bear – this may require a manoeuvre such as ♖e3-g3. A pawn attack naturally creates space for the rooks to operate effectively from the first rank.

The relative position of the kings is also important. When the kings are castled on the same side, pawn attacks are less likely, as these expose the attacker's own king. Only if the centre is blocked, or if the attacker has a very solid central structure, can he contemplate a pawn attack. On the other hand, opposite-side castling leads to pawn attacks with much greater frequency. The main question then is how many pawns to advance. Too many, and the attack will proceed at a snail's pace. The basic rule is that the attacker should advance just enough pawns to create a decisive weakening in the opposing castled position – any more are redundant. Very often, just a single pawn is sufficient. In the following game, two pawns are enough to do the job, as they converge on the g6-square.

Game 10

J. Nunn – C. Ward

British League (4NCL) 1997/8

Sicilian Defence, Dragon Variation

| 1 | e4 | c5 |
| 2 | ♘f3 | |

For comments on the moves up to here, see Game 8.

| 2 | ... | d6 |

This move is an equally good alternative to 2...♘c6, as played in Games 8 and 9. Black intends to play ...♘f6, attacking the e4-pawn, but first prevents the reply e5.

| 3 | d4 | |

Just as in Games 8 and 9, White is prepared to exchange off a central pawn to speed up the development of his minor pieces.

| 3 | ... | cxd4 |

Black is also satisfied with this exchange, which gives him a majority of pawns in the centre and a half-open c-file.

| 4 | ♘xd4 | ♘f6 |

A natural developing move, which also attacks e4.

5 ♘c3

The most flexible way to defend e4.

5 ... g6

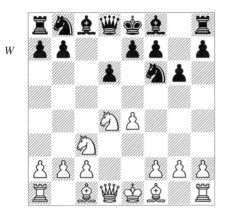

This move introduces the Dragon Variation, one of the most controversial opening systems. The basic idea is logical enough: Black wants to develop his bishop actively on the long diagonal, rather than on e7, as occurs in most other lines of the Sicilian. White can counter the Dragon in numerous ways, but the sharpest and, according to theory, best plan is to aim for 0-0-0 and a direct attack against Black's king. This leads to very double-edged play, with White's kingside attack and Black's queenside counterattack racing each other to strike first. Dragon players tend to be fanatical in their support for the opening. Playing the Dragon is obviously highly addictive, because many Dragon players who start out as occasional users prove unable to throw off the habit and get stuck with the opening for the rest of their lives. The cause of the Dragon was advanced when Kasparov used it in his PCA World Championship match against Anand in 1995, but despite this endorsement it has only caught on amongst a minority of leading grandmasters. Either they regard it as too risky, or perhaps they fear becoming wedded to a particular opening.

6 ♗e3

If White wants to launch an attack against the black king, then 0-0-0 will be essential, so White immediately starts to develop his queenside pieces. His basic attacking plan will contain two key elements:

1) the advance of the h-pawn to soften up Black's kingside and bring the h1-rook into the attack from its initial square;

2) playing ♗h6 to eliminate the g7-bishop, which is both the main defender of Black's kingside and a very useful piece for supporting Black's queenside counterattack. This method of attacking a kingside fianchettoed position is not restricted to the Dragon, and it often occurs in the Pirc Defence (1 e4 d6) and certain lines of the King's Indian Defence (especially the Sämisch – see Game 14).

6 ... ♗g7

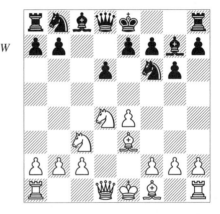

The Dragon bishop settles onto its favourite diagonal. Although at the moment many pieces lie between g7 and the white queenside, innumerable games have been decided by the power of the Dragon bishop, and all players facing the Dragon have learnt to treat it with respect. The ideal solution, from White's point of view, is to exchange the bishop with ♗h6, but this may not be so easy to achieve under favourable circumstances. In the Dragon, the dark squares hold a particular importance, and both sides will be keen to avoid the exchange of their dark-squared bishop (except possibly in return for the opposing dark-squared bishop).

7 f3

This is a necessary precaution. If White plays 7 ♕d2, then Black can harass White's dark-squared bishop by 7...♘g4. Note that Black could not have played 6...♘g4 because the reply 7 ♗b5+ would have cost Black material. It is interesting to observe that in the lines of the Pirc and King's Indian embodying the same strategy, White also feels it necessary to play the precautionary f3. In all cases the purpose is not only to secure the dark-squared bishop, but also to solidify the centre in preparation for a flank attack.

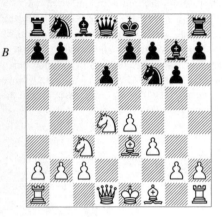

7 ... ♘c6

The most natural square for the knight, since the attack on d4 will make it harder for White to arrange ♗h6.

8 ♕d2

White prepares both queenside castling and an eventual ♗h6.

8 ... 0-0

Even though Black is well aware of White's intentions, there is no better place for his king.

9 ♗c4

This move might appear inconsistent. Why does not White just get on with the job and play 9 0-0-0 without further ado? The answer is that Black is then able to steer the game into new channels by playing 9...d5. It is not clear whether White has any advantage in that case, but it is clear that White has been deflected from the plan of a direct attack down the h-file. Therefore, White often prefers to play the text-move, which rules out ...d5. Another plus point is that the bishop is aimed at Black's kingside. There are two main negative points. The first is that White has to spend two tempi moving his bishop, since ♗b3 will be inevitable sooner or later. The second is that the bishop may itself become vulnerable to attack, for example if Black manages to push his a- and b-pawns. The pros and cons more or less balance each other, which explains why both 9 0-0-0 and 9 ♗c4 are often seen in practice.

9 ... ♗d7

The half-open c-file will be one of Black's main avenues of attack, so it makes sense to clear c8 for one of the rooks.

10 0-0-0

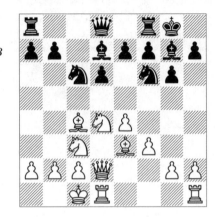

Opposite-side castling usually leads to sharp play. When the kings are castled on the same side, an attack involving pawns entails some risk, as the pawns that are being advanced are those which are defending one's own king. There is no such inhibiting factor when the kings are on opposite sides of the board, and it is quite normal for both players to launch an attack as soon as possible. Such a situation is like a race; whichever player manages to strike a real blow first is likely to win. There are two additional points to make. Winning material is of less significance in such situations than it normally is. It is no good gaining material if the result is the collapse of one's attack, leaving the opponent free to go for mate. Secondly, having to pull one's pieces back from the attack for defensive purposes is often equivalent to resignation, for then the opponent has all the time he needs to break through. This does not mean that no defensive moves at all should be made; for example, it is clearly worthwhile to make a defensive move if it delays the enemy attack by two moves. It does mean, however, that each defensive move must be carefully considered to see if it is worth the tempo it consumes.

10 ... ♕a5

This slightly unusual move is a lifelong favourite of Chris Ward. The idea is to move the f8-rook to c8, which has the advantage that the other rook can also join in the attack, for example by supporting ...b5 with ...♖ab8. A second advantage is that Black can usually retain his key 'Dragon' bishop by answering ♗h6 by ...♗h8. The disadvantages are twofold: first of all, the f8-rook is sometimes useful for defensive purposes and moving it away from the kingside leaves that part of the board looking a little short of defenders. Secondly, it isn't really clear that a5 is a good square for the queen, since in some lines it is vulnerable to attack. We shall see how all these factors play a part in the game.

Quite honestly, I regard this system as somewhat dubious for Black – in fact, it is quite hard to put one's finger on an error by Black in this game, other than his choice of opening variation.

The most common line is 10...♘e5 11 ♗b3 ♖c8.

11 h4

White wastes no time in starting his attack.

11 ... ♘e5

This is the normal square for the knight in this variation. In some cases Black will eventually play ...♘c4 to force the exchange of White's light-squared bishop, while in other lines the knight simply stays on e5, defending some squares on the kingside while retaining the option of helping on the queenside.

12 ♗b3 ♖fc8

Black follows the plan initiated at move 10.

13 g4

White has quite a wide range of moves here. Perhaps the most direct is 13 h5. It is quite normal in the Dragon for White to offer his h-pawn, since in taking it Black not only loses time with his knight, but also opens up the h-file. After 13...♘xh5, it is tempting to play 14 ♗h6 since at this moment Black cannot avoid the exchange of bishops by 14...♗h8 due to 15 ♖xh5 gxh5 16 ♕g5+, when White wins Black's queen. However, Black has a stronger reply in the surprising move 14...♘d3+ (14...♗xh6 is also playable), which leads to a satisfactory position for Black after 15 ♔b1 ♘xb2 16 ♔xb2 ♗xh6 17 ♕xh6 ♖xc3.

Therefore, the most popular move for White here is 13 ♔b1, again aiming to play h5, but having moved White's king out of harm's way first. This move raises the interesting question as to when White should play a consolidating move such as ♔b1. One should certainly give

far more thought to such moves in opposite-side castling situations than one would to, say, ♔h1 when both kings are on the kingside. When the kings are on opposite sides every tempo is vital, and so a move such as ♔b1 should not be played without a concrete reason. A typical reason would be to anticipate the exchange sacrifice ...♖xc3, bxc3 ♕xc3, when ♔b1 is normally forced in any case because of the threatened check on a1. If White is going to have to play ♔b1 anyway, it might be less committal to get it out of the way immediately. In the current position there is certainly some point to 13 ♔b1; we have already seen one line with an unexpected check to the king on c1, and if White plays ♗h6 at some stage, Black might well reply ...♗xh6 and ...♖xc3. However, the arguments are quite finely balanced.

Just before playing this game, I recalled a conversation I had with Chris Ward a few months earlier. We were having breakfast together the day after one of our battles in the Dragon (on that occasion, I had played 13 h5). Chris remarked that it was surprising 13 ♔b1 was so popular, as 13 g4 looked like a more useful move. On thinking about this, it seemed a valid point, so I decided to give his own recommendation a try! The move g4 aims primarily to play h5 without sacrificing a pawn, but it has some other good points: it allows the white queen to switch to h2, and in some lines it supports the piece sacrifice ♘f5.

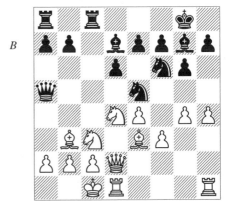

13 ... b5

There are three possible plans here for Black. The most obvious is 13...♘c4 14 ♗xc4 ♖xc4, but after 15 h5 ♖ac8 16 ♘b3 ♕a6 17 hxg6 fxg6

18 e5 White has a dangerous attack, because 18...dxe5 loses a piece to 19 g5, while if the f6-knight moves White can reply 19 ♕h2.

Another option is the surprising 13...♖c4!?. The lines after this move provide a good illustration of typical Dragon themes:

1) 14 ♗xc4 is dubious, as Black is able to break through on the dark squares: 14...♘xc4 15 ♕d3 ♕b4 16 ♘b3 ♘xe4! (a surprising sacrifice on a triply defended square) 17 fxe4 (17 ♘xe4 ♘xb2 18 ♕d5 ♕a3 gives Black a very dangerous attack in return for the rook, while 17 ♕xe4 ♗xc3 18 ♗d4 ♘xb2 19 ♗xc3 ♕xc3 is just bad for White) 17...♗xc3 18 ♗d4 (18 ♕xc3 ♕xc3 19 bxc3 ♘xe3 favours Black) 18...♗xd4 19 ♕xd4 ♗xg4 is unclear. Black has two pawns for the exchange but White still has some attacking chances.

2) 14 g5! ♘h5 (14...♖xd4? 15 ♗xd4 ♘xf3 16 ♕f2! ♘xd4 17 ♖xd4 and the weakness of f7 is fatal for Black) 15 f4 ♖xd4 (15...♘f3? 16 ♘xf3 ♖xc3 looks like another typical Dragon combination based on a dark-squared breakthrough; however, such combinations don't always work: here 17 e5! causes Black's position to collapse) 16 ♕xd4 ♘g4 17 e5 (17 ♕d3!? is also possible) 17...♘g3 18 ♖he1 ♘f5 19 ♕d2 ♘fxe3 20 ♖xe3 ♘xe3 21 ♕xe3 with some advantage to White.

With the move played, Black again aims to play ...♘c4, but now with the idea of recapturing on c4 with the pawn. This will give Black a ready-made attack along the b-file. The two problems with this plan are firstly that it is a little slow and secondly that, thanks to White's omission of ♔b1, a black queen arriving on b2 may not be mate.

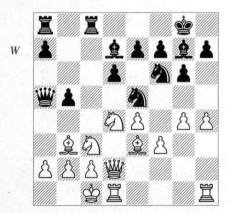

14   h5
White gets on with the attack.

14   ...   ♘c4

15   ♗xc4

This is best. After 15 ♕d3 ♘e5 White has nothing better than to repeat moves, since playing 16 ♕e2 positively invites Black to sacrifice on c3.

15   ...   bxc4

Now White has two free moves before Black lines up against b2.

16   ♗h6

A logical step. Either Black's bishop is exchanged, or White transfers his bishop to a more active square with gain of tempo. Note that White doesn't have to worry any more about ...♖xc3, so there is no problem about the white queen being drawn away if Black plays ...♗xh6.

16   ...   ♗h8

This is forced as here Black cannot allow his defensive bishop to be exchanged; for example, 16...♖ab8 17 ♗xg7 ♔xg7 18 hxg6 fxg6 19 ♕h6+ ♔g8 20 g5 ♘h5 21 ♖xh5 gxh5 22 g6 hxg6 23 ♕xg6+ ♔f8 24 ♖g1 mates, or 16...♗xh6 17 ♕xh6 g5 18 ♘f5 with a winning position.

17   ♘f5

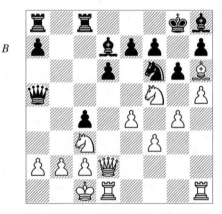

We have reached a critical moment as White is now threatening mate in one on e7.

17   ...   ♖e8

This is perhaps most testing, although the resulting complications favour White. The alternative is 17...♗xf5, but this also appears unsatisfactory for Black in view of 18 exf5! (18 gxf5 ♖ab8 19 hxg6 fxg6 20 fxg6 hxg6 21 ♖dg1 ♔f7 22 ♕g2 ♖g8 is unclear as White's attack has been brought to a halt) 18...♖ab8 19 hxg6 fxg6 (19...hxg6 20 fxg6 ♕b4 21 ♕e3! ♕xb2+ 22 ♔d2 gives White a clear advantage) 20 ♕e3 (the key advantage of playing exf5 rather than gxf5 is that White is now threatening mate in one) 20...♕e5 21 ♕xe5 dxe5 22 g5 ♘e8 23 ♘d5 and the endgame favours White.

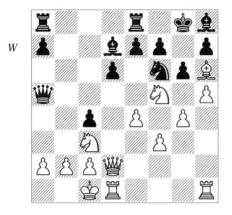

18   ♕g5!

Before the game, I looked at some recent copies of *Informator* to see if there had been any important games with the 10...♕a5 line. My eye was caught by the postal game Pavlov-Vaskin, which had continued 18 ♗g7 ♗xf5 19 ♗xh8 ♔xh8 20 exf5 ♖g8 21 ♖de1 ♖ae8 22 hxg6 fxg6 23 ♕h6 ♖g7 24 fxg6 ♖b8. Here White played 25 ♕f4 ♕b4 26 ♘d1 (not 26 ♖xe7? ♕xb2+ 27 ♔d2 ♕xc3+) and won after a long, hard struggle. It didn't take long to spot that Black is just dead lost after 25 ♕h4!. This again threatens 26 ♖xe7 ♖xe7 27 ♕xf6+, against which Black has scant defence. If Black plays 25...♕b4 as in the game, then White wins by 26 ♖xe7 ♕xb2+ 27 ♔d2 since Black no longer has the sacrifice on c3.

At the board I was mentally rubbing my hands with glee at the thought of springing this move on Chris Ward, when I decided to check the earlier moves in this line. I immediately received a dash of cold water; after 18 ♗g7, Black can simply reply 18...gxf5, meeting 19 ♕g5 with 19...h6! 20 ♗xh6+ ♔h7, when Black is a piece up for very little. Clearly Chris had spotted this and was prepared with his own surprise. Unfortunately for him, the position is in fact bad for Black, provided White finds the correct 18th move. After the game I looked again at my *Informator* and spotted a little note I hadn't

noticed before, which gave 18...gxf5 as unclear after 19 ♕g5 h6 or 19 gxf5 ♗xg7 20 h6 ♗f8, with this last move being given the 'only move' symbol. As already noted, the first of these lines leaves Black a piece up for almost nothing, while the second is even more ludicrous. If Black plays 20...♗h8 21 ♖hg1+ ♔f8 instead of 20...♗f8, then he is two pieces up for nothing. White can only create a threat by tripling on the g-file, but even if he manages this, Black just plays ...e6 and the whole attack collapses. If anybody requires a stark warning that published analysis should always be checked carefully, then this is it.

Luckily for me, it didn't take long to find the powerful text-move. The threat of ♘xe7+ forces Black to move his queen, but the net effect is that White has transferred his queen to a more aggressive position with gain of tempo.

18   ...   ♕b6

Of course, Black puts his queen on the b-file so as continue his attack against b2 but, as noted above, ...♕xb2+ is not the end of the world for White and in many cases it can simply be ignored.

19   hxg6

Now the time is ripe for the ♗g7 combination, but first of all White opens the h-file.

19   ...   fxg6

19...hxg6 20 ♗f8! is instantly decisive, so this is forced.

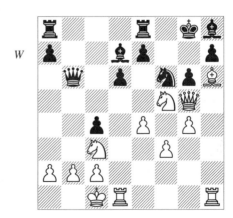

20   ♗g7!

One could not wish for a more vivid demonstration of the importance of eliminating Black's defensive bishop. White is prepared to sacrifice a piece to get rid of it.

20   ...   ♗xg7

20...♖ab8 21 ♗xh8 ♕xb2+ 22 ♔d2 ♔xh8 loses to 23 ♖xh7+! (23 ♘xe7 is also very strong; for example, 23...♖xe7 24 ♕xf6+ ♖g7 25 ♖b1) 23...♘xh7 24 ♖h1 (threatening 25 ♖xh7+, amongst other things) 24...♗xf5 25 ♕h6 ♔g8 26 ♕xh7+ ♔f8 27 gxf5 with a quick mate to follow.

20...♗xf5 21 ♗xh8 ♔xh8 22 gxf5 is also very awkward for Black; for example, 22...♖ab8 23 fxg6 ♕xb2+ 24 ♔d2 (threatening 25 ♖xh7+ ♘xh7 26 ♕h6) 24...♕b6 (24...♖g8 25 ♕xf6+!) 25 ♔e2! (stopping any annoying checks and renewing the threat) 25...♖b7 26 ♘d5 with a winning attack.

21   ♘xg7

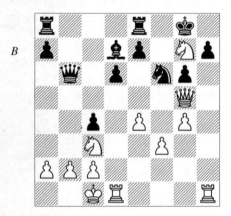

21   ...   ♖eb8

Black decides to decline the offered piece. After 21...♔xg7 22 ♘d5! there is no good square for the queen:

1) 22...♕a5 23 ♕h6+ ♔f7 24 ♘xf6 ♔xf6 (24...exf6 25 ♖xd6 ♗e6 26 ♕xh7+ ♔f8 27 ♖xe6 ♖xe6 28 ♕b7! and White takes the a8-rook with check) 25 ♖d5 ♕b6 26 g5+ winning.

2) 22...♕b7 23 ♘xf6 exf6 24 ♕h6+ ♔f7 25 ♕xh7+ ♔e6 26 ♕xg6 with a winning attack.

3) 22...♕c5 23 ♕h6+ ♔f7 24 g5! ♘h5 (24...♘xd5 25 ♕xh7+ wins for White, as does 24...♘g8 25 ♕xh7+ ♔f8 26 ♕xg6) 25 ♖xh5 gxh5 26 ♕xh7+ ♔f8 27 g6 ♗e6 28 ♕h8+ ♗g8 29 ♕h6#.

4) 22...♕b5 23 ♕h6+ ♔f7 24 g5 wins as after 22...♕c5.

22   ♘h5!

White ignores Black's threat to b2 and concentrates on whittling away Black's kingside

defenders. Once the f6-knight has gone, White's threats down the h-file will be extremely strong. Note that 22 ♘f5 is wrong, as Black can eliminate the knight with his bishop, which is not a vital defensive piece.

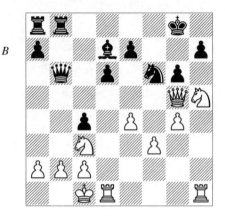

22   ...   ♘xh5

22...♕xb2+ 23 ♔d2 doesn't help, since in some lines White can actually use the b-file for his attack:

1) 23...♖f8 24 ♘xf6+ ♖xf6 (24...exf6 25 ♕d5+ ♔h8 26 ♖b1 ♕a3 27 ♖b7 ♖ad8 28 ♕e6! is a neat variation that wins for White) 25 ♕d5+ ♔g7 26 ♕xa8 ♖xf3 27 ♖xh7+! (otherwise White might even lose) 27...♔xh7 28 ♖h1+ ♔g7 29 ♕h8+ ♔f7 30 ♖h7+ ♔e6 31 ♖xe7+ ♔xe7 32 ♘d5+ winning the queen.

2) 23...♘xh5 24 gxh5 and now:

2a) 24...♗e8 loses to 25 hxg6 ♗xg6 26 ♖xh7 ♔xh7 27 ♖h1+ ♔g7 28 ♕xe7+ ♔g8 29 ♕f6.

2b) 24...♕b6 25 ♔e2! ♕b2 (25...♗e8 is also met by 26 ♘d5) 26 ♘d5 and White wins.

3) 23...♕b6 24 ♘xf6+ exf6 25 ♕d5+ ♔g7 26 ♖xh7+! ♔xh7 27 ♕f7+ ♔h6 28 ♖h1+ ♔g5 29 f4+ ♔xg4 30 ♕xg6+ ♔f3 31 ♕h5+ ♗g4 32 ♖h3+ ♔xf4 33 ♘d5+ ♔xe4 34 ♘xf6+ ♔f4 35 ♕xg4+, etc.

23   gxh5   ♗e8

23...♕xb2+ 24 ♔d2 ♗e8 transposes to line '2a' of the previous note.

24   b3!

The simplest and most effective move. Now that Black's dangerous dark-squared bishop has gone, White can afford to play this defensive move, which brings Black's queenside play to a dead halt. White, on the other hand, retains a massive attack on the kingside – the immediate threat is 25 ♘d5.

24 hxg6 ♗xg6 25 ♖xh7 ♔xh7 26 ♖h1+ ♔g7 27 ♕xe7+ ♗f7 only leads to a draw here, since Black's queen is controlling g1.

| 24 | ... | cxb3 |
| 25 | axb3 | |

There is no real defence to ♘d5.

| 25 | ... | ♕c5 |

25...e6 26 ♕f6 and 25...♗f7 26 hxg6 ♗xg6 27 ♘d5 are also hopeless for Black.

| 26 | ♘d5 | |

With a double attack against e7.

| 26 | ... | ♖b7 |

26...♕a3+ 27 ♔d2 ♕a5+ 28 b4 brings the checks to an end. After 28...♖xb4 we have an echo of the idea at move 18 in that White can win Black's queen with a knight check.

| 27 | ♘xe7+ | |

Picking up the exchange.

| 27 | ... | ♖xe7 |

Alternatively, 27...♔g7 (27...♔f7 28 hxg6+ hxg6 29 ♖h7+) 28 ♘f5+ ♔g8 29 hxg6 ♗xg6 30 ♕f6 ♗xf5 31 ♖dg1+ ♗g6 32 ♖xg6+ hxg6 33 ♖h8#.

| 28 | ♕xe7 | |

Black's material situation is hopeless.

28	...	♖c8
29	♖h2	gxh5
30	♖g2+	♗g6
31	♖xd6	♕e3+
32	♖gd2	♖f8
33	♖d8	♖xd8
34	♕xd8+	♔g7
35	♕d4+	

Perhaps White could have won more quickly by another method, but it can't be wrong to liquidate to a trivially won ending.

35	...	♕xd4
36	♖xd4	h4
37	♔d2	h3
38	♔e3	♔h6
39	♔f4	1-0

This game was decided at a relatively early stage. Having chosen a very sharp opening, Black went in for a slightly unusual line. To begin with, White simply followed the standard attacking plan against a kingside fianchetto. It was only at move 18 that White really had to think hard and find the most accurate way to continue. By this stage White had built up an impressive array of attacking pieces on the kingside, but it was still not so easy to break through. White's 20th and 22nd moves were the key; between them these two moves eliminated Black's two main kingside defenders. After this Black was always in trouble, and soon the attack broke through.

The lessons here are:

1) Opposite-side castling greatly sharpens the play. In the ensuing attacking race, every tempo is vital.

2) The plan of h4-h5 and ♗h6 is a typical method of attacking a kingside fianchettoed position.

3) It may be worth considerable material to eliminate a key defensive piece.

4) Don't believe everything you see in print.

The Deadly Long Diagonal

One of the most dangerous attacking avenues is the long diagonal leading to the castled position. These days attacks based at least partly on the long diagonal are common because of the popularity of fianchetto openings. Such attacks can arise in two ways. First of all, Black might play an opening such as the King's Indian Defence, which is based on the fianchetto of a bishop at g7. If White later castles queenside (as often occurs in the Sämisch Variation – see Game 14), this bishop may provide the basis for a vicious attack against White's queenside castled position.

Secondly, the side carrying out the fianchetto may become the victim of a long-diagonal attack. If the fianchettoed bishop in front of a castled position is eliminated, then the king may become very exposed due to the resulting network of weak squares. Then an attack along the long diagonal may not be far away.

In the following game, both the above features make an appearance, albeit in a slightly unusual form. White plays g3, as if he were intending to fianchetto, but then the light-squared bishop goes elsewhere and it is White's king rather than his bishop that ends up on g2. This exposes White to a typical attack based on a bishop-and-queen line-up on the long diagonal. The analysis of this game shows how dangerous such an attack can be, and how it may be worth a considerable material sacrifice to bring such an attack to fruition.

Game 11

J. Timman – J. Polgar

Sigeman & Co. tournament, Malmö 2000

Queen's Indian Defence, 4 g3 ♗a6

1   ♘f3

For comments on this move, see Game 1.

1   ...   ♘f6

Black responds to White's flexible first move with an equally flexible move. Neither side is yet committed in the centre and play can evolve in many different directions.

2   c4

White starts to stake out a claim in the centre.

2   ...   b6

Black's aim is to develop her light-squared bishop to the long diagonal, thereby avoiding the problem of this bishop being shut in behind some pawns, as often occurs when Black plays ...e6 and ...d5. The bishop will be quite well placed on b7, not only occupying a useful diagonal, but also exerting control over e4 and thus preventing White from forming a 'two-abreast' pawn-centre on d4 and e4.

3   d4

White expands in the centre. If he can play e4 as well then he will have the advantage, but in view of Black's control of e4, this is unlikely to be possible.

3   ...   e6

Black transposes into a standard opening, the Queen's Indian Defence, which more often arises via the move-order 1 d4 ♘f6 2 c4 e6 3 ♘f3 b6. The move ...e6 enables the development of the dark-squared bishop, when Black will be ready to castle.

4   g3

This is the most popular line against the Queen's Indian by quite a large margin. White takes immediate steps to neutralize the effect of Black's bishop on the long diagonal, and at the same time makes progress towards castling kingside. The other important lines are 4 a3, 4

e3 and 4 ♘c3. One of the curious features of this game is that while it appears inevitable that White will play ♗g2 sooner or later, in fact he never gets round to it!

4   ...   ♗a6

At first sight this looks like a beginner's move. Black puts her bishop on a strange square, for the sole purpose of attacking an easily defended pawn. However, despite its odd appearance, this is a perfectly reasonable alternative to the more obvious 4...♗b7 (both are about equally popular). According to circumstances, Black will either leave the bishop on a6, or drop it back to b7 after extracting some concession from White.

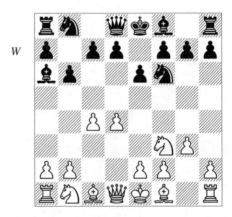

5   ♕b3

White's problem is that all the available methods of defending the c4-pawn have some drawbacks. First of all, playing g3 virtually commits his bishop to g2, so it is no good defending the c4-pawn by playing 5 e3. Secondly, many of the moves defending c4 (such as 5 ♘bd2, 5 ♕a4 and 5 ♕c2) weaken White's control of d4, and so allow Black to strike in the centre with 5...c5. Finally, the most natural move, 5 b3, allows Black a further disruptive manoeuvre: 5...♝b4+ 6 ♝d2 (6 ♘bd2? ♝c3 7 ♖b1 ♝b7 is just bad for White) 6...♝e7 and now:

1) 7 ♘c3 d5 again leaves White with no reasonable way to defend c4. If White has to play cxd5, then after ...exd5 Black has a satisfactory position. The black bishop is actively placed on a6, and White has been forced to spend a tempo on the useless move b3.

2) After 7 ♝g2 c6 the point of Black's play is revealed. After the coming ...d5, the most natural way to defend c4 would be by ♘bd2, but White's bishop is blocking this square. The most common line is 8 ♝c3 (to free d2) 8...d5 9 ♘e5 (counterattacking c6) 9...♘fd7 10 ♘xd7 ♘xd7 11 ♘d2, when Black's preliminary check on b4 means that White's bishop is on c3 rather than b2, a difference which favours Black as the bishop is blocking the c-file.

The text-move is rather unusual. White defends the c4-pawn, while at the same time retaining control over d5 so as to be able to meet 5...c5 by 6 d5. The defect is that the queen is exposed to attack on b3.

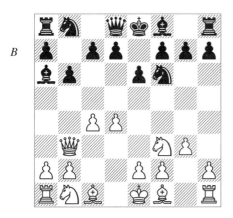

5 ... ♘c6

Another disruptive move. Black threatens 6...♘a5, and White is forced to spend time meeting this threat. However, despite the gain of time, this move does have some drawbacks. Sooner or later, Black will probably counter in the centre with ...d5, and after an exchange of pawns on d5 (cxd5 exd5), the knight may be clumsily placed on c6, blocking the natural move ...c5.

6 ♝d2

White restrains Black's ...♘a5. Although one can hardly speak of problems for White yet, his plan of development appears somewhat artificial because he has to spend so many tempi just responding to Black's threats. However, after the alternative 6 ♘bd2 ♘a5 the white queen is driven away from its control of d5, and so Black can once again play ...c5; for example, 7 ♕c2 c5 or 7 ♕a4 ♝b7 8 ♝g2 c5.

6 ... ♝b7

Black decides that her bishop has done its duty in forcing White to play some rather artificial moves, so she drops it back to the long diagonal, at the same time threatening 7...♘xd4. This is only the first of many threats to arise along the long light-square diagonal.

In fact 6...♘a5 7 ♝xa5 bxa5 is not entirely out of the question; in return for the (admittedly quite serious) pawn weaknesses, Black obtains the two bishops and a half-open b-file. It is hard to judge such unbalanced positions but in this case, with the position far from open, Black's piece activity probably doesn't completely compensate for the structural weaknesses.

7 ♝c3

Once again White has to take time out to counter Black's threat, but now White is ready to continue his development and consolidate his position in the centre by ♘bd2, ♝g2, etc.

7 ... ♘e4

A further irritating little move, threatening 8...♘xc3, when 9 ♕xc3?? ♝b4, 9 bxc3 ♘a5 and 9 ♘xc3 ♘xd4 all cost White material. Thus he must play another defensive move.

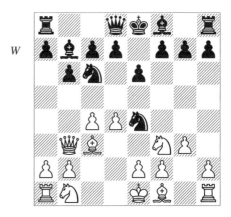

8 a3

So far Black has been making all the running, and White must take care lest he fall dangerously behind in development. However, without any real development to back up Black's threats, they have never posed any serious danger to White. Indeed, one must take care before making one- or two-move threats in the opening. They are usually quite easy to counter, and it may well be that the opponent can meet them in a way that improves his position, for example by furthering his development. Judit Polgar has not fallen into this trap, since in this case Black obtains the concrete gain of the two bishops in return for her manoeuvres.

8   ...   ♘xc3

Black cannot afford to wait, because White was threatening to push forward in the centre by d5.

9   ♕xc3

Forced, because 9 ♘xc3? loses a pawn after 9...♘xd4, while 9 bxc3 e5 is also very unpleasant for White. The move played prevents ...e5 and renews the threat of d5.

9   ...   ♗e7

Black is able to meet the threat by simple development: if now 10 d5, then 10...♗f6 followed by ...♘e5, when Black's bishops are becoming very active.

10   ♕d3?!

10 e4 is premature, due to 10...f5! (highlighting White's failure to secure the long diagonal with ♗g2) 11 d5 (11 exf5 ♘xd4 12 ♕xd4 ♗xf3 13 ♖g1 0-0 is very good for Black; 11 ♘bd2 fxe4 12 ♘xe4 0-0 is fine for Black due to her active pieces and lead in development) 11...♗f6 12 ♕e3 (12 e5 ♘xe5 13 ♘xe5 d6 favours Black) 12...exd5 13 exd5+ ♘e7 14 ♘c3 0-0 and Black's dark-squared bishop is quite powerful.

The text-move is critical, because White renews his threat to play d5, and clears c3 for his knight to move out to support the centre. However, there is a nasty tactical surprise in store for White and it would have been better to play 10 ♗g2 ♗f6 11 e3 ♘e7 12 ♕d3 c5, although even in this case Black has absolutely no problems.

10   ...   d5

This is more or less essential to prevent White's central expansion. After 10...♗f6, for example, 11 e4 d6 12 ♘c3 gives White a massive grip on the centre, which is far more important than Black's possession of the two bishops.

11   cxd5

White takes the chance to establish a majority of pawns in the centre. The alternatives are no better; for example, 11 ♘c3 (not 11 ♗g2? dxc4 12 ♕xc4 ♘xd4) and now:

1) 11...dxc4 12 ♕xc4 ♘xd4 is tempting, but not so clear after 13 0-0-0 c5 14 ♘xd4 cxd4 15 ♕a4+ (15 ♖xd4 ♕c8) 15...♕d7 16 ♕xd7+ ♔xd7 17 ♖xd4+ ♔c7 18 ♖c4+ with a likely draw by perpetual check.

2) 11...♗a6! gives Black an edge with no risk: 12 ♕c2 (12 b3 ♘a5 is unpleasant since 13 ♘d2 loses to 13...♘xb3) 12...♗xc4 13 ♕a4 ♕d7 14 b3 b5 15 ♘xb5 ♗xb5 16 ♕xb5 ♖b8 17 ♕a4 ♘d8 18 ♕xd7+ ♔xd7 19 b4 a5 is fine for Black.

11   ...   ♕xd5

11...exd5 12 ♘c3 is wrong because sooner or later the pressure against d5 will force Black to move her c6-knight, which both loses time and allows White's f3-knight to occupy e5.

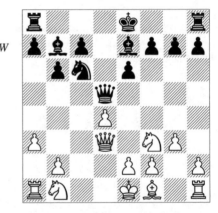

After the text-move, Black has considerable piece activity, but White has superior control of the centre. It is impossible to judge which will be the dominant factor on general principles; everything depends on the particular features of the position. In this case there is a tactical finesse which tips the balance in Black's favour.

12   e4

This is certainly not the move White wanted to play, since he is unlikely to be able to justify such an aggressive move when he is far behind in development. 12 ♘c3 appears more natural, but this runs into the unpleasant 12...♘e5! 13 dxe5 ♕xd3 14 exd3 ♗xf3 15 ♖g1 0-0-0 with a massive advantage for Black. The move 12 ♘c3 had been played in the earlier game Epishin-Razuvaev, Russian Championship, St Petersburg 1998, but Black had not noticed the reply 12...♘e5!. This again shows the danger of following 'theory' without checking it for yourself.

12   ...   ♕a5+

Black plays for rapid development.

13   ♘bd2

After 13 ♘c3 0-0-0 it is too late for White to develop quietly by 14 ♗g2 since 14...♗f6 exerts intolerable pressure against d4. On the other hand, 14 0-0-0 allows a very tempting sacrifice: 14...♗xa3 15 bxa3 (15 d5 exd5 16 exd5 ♘b4 17 ♕f5+ ♔b8 favours Black) 15...♕xa3+ 16 ♔d2 (16 ♔b1 loses after 16...♕b3+ 17 ♔c1 ♘b4) 16...f5 with two pawns and a dangerous attack for the piece.

The text-move leaves the c-file open for White's counterplay.

13   ...   0-0-0

Again Black plays for development and to inconvenience White's king while it is still in the centre.

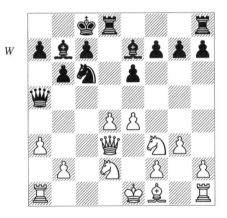

14   ♖c1

White must focus on his c-file counterplay, as after 14 ♗g2 f5! he again suffers along the diagonal: 15 exf5 ♘xd4 16 ♘xd4 ♗xg2 17 ♖g1 ♗b7 and White's position is a wreck. 14 0-0-0 is just as bad in view of 14...♘xd4 15 ♘xd4 ♕c5+ 16 ♘c4 ♗f6 17 ♘b3 ♖xd3 18 ♘xc5 ♖xd1+ 19 ♔xd1 bxc5.

The text-move aims to chase Black's queen by b4, and also to pin the c6-knight against a mate on c7.

14   ...   f5!?

The sharpest continuation, again exposing the weak long diagonal. 14...♘xd4? 15 ♘xd4 e5 fails to 16 ♕c2 threatening mate, but 14...♗f6 is also quite good for Black: 15 b4 (15 ♕c2 ♔b8 and 15 ♕c3 ♗xd4 16 ♘xd4 ♖xd4 are very good for Black) 15...♕a4 16 ♕c3 (16 ♕c4 ♖d7 leaves Black in control) 16...♗xd4 17 ♘xd4 ♖xd4 18 b5 ♖xe4+ 19 ♘xe4 ♕xe4+ 20 ♔d2 ♕xh1 21 bxc6 ♕d5+ 22 ♔e3 (22 ♔e1 loses to 22...♕e4+ 23 ♗e2 ♗a6) 22...♗a8 23 ♕xg7 ♖d8 24 ♕c3 and Black is a pawn up, although the buried bishop on a8 gives White some compensation.

15   b4

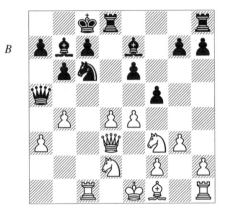

White must play for tactics, since his position is collapsing.

15   ...   fxe4

Best, as 15...♕a4 16 ♕c4 ♖d7 (16...fxe4? allows White to turn the position around by 17 ♘e5 ♖d6 18 ♗g2, when the pin along the c-file is almost unbreakable) 17 ♕xe6 is unclear. The sacrifice 15...♘xb4 16 axb4 ♗xb4 is inadvisable; after 17 ♕c2 c5 18 ♗d3 fxe4 19 ♗xe4 ♗xd2+ 20 ♘xd2 ♖xd4 21 ♗xb7+ ♔xb7 22 ♔e2 White crawls away from his immediate problems.

16   ♕c3

The only move, since 16 ♕xe4? ♕xa3! 17 ♖xc6 ♗xb4 and 16 ♘xe4? ♕f5 are crushing for Black. White must stake everything on the c-file pin.

16   ...   ♕d5

In contrast to the note to Black's 15th move, here Black's queen can occupy an active central position, emphasizing her pressure along the long diagonal.

17 ♘e5

The critical line; White simply plays to win the pinned knight. 17 ♗c4 also does not solve White's problems; after 17...♕f5 18 ♗a6 (18 b5 exf3 19 bxc6 ♗a8 20 0-0 ♗g5 is also very good for Black) 18...♗xa6 19 ♕xc6 ♔b8! 20 ♕xc7+ (20 ♕xe4 loses to 20...♕xe4+ 21 ♘xe4 ♗b7) 20...♔a8 21 ♕e7 ♖c8, followed by ...exf3, Black has a decisive attack against the white king, which is trapped in the centre.

17 ... e3

This sharp continuation should favour Black, but there is another, simpler possibility, which is about equally good: 17...♗g5 18 ♘xc6 e3 19 fxe3 (19 ♘e7+ ♔b8 20 ♘xd5 exd2+ 21 ♕xd2 ♗xd2+ 22 ♔xd2 ♖xd5 23 ♗c4 ♖xd4+ 24 ♔c3 ♖xc4+ 25 ♔xc4 ♗xh1 26 ♖xh1 ♖d8 and White has only slight compensation for the minus pawn) 19...♕xh1 20 ♘e5 (20 ♘xd8 ♗xd8 is also very good for Black) 20...♔b8! (20...c6 21 ♘xc6 ♗xc6 22 ♕xc6+ ♕xc6 23 ♖xc6+ ♔b8 24 ♔e2 ♖he8 25 ♘e4 ♗h6 26 ♗h3 is unclear) 21 ♘f7 ♕xh2 22 ♕xc7+ ♔a8 23 ♘xh8 ♖xh8, when Black's active bishops and safer king give her a clear advantage.

18 ♘df3

The only move, since d2 and h1 were both attacked.

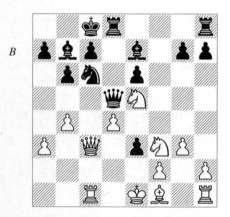

18 ... exf2+?

The immediate 18...♖hf8! is stronger: 19 ♗e2 (19 fxe3 ♖xf3 20 ♘xc6 ♗xc6 21 ♕xc6 ♕xc6 22 ♖xc6 ♖xe3+ 23 ♔f2 ♖xa3 and 19 ♘xc6 ♕xf3 20 ♘xe7+ ♔b8 are winning for Black) 19...exf2+ 20 ♔f1 (20 ♔xf2 loses to 20...♕xd4+ 21 ♕xd4 ♘xd4) 20...♗c5! (a tactical idea similar to that occurring later in the game; 20...♗g5 is wrong as after 21 b5 ♗xc1 22 bxc6 ♗h6 23 cxb7+ ♔xb7 24 ♗c4 ♕e4 25 ♗d3 ♕d5 26 ♕c2 White, who has taken over control of the long diagonal, has the advantage) 21 ♘xc6 (21 bxc5 ♘xe5 22 cxb6 ♖d7 23 dxe5 ♖xf3 24 ♗xf3 ♕xf3 25 ♕xf3 ♗xf3 26 ♔xf2 ♗xh1 27 ♖xh1 axb6 should be winning for Black, while after 21 dxc5 ♘xe5 22 cxb6 ♕c6 23 ♕xc6 ♘xc6 24 bxc7 ♖d7 White will lose material on the kingside) 21...♗xc6 22 dxc5 ♖xf3 23 ♗xf3 ♕xf3 24 ♕xf3 ♗xf3 25 ♔xf2 ♗xh1 26 ♖xh1 bxc5 27 bxc5 ♖d3 and Black should win this ending.

19 ♔xf2 ♖hf8
20 ♔g2!

20 ♗e2 ♕xd4+ 21 ♕xd4 ♘xd4 wins for Black, while 20 ♘xc6 ♗xc6 21 ♗e2 ♔d7! 22 b5 ♗b7 23 ♖hf1 (23 ♕xc7+ ♔e8 24 ♕c3 ♗f6 gives Black a crushing attack) 23...♗d6 leaves Black a pawn up with a good position.

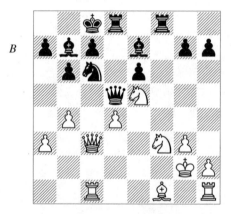

The text-move is only possible because Black exchanged on f2 too soon. Now White genuinely threatens to play 21 ♘xc6, because after 21...♗xc6 22 ♕xc6 Black cannot win a piece at f3. Hence the c6-knight is falling and Black has to find a way to unleash her threats on the long diagonal, threats which are temporarily held at bay by the c-file pin. The complexity of the position is such that even such an excellent tactician as Judit Polgar failed to find the correct answer.

20 ... g5?

This is a remarkable idea, but it could have been refuted by accurate play. Black had two superior alternatives:

1) 20...♗g5 and now:

1a) 21 ♖c2? ♗d2!! (a stunning blow; which-ever way the bishop is captured, the mate threat to c7 disappears, and so the c6-knight is freed to unleash the long-diagonal threats) 22 ♘xc6 (22 ♖xd2 ♘xe5 and 22 ♕xd2 ♘xe5 win for Black) 22...♗xc3 23 ♘e7+ ♔b8 24 ♘xd5 ♗xd4 25 ♘xd4 ♗xd5+ 26 ♔g1 ♖d6 with a winning position for Black.

1b) 21 ♘xc6 (the best chance) 21...♕xf3+ 22 ♕xf3 ♖xf3 with a final branch:

1b1) 23 ♔xf3 ♗xc1 24 ♗a6 ♖f8+ 25 ♔e4 ♗xa3 26 b5 ♗d6! (after 26...♗xa6 27 bxa6 ♔d7 28 ♘e5+ it is hard to see how Black is going to win despite the two extra pawns) 27 ♖a1 ♗xa6 28 ♖xa6 ♖f5 29 ♘xa7+ ♔d7 with excellent winning prospects for Black.

1b2) 23 ♗a6 ♗xa6 (23...♖df8 24 ♘xa7+ ♔b8 25 ♘c6+ ♗xc6 26 ♖xc6 ♖xa3 27 ♖f1 also offers White some drawing chances) 24 ♔xf3 ♖f8+ 25 ♔e4 ♗xc1 26 ♖xc1 ♗b7 and Black will be a pawn up in a rook ending.

2) 20...♖xf3! (this is the most clear-cut) 21 ♘xf3 (21 ♕xf3? loses to 21...♘xe5) 21...b5! (this odd-looking move is quite effective; it prevents both b5 and ♗c4, and threatens to free the c6-knight by ...♗d6; 21...♔b8 22 ♗c4 ♕d6 23 ♗a6 is less clear) 22 ♗e2 (22 ♔g1 ♗f6 23 ♗g2 ♕d6 24 ♕c5 ♘xd4 25 ♕xd6 ♖xd6 26 ♘xd4 ♗xd4+ 27 ♔f1 ♗b2 28 ♗xb7+ ♔xb7 29 ♖c5 ♔b6 is very good for Black, while 22 ♗d3 loses to 22...♖f8 23 ♖hf1 g5 24 g4 h5 25 h3 ♗d6) 22...g5 23 h3 h5 24 g4 ♗d6 and Black has extremely strong kingside pressure in return for a slight material disadvantage. It is perhaps going too far to claim that Black is clearly winning, but it is certainly fair to say that White is in serious trouble.

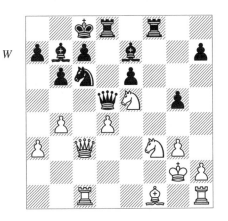

21   ♘xc6

White correctly accepts the offer. The alternatives are bad:

1) 21 h3? ♗c5! 22 ♘xc6 (22 ♗c4 loses to 22...♕xd4 23 ♗xe6+ ♔b8 24 ♘xd4 ♘xd4+ 25 ♘f3 ♖xf3) 22...♗xc6 and Black wins easily.

2) 21 ♗e2? is met by 21...♗c5! (21...g4? 22 ♘xc6 ♗xc6 23 ♕xc6 ♕xc6 24 ♖xc6 gxf3+ 25 ♗xf3 ♖xd4 26 ♖xe6 looks like a draw) and now:

2a) 22 bxc5 ♘xe5 23 cxb6 ♘c6 24 ♗c4 (24 bxc7 loses to 24...♖d7) 24...♕d6 25 bxa7 g4 26 ♗a6 ♘xa7 27 ♗xb7+ ♔xb7 28 ♕b3+ (28 ♘h4 ♕d5+ 29 ♔g1 ♘b5 is decisive) 28...♔a8 29 ♘h4 ♕xd4 30 ♖hf1 ♖xf1 31 ♖xf1 ♕d5+ 32 ♕xd5+ exd5 and the two connected passed pawns should decide the game.

2b) 22 ♘xc6 ♗xc6 23 bxc5 g4 24 ♖hf1 gxf3+ 25 ♗xf3 ♖xf3 26 ♖xf3 bxc5 27 dxc5 ♕xf3+ 28 ♕xf3 ♖d2+ wins for Black.

2c) 22 ♗c4 ♘xe5 23 ♗xd5 ♗xd5 24 dxc5 (24 dxe5 ♗xf3+ 25 ♕xf3 ♖d2+ 26 ♔h3 ♖xf3 27 bxc5 ♖xa3 with two extra pawns) 24...♖xf3 25 ♕xe5 ♖e3+ 26 ♕xd5 exd5 should be a win.

3) 21 b5? ♕a2+ and now:

3a) 22 ♔g1 ♗c5! 23 ♘xc6 (23 dxc5 ♘xe5 24 ♕xe5 ♖xf3 and 23 bxc6 ♗xd4+ 24 ♕xd4 ♖xd4 25 cxb7+ ♔xb7 26 ♗g2 ♖e4! are winning for Black) 23...♖xd4 24 ♘cxd4 ♖xf3 and Black wins.

3b) 22 ♔h3 g4+ 23 ♔xg4 (23 ♘xg4 loses to 23...♖xf3 24 ♕xf3 ♘xd4 25 ♕f4 e5! 26 ♕xe5 ♘e6) 23...♘xe5+ 24 ♘xe5 ♗d6 25 ♘c6 ♕f2 with a winning attack for Black.

21   ...   ♖d7

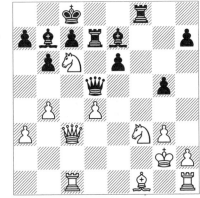

A remarkably calm move, covering the mate on c7 and defending the bishop on e7. At first sight, it seems as if White should have little trouble defending, since there is no obvious way to remove the blockading knight on c6. However, White's task is harder than it looks.

22   g4?!

Although White retains the advantage after this move, it is not the best. The alternatives are:

1) 22 ♗b5? is wrong: 22...g4 23 ♘xa7+ ♔b8 24 ♗xd7 (24 ♘c6+ ♔a8 transposes) 24...♖xf3 25 ♗c6 ♖xc3+ 26 ♗xd5 ♗xd5+ 27 ♔f2 ♖f3+ 28 ♔e2 ♗g5 29 ♘c6+ ♔b7 30 ♘e5 ♖e3+ 31 ♔f2 ♖xa3 with an easy win for Black.

2) 22 ♗e2 leads to a favourable ending for White after 22...g4 23 ♘xa7+ ♔b8 (23...♔d8 24 ♘c6+ ♔e8 25 ♖hf1 is also good for White) 24 ♘c6+ ♔a8 (24...♗xc6 25 ♕xc6 ♕xc6 26 ♖xc6 gxf3+ 27 ♗xf3 ♖xd4 28 ♖xe6 ♖d2+ 29 ♖e2 and 24...♔c8 25 ♖hf1 ♕e4 26 ♕c2 ♗xc6 27 ♕xc6 gxf3+ 28 ♗xf3 ♕xc6 29 ♖xc6 ♖xd4 30 ♖xe6 leave White with an extra pawn) 25 ♖hf1 ♗f6 26 ♕c2 ♗xc6 27 ♕xc6+ ♕xc6 28 ♖xc6 gxf3+ 29 ♖xf3 and again White keeps his extra pawn. White has a clear advantage in all these endings, although the presence of opposite-coloured bishops offers Black some drawing chances.

3) 22 h3! h5 23 ♘xa7+ ♔b8 24 ♘c6+ ♔a8 25 g4 transposes to line '4'.

4) 22 ♘xa7+! is probably the strongest move. White will check on a7 and c6, and if the king returns to c8 White continues as in the game but with a useful extra pawn. Timman was probably worried that the king would flee to a8, but there it is exposed to new threats along the a-file. The analysis runs 22...♔b8 (22...♔d8 23 ♘c6+ ♔e8 24 h3 h5 25 g4 ♗c5 26 ♗b5 is winning for White as Black does not have the move ...♖df7, which saves the day when the king is on a8) 23 ♘c6+ and now:

4a) 23...♔c8 24 g4! (24 ♗e2 g4 25 ♖hf1 transposes to line '2') continues as in the game, but with an extra pawn for White.

4b) 23...♔a8 and now:

4b1) 24 ♗b5? g4 25 ♗e2 ♗c5 is good for Black.

4b2) 24 g4?! ♗c5 25 ♗b5 (25 b5 ♕e4 26 dxc5 ♖df7 27 h3 ♗xc6 28 bxc6 ♖xf3 29 ♕c4 ♖f2+ 30 ♔g1 ♖xf1+ 31 ♖xf1 ♕xc4 32 ♖xf8+ ♔a7 33 cxb6+ ♔xb6 and Black is slightly better) 25...♗xd4 26 ♘cxd4 (26 ♕d3 e5 27

♖hf1 e4 28 ♕xd4 exf3+ 29 ♔g3 ♕xd4 30 ♘xd4 ♖xd4 31 ♖xc7 is equal) 26...♕xd4 27 ♗c6 ♕xg4+ 28 ♔f2 ♖df7 29 ♗xb7+ ♔xb7 30 ♕c6+ ♔b8 31 ♖c3 ♕h3 32 ♔e1 ♖xf3 33 ♕xc7+ ♔a8 34 ♕c6+ ♔a7 with a draw.

4b3) 24 ♗e2 g4 again transposes to line '2'.

4b4) 24 h3! h5 25 g4 ♗c5 26 b5! (not 26 ♗b5 ♖df7 27 ♖hf1 hxg4 28 hxg4 ♗d6 29 ♘ce5 ♗xe5 30 ♗c6 ♗xc6 31 ♕xc6+ ♕xc6 32 ♖xc6 ♗d6, when Black is slightly better as White's pawns will come under fire after ...♖f4) 26...hxg4 (26...♖df7 27 ♗c4 ♗xc6 28 ♗xd5 ♗xd5 29 ♖hf1 should be winning for White) 27 hxg4 ♗xd4 (27...♖df7 28 ♖h3) 28 ♕d3 e5 29 ♖c4 (White exploits the exposed black king) 29...♕xb5 30 ♖h6 (as always, maintaining the blockade on c6 is very important) 30...♖df7 31 ♗e2 and Black does not have enough compensation for the piece. One line is 31...♗c5 32 ♖b4! ♕xc6 33 ♖xc6 ♗xc6 34 ♖e4 ♔b8 (or 34...♖f4 35 ♖xf4 ♖xf4 36 ♔h2) 35 ♘xe5 ♗xe4+ 36 ♕xe4, when White has a decisive advantage.

22   ...   ♗c5!

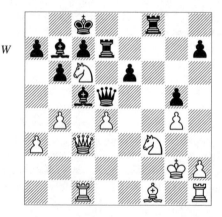

This startling move is the point behind Black's play. She wants to remove the blockade on c6 and conquer the long diagonal after all.

23   ♗b5!

The best reply, forcing the exchange of Black's dangerous light-squared bishop. Other moves are bad:

1) 23 ♗a6? ♗xa6 24 b5 h5 25 h3 hxg4 26 hxg4 ♕e4 27 ♖h3 ♗d6 wins for Black.

2) 23 b5? ♕e4! 24 h3 ♖xd4 25 ♘cxd4 ♕xd4 26 ♕xd4 ♗xf3+ 27 ♔h2 ♗xd4 28 ♗g2 and Black is slightly better after 28...♗xg2 29

♔xg2 ♖f2+ 30 ♔g3 ♖a2 or 28...♗e2 29 ♗c6 e5.

3) 23 bxc5?! ♕xc6 24 ♗e2 (24 d5? loses after 24...♖xd5 25 ♗e2 ♖d2! 26 ♕xd2 ♖xf3) 24...♖xd4 25 cxb6 (25 h3?! ♖e4 26 ♗d1 ♖c4! 27 ♕xc4 ♖xf3 28 cxb6 ♕xc4 29 ♖xc4 ♖f4+ 30 ♔h2 ♖xc4 31 ♖e1 axb6 32 ♗b3 ♖c3 33 ♗xe6+ ♔d8 gives Black good winning chances thanks to the extra pawn) 25...♖xg4+ 26 ♔h3 ♕xc3 27 ♖xc3 ♖e4 28 ♖xc7+ ♔b8 29 ♗d1 g4+ 30 ♔g3 ♗d5! 31 ♖c3 gxf3 32 ♗xf3 leads to a draw.

23	...	♗xc6
24	♗xc6	♕xc6

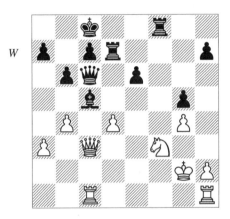

25 ♖hf1?

White misses his last chance to keep the advantage. The other possibilities are:

1) 25 ♖hd1? ♕e4 wins for Black.

2) 25 ♖cd1? h5 26 h3 ♖df7 27 ♖d3 (27 ♖hf1 loses to 27...hxg4 28 hxg4 ♕e4) 27...♕b5 (threatening 28...♖xf3 29 ♖xf3 ♕e2+) 28 ♖e1 hxg4 29 hxg4 ♗d6 30 ♖xe6 ♔b8 followed by some combination of ...♖f4 and ...♕d5, with a winning attack.

3) 25 h3 and now:

3a) 25...♕b5 26 bxc5 (26 ♖he1 ♗d6 27 ♕c6 ♕xc6 28 ♖xc6 is slightly better for Black) 26...♕e2+ 27 ♔g3 ♖xd4 28 cxb6 ♖xf3+ 29 ♕xf3 ♖d3 30 ♖xc7+ ♔d8 31 ♖f7 with an equal position.

3b) 25...♖xd4 26 bxc5 ♕d5 27 cxb6 ♖c4 28 ♕e3 ♖xf3 29 ♕xf3 ♕d2+ 30 ♕f2 ♕d5+ 31 ♕f3 draws.

4) 25 bxc5! and now:

4a) 25...♕e4 26 ♖hf1 ♕xg4+ 27 ♔h1 ♕e4 28 ♖ce1 ♕c6 29 ♔g1 ♖df7 30 ♘d2 and the attack collapses.

4b) 25...h5 26 h3! (26 cxb6 ♕e4 27 ♖he1 ♕xg4+ 28 ♔f2 axb6 29 ♖e3 ♕xd4 30 ♕xd4 ♖xd4 31 ♔e2 ♖g4 32 ♖xe6 ♖g2+ 33 ♔e3 g4 and in view of the reduced material, a draw is almost inevitable) 26...hxg4 27 hxg4 ♕e4 28 ♖h3 ♕xg4+ 29 ♖g3 and Black's compensation is inadequate.

4c) 25...♖xd4 26 ♖hf1! (26 h3 ♕d5 27 cxb6 ♖c4 28 ♕e3 ♖xf3 29 ♕xf3 ♕d2+ 30 ♕f2 ♕d5+ 31 ♕f3 is a draw, while 26 ♔g3? ♕e4! 27 ♘xd4 ♕f4+ 28 ♔h3 h5 29 ♖cg1 hxg4+ 30 ♖xg4 ♖h8+ 31 ♔g2 ♕xg4+ 32 ♔f2 ♖h3 33 ♘f3 ♕f4 is good for Black) 26...♖xg4+ 27 ♔h3 h5 (27...♖gf4 28 ♘e5 ♕xc5 29 ♕xc5 bxc5 30 ♖xf4 ♖xf4 31 ♖xc5 gives White the advantage in view of the numerous weak black pawns) 28 cxb6 ♕xc3 (28...♕xb6 29 ♘e5 ♖gf4 30 ♖xf4 ♖xf4 favours White) 29 b7+ ♔b8 30 ♖xc3 ♖gf4 31 ♔g2 g4 (31...♖g4+ 32 ♔f2 ♖gf4 33 ♔e2 does not help Black) 32 ♘d2 ♔xb7 33 ♖xf4 ♖xf4 34 ♔g3 and again White has a definite advantage.

25 ... h5!

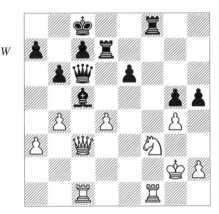

Suddenly the balance tips in Black's favour.

26 ♔g1

Black wins after 26 h3? hxg4 27 hxg4 ♕e4 28 dxc5 ♕xg4+ 29 ♔f2 ♖d2+ 30 ♔e1 ♕e4+ 31 ♔xd2 ♖d8+ 32 ♘d4 ♖xd4+ 33 ♕xd4 ♕xd4+ 34 ♔c2 bxc5, while 26 gxh5 g4 27 bxc5 gxf3+ 28 ♖xf3 bxc5 gives Black a large advantage.

26 ... ♖xf3

Not 26...♖df7? 27 ♘d2 ♖f4 28 h3 ♗xd4+ 29 ♕xd4 ♕xc1 30 ♕xf4 ♖xf4 31 ♖xc1 hxg4, when White is slightly better.

27	♕xf3	♕xf3
28	♖xf3	hxg4

28...♗xd4+ 29 ♔g2 hxg4 is less accurate owing to 30 ♖f8+ ♔b7 31 ♖d1.

After the text-move Black has a clear endgame advantage, although by accurate defence White can retain some drawing chances. However, after the earlier complications White was in severe time-trouble and this seals his fate.

29   ♖g3

It looks obvious to go for the g4-pawn, but the rook ends up offside. An alternative defensive plan is 29 ♖d3 ♗xd4+ 30 ♔g2, when it is hard for Black to free himself without allowing an exchange of rooks, which markedly increases White's drawing chances.

29   ...   ♗xd4+

30   ♔h1

The alternative 30 ♔g2 ♗e5 31 ♖xg4 ♖d2+ 32 ♔f3 ♖a2 33 ♖xg5 ♖xa3+ 34 ♔g2 ♖a2+ 35 ♔f3 ♗xh2 also leaves Black in a dominant position.

30   ...   ♗e5

31   ♖xg4   ♗f4

In this line Black only obtains two pawns for the exchange, but nevertheless White is struggling. Black's bishop occupies an excellent square, White's queenside pawns are weak and his rooks are poorly coordinated.

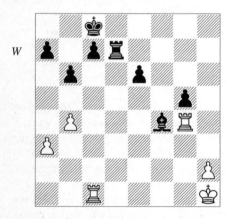

32   ♖c2?

This is a mistake. Black's threat is to secure her bishop with ...e5, and then play ...♖d3, attacking the queenside pawns. Therefore White's rook belongs on the third rank, a fact which he belatedly recognizes next move. After 32 ♖c3 White retains some drawing chances; for example, 32...e5 (32...♖d1+ 33 ♖g1 ♖d5 34 ♖g4 renews the threat of h4) 33 h4 gxh4 34 ♖xh4 ♗g7

35 b5 ♔b7 36 a4 and Black cannot easily make a passed pawn on the queenside.

32   ...   e5

Now Black threatens ...♖d3.

33   ♖c3

The loss of a tempo is important since Black can now push her passed e-pawn to the sixth rank. 33 h4 just drops a pawn to 33...♖h7.

33   ...   e4

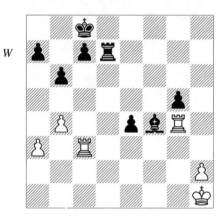

34   ♖c4?!

34 h4 is the critical line, but after 34...♖d1+ (34...♗d2 35 ♖h3 e3 36 ♖e4 gxh4 37 ♖hxh4 a6 38 a4 and 34...e3 35 ♖c1 e2 36 ♖e1 ♖d1 37 ♖gg1 are rather unclear) 35 ♖g1 (35 ♔g2 e3 36 ♔f3 ♖f1+ 37 ♔e2 ♖f2+ 38 ♔e1 gxh4 39 ♖xh4 ♗g3 wins for Black) 35...♖d2 36 ♖h3 e3 37 hxg5 e2 38 ♖h8+ (38 ♖h7 ♗e3 39 ♖e7 ♗xg1 40 ♔xg1 ♖d5 41 ♔f2 ♖xg5 42 ♖xe2 must be a win for Black in view of the distant white king) 38...♔d7 39 ♖h7+ ♔d6 40 ♖h8 (40 ♖h6+ ♔e5 41 ♖h8 ♔e4 is decisive) 40...♗xg5 41 ♖h2 ♗f4 42 ♖hg2 ♔c6 43 ♖e1 ♔b5 44 ♖exe2 ♖xe2 45 ♖xe2 ♔a4 46 ♖e4 ♗d6 47 ♖e3 c5 Black wins.

34   ...   e3

Now it should be all over.

35   ♖e4   c5?

This error by Black could have had serious consequences. 35...♖d1+! 36 ♖g1 ♖d2 37 ♖g2 c5! was the correct sequence, in order to be able to meet 38 ♖e8+ with 38...♔d7. The continuation might be 38 bxc5 bxc5 39 ♖c4 ♔b7 40 h4 ♖d4 41 ♖xc5 (or else ...♔c6-d5 wins) 41...♖d1+ 42 ♖g1 e2 43 ♖b5+ ♔c6 44 ♖b1 ♖xb1 45 ♖xb1 ♗d2 46 hxg5 e1♕+ 47 ♖xe1 ♗xe1 and Black wins.

36   bxc5   bxc5

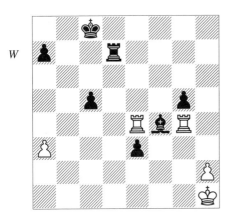

W

	37	**h4?**

Missing 37 ♖e8+! ♔c7 (37...♖d8 38 ♖xd8+ ♔xd8 39 ♔g1 is OK for White; 37...♔b7 38 h4 c4 39 hxg5 is also fine for White as 39...c3? 40 ♖xf4 c2 41 ♖b4+ ♔a6 42 ♖c4 ♖d1+ 43 ♔g2 c1♕ 44 ♖xc1 ♖xc1 45 ♖xe3 even wins for him) 38 h4, which might very well have saved White; e.g., 38...♖d5 39 ♔g2 or 38...♖h7 39 ♖e4.

37	...	**♖d4**

Now everything is back on track.

38	**♖xd4**	**cxd4**
39	**♔g2**	**d3**
40	**♔f3**	**e2**

0-1

Despite its inaccuracies, this was a fascinating struggle in all its phases and a good illustration of the attacking possibilities offered by a weakened fianchetto position.

The lessons here are:

1) A fianchetto position may be a serious weakness if the bishop is missing.

2) A bishop and queen lined up on a long diagonal are a formidable attacking force.

3) It is important not to get carried away when attacking. A simple but strong continuation may be more effective than a spectacular but unclear sacrifice.

4) Time-trouble leads to mistakes – avoid it!

2.2 Defensive Play

For every attacker there must be a defender, so defence is just as important a topic as attack. While in some ways the principles the defender must adopt are simply the converse of those for the attacker, there are a number of special topics which deserve particular attention.

The first of these is partly psychological. Many defenders panic when they see the attack coming, and either create self-inflicted weakness that only serve to strengthen the attack, or embark on a panicky and poorly-considered attempt at counterattack. Game 12 is an example of correct defence, dealing with the opponent's threats in the most economical manner possible and using any spare tempi to further a counter-attack.

In a sacrificial attack, the attacker may have made positional concessions as well as material ones, so the possibility of a counter-sacrifice to fend off the attack is a standard defensive idea. If material equality is restored, then positional factors become important and it may well be that these favour the defender. In some cases the defender may be happy to counter-sacrifice even more material than the attacker offered initially, if the positional factors are greatly in his favour. Game 13 is an example of this.

Some of the sharpest positions in chess arise when attack faces counter-attack – a slight slip can mean instant disaster. The interplay between the different parts of the board means that pieces sometimes have to serve both attacking and defensive functions. An example is the white queen on h6, which can nevertheless come back to c1 or d2 for defensive purposes. Game 14 examines such a situation.

Finally, everybody sometimes has to handle a defensive position that is genuinely bad. In this case the defender has to hang on by his fingertips, always making things as hard as possible for the opponent and waiting patiently for a slip. If a chance does come along, the defender must remain alert enough to spot it and seize the opportunity. Game 15 is an example of such 'grim defence'. This type of defence is psychologically difficult, and some players are better suited to it than others, but it gives a great sense of satisfaction when it does succeed.

Don't Panic

The sight of the opponent funnelling pieces towards one's king is enough to worry all but the most resilient player. There aren't many defenders who do not think, at least for a moment, about being on the wrong end of a brilliancy. And all the time one is aware that a single slip may bring about instant disaster. Psychology plays a relatively large part in such tense situations. Whether attacking or defending, the player who can keep his nerves under control, assess the position objectively and keep a clear head stands much better chances than one whose decisions are based on rushes of adrenaline.

I will not pretend that defensive play is easy; on the contrary, it is probably more difficult than conducting an attack. However, the defender does have some things in his favour. Attackers are constantly on the lookout for a knockout blow. If a resilient defender denies the attacker a forced win, move after move, the attacker often fears that he will not after all succeed; then he may become desperate and make a rash move. This may take the form of an unsound sacrifice or a decision to call off the attack, when the defender may take over the initiative. Attackers are also far more alert to their own tactical possibilities than those of their opponent. Chess history is littered with examples of attacks that would have succeeded, had not a back-rank mating idea tipped the balance in the defender's favour.

In the following game, Lanka is faced with an extremely dangerous attack, but he conducts the defence superbly. Eventually White's attack collapses, and the counterattack tears his position to shreds.

Game 12
M. Rõtšagov – Z. Lanka
European Team Championship, Debrecen 1992
Sicilian Defence, Velimirović Attack

1	e4	c5
2	♘f3	♘c6
3	d4	cxd4
4	♘xd4	

For comments on the moves up to here, see Game 9.

4	...	♘f6

In Game 9 Black played the slightly unusual 4...e5. The text-move, 4...♘f6, is a far more common continuation, and leads to some of the main theoretical battlegrounds in the Sicilian.

5	♘c3	

The most natural way to defend the e-pawn.

5	...	d6

This is the Classical System of the Sicilian, in which Black develops his knights to their most natural squares. The main alternatives are 5...e5 (Game 23), which gains time by chasing White's knight but weakens the d5-square, and 5...e6 (Game 20).

6	♗c4	

White has a wide range of systems here. The most common is 6 ♗g5, which aims for ♕d2 and 0-0-0. Since Black usually castles kingside, a situation with kings on opposite flanks arises. As we know from Game 10, this often leads to very sharp play. 6 ♗e2 is a more positional alternative, intending kingside castling.

B

The move played keeps White's options open: he may continue with kingside castling, or he may play ♗e3, ♕e2 and 0-0-0. The development of the bishop at c4 became popular after it was successfully employed by Bobby Fischer (World Champion, 1972-5) and is now quite common against various Sicilian systems.

6   ...   e6

This serves a number of purposes. First of all, it enables the development of the dark-squared bishop, essential if Black is to castle kingside. Secondly, the solid pawn-chain f7-e6 acts to restrict the activity of the c4-bishop. The success or failure of White's opening play often depends on the activity of this bishop. If Black can keep it under lock and key then he has good chances in the middlegame, but if White can unleash its potential by opening up the a2-g8 diagonal then he will have a very dangerous attack. There are two main methods White can employ to achieve this. The first is the advance f4-f5, to exert pressure on the e6-pawn. If Black is forced to play ...exf5 or ...e5, then the scope of White's light-squared bishop is increased. The second is some sort of sacrificial break-through, usually on e6 but sometimes on d5. In lines with ♗c4, Black must take considerable care to avoid falling prey to this latter idea.

7   ♗e3

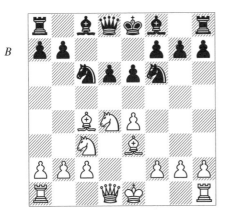

White continues his development, while at the same time retaining the option of castling on either side.

7   ...   ♗e7

Black develops a piece and prepares to play ...0-0.

8   ♕e2

This move strongly indicates that White intends castling queenside. If White wants to castle kingside, then he should play either 8 0-0 or 8 ♗b3 followed by 9 0-0. His plan in that case would be to play f4, followed either by the thematic f5, or by e5, which opens lines for the attack.

By committing himself to the double-edged 0-0-0, White ups the stakes. Neither player will be able to continue positionally since tactical factors will predominate in the race of the two attacks.

8   ...   a6

When White's rook arrives on d1, Black's queen will be very uncomfortably placed on d8, and will have to move off the d-file. The most natural square for the queen is c7, so this little preparatory move, preventing a white knight jumping in to b5, is essential. The pawn move serves a second purpose in that it prepares an eventual ...b5, which will be a useful addition to Black's queenside counterattack.

9   0-0-0   ♕c7

Although White had no immediate threat along the d-file, a queen move will be essential at some point, so Black maintains maximum flexibility by playing it straight away.

10   ♗b3

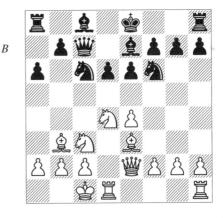

The logic behind this move is similar. There was no immediate threat against the c4-bishop, but its vulnerable position on the half-open c-file means that this retreat will be necessary sooner or later.

10   ...   0-0

Now the stage is set for the competing attacks to get under way, White's on the kingside and Black's on the queenside. Black can also play to defer castling, so as to avoid giving White a target to aim at. This alternative plan would run 10...♘a5 11 g4 b5 12 g5 and now we have an illustration of how careful Black must be about possible sacrifices on e6. The careless 12...♘d7? would allow 13 ♗xe6! fxe6 14 ♘xe6 with an enormous attack for the piece; for example, 14...♕c4 15 ♘xg7+ ♔f8 (15...♔f7 16 ♕h5+ is the same) 16 ♕h5! ♔xg7 17 ♗d4+ ♘e5 18 f4 ♘c6 19 fxe5 ♘xd4 (19...dxe5 20 ♕h6+ ♔g8 21 g6 is decisive) 20 exd6 and White's attack is too strong after 20...♗f8 21 ♖xd4! ♕xd4 22 ♖f1 ♗f5 23 ♖xf5 or 20...♗d8 21 ♖hf1 h6 22 gxh6+ ♖xh6 23 ♕e5+! ♗f6 (23...♔h7 24 ♖f8) 24 ♖xf6 ♖xf6 25 ♖g1+. Thus Black must eliminate the b3-bishop before retreating the knight. After 12...♘xb3+ 13 axb3 ♘d7 there is no sacrifice on e6 and the position is roughly equal.

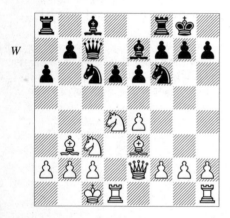

11   ♖hg1

White must decide how to launch his attack. The most obvious method is to play 11 f4, but this has the defect that after 11...♘xd4 White is forced to take back with the rook, since 12 ♗xd4 fails to 12...e5 followed by ...♗g4. After 12 ♖xd4 ♘d7 13 f5 ♘c5 White's plan to activate his b3-bishop has not succeeded. Black has maintained his pawn on e6, and the rook on d4 is exposed to attack by ...♗f6.

Therefore, White's normal plan here is to push the g-pawn. When the pawn arrives on g5, Black's defensive knight will be driven away. Then h7 will be vulnerable and White can aim for mate by ♕h5 and ♖hg1-g3-h3. This is obviously a dangerous plan, but of course it takes

several moves to execute, which gives Black time to make progress with his own attack. Also, as we shall see, Black can fight a delaying action on the kingside which slows White down even further.

One might ask why White does not play the immediate 11 g4. In fact, this is also a perfectly reasonable plan. Just as after 11 f4, White has to meet 11...♘xd4 with 12 ♖xd4 (12 ♗xd4? e5), when 12...e5 may be met by 13 ♖c4. It is not clear whether the tempo White saves by missing out ♖hg1 is more important than the clumsily placed rook on d4, and both 11 g4 and 11 ♖hg1 are popular in practice. In this game White prefers the preparatory 11 ♖hg1, so as to ensure that the pawn will be defended on g4 and therefore that White will be able to meet ...♘xd4 with the more natural ♗xd4.

11   ...   ♘d7

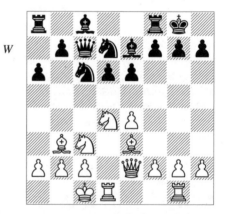

At first sight this voluntary retreat looks odd, but Black is not losing any time, because once White has spent a tempo on ♖hg1 he is not going to forego the advance g4-g5, when the knight will have to move in any case. The advantage of playing the knight to c5 straight away is that it enables Black to follow up with ...♗d7 and ...♖fc8, building up pressure along the c-file without delay. Black cannot play ...♗d7 before ...♘d7 because then his f6-knight would have to retreat to the passive square e8 after White plays g4-g5.

12   g4

The attack begins. White is five moves away from delivering mate (g5, ♕h5, ♖g3, ♖h3 and ♕xh7#) and at first sight Black is unlikely to get far enough on the queenside to deflect White from this brutal but effective plan. However, provided Black obeys the basic principles of defence against an attack on the king, he can maintain the balance. Although you will rarely find it in textbooks, the first such principle should be 'Don't Panic', because if you don't follow this principle then none of the other ones will do you any good. Even really dangerous-looking attacks can often be countered provided the defender keeps a cool head and makes the most of his chances. All too often, the defender panics and ruins his own position.

The second principle is not to create unnecessary weaknesses. In particular, unnecessary pawn moves in front of the king should be avoided. Not only do such moves waste time, they often help the attacker. Each pawn move restricts the defender's options and makes it easier for the attacker to pinpoint the most vulnerable square to attack. The longer such pawn moves can be delayed, the longer the attacker is kept in the dark as to the defender's intentions.

The third principle is to get on with your own counterplay. Obviously, you must deal with the most serious threats on the side where you are being attacked, but any spare tempi should be spent on counterattack rather than defence. In this game, for example, it is clear that White's attacking build-up will, if given a free hand, eventually break through on the kingside. Black must therefore adopt a two-pronged strategy: holding White up where possible, but also furthering his own play on the queenside.

12 ... ♘c5

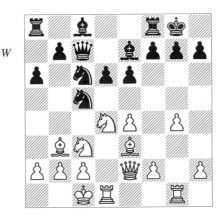

Here the knight is very well placed. It supports e6, exerts pressure on e4, and stands ready

to eliminate the b3-bishop at a moment's notice should that prove necessary.

13 g5

This appears a perfectly natural continuation of White's plan but, as we shall see, White has few chances of an advantage in the subsequent play. Therefore, in more recent games White has tried the radical 13 ♘f5. I will not go into detailed questions of opening theory in this book; suffice it to say that at the time of writing best play appears to be 13...b5 14 ♗d5!? ♗b7 15 g5 ♖fc8 16 ♖g3 ♗f8 17 ♕h5 g6 18 ♘h6+ ♔h8 19 ♕h4 b4 20 ♘g4 bxc3 21 ♖h3 f5 22 ♘f6 h6 23 ♕xh6+ ♗xh6 24 ♖xh6+ ♔g7 25 ♖h7+ ♔f8 26 ♖h8+ with a draw by perpetual check. This immensely complicated line is another example of cool and resourceful defence by Black, and it is well worth checking the details.

13 ... ♗d7

Black is not deflected by the gathering storm on the kingside and quietly brings his last minor piece into play, at the same time freeing c8 for a rook.

14 ♕h5

It starts to look rather ominous on the kingside, since Black's minor pieces are mostly on the other side of the board. However, there are as yet no open lines on the kingside, so White still has some way to go before he breaks through.

14 ... ♖fc8

Accuracy is essential. Black's defensive plan involves ...g6, meeting ♕h6 by ...♗f8, so it is necessary to clear f8 for the bishop.

15 ♖g3

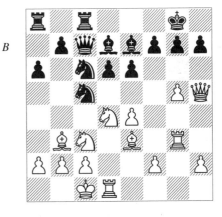

At last White has a threat that cannot be ignored: 16 ♖h3. A quick glance is enough to show that Black has no way of defending h7 directly, so he has to operate indirectly.

15 ... g6

Thus far Black has resolutely refused to touch the pawns in front of his king, but now he is compelled to take action. It is important that Black did not exchange on d4 earlier. Had he done so, White would have recaptured with the bishop and now ...g6 would be impossible, as White could mate by ♕xh7+ followed by ♖h3+ and ♖h8#.

16 ♕h6

Better than 16 ♕h4, as then ♖h3 could be met by ...h5.

16 ... ♗f8

The queen must be expelled from h6 or else ♖h3 will be deadly.

17 ♕h4

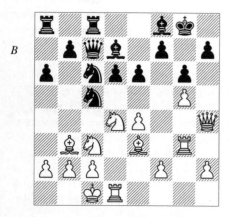

17 ... ♘xd4

Black's defensive idea is to meet ♖h3 by ...h5, and after gxh6 to play ...♔h7. With the h-file sealed by White's own pawn, his attack will be stymied for the time being and this will give Black the chance to make further progress on the queenside. The plan of blocking the pawn with a king on h7 clearly won't work if White can check the king by playing a knight to g5 (or f6), so it is essential to eliminate the d4-knight to prevent ♘f3-g5. As mentioned above, playing ...♘xd4 too early would have undermined Black's defensive plan, so his timing had to be spot-on.

17...♗e7 is an alternative idea, pinning the g5-pawn so as to meet 18 ♖h3 by 18...h5. However, quite apart from allowing White a draw by repetition, it is riskier as White can pursue the

attack by other means, for example by 18 f4. Then the game Martin Gonzalez-Corral Blanco, Linares 1991 continued 18...b5 19 ♘f5 ♘xb3+ 20 axb3 h5 21 ♘h6+ ♔h7 22 f5 ♘e5 23 ♘xf7! ♘xf7 24 fxg6+ ♔xg6 25 ♖f1 with a massive attack for White which soon proved decisive.

18 ♖xd4

The best recapture. After 18 ♗xd4 ♘xb3+ 19 axb3 White threatens 20 ♕xh7+, but Black can easily meet this by 19...e5, which covers h3 and gains time by attacking the bishop. Thanks to the mate on c2, White is not able to reply 20 ♘d5 – Black's plan of playing ...♖fc8 shows its worth by preventing the knight from joining the attack. After 19...e5, it is no longer clear how White can break through on the kingside, while Black's queenside counterattack starts to look extremely promising. A typical line would be 20 ♗e3 (20 ♗b6 is a tricky move, as 20...♕xb6 loses to 21 ♘d5, but after 20...♕c6! 21 ♖d2 ♗e6 White has not solved any of his problems) 20...b5 21 ♖d2 ♗e6 22 ♘d5 (by forcing the exchange of the e6-bishop, White gains access to h3, but it is all too slow) 22...♗xd5 23 exd5 ♗g7! (Black's queenside attack is now so strong that he can afford to give away the h7-pawn) 24 ♖h3 a5 25 ♕xh7+ ♔f8 (White's other pieces do not cooperate well with the queen on h7, so although White can pick up a couple of pawns he cannot generate a really serious threat) 26 ♖f3 a4 27 b4 (27 ♔d1 loses to 27...axb3 28 cxb3 ♖a1+ 29 ♔e2 ♕c1) 27...a3 28 bxa3 ♖xa3 and Black wins.

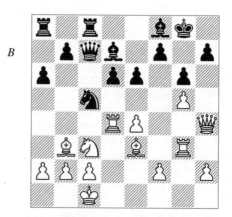

18 ... b5!

Here Black need not eliminate the b3-bishop and so he gains extra attacking ideas such as

...a5-a4 trapping the bishop. 18...♘xb3+?! 19 axb3 e5 20 ♖d2 is inaccurate because White would be a tempo ahead of the note to his 18th move.

19 ♖h3

White has nothing better than to execute his threat since otherwise Black would just improve his position by 19...♗g7.

19 ... h5
20 gxh6 ♔h7

It is not easy for White to make further progress on the kingside. His knight cannot easily reach g5 or f6 – not only would this require several moves, but there is also a lurking mate on c2. Advancing the h-pawn is rather slow as White would have to shift his major pieces off the h-file first.

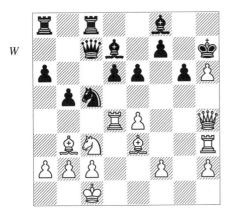

21 ♕f6?!

Up to now our emphasis has been on Black's need for accuracy. It is certainly true that a mistake by the defender is often punished quite quickly (by mate!), but a slip by the attacker can also have serious consequences. Up to this point White has conducted his attack accurately and consistently, but now he starts to lose his way. On f6 the queen generates some tactical threats, but this move is also very committal. If the queen has to retreat, then the time White has wasted will probably prove fatal. It is White's failure to follow up this move with the necessary aggression that proves disastrous, but in practical terms it would probably have been better to adopt a less one-sided approach.

21 ♖d2?!, to free the knight, is also poor, as after 21...♗c6! White will not have time to move the knight anywhere useful; for example,

22 ♗d4 (22 ♕f6 ♕e7!) 22...b4 23 ♘d5!? ♘xb3+ 24 axb3 ♗xd5 (24...exd5?? loses to 25 ♕f6) 25 exd5 e5 26 ♗e3 a5 favours Black.

21 f4!? is best, since pushing the pawn to f5 is the quickest way to open up lines on the kingside. After 21...♕d8! (21...♘xb3+ 22 axb3 e5 23 fxe5 dxe5 24 ♖xd7 ♕xd7 25 ♘d5 gives White good play for the exchange) White should avoid 22 ♕xd8 ♖xd8 as he has no attacking chances left while Black has the awkward threat of ...a5-a4. One line is 23 ♖g3 a5 24 a4 b4 25 ♘b5 ♘xb3+ 26 cxb3 ♖ac8+ 27 ♔b1 d5!, when White's poorly coordinated position is disintegrating. Therefore White should keep the queens on with 22 ♕f2 or 22 ♕g3, when the position remains unclear, although in either case the burden is on White to prove that he really has a good way to meet 22...a5.

21 ... ♗e8

21...♗c6? 22 ♖f3! ♖a7 23 h4 is dangerous for Black, since in this position he is unable to expel White's queen by ...♘d7.

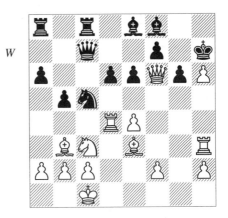

22 ♗g5?

Although this stops ...♕e7, after Black's obvious reply White has to retreat his queen, when Black takes over the initiative with a vengeance. 22 ♖d2 ♕e7! 23 ♕xe7 ♗xe7 would also favour Black, so White should have tried 22 e5!. This opens up the possibility of playing the knight to the kingside via e4, and by allowing ♖dh4 it sets up various tactical ideas based on a queen sacrifice at g7. Black has to continue very accurately:

1) 22...dxe5? allows White to force a beautiful win by 23 ♖dh4 ♘d7 24 ♕g7+! ♗xg7 25 hxg7+ ♔xg7 26 ♗h6+ ♔f6 (26...♔g8 27 ♗g5

also mates) 27 ♗g5+! ♔f5 (27...♔xg5 28 ♘e4+ ♔f5 29 ♜f3#) 28 ♘e4 with a quick mate.

2) 22...♘d7 23 exd6 ♘xf6 (23...♛xc3 24 ♛g7+ ♗xg7 25 hxg7+ ♔xg7 26 bxc3 favours White) 24 dxc7 ♜xc7 leads to a roughly equal ending.

3) If Black wants to play for a win, he should try the cold-blooded 22...d5!?. This keeps the knight out of e4, and threatens ...♘d7 followed by the capture of the e5-pawn, when the attack falls apart. White can reply:

3a) 23 ♗g5 is no good in view of 23...♘d7.

3b) 23 ♜f4 ♘d7 24 ♘xd5 exd5 25 ♛xf7+ ♗xf7 26 ♜xf7+ ♔h8 27 e6 ♗c5 28 exd7 ♜f8 and the attack is refuted.

3c) 23 ♜dh4! ♘d7 (23...♛e7 24 ♛f4 is dangerous for Black) 24 ♛g7+ ♗xg7 25 hxg7+ ♔xg7 26 ♜h7+ (not 26 ♗h6+? ♔g8 27 ♗f4 ♘f8 28 ♘xd5 exd5 29 e6 ♛xf4+ 30 ♜xf4 ♘xe6, when Black wins) 26...♔f8 27 ♜h8+ (27 ♗g5? ♛xe5 defends) 27...♔e7 28 ♗g5+ and now both 28...f6 29 ♜8h7+ ♗f7 30 exf6+ ♘xf6 31 ♜e3 and 28...♘f6 29 ♗xf6+ ♔d7 30 ♜d3 ♛c6 31 ♜h7 are rather murky. In both cases White ends up with two minor pieces for the queen, which is normally far from enough. However, White also retains a considerable initiative and strong pressure on the dark squares. Assessing such a position is very difficult: I think Black cannot be worse, but it is possible that White's compensation is enough to hold the balance.

> **22   ...   ♘d7**

The care Black has to take in this position is illustrated by the error 22...a5?, which gives White an extra tempo to bring his knight into the attack. White wins by force with 23 e5! ♘d7 (23...dxe5 loses to 24 ♜dh4! followed by 25 ♛g7+!) 24 ♘e4 d5 (24...♘xf6 loses to 25 ♗xf6) 25 ♛g7+! ♗xg7 26 hxg7+ ♔xg7 27 ♗h6+! ♔g8 28 ♘f6+ ♘xf6 29 exf6 ♛e5 30 ♗g7 ♛g5+ 31 ♜f4!! (31 ♔d1 ♛h5+ 32 ♜xh5 gxh5 33 ♜h4 ♔h7 is less clear-cut) 31...♛h5 (31...♛xf4+ 32 ♔b1 mates) 32 ♜fh4! ♔h7 33 c3 ♜c4 (or 33...e5 34 ♜xh5+ gxh5 35 ♜xh5+ ♔g6 36 ♜xe5) 34 ♜xh5+ gxh5 35 ♗c2+ ♜e4 36 f3 – a beautiful line.

After the text-move, White must retreat his queen, the possibility of a sacrifice on g7 disappears and White's attack evaporates with incredible speed.

> **23   ♛f3   b4**

In meeting Black's threats, White is handicapped by the fact that his pieces have been arranged for an attack, and cannot easily be switched to defensive duties.

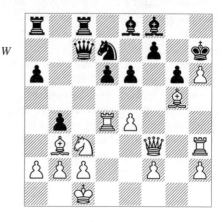

> **24   ♘b1**

The alternatives are also unattractive:

1) 24 ♜xb4? ♛c5 forks b4 and g5.

2) 24 ♘e2 a5 25 c3 a4 26 ♗c2 b3 27 axb3 axb3 28 ♗xb3 ♛a5 29 ♜g3 ♜ab8 30 ♔c2 ♘c5 and Black's attack is decisive.

3) 24 ♘a4 (trying to block the advance of Black's a-pawn) 24...♘e5 25 ♛e3 ♛a5 26 f4 ♗xa4 27 fxe5 ♗xb3 28 ♛xb3 ♛xe5 29 ♗e3 a5 and Black is clearly better. White's pawn-structure is wrecked and after ...♜c7 followed by ...♜ac8 Black also has good attacking prospects on the queenside.

> **24   ...   a5**

Long ago, I mentioned that the success of White's attack often depends on whether he can activate the b3-bishop. White has definitely failed in this respect, and the time it takes him to rescue this bishop from Black's advancing pawns only helps accelerate Black's counterattack.

> **25   ♘d2**

White saves the bishop by securing the c4-square.

> **25   ...   a4**
> **26   ♗c4   b3!**

Black should not be deflected from his attack by the prospect of material gain. After 26...♘e5 27 ♛f6 ♗b5?, for example, 28 ♗f4! causes confusion by setting up the deadly threat of ♗xe5 followed by ♘f3 (e.g. 28...♗xc4? 29 ♗xe5 dxe5 30 ♘f3 mating). The move played sacrifices a pawn, but opens up lines on the queenside.

27 axb3

Black also wins after 27 cxb3 axb3 28 axb3 (28 a3 ♘b6) 28...♖a1+ 29 ♔c2 (29 ♘b1 ♕a5) 29...♕a5 30 ♕g2 ♘e5 with a crushing attack.

27 ... a3

By now Black even has a choice of effective continuations: 27...axb3 28 ♗xb3 ♕b6 is also good.

28 bxa3 ♕c5

After this, Black soon regains the two sacrificed pawns, while maintaining his attack.

29 ♗e3

29 ♗f6 ♕xa3+ 30 ♔d1 ♕b2 is similar to the game.

29 ... ♕xa3+

30 ♔d1 ♕b2

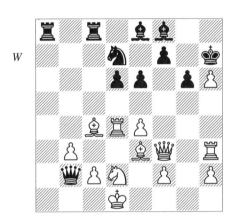

W

White's position is in total disarray. His rooks are especially ineffective, having been left stranded by the ebbing of White's attacking tide.

31 ♕g2

If White tries to flee with his king by 31 ♔e2 ♕xc2 32 ♔f1, Black continues 32...♘e5 33 ♕f6 (33 ♕e2 ♘xc4 34 bxc4 e5 35 ♖d3 ♖xc4! also wins for Black) 33...♘g4 34 ♕f3 e5 35 ♖d5 (35 ♖d3 ♖xc4) 35...♘xe3+ 36 ♕xe3 ♗d7 37 ♖f3 ♗e6 with decisive threats; for example, 38 ♖d3 ♖a1+ 39 ♔g2 ♖xc4 40 ♘xc4 ♕b1 and there is no real answer to 41...♕g1#.

31 ... ♖a1+

32 ♔e2 ♕xc2

Material equality is restored but the game is effectively over.

33 f4

Or 33 ♔f3 e5 34 ♗d3 (34 ♖d5 loses after 34...♘f6) 34...exd4 35 ♗xc2 ♘e5+ 36 ♔e2 ♖xc2 37 ♗xd4 ♗b5+ 38 ♔e3 ♖e1+ 39 ♔f4 ♖xd2 with a large material advantage and a crushing attack.

33 ... e5

34 ♖d3

34 fxe5 loses to 34...♕d1+ 35 ♔f2 ♕e1+ 36 ♔f3 ♘xe5+ 37 ♔f4 ♗d7.

34 ... ♘f6!

The most effective finish. The main threat is 35...♘g4, with ...♕d1# to come.

35 ♖g3

After 35 fxe5 ♘g4 36 ♖c3 ♕d1+ 37 ♔d3 ♘xe5+ 38 ♔d4 ♘c6+ 39 ♔d3 ♘b4+ 40 ♔d4 ♗e7 41 ♖f3 ♗d8 the white king falls.

35 ... d5!

An absolutely thematic finish. The only black pieces not participating in the attack are his bishops, and blowing open the centre lets them join in the fun.

36 ♗xd5

Or 36 exd5 e4 37 ♖d4 ♕d1+ 38 ♔f2 ♕e1#.

36 ... ♗b5

37 ♗c4 ♖xc4

Simple and effective. White ends up in *two* deadly pins.

38 bxc4 ♗xc4

39 ♗b6 ♗b4

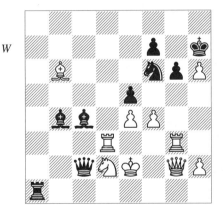

W

A painful picture for White. The glory days of his attack are but a distant memory and White's own king is mercilessly punished for his failures.

40 ♖e3 ♕xd2+

40...♗xd2 41 ♔f3 ♗xd3 would have won virtually all White's pieces, but of course at this stage it doesn't make any difference how Black chooses to win.

41	♔f3	♗xd3
42	♕xd2	♗xd2
43	♖xd3	♗xf4
44	♗d8	♖a6

0-1

Lanka succeeded in this game because he constructed his defence following all the basic principles of defensive play. He avoiding weakening moves, and arranged his pieces not only for immediate defensive purposes but also with an eye to his longer-term counterattacking possibilities. At several points he had to play with great accuracy – one slip could have been fatal. For a long time the balance between attack and defence was preserved, but finally Rõtšagov was the one to go wrong. He fell victim to that frequently fatal disease – inconsistency. Having committed himself entirely to an attack, at the critical moment Rõtšagov was unwilling to accept the inevitable consequence of his preceding play, namely the sacrifice of his queen.

Once he had lost his nerve, the attack faltered and Lanka's punishment was swift and severe.

It may seem surprising how quickly the attacker's position collapses in cases like this, but it is a quite normal consequence of the commitments the attacker has made in launching his attack. Weakening pawn advances, misplaced pieces and the abandonment of the centre to launch a flank attack are all typical commitments by the attacker which may later return to haunt him if the attack fails.

The lessons here are:

1) Keep calm when faced by an attack on the king. Presumably going into a panic must have some evolutionary purpose, but it isn't very helpful when playing chess!

2) Wait for your opponent to force weaknesses – don't concede them voluntarily.

3) Whenever you get a spare moment, press ahead with your counterplay.

4) When you have taken over the initiative, press home the attack ruthlessly – don't give your opponent time to rebuild his attack.

The Defensive Sacrifice

It is considered quite normal for the attacker to sacrifice, but the concept of a defensive sacrifice is perhaps less familiar. Note that I am not talking about the defender returning material which had earlier been sacrificed by the attacker, but about the case in which the defender is prepared to be at a material disadvantage. The basis for such sacrifices usually lies in the positional commitments incurred by the attacker. These typically involve decentralization, pawn weaknesses and exposure of the attacker's own king (e.g. by pawn advances in front of the king). If the defender is able to stop the attack by means of a sacrifice, these positional defects may provide ample compensation. Typically, such a sacrifice involves the elimination of a key attacking unit. Perhaps the commonest case is the sacrifice of an exchange, but it is not unusual for a queen to be offered in return for a rook and a minor piece, as in the following game.

Game 13

B. Lalić – A. Khalifman

Open tournament, Linares 1997

Benko Gambit

| 1 | d4 |

For comments on this move, see Game 2.

| 1 | ... | ♘f6 |

This flexible move is the most popular response to 1 d4. It can introduce a wide range of

openings, ranging from the Orthodox Queen's Gambit (if Black later plays ...e6 and ...d5) to more modern openings such as the King's Indian (see Game 14, amongst others). Black aims to stop, at least temporarily, White setting up an ideal centre with pawns on d4 and e4. The move ...♘f6 is not especially committal because the g8-knight is usually best posted on f6, so Black is able to keep his options open as regards his central pawn-structure.

2   c4

Again, the most common reply. White intends to play ♘c3, when he is ready to occupy the centre with e4. At first sight White could save time by playing 2 ♘c3, but in this case Black can reply 2...d5, when White is unable to challenge the d5-pawn by either e4 or c4. Then Black would have a relatively easy time of it, whereas by playing c4 first White makes the positional threat of ♘c3 followed by e4 harder to meet.

2   ...   c5

Black has to make a decision about his intended plan in the centre. 2...d5 is not a good response, because after 3 cxd5 ♘xd5 4 ♘f3, followed by e4, White gains an advantage in the centre. However, Black has a number of reasonable replies. He can play 2...e6, with the aim of meeting 3 ♘c3 by either 3...d5 (the Queen's Gambit Declined) or 3...♗b4 (the Nimzo-Indian Defence), both of which prevent White's intended e4. It is also possible for Black to ignore White's threat and play 2...g6. A third option, which Black adopts in this game, is to challenge White's d4-pawn with 2...c5. This move can lead to two popular openings, the Benoni and the Benko Gambit.

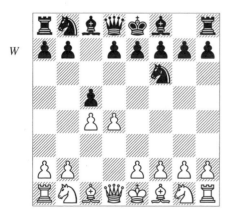

3   d5

This is the most critical response. 3 dxc5 is weak, because Black can easily regain the pawn after 3...e6, when White has surrendered his central d-pawn for Black's c-pawn. However, 3 ♘f3 is perfectly playable; although this again allows the exchange of d-pawn for c-pawn, in this case White obtains a lead in development as compensation.

3   ...   b5

This is the key move of the Benko Gambit. Black offers a pawn in order to open lines for his pieces on the queenside and to undermine White central pawn-chain on c4 and d5. This opening is another example of the modern style of gambit play (see Game 5). Black does not aim for a quick attack against the white king, but rather hopes for compensation in the form of lasting positional pressure. The main alternative is 3...e6, leading to the Benoni.

4   cxb5

White accepts the gambit, at least temporarily. It is also possible to decline the gambit by 4 ♘f3 or 4 a4, but most leading players prefer to take the pawn.

4   ...   a6

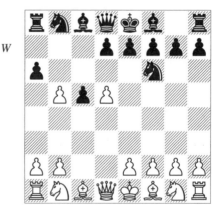

This is the logical follow-up to Black's previous move. If play now continues 5 bxa6 ♗xa6, then we can see what Black is aiming for with his pawn sacrifice. He has two half-open files on the queenside, which he can use to exert pressure against White's a- and b-pawns. This might seem a far-off prospect, but after ...d6, ...g6, ...♗g7, ...0-0, ...♘bd7, a queen move and ...♖fb8 it can easily become a reality. The development of the bishop at g7 is an integral part of Black's plan, as this further enhances the pressure on White's queenside. However, all this potential would come to nothing if White could complete his development with ease. In fact, it is by no means straightforward for White to get his kingside pieces out. If White moves his e-pawn, then the exchange of bishops on f1 will deprive White of the right to castle, when White will require several more tempi to sort out his kingside pieces. White can, it is true, play ♘f3, g3, ♗g2 and 0-0 but this leaves Black's a6-bishop unopposed on the a6-f1 diagonal.

5   f3

Although many players try to hang on to the gambit pawn, there is a school of thought to the effect that White should immediately return the pawn and use the tempo Black must spend on ...axb5 for development. The two most popular lines based on this strategy are 5 ♘c3 and the move adopted in this game, 5 f3. The former might appear more natural, but after 5 ♘c3 axb5 6 e4 b4 White's knight is driven away to the awkward square b5. The text-move also prepares e4, but in a more secure manner.

5   ...   e6

Black tries to take advantage of White's rather slow plan to counterattack in the centre. The alternative is 5...axb5 6 e4 ♕a5+ 7 ♗d2 b4 8 ♘a3, but then White has made good use of the delay in developing his queen's knight, since it can immediately settle on c4.

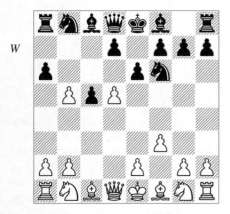

6   e4

The only consistent move.

6   ...   exd5

This looks most natural, but 6...c4!? is also playable, offering a second pawn in order to open the a7-g1 diagonal and thereby trap the white king in the centre more or less permanently.

7   e5

The most dangerous move, leading to extremely sharp and double-edged positions. It is also possible to play 7 exd5 ♗d6 8 ♕e2+ (forced, or else ...0-0 gives Black a strong attack) 8...♔f8 9 ♘c3 axb5 10 ♘xb5 (10 ♕xb5 ♘a6, intending ...♘b4 and ...♗a6, is more dangerous for White) 10...♗a6 11 ♕d2 ♕e7+ 12 ♔d1 with a very unclear position.

7   ...   ♕e7

Black must insert this before moving the knight, since an immediate knight move can be met by ♕xd5.

8   ♕e2

Now the f6-knight must move, and 8...♘h5 9 g4 costs a piece, so Black is forced to retreat the knight to its original square. 8 f4 is weak as Black can just reply 8...d6.

8   ...   ♘g8

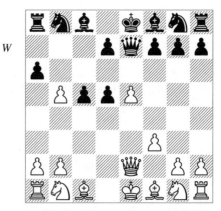

After this more or less forced sequence, it's time to take stock of the position. Material equality has been restored, but other features of the position are at least as important as the material balance. Both sides have great difficulties with their kingside development owing to the awkward positions of the two queens. Thus neither player will be able to castle kingside in the near future. Black, however, also has problems with his queenside development as his b8-knight cannot move while White's pawn remains on b5. The most obvious weakness in either position is the d5-pawn, which White can attack by ♘c3, ♘h3-f4 and possibly 0-0-0. Clearly, if a white knight lands on d5 then Black will be in serious trouble. Thus White's plan will be based on a quick attack, aimed mainly at conquering d5. Black will have to defend for the moment, but there are chances for a later counterattack. It will take White too long to arrange 0-0, so he has no safe spot for his own king.

9   ♘c3

Immediately taking aim at d5.

9   ...   ♗b7

Black must defend the key square.

10   ♘h3

White already has a deadly threat: 11 ♘f4, when d5 falls.

10   ...   c4!?

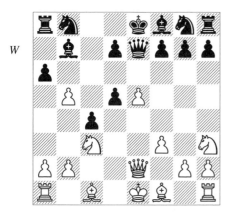

At first sight this looks odd, since in such a sharp position one would expect a developing move. However, Black simply doesn't have a reasonable developing move available. The text-move serves several purposes. The main point is to allow Black's queen to move to c5 or b4, not only activating the queen but also releasing the log-jam of pieces on the kingside. Black is also aiming to play ...axb5, releasing the queenside as well. The pressure is on White to take quick action before Black solves his development problems.

11   ♗e3

To prevent ...♕c5. After 11 ♘f4 ♕c5, followed by ...d4, Black has no problems.

11   ...   axb5

Only this move can justify Black's play. Black opens the a-file for his rook and frees the b8-knight. Moreover, in case White plays 0-0-0, Black's queenside pawn-mass could form the basis of an attack against White's king. The alternatives are much weaker:

1) 11...♕b4 12 b6! (White prevents the capture on b5) 12...♗c5 13 0-0-0 ♕xb6 14 ♗xc5

♕xc5 15 ♘f4!? ♘e7 16 ♕d2 regains the pawn with a definite positional advantage for White.

2) 11...♕xe5 is too risky, as 12 0-0-0 ♘f6 (12...♘e7 13 ♕d2 is similar) 13 ♕d2 followed by ♗f4 (or ♗d4) and ♖e1+ gives White an enormous attack.

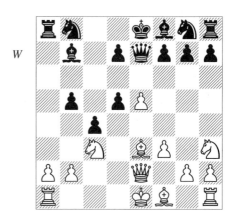

12   0-0-0

12 ♘f4 may be met by 12...♕xe5!, when thanks to the extra tempo ...axb5 Black has enough counterplay on the queenside to keep White at bay: 13 0-0-0 ♘e7 14 ♕d2 b4 15 ♘cxd5 ♘xd5 16 ♘xd5 c3! 17 bxc3 ♗xd5 18 ♕xd5 ♕xe3+ 19 ♔b1 ♖a7 and White does not have enough for the piece.

12 ♘xb5?! is too slow; it is not worth two tempi to remove the b5-pawn. After 12...♕b4+ 13 ♘c3 ♗c5 14 0-0-0 ♘e7 Black is ready to castle, when it will be White's king which is more exposed to attack.

12   ...   ♕b4!

During this phase Black is walking a very fine line and the slightest misstep will cost him the game. This move puts the queen in an aggressive position and clears e7 in order to support d5 with ...♘e7. The greedy 12...♕xe5? is once again wrong, since 13 f4 ♕e7 14 ♖xd5! d6 15 ♖xb5 restores material equality with a large lead in development for White.

13   ♘f4

13 ♖xd5 again looks very good, but it is met by the surprising 13...♕xc3+! 14 bxc3 ♗xd5. This type of sacrifice, which also occurs in the game, is another point behind ...♕b4. We will discuss the merits of a similar queen sacrifice in the note to Black's 15th move; suffice it to say that it is also effective after 13 ♖xd5.

13   ...   ♘e7

Forced, as the d5-pawn was threatened.

14   ♗b6

14 ♖xd5 would again be met by 14...♕xc3+ 15 bxc3 ♘xd5 so White instead plays to trap Black's queen. The immediate threat is ♕c2, followed by a3, which may appear slow but is actually quite dangerous.

14 ♕f2!? is another attempt to embarrass Black's queen, and in view of the result of this game it might well be White's strongest move. The threat is 15 ♗d2, when there is no way to prevent a discovered attack against the queen. Black has several possible replies, such as 14...♕a5 and 14...♘a6. One can only say that the resulting positions are unclear.

14   ...   h5!

Sometimes defence requires a considerable degree of imagination. With most of Black's pieces tied down to defending d5, it is not easy for Black to come up with a useful move. This advance, odd though it looks, fills the bill admirably. Black prevents 15 ♕c2, because 15...♖h6 attacks the b6-bishop. In any case Black may well play ...♖h6, activating the rook along the almost empty third rank. If this rook can be switched to the queenside, then Black will have developed an attack against White's king without the normal prelude of minor-piece development.

14...♖a6? is inferior as 15 ♗c7 ♘bc6 16 ♗d6 ♕a5 17 ♘fxd5 ♘xd5 18 ♘xd5 gives White a very strong attack.

15   ♖xd5

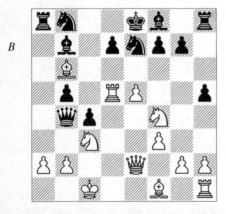

Of course, you have seen some similar lines in the earlier notes, so this move won't come as a complete shock. Nevertheless, it looks very strong. It takes only a few minutes to see that the arrival of a knight on d5 is catastrophic for Black, so this rook cannot be taken. On the other hand, a vital pawn has disappeared and b5 is under attack, so what is Black to do? Up to now Black has been restricted to responding to White's threats – most of his moves have been primarily defensive. Yet all the time he has managed to keep open the possibility of eventual counterplay. The rook on a8 and queenside pawn-mass might eventually form part of an attack on White's king. Even the move ...h5, which was mainly designed to prevent ♕c2, introduced an attacking idea in the shape of ...♖h6-a6. Just at this moment Black has the chance, by means of a sacrifice, to snuff out White's attack, when his own potential attacking possibilities can come to the fore.

15   ...   ♕xc3+!

Again, having seen this type of sacrifice in the earlier notes, you won't be too surprised by its appearance here, but it is worth considering how remarkable this idea is. Black's development is not exactly textbook stuff, with his king stuck in the centre and four other pieces still on their original squares. Yet here he is, not only returning the sacrificed pawn, but even making a sacrifice of his own. How can this be justified? The answer is that Black's sacrifice eliminates White's most dangerous attacking pieces, leaving White struggling with his positional defects. His two main problems are his exposed king and his inactive kingside pieces. These defects are not accidental, but an inevitable consequence of White's decision to embark on an early attack. He could not have launched his attack without the committal moves ♕e2 and 0-0-0, yet it is precisely these moves which now return to trouble him. Black has few positional problems. True, his king is still in the centre, but in many lines this can be easily solved by ...♗a3+ and ...0-0. Otherwise Black can be happy with the general structure of his position; the b5-c4 pawn-chain restricts White's f1-bishop, his a8-rook is already in play and his remaining minor pieces are easily developed.

From the objective point of view, Black is not yet better. However, White suddenly has to adjust to a different type of struggle, in which it is Black who has the initiative and White who must defend accurately. Such an adjustment is much more difficult than the switch in the reverse direction, from defensive to attacking play, and here it proves too much for White.

16   bxc3   ⟁xd5

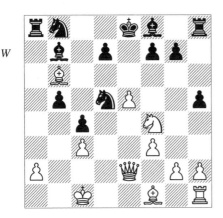

17   ⟁xd5?

The general structure of the position affords Black ample compensation for his sacrifice, so White should be seeking to exploit the particular features of the diagram position. The apparently natural exchange of knights is in fact a serious error, since Black is then able to put his positional assets to use without interference by White.

The critical move is 17 ♕e4!, exploiting the undefended bishop on b7. After 17...♗a3+ 18 ♔d2 ⟁xb6 19 ♕xb7 ♗c5 20 ⟁d5 ♖xa2+ White can play:

1) 21 ♔c1? 0-0 22 ⟁xb6 ⟁c6!. Here Black has only a rook for the queen, but he has at least a draw based on ...⟁a5, followed by ...⟁b3+ and perpetual check on a1 and a2. Surprisingly, however, Black need not be satisfied with a draw and can well play on. For example, 23 ⟁c8 (White must give up his queen after 23 ⟁d5 ♖fa8 or 23 ⟁d7 ♗e3+ 24 ♔b1 ♖fa8) 23...⟁a5 24 ♕xd7 ⟁b3+ 25 ♔b1 ♖d2!, followed by ...♗a3, leaves White in trouble.

2) 21 ♔d1 (a much better defence, denying Black the bishop check on e3 which was so important in line '1') 21...0-0 22 ⟁xb6 ♗xb6 (22...⟁c6 23 ⟁xd7 favours White) 23 ♕xb6 ⟁c6 reaches a fascinating position in which Black has only a rook and a pawn for the queen, but White has serious problems developing his kingside pieces. White can try:

2a) 24 ♔e1 b4 25 cxb4 ♖b8 26 ♕e3 ♖xb4 27 ♕c1 ⟁xe5 is fine for Black.

2b) 24 ♖g1 ♖b8 25 ♕c5 ♖ba8 26 f4 (26 ♗e2? ♖a1+ 27 ♔d2 ♖8a2+ wins for Black) 26...♖b2 27 ♔c1 ♖b3 and Black has enough compensation.

2c) 24 ♔c1 ⟁xe5 (24...b4 25 cxb4 ♖b8 26 ♕c7 ♖a7 27 ♕d6 ♖xb4 28 ♔d2! favours White) 25 ♕xb5 ♖e8! 26 f4 ⟁g4 27 ♗xc4 ♖a1+ 28 ♔b2 ♖xh1 is slightly better for White, but should probably be a draw.

It seems likely that the sudden change from attack to defence confused White, and the critical position arose before he had fully grasped the key features of the new situation.

17   ...   ♗xd5

Suddenly White's problems become clear. It takes Black only a few moves (...♗a3+, ...0-0, ...⟁c6 and ...♖fb8) to launch a decisive attack on the white king, so White must act quickly, but what can he do with his kingside pieces bottled up?

18   ♕d2

White decides simply to bring his kingside pieces out. The alternative was to play for the exchange of dark-squared bishops, but this costs valuable time: 18 ♔b1 ⟁c6 19 ♕e3 (intending to play ♗c5) 19...b4 is also unpleasant for White; for example, 20 ♗c5 ♗xc5 21 ♕xc5 ♖a5 22 ♕d6 ♖h6 23 ♕c7 bxc3 24 ♗e2 ♖b5+ 25 ♔c1 ⟁d4 26 ♗xc4 ♖c6 with a winning attack.

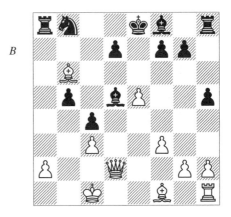

18   ...   ♗e6

This is a flexible square for the bishop; it defends c4 in case of ...b4, and can switch to f5 if necessary.

19   &e2

There is nothing better. 19 &c7 &a3+ 20 &b1 0-0 followed by ...&c6 also gives Black a dangerous attack, while 19 &b1 &c6 20 &e3 leaves White a tempo down over the previous note.

19   ...   &c6

The most flexible move. Black should not play ...&a3+ too early, as he may do better by leaving the a-file open. An unusual feature of this attack is the way Black's pieces take part from their original squares (see also Game 9).

20   f4

Now the plan of exchanging bishops is hopeless in view of 20 &c7 b4 21 &d6 &xd6 22 &xd6 &xa2 and Black wins. The text-move aims to give the e2-bishop a good square on f3 and introduces the possibility of playing for f5.

20   ...   b4

Black does not waste time but powers ahead with his attack.

21   f5

White tries to deflect the bishop from e6 and thus play &xc4. Black wins after the alternative 21 cxb4 &xb4 22 &d4 &xa2+ 23 &d1 c3 24 &c2 (24 &xc3 &c8) 24...&b8.

21   ...   bxc3
22   &xc3   &a3

Putting the question to White's queen. The alternative 22...&xf5 23 &xc4 is less clear.

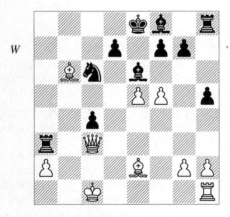

W

23   &b2?

Up to here White has defended well, but after this error the black attack crashes through. The alternatives were:

1) 23 &c2? &b4 24 &e4 &d5 and now:

1a) 25 &h4 (the threat of mate at d8 does not save White) 25...&xa2+ 26 &d2 (26 &b2 loses to 26...c3+ 27 &b1 &b3+ 28 &a1 &e7 29 f6 &b4) 26...&e7 27 f6 g5! 28 &xg5 &b4+ 29 &c2 (29 &d1 &c3+ followed by ...&e4+ reveals the point of luring the white queen to g5) 29...&e4+ 30 &d1 &c3+ 31 &e1 &d3 and Black wins.

1b) 25 &d4 &xa2+ 26 &c2 (26 &b2 loses to 26...c3+ 27 &b1 &b3+ 28 &a1 &b4 29 &d3 &e7 30 f6 0-0! 31 fxe7 &a8+ 32 &a7 &xd3, while 26 &b1 &e4+! 27 &a1 &c3+ 28 &b2 &a2+! 29 &xc3 &c2# leads to mate) 26...&b4+ 27 &b1 &b3+ 28 &c1 g6! wins for Black.

2) 23 &a1? &d5 24 &d1 &b4 is very strong; for example, 25 &d4 &xa2+ 26 &c2 &b4+ 27 &b1 c3 and Black wins.

3) 23 &e1! was the only way to continue the game, putting the queen out of harm's way for the moment. After 23...&xf5 (both 23...&xa2? 24 fxe6 &a1+ 25 &c2 &xe1 26 exf7+ &xf7 27 &xc4+ &g6 28 &xe1 and 23...&b4 24 &f2 &d5 25 &f3 are fine for White) 24 &xc4 &b4 25 &f2 (25 &f1 g6 is much the same) 25...g6! (not 25...&c3+ 26 &b2 &c2+ 27 &xc2 &xc2 28 &xc2 &xe5 29 &b5, when the active bishops and passed a-pawn balance Black's extra pawn) Black will successfully castle, enabling his other rook to join the attack. Black retains strong pressure, but White is not dead.

23   ...   c3

Now there is no decent square for the queen.

24   &b5

After this Black winds up his attack with a nice tactical finish. 24 &c2 &b4 and 24 &b1 &xa2 25 &e4 &b3 are more prosaic wins.

24   ...   &xf5
25   &f1

Or 25 &c4 g6 26 &e3 &a5 27 &b3 &a3+ 28 &d1 c2+ 29 &d2 0-0 and Black wins.

25   ...   &xa2!

This attractive piece sacrifice rounds off a well-played attack by Khalifman.

26   &xf5   &b4

Black threatens mate in one.

27   &a5

27 &d3 &a1+ 28 &b1 c2 29 &xb4 &xb4 30 &xc2 &h6 gives Black a decisive material advantage. The text-move attempts to return the queen, but Black does not need to take it straight away.

27   ...   g6!

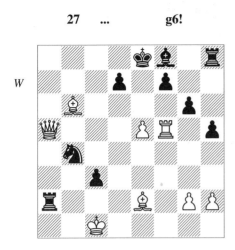

0-1

A thematic finish. The bishop strikes the decisive blow without ever moving from its original square.

White cannot avoid heavy loss of material; for example, 28 ♖f3 ♗h6+ 29 ♔e3 ♖xa5 with an extra rook for Black.

This game is a model example of how to turn defence into counterattack. Faced with a sharp and aggressive opening by White, Khalifman was at first restricted to passive defence. However, White's double-edged play involved making concessions, particularly with respect to his king position, and this gave Black the chance to seize the initiative with a positional queen sacrifice. After an error at move 17, Black developed a very strong attack with his king in the centre and most of his pieces still on their original squares. Lalić found himself under continuing pressure and when he made a slip on move 23, Khalifman was able to drive his attack home in spectacular style.

The lessons here are:

1) Very aggressive openings usually involve the attacker accepting some risk – either material sacrifice or positional weaknesses. If you are the defender, bear in mind that if you can survive the initial onslaught, the tide may turn in your favour.

2) A dangerous attack can sometimes be defused by a sacrifice to eliminate key attacking units.

3) It is psychologically difficult to switch from attacking to defensive play. Mistakes are common in the aftermath of such a switch.

4) Not all attacks are based on the standard formula: develop your pieces, move them towards the enemy king, force weaknesses and mate. General principles offer useful guidelines, but it is the actual position on the board that matters. In this game Black was very successful with his 'non-standard' attack.

Defence and Counter-Attack

When the scenario of kingside attack vs queenside attack is being played out, it is quite easy to fall into the trap of mentally dividing the board into the two halves. Take a look at the diagram on page 108 (after 18 ♖h2). Here it seems that there is a clear division. White is attacking down the h-file with the aim of giving mate on h7 or h8, while Black is striving to generate threats on the other side of the board. One might then mentally assign each piece to a particular half of the board. The white queen, for example, is the spearhead of White's kingside assault, while Black's queen and knight seem equally clearly to be part of the queenside activity. Yet there are many dangers in artificially compartmentalizing the board like this, because the interaction between the various parts of the board is ignored. What about the white rook on h2, for example? Is its main role on the kingside or the queenside? In fact, both are equally important. The rook is covering the mate on b2, but at any moment it might play a decisive role along the h-file. Mentally chopping the board into pieces can easily lead to oversights. If the white queen has been mentally assigned to the kingside, it would be easy to overlook that its control of c1 might play a vital defensive role in one line (for example, at the end of note '2a' to White's 15th move). It is said that long diagonal moves backward are hard to see; here there is an additional difficulty in spotting the possible change of function of the white queen. This comment applies equally to the black queen; in note '4' to White's 23rd move, for example, the queen suddenly arrives back on f6 to save the black king.

In this game the interaction between the kingside and queenside play is particularly intense; pieces are made to work hard performing multiple functions, and nothing can be taken for granted.

Game 14
Bu Xiangzhi – Ye Jiangchuan
Shenyang 1999
King's Indian Defence, Sämisch Variation

	1	d4	♘f6
	2	c4	

For comments on the moves up to this point, see Game 13.

	2	...	g6

This was mentioned as a possibility in the notes to Game 13. Black ignores White's threat to force through e4 and concentrates on quick piece development and early castling.

3   ♘c3

White continues with his plan to support the advance e4.

	3	...	♗g7

The main alternative is to act directly in the centre by 3...d5 (the Grünfeld Defence). One of the main lines of the Grünfeld runs 4 cxd5 ♘xd5 5 e4 ♘xc3 6 bxc3 ♗g7. In this variation White has managed to force through e4 and has even gained a 2 vs 1 pawn-majority in the centre, but at the cost of some time. Black can use this time to assault the d4-pawn by ...c5 and ...♘c6. If the pawn is forced to move, then the g7-bishop will become more active. As so often in chess, it is a matter of balancing one advantage against another – in this case White's superior centre against Black's lead in development. See Game 29 for more on this opening.

The text-move introduces the King's Indian Defence, an opening that became especially popular when Kasparov scored some notable victories with it.

4   e4

White, of course, follows his intended plan. His centre looks imposing, but he will have to catch up in development and this will give Black time to start his own play in the centre.

	4	...	d6

Black intends to organize his central play on the dark squares, for example by ...0-0, ...e5 and ...♘c6 to exert pressure on the d4-pawn. Note that the text-move effectively prevents e5 by

White, since 5 e5 dxe5 6 dxe5 ♕xd1+ 7 ♘xd1 (7 ♔xd1 ♘g4 wins a pawn) 7...♘fd7 8 f4 f6 is obviously fine for Black.

5   f3

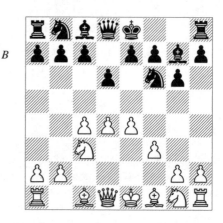

B

At first sight this resembles a beginner's move. Instead of developing a piece, White moves yet another pawn, at the same time taking away the best square from the g1-knight. Of course White supports e4, but this pawn was not attacked. Despite this, 5 f3 (called the Sämisch Variation) is considered one of White's most dangerous lines against the King's Indian, and it has been employed by Botvinnik, Petrosian, Karpov and Kramnik, amongst many other leading players. What, then, is the venom hidden in this apparently harmless move? In the note to Black's 4th move, I mentioned that Black typically tries to exert pressure against the d4-pawn. White would like to support the d4-pawn by ♗e3, but this bishop can be dislodged by ...♘g4. Thus the move f3 is necessary preparation for the manoeuvre ♗e3 and ♕d2. If the d4-pawn requires further support, then ♘ge2 is possible. Unusually for the King's Indian, White often castles queenside in the Sämisch. This sharpens the struggle, since White may choose to launch a kingside attack by h4-h5 and ♗h6 (much as in the Sicilian Dragon – see Game 10). A solid centre is a prerequisite for a flank attack, and White's solid defence of d4 and e4 provides a reasonable foundation for kingside action. The dark side of White's plan is that it is quite time-consuming, and his kingside pieces often have to stay at home for some time. Moreover, the move f3 slightly weakens the dark squares, so White must take care that Black is not able to exploit this.

>   **5   ...   0-0**

The natural move; Black completes his kingside development.

>   **6   ♗e3**

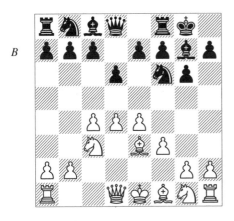

This is the logical follow-up to White's previous move.

>   **6   ...   e5**

Black has to decide how to act in the centre – he has quite a wide range of possible plans. The first idea is simply to continue with his normal central play against d4. In this case 6...c5 (Black gets adequate compensation if White wins a pawn on c5) or the text-move is indicated. Another plan is to expand on the queenside, so as to set up a possible counterattack there in anticipation of White's 0-0-0. In this case Black might play 6...c6, followed by ...a6 and ...b5. Just to confuse the issue, there are some hybrid plans in which Black aims for both ...b5 and ...e5. As we shall see, Black adopts a such a hybrid plan in the main game.

>   **7   ♘ge2**

Further support for d4 is necessary, as Black was threatening 7...exd4 8 ♗xd4 ♘c6. In view of his shaky dark squares, White cannot afford

to let his dark-squared bishop be exchanged for a knight, and so the bishop would have to retreat from d4 with loss of time. The text-move permits White to recapture on d4 with a knight.

>   **7   ...   c6**

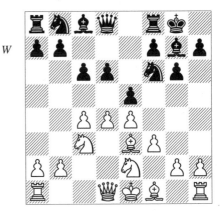

A good, flexible move. White's pieces are kept out of d5, Black prepares a possible development of his queen to a5, and he is ready for further queenside action by ...a6 and ...b5.

>   **8   ♕d2**

For the moment everything is secure in the centre, so White can complete his queenside development.

>   **8   ...   ♘bd7**

After White's 0-0-0, there will be a threat of dxe5, so Black further supports his strongpoint in the centre.

>   **9   0-0-0   a6**

Now that White's king is committed to the queenside, Black's natural plan is to prepare expansion via ...b5.

>   **10   ♗h6**

White has to make a fundamental choice about how to proceed. There are basically two strategies: to play in the centre, or to launch a kingside attack. If White wants to play in the centre, he has to face the problem of developing his kingside pieces. The roadblock is the knight on e2, which locks in the bishop. The knight could move to g3, but there it has little future if White is not going to attack on the kingside. Therefore 10 ♔b1 is the most natural move, preparing ♘c1 and possibly ♘b3. This line is indeed the most popular in practice, because White has chances for an advantage without incurring any great risk.

If White wants to play for a kingside attack, he might try 10 g4 or 10 h4, but since the exchange of the g7-bishop is almost certain to be necessary sooner or later, it is most flexible to start with the text-move.

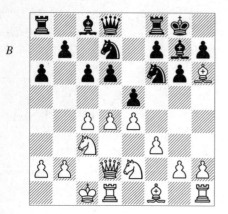

B

10   ...   ♗xh6

The problem of whether to meet ♗h6 with ...♗xh6 occurs in several openings – for example, the Sicilian Dragon (see Game 10) and the Pirc, as well as the King's Indian. In terms of tempi it usually makes no difference. We can see this if we look at the following sequences (in which Black's tempi are indicated by B1, B2, etc.): 1...♗xh6 2 ♕xh6 B1 3 h4 B2 4 h5 B3 5 hxg6 fxg6 and 1...B1 2 ♗xg7 ♔xg7 3 h4 B2 4 h5 B3 5 hxg6 fxg6 6 ♕h6+ ♔g8. These sequences end up with the same position, although the second takes one move longer. It is therefore necessary to see if there are any factors peculiar to the given position which favour one or the other. For example, if it might be better to retreat the king to h8 after ♕h6+, then the second sequence could be preferable. In the current position it doesn't matter much if Black plays ...♗xh6 straight away or not, as he can usually still play it later. However, he should not leave it too long; for example, after 10...b5 11 h4 ♕a5 12 h5 b4 13 ♘b1 ♕xa2 14 ♘g3 it is Black's last chance to transpose to the line considered in the note to White's 13th move. If he delays further with 14...exd4?, then 15 ♗xg7! ♔xg7 16 ♕xd4 gives White a clear advantage. The d6-pawn will be captured, after which e5 will be very strong.

In this discussion, we assume that a white knight cannot easily reach g5. If it can, then it is

usually very unwise to play ...♗xh6, as the combination of a queen on h6 and a knight on g5 is very dangerous.

11   ♕xh6   b5

Black should not delay in starting his counterplay.

12   h4

As we have mentioned earlier, launching an attack on the castled king usually involves a fair degree of commitment. Here the commitments are the decentralized queen and the time it takes to open the h-file. If the attack collapses, White may have to bring his queen back to the centre, in which case all the time he has spent will be wasted.

12   ...   ♕a5

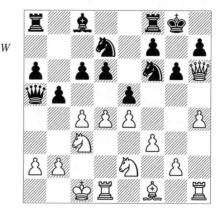

W

Black's kingside will not defend itself for ever, so (just as in Game 12) he has to strike a balance between direct kingside defence and furthering his queenside counterplay. Black's pieces are at the moment not especially well placed for a queenside attack, and he will need to involve his queen and at least one minor piece in order to create some serious threats. Note that White cannot defend his queenside directly by 13 ♔b1?? because 13...b4 wins a piece.

13   g4!?

At first sight this looks like a waste of time, because it is perfectly possible to play h5 without any further preparation. However, White has an interesting idea in mind, which we can only understand if we take a look at what happens after the immediate 13 h5. Black continues 13...b4 14 ♘b1 ♕xa2 and now:

1) White should not exchange prematurely on g6, because this gives Black extra defensive

possibilities along the second rank; for example, 15 hxg6 fxg6 16 ♖d2 ♕xc4+ 17 ♖c2 ♕f7 and Black stands well.

2) The direct attempt 15 ♘g3 leads to a forced draw by perpetual check after 15...♘b6 16 c5 (an attempt to displace the knight from f6, so that hxg6 would lead to mate) 16...♘c4 (16...♘a4 also seems adequate for a draw in view of 17 ♖d2 exd4 18 e5 ♘xc5 {but not 18...dxe5? due to 19 ♘e4 ♕e6 20 hxg6 fxg6 21 ♘xf6+ ♖xf6 22 ♕xh7+ ♔f8 23 ♕c7, when White has a clear advantage} 19 exf6 ♘b3+ 20 ♔c2 ♘a1+ 21 ♔c1 ♘b3+) 17 ♖d2 ♘a5! (after 17...♘xd2? 18 ♘xd2 ♕a1+ 19 ♘b1 White has a dangerous attack, since the elimination of Black's knight has brought his attack to a halt, at least for the moment) 18 cxd6 ♘b3+ 19 ♔c2 ♘a1+ 20 ♔c1 ♘b3+. This sequence occurred in the game Beliavsky-Kasparov, Linares 1993.

3) White can also try 15 ♖d2 first, and this introduces some new ideas for both sides:

3a) 15...♘b6 16 c5 (16 ♕g5 ♕xc4+ 17 ♖c2 ♕e6 18 ♖xc6 ♘fd7! 19 d5 ♘xd5! 20 exd5 ♕xd5 21 ♖c2 ♘c5 gives Black three pawns and a dangerous attack for the piece) 16...♘c4 17 cxd6 (17 ♖c2 ♘a5 favours Black) 17...♘a5 has been believed to result in the familiar draw by ...♘b3+ and ...♘a1+, or if 18 ♖d3, then 18...♘c4 forces a repetition. Indeed, the game T.Pähtz-Cvitan, Bad Wörishofen 1994 concluded 18 dxe5 ♘b3+ 19 ♔c2 ♘a1+ 20 ♔c1 ♘b3+ 21 ♔c2 ½-½. However, 18 hxg6! fxg6 (18...♘b3+ 19 ♔c2 ♘a1+ 20 ♔d1! is similar) 19 dxe5 is very awkward for Black. Then 19...♘b3+ 20 ♔c2 ♘a1+ 21 ♔d1! ♕xb1+ 22 ♘c1 wins for White, as Black cannot meet the threats of 23 ♗c4+, 23 ♗d3 and 23 exf6, but Black's alternative 19th moves also fail to give him a satisfactory position.

3b) 15...♕xc4+ 16 ♖c2 ♕d3!? is an untested suggestion of Gallagher. The queen appears precariously placed on d3, but there is no obvious way for White to exploit this.

The point of 13 g4 is not so much to support h5, but to open the second rank to allow White to defend the b2-pawn by ♖h2. Then the d1-rook will be free to move to d3, ready to meet ...♘b3+ by the exchange sacrifice ♖xb3. White hopes Black's counterattack will come to nothing without this perpetual, leaving White in the driving seat. The idea of using the rook on h2

for both attack and defence is ingenious. In this game it fails, but only because of a later slip by White.

| | 13 | ... | **b4** |

13...♘b6? is a mistake because of 14 dxe5 dxe5 15 ♖d6!.

| | **14** | **♘b1** | **♘b6** |

14...♕xa2 15 ♘g3 ♘b6 transposes to the following note.

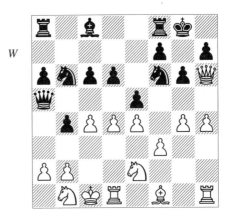

15 dxe5?!

The opening of the d-file helps Black more than White, since in many lines White's king is chased onto the open file. It is true that White can still draw after this move, but only by very accurate play.

The critical line runs 15 ♘g3 ♕xa2 16 h5 ♘xc4 17 ♖h2 and now:

1) 17...♘a5 allows White to put his plan into action: 18 ♖d3! ♘b3+ 19 ♖xb3 (this is a defensive sacrifice of the type we saw in Game 13; a key attacking piece is eliminated, and the black attack grinds to a halt) 19...♕xb3 20 ♘d2 (White has a very dangerous attack) 20...♕a2 (20...♕e6 21 ♘f5! gxf5 22 gxf5 and 20...♕a4 21 dxe5 dxe5 22 hxg6 fxg6 23 ♗c4+ ♖f7 24 ♘h5 are both winning for White) 21 hxg6 ♕a1+ 22 ♘b1 fxg6 23 dxe5 and Black is in serious trouble as he cannot play ...dxe5 due to ♗c4+.

2) 17...♘a3! (this move exposes the weak point of defending b2 from h2 – the rook is undefended on h2) 18 ♗d3 ♘xb1 19 hxg6 (19 g5 ♘g4 20 fxg4 ♘a3 21 hxg6 ♕a1+ 22 ♔d2 ♕xb2+ 23 ♔e1 is a draw) 19...fxg6 20 g5 with enormous complications:

2a) 20...♘c3 21 bxc3! (21 ♖dh1 exd4 22 gxf6 ♖a7 23 ♕xh7+!? ♖xh7 24 ♖xh7 ♕a1+ 25

♔d2 ♕xh1 26 ♖g7+ ♚h8 27 ♘xh1 is also
murky) 21...♕a1+ 22 ♔d2 ♕xc3+ 23 ♚e2 and
although Black gets four pawns for the piece,
none of the pawns is really dangerous, while
White's residual attacking chances are still significant. White wins after 23...♘h5 24 ♘xh5
gxh5 25 g6, while 23...♖a7 24 gxf6 ♖xf6 25
♖c1! also favours White.

2b) 20...♘a3! (this is better, because Black's
queen ends up on a3 rather than c3, and so is not
exposed to the tempo-gaining ♖c1) 21 bxa3
♕xa3+ 22 ♔d2 ♖a7 23 gxf6 ♖xf6 24 ♖c1 ♗e6
with a totally unclear position.

Perhaps put off by the result of this game,
nobody seems to have cared to repeat White's
idea, but on the basis of this analysis it deserves
another try.

15	...	dxe5
16	♘g3	

16 ♖d6, which was successful in the note to
Black's 13th move, no longer works due to
16...♘xc4 17 ♖xf6 ♕xa2, when there is no way
to defend b2.

16	...	♕xa2

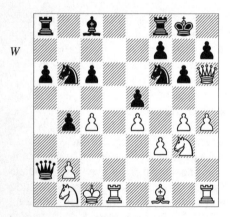

W

17	h5

17 g5 is a mistake; it does not help White's
kingside chances and only drives the f6-knight
to join in Black's queenside attack: 17...♘xc4
18 ♖h2 ♘d7 19 ♗xc4 (19 h5 loses to 19...♘c5)
19...♕xc4+ 20 ♖c2 ♕b5 21 h5 ♘c5 22 ♘d2
♕a5! and Black wins.

17	...	♘xc4
18	♖h2!	

The only consistent move. 18 ♗xc4 is bad
as 18...♕xc4+ 19 ♔d2 ♘xg4 20 fxg4 ♖d8+ 21
♔e3 ♗xg4 gives Black a decisive attack; the

immediate threat is 22...♕c5+ and mate next
move. 18 ♖d2 is inconsistent with White's
plan. Then Black can force his usual draw by
18...♘a5 19 hxg6 ♘b3+ 20 ♔c2 ♘a1+, but he
can also very well play for a win by 18...♖a7!
19 hxg6 fxg6 20 g5 (20 ♗xc4+ ♕xc4+ 21 ♖c2
♕d3 22 g5 ♘g4! 23 fxg4 ♕xg3 wins for Black)
20...♘xd2 21 ♘xd2 ♕a1+ 22 ♘b1 ♘d5! (a
neat method of blocking the a2-g8 diagonal) 23
♗c4 (23 exd5 cxd5 followed by ...♖c7+ is an
easy win for Black) 23...♖c7! and White cannot
reinforce his attack. This line provides another
example of a rook operating both defensively
along a rank and aggressively along a file.

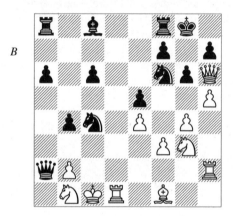

B

18	...	♘a3!

Once again, this stroke saves Black – indeed,
in this position, it forces White to respond accurately.

19	♗d3

Not 19 ♘xa3? bxa3 20 hxg6 fxg6 21 bxa3
♕xa3+ 22 ♔c2 ♗e6, when Black's attack
strikes first.

19	...	♘xb1

A critical moment. Black has no immediately deadly threats, so White has a tempo to
spend on reinforcing his attack. How can he
best utilize this tempo?

20	hxg6?

White makes the wrong choice. Opening the
second rank makes it easier for Black to defend
g7 and h7, and the balance starts to tip in Black's
favour. 20 ♗xb1 is also inferior; after 20...♕c4+
21 ♖c2 (21 ♗c2 loses to 21...b3 22 ♖d6 bxc2
23 ♖xf6 ♕a2 24 ♔xc2 ♖b8) 21...♕b3 22 ♘f5
(22 ♖xc6 ♕xf3 23 ♖d3 ♕f4+ 24 ♕xf4 exf4 25
♖xf6 fxg3 26 ♖xg3 ♗e6 gives Black a large

endgame advantage) 22...♗xf5 23 exf5 (23 gxf5 ♘xh5) 23...♖ad8 White's attack is collapsing; for example, 24 hxg6 ♖xd1+ 25 ♔xd1 ♕xf3+ 26 ♔e1 ♕g3+ 27 ♔f1 fxg6.

20 g5! is correct. There are many ways for Black to force a draw, but there is no route to an advantage. The trickiest line runs 20...♘c3 (20...♘g4 21 fxg4 ♘a3 22 hxg6 ♕a1+ 23 ♔d2 ♕xb2+ 24 ♔e3 ♕d4+ 25 ♔d2 is a draw) 21 ♖dh1! (21 bxc3? loses to 21...♕a1+ 22 ♔d2 ♕xc3+ 23 ♔e2 ♘g4 24 fxg4 ♗xg4+ 25 ♔e3 ♗xd1 26 hxg6 ♕c1+) 21...♘g4 (21...♕a1+ 22 ♔c2 ♕a4+ 23 ♔c1 is an immediate perpetual) 22 fxg4 ♖a7 (now Black only needs a couple of tempi to put a rook on the d-file and deliver mate, but White is just in time) 23 ♘f5! (23 bxc3? ♕a1+ 24 ♔d2 ♕xc3+ 25 ♔e3 ♖d8 26 ♖d1 ♗xg4 is a win for Black) 23...gxf5 24 gxf5 and it is time for Black to give perpetual check by 24...♕a1+ 25 ♔c2 ♕a4+ 26 ♔c1, or else he might even lose. In these lines, the defensive powers of the rook on h2 save White again and again.

20	...	**fxg6**
21	**g5**	

21 ♗xb1 ♕c4+ 22 ♖c2 ♕b3 is very good for Black, much as in the note to White's 20th move.

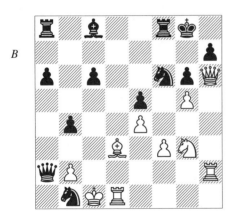

B

21	...	**♖d8!**

Thanks to White's error, Black is suddenly able to switch to the attack himself. Sooner or later, White's king will be chased onto the d-file; when that happens, the rook will be usefully posted on d8. 21...♘c3 is wrong since 22 bxc3 ♕a1+ 23 ♔d2 ♕xc3+ 24 ♔e2 favours White.

22	**gxf6**	

22 ♗c2 doesn't help in view of 22...♖xd1+ 23 ♗xd1 (23 ♔xd1 loses to 23...♕xb2 24 gxf6 ♖a7) 23...♖a7! (23...♘c3 24 bxc3 ♕a1+ 25 ♔d2 is less clear) 24 gxf6 ♘c3! 25 bxc3 (25 ♗b3+ ♕xb3 26 ♖d2 ♘d5! 27 exd5 cxd5 should win for Black) 25...♕a1+ 26 ♔d2 (26 ♔c2 b3+ 27 ♔xb3 ♕xd1+ 28 ♔a3 ♗e6 is decisive) 26...♖d7+ 27 ♔e3 ♕xd1 and Black wins.

22	...	**♖a7!**

This move is only possible thanks to White's premature pawn exchange on g6. In an echo of White's earlier ♖h2, Black's rook provides a sturdy defence along the second rank.

The interaction of attack and defence in this game is quite complex. Neither side can afford to proceed with his attack without taking into account the actions of the opponent.

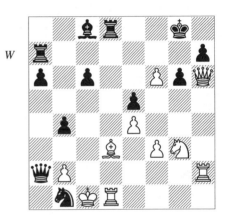

W

23	**♕g5?**	

After this, Black wins fairly easily. Some of the alternatives offered better practical chances, although there is nothing fully satisfactory for White:

1) 23 ♖c2? ♗e6 (23...♘c3?? 24 ♗c4+) 24 ♘f5 ♕a1 and Black wins at once.

2) 23 ♕e3 ♖ad7 24 ♕b6 (24 ♗c2? loses to 24...♖xd1+ 25 ♗xd1 ♘c3) 24...♘c3 25 bxc3 ♕a1+ 26 ♔c2 ♕xc3+ 27 ♔b1 ♖xd3 28 ♕xd8+ ♖xd8 29 ♖xd8+ ♔f7 30 ♖xc8 ♕e1+ 31 ♔b2 ♕xg3 32 ♖xh7+ ♔xf6 33 ♖xc6+ ♔g5 gives Black excellent winning chances.

3) 23 b3 is a better move which requires accurate handling by Black: 23...♕xb3 24 ♗c2 ♖xd1+ 25 ♗xd1 ♕d3 26 ♗e2 (after 26 ♗c2, 26...♕a3+ 27 ♔xb1 ♗e6 comes to the same thing, but Black must avoid the tempting move

26...♕xf3 since 27 ♘f5! gxf5 28 f7+! ♖xf7 29 ♕g5+ ♖g7 30 ♕d8+ forces perpetual check) 26...♕c3+ 27 ♔xb1 ♗e6 and Black has the advantage since he has three pawns for the piece, plus threats against the exposed white king. One possible line is 28 ♗d1 ♕d3+ 29 ♗c2 (29 ♔c1 ♖d7 30 f7+ ♖xf7 31 ♖d2 ♕a3+ 32 ♔b1 ♖d7 favours Black) 29...♕a3 30 ♕g5 (30 ♗d1 ♖d7) 30...♗a2+ 31 ♔a1 ♖d7! cutting the king's escape route off and winning easily.

4) 23 ♘f5! is probably the best chance. After 23...♗xf5 (23...♖xd3? 24 ♖g1 gives White a very dangerous attack) 24 exf5 ♘a3! (24...♖xd3? 25 ♖g1 wins for White) 25 ♔d2 (25 bxa3 ♕a1+ 26 ♔d2 ♖xd3+ 27 ♔xd3 ♕xd1+ 28 ♔e3 ♖d7 and Black wins) 25...e4! 26 fxe4 (26 ♔e1 loses to 26...♖xd3) 26...♕xb2+ 27 ♔e1 ♕xf6 28 fxg6 ♔h8 Black has the advantage, although White has drawing chances thanks to Black's rather exposed king and the reduction in the number of pawns.

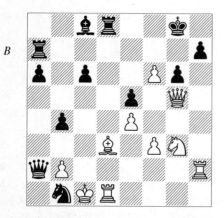

B

23   ...   ♖xd3!

This tactical shot forces a liquidation that takes the sting out of White's attack and leaves Black with a safe material advantage.

24   ♖xd3   ♕c4+
25   ♔xb1

Or 25 ♖c2 ♕xd3 26 ♕xe5 ♔f7! 27 ♕c5 (27 ♔xb1 b3) 27...♖d7 28 ♔xb1 b3 29 ♕c4+ ♕xc4 30 ♖xc4 ♖d1+ 31 ♖c1 ♖xc1+ 32 ♔xc1 ♔xf6 with a winning ending for Black.

25   ...   ♕xd3+
26   ♔c1   ♖d7

Suddenly Black is two pawns up and has strong threats against White's king.

27   f7+

This is just desperation.

27	...	♖xf7
28	♖d2	♕xf3
29	♖d8+	♖f8

0-1

Four extra pawns is too many.

This was an exceptionally complex and interesting game from which both players emerged with credit. White adopted a sharp opening and launched a direct kingside attack as soon as it was reasonable to do so. Black counterattacked on the other flank, but the attacks did not operate independently of each other; on the contrary, at every stage both players made an effort to combine attacking play on one wing with defensive play on the other. White made two errors, both involving pawn captures and both of a similar nature. The exchange on e5 was wrong because Black was better able to use the open d-file. The exchange on g6 was wrong because it opened the second rank and so made it easier for Black to defend the kingside. When there is a potential pawn exchange, there is often a temptation to make it sooner rather than later. The reason is that it is time-consuming to consider in each line what might happen with and without the exchange, and if the exchange is delayed, there is also the possibility that the opponent might exchange pawns instead. It often seems easier to clear the situation up by exchanging pawns, as it greatly simplifies all the calculations. Yet in making such a decision, one must make sure that it is justified in chess terms and is not simply laziness.

Once Black had his chance, he reacted with vigour, trying to cut the white king off along the d-file. White could still have fought, but now that the position had turned against him, he was unable to put up the greatest resistance and collapsed comparatively quickly.

The lessons here are:

1) In several openings, White launches an attack against Black's fianchettoed kingside position. Many ideas are common to all such attacks, and it is important to be aware of typical plans for both sides.

2) A rook can prove an effective defender along the second rank, while still continuing to operate aggressively along a file.

3) Avoid laziness. Clarifying the position might be a good idea, but making a pawn exchange too early can reduce one's options later.

4) Even though games are often decided by messy tactics, basic principles are frequently a useful guide to the right move. Here White did not really gain anything by exchanging so soon on g6; the opening of the second rank was always likely to prove of more value to Black than White.

Grim Defence

In our previous examples, we have dealt mainly with cases in which there was a balance between attack and defence, or between attack and counterattack – in other words the defender was not objectively worse. In an ideal world, this would always be the case, but as we all know, it is sometimes necessary to defend positions that are objectively inferior. Of such cases, the most unpleasant are those in which there is only a distant prospect of counterplay. Then one is reduced to trying to anticipate the opponent's threats, and fending them off as they arrive. However, even then one should not give up hope. Of course, since the position is actually inferior, if the opponent plays accurately then he will probably win, but one should certainly not make it easy. The first rule is not to become depressed; perhaps the position is lost, but one should resolve to put every possible obstruction in the opponent's path. Poor defence is quite common, and your opponent, unused to a resolute rearguard action, will probably be anticipating a quick victory. When it does not come, he may panic and then the errors can creep in. Another good idea is, if possible, to offer your opponent plenty of choices. This will cause him to consume time on the clock and increase the chances of confusing him.

In the following game, Anand puts these principles into action so effectively that even such a strong player as Kramnik loses his way in the complications.

Game 15
V. Kramnik – V. Anand
Belgrade 1997
Queen's Gambit Declined, Semi-Slav Defence

1	♘f3	♘f6
2	c4	

For comments on the moves up to here, see Game 11.

| 2 | ... | e6 |

With this move, Black indicates that he will probably aim for central play on the light squares, based around the move ...d5.

| 3 | ♘c3 |

The particular move-order chosen in the opening often depends as much on psychology as on objective chess considerations. Of course, 3 d4 is a perfectly playable alternative, arriving at a common position that is more often reached by 1 d4 ♘f6 2 c4 e6 3 ♘f3. However, this allows Black to continue with 3...b6 (the Queen's Indian Defence) or 3...♗b4+ (the Bogo-Indian Defence). Both these popular openings are regarded as being very solid for Black, and White

has to work hard to prove even a slight advantage against them. Kramnik's move is quite cunning; he delays d4, and so prevents Black from adopting one of these ultra-solid defences. Black can, of course, play 3...b6 or 3...♗b4 even after 3 ♘c3, but White is then by no means committed to playing d4, and indeed many players believe that White has better chances of an advantage without d4.

| 3 | ... | d5 |

Anand decides to play directly in the centre. Black now threatens ...d4, so White's options are limited to the text-move, transposing to a standard Queen's Gambit position, and 4 e3.

| 4 | d4 |

So, by a slightly circuitous route, we have arrived at one of those classical opening positions which have been played in top-level chess for over a century. Despite the enormous amount of practical experience with this position, there are still new discoveries to be made.

4   ...   c6

Black adopts the Semi-Slav pawn-structure, which we have already seen in Game 2 (although in that case White had not played ♘c3). The pawns on c6 and e6 provide exceptionally solid support for the d5-pawn, allowing Black to develop by ...♗d6, ...♘bd7 and ...0-0. Curiously, the Semi-Slav had been one of Kramnik's favourite openings for many years, so Anand's choice of opening was a little provocative.

Black's main alternatives are 4...♗e7 and 4...♘bd7, which lead to the Orthodox Queen's Gambit.

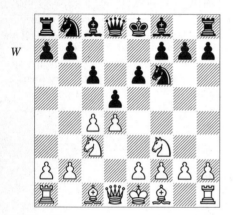

5   ♗g5

This is the most aggressive system for White, and the only one which really disrupts Black's plan of development (as outlined in the previous note). The main alternative is 5 e3, which, although relatively quiet, can still give rise to some complicated positions.

5   ...   h6

This move introduces the Moscow Variation. The main alternatives are 5...♘bd7, which transposes into lines of the Orthodox Queen's Gambit, and 5...dxc4, which leads to the fearsomely complicated Botvinnik System after 6 e4 b5 7 e5 h6 8 ♗h4.

6   ♗h4

For many years, 6 ♗xf6 ♕xf6 7 e3 was held to be White's best line against the Moscow Variation. It is certainly true that White obtains a considerable lead in development, especially as Black's queen will probably have to move again at some stage. However, Black also has a

major asset in the shape of the two bishops. Although the light-squared bishop is currently rather inactive, given time Black will bring it into play. Therefore White has to make the most of his temporary initiative, or else Black will complete his development and be at least equal. It turns out that it is not so easy for White to achieve this; Black's solid pawn-structure operates in his favour, making it hard for White to open the game up quickly. Moreover, opening up the position also helps activate Black's bishop-pair, so aggressive play by White can prove double-edged. As a result of White's failures with 6 ♗xf6, the more dynamic text-move became popular. While it offers White good attacking possibilities, it is also riskier as Black can win a pawn.

6   ...   dxc4

Black can still reach a normal Queen's Gambit by 6...♗e7 or 6...♘bd7, but there is no doubt that the text-move is the critical test of White's opening. Black grabs a pawn and intends to keep it!

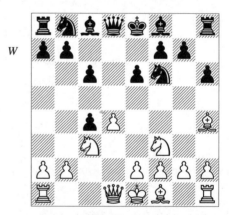

7   e4

The most natural move. Black's capture on c4 may net him a pawn, but it does give White a relatively free hand in the centre. The main alternative is 7 a4, to make it harder for Black to keep his extra pawn with ...b5. However, it is worth noting that even this does not guarantee that White will regain his pawn, since Black may continue 7...♗b4 8 e3 b5.

7   ...   g5

Black can transpose to the Botvinnik System by 7...b5 (see the note to Black's 5th move), but given that Black passed by the chance to reach the Botvinnik at move five, it is unlikely that he will change his mind now.

8   ♗g3   b5

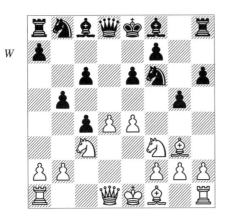

The only reasonable move. Black has made several concessions, such as surrendering the centre and weakening his kingside, so he must keep the extra pawn to justify his play.

9   ♗e2

Once again, I must return to the theme of modern gambit play (see also Games 5 and 13). Many contemporary gambits are not based on the idea of launching a quick attack against the enemy king. This is just such a case since White's compensation lies mainly in positional factors. Black has compromised his pawn-structure on both wings, and has given White a firm grip on the centre. It is true that since Black's king has no obviously safe spot, White's compensation may evolve into a direct attack on the king, but that is a consequence of the compensation rather than its primary element. It follows that White has no need to hurry and he therefore quietly completes his development, while leaving Black to face the problem of coordinating his position.

9   ...   ♗b7

This is the most popular move. It is natural for Black to develop his queenside pieces first, because it is hard to imagine them going anywhere apart from b7 and d7, so Black is not committing himself unduly. In contrast, the best square for the f8-bishop is not yet clear, so for the moment Black keeps it at home. Black should not invert his moves, because 9...♘bd7 allows a powerful central breakthrough by 10 d5!, exploiting the weak c6-square.

10   e5?!

White has a number of dangerous attacking ideas, and it is not clear which is best. The flexible 10 0-0 is popular, while the direct 10 h4 g4 11 ♘e5 h5 12 0-0 also gives White a dangerous initiative. My own view is that this pawn sacrifice is quite unpleasant for Black, but perhaps that is because I am an attacking player and so naturally tend to prefer the white side. A strong defensive player might take the opposite point of view – chess is not an exact science and there is plenty of room for personal differences.

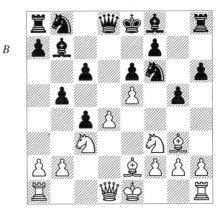

Kramnik's move aims for a more rapid attack than the (relatively!) positional 10 0-0. Playing e5 takes away a useful square from the f3-knight, and blocks in the g3-bishop, so in order to justify it White has to follow up energetically. It seems to me, though, that this wasn't really necessary and White could have obtained a promising initiative by less committal methods.

10   ...   ♘h5

This invites White to make a piece sacrifice. The alternative is 10...♘d5; after 11 h4 g4 12 ♘d2 the position is unclear – White has enough compensation for the pawn, but it is not clear whether he can claim an advantage.

11   a4?!

White could play the immediate sacrifice with 11 ♘xg5 ♘xg3 12 ♘xf7 ♔xf7 13 fxg3 ♔g8 14 0-0 ♘d7 (14...♘a6? 15 ♘e4 ♗g7 16 ♗h5! gives White a decisive attack), giving the same position as in the game, but without ...a6 and a4. This difference favours Black since, as we shall see, the possibility of capturing on b5 is an important option for White. The immediate sacrifice may be evaluated as unclear, whereas the sacrifice with ...a6 and a4 favours White.

The text-move aims to induce ...a6, in order to reach the more favourable form of the sacrifice. However, in playing a4 Kramnik gives Black the chance to avoid the sacrifice altogether.

11   ...   a6?

Anand falls in with Kramnik's plan and soon finds himself in a critical position. There were two reasonable alternatives:

1) 11...♘xg3 rules out the sacrifice on g5, but after 12 hxg3 (12 fxg3 a6 is now fine for Black) 12...♗b4 13 ♔f1, intending 14 ♘e4, White has good compensation for the pawn.

2) 11...b4! is the safest option. After 12 ♘e4 c5 (12...g4 13 ♘fd2 ♕xd4 14 ♗xc4 ♘xg3 15 hxg3 ♘d7 is more double-edged, but may be playable) 13 ♘xc5 ♗xc5 14 dxc5 ♕xd1+ 15 ♖xd1 ♘d7 the endgame is fine for Black.

12   ♘xg5!

Kramnik starts a very dangerous attack.

12   ...   ♘xg3

Forced, or else White regains the pawn with a large positional advantage.

13   ♘xf7

Forcing the king onto the f-file, which is about to be opened.

13   ...   ♔xf7

14   fxg3

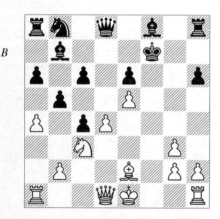

Of course, White takes this way so as operate with his rook on the open f-file. In return for the piece, White has just one pawn, but Black clearly has many problems to solve. Five of his pieces remain on their original squares, and all White's pieces except the a1-rook are ready to join in the attack. A particular worry for Black

is that the f6- and f7-squares are weak, thus providing potential entry points for a white rook. If one adds in the possibilities of ♗h5, ♕g4 and ♘e4 then things look ominous for Black. There is no doubt that Black is worse here, and moreover the position is of a type which is very difficult to play in practice and would certainly have proved too much for most players. The position is particularly complicated because both sides have several reasonable alternatives at virtually every move and because the unbalanced situation makes it hard to assess any position accurately. One should view the ensuing inaccuracies in the light of these complexities – I am sure that only a few players in the world could have done so well as Anand and Kramnik.

Having landed himself in this awkward position, Anand defends with great accuracy over the next few moves. In a grim position such as this, the basic rules are not to give up, and to put the maximum difficulty in the way of the opponent by not allowing him a clear-cut win.

14   ...   ♔g8

Already, on the very first move after the sacrifice, Black faces a difficult choice. Should the king try to flee to the queenside, or hide on the kingside? The former would provide the best solution to Black's problems, but it involves giving up the e-pawn; after 14...♔e8 15 0-0 ♔d7 16 ♖f7+ ♔e7 (or 16...♔c8 17 ♗g4 ♕e8 18 ♖f6 and e6 falls) 17 ♗g4 ♔c7 18 ♗xe6 ♖f8 19 ♖g7 ♘d7 (19...♔b6 20 d5 ♗c5+ 21 ♔h1 is very good for White, e.g. 21...cxd5 22 a5+ ♔a7 23 ♗xd5) 20 ♕h5 ♔b8 21 ♖d1 White has two pawns and very strong pressure for the piece. At the very least, White can expect to get a third pawn (on h6) while retaining many of his threats.

14...♘d7 is also dubious, because after 15 ♗h5+ Black cannot move to g8 and so must put his king on an inferior square. The various possibilities are:

1) 15...♔g8?? loses to 16 ♕g4+ ♕g5 17 ♕xe6+.

2) 15...♔e7 16 0-0 ♘xe5 (16...♕b6 17 a5 ♕a7 18 ♕g4 ♘xe5 19 ♕e4 ♘d7 20 ♖ad1 is clearly better for White) 17 dxe5 ♕xd1 18 ♖axd1 ♖h7 19 ♘e4 and White wins.

3) 15...♔g7 is relatively best, but now Black will have to waste time moving his king again

to free the h8-rook. After 16 0-0 (16 ♕g4+ ♕g5 17 ♕xe6 ♕xh5 18 ♕xd7+ ♕f7 19 ♕g4+ ♕g6 is only a draw) 16...♖h7 White can try:

3a) 17 ♗g6 ♔xg6 18 ♕g4+ ♕g5 19 ♕xe6+ ♔g7 is perpetual check.

3b) 17 ♖f7+ ♔h8 18 ♖xh7+ ♔xh7 19 ♕c2+ ♔h8 20 ♖f1 ♗g7 (20...♕g5 21 ♖f7 ♗g7 22 ♕e2 ♕c1+ 23 ♖f1 ♕g5 24 ♘e4 ♕d8 25 ♘d6 is good for White) 21 ♖f7 ♘f8 is unclear.

3c) 17 ♘e2! is the most unpleasant move, targeting both e6 and g6. After, for example, 17...♔h8 18 ♘f4 ♗b4 19 ♗g6 ♖e7 20 ♕h5 ♗d2 21 ♗f7! White has a clear advantage.

15   0-0

If Black has to surrender his e6-pawn, then White will certainly have excellent compensation for the piece, so holding on to this key pawn is his first task.

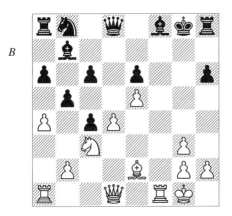

15   ...   ♘d7

Black wants to meet ♗g4 by ...♕e7 and ♗h5 by ...♖h7. Since these defences are already in place, he can afford to spend a tempo developing a piece, at the same time covering the sensitive f6-square. Instead, 15...c5!? is premature. Then White can try:

1) 16 ♕c2 ♖h7 is unclear.

2) 16 ♗g4 ♕xd4+ (16...♗c8 17 d5 b4 18 ♘e4 ♗g7 19 ♘d6 is good for White) 17 ♕xd4 cxd4 18 ♗xe6+ ♔h7 19 ♖f7+ (19 ♘d5 ♗g7) 19...♗g7 20 ♗f5+ ♔g8 21 ♖xb7 dxc3 22 bxc3 ♘c6 23 axb5 ♘xe5 24 bxa6 gives White some advantage.

3) 16 d5! exd5 17 ♗f3 ♗g7 18 ♗xd5+ ♗xd5 19 ♘xd5 ♖h7 20 ♘c7 ♕xc7 21 ♕d5+ ♔h8 22 ♖f7 ♕c8 23 ♕xa8 and Black is in serious trouble.

In the long run Black would certainly like to play ...c5 to activate the otherwise dead bishop on b7, but he must first fend off White's immediate threats.

16   ♗g4

White can force a draw by 16 ♗xc4 bxc4 17 ♕g4+ ♗g7 18 ♕xe6+ ♔h7 19 ♕f5+, but not surprisingly Kramnik goes for more.

16 ♗h5 ♖h7 17 ♕g4+ ♔h8 18 ♕xe6 wins the e6-pawn, but at the cost of dissipating White's initiative. Black would then have the chance to activate his bishop by 18...c5 with good prospects, since 19 d5 ♖e7 costs White the e5-pawn.

16   ...   ♕e7

Once again, Black cannot afford to jettison the e6-pawn, since 16...♖h7 17 ♗xe6+ ♔h8 18 ♕h5 leaves Black badly tied up, while White now has two pawns for the piece.

17   ♘e4?!

This is a natural move, since d6 is now available for the knight, but it is probably inaccurate. 17 ♕c2! is a dangerous alternative, after which Black would face serious difficulties. 17...♖h7 is bad, since after 18 ♕g6+ ♔h8 19 ♗xe6 ♕g5 20 ♕e4 White avoids the exchange of queens, and without his e6-pawn Black is bound to be struggling. One line might be 20...♖b8 21 ♖f5 ♕e7 22 ♗xd7 ♕xd7 23 ♖af1 ♔g8 24 e6 ♕d6 25 ♖f7 ♗g7 26 ♔h1, when White has a winning position. Other moves are little better; for example, 17...♗g7 18 ♕g6 ♖e8 19 ♘e4 or 17...♕e8 (preventing ♕g6+) 18 ♘e4! (now that the white queen is not on d1, White cannot reply ♗h5, but this alternative is very strong) 18...♖h7 19 ♖f6 and again the e6-pawn falls, since 19...♖e7? loses to 20 ♘d6.

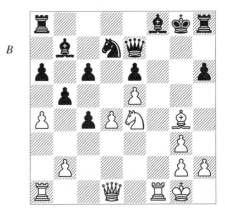

17   ...   ♖h7?!

Anand rejected 17...c5 but it might have been the best move. After the reply 18 ♘d6 Black has:

1) 18...cxd4? 19 ♖f7! (19 ♘xb7 ♘xe5! 20 ♕xd4 ♗g7 21 ♕e4 ♘xg4 22 ♕xg4 ♕xb7 23 ♕xe6+ ♔h7 24 ♖f7 ♕c8 is probably a draw) 19...♕xf7 20 ♘xf7 ♔xf7 21 ♗f3! ♗d5 22 ♗xd5 exd5 23 ♕f3+ ♔e6 (23...♔e7 24 ♕xd5) 24 ♖f1 and White's attack is too strong.

2) 18...♗d5? 19 ♗f3! (19 ♖f7 ♕d8! 20 ♕c2 ♕g5 is unclear) and now:

2a) 19...♗g7? 20 ♘f5! ♕e8 21 ♗h5 ♕d8 22 ♘xg7 ♔xg7 23 ♖f7+ ♔g8 24 h4 ♖h7 25 ♕g4+ ♔h8 26 ♖xh7+ ♔xh7 27 ♕g6+ ♔h8 28 ♕xh6+ ♔g8 29 ♗f7+! ♔xf7 30 ♖f1+ ♔g8 31 ♕g6+ ♔h8 32 ♖f7 mating.

2b) 19...cxd4?! 20 ♗xd5 exd5 21 ♕g4+ ♗g7 22 ♖f7 ♕xe5 23 ♕xd7 and although White remains a pawn down, his attack is a far more important factor; for example, 23...♗f6 (23...d3 loses to 24 ♖e7 ♕d4+ 25 ♔h1 d2 26 ♖d1) 24 ♖xf6 ♕xf6 25 ♖f1 ♕g6 26 ♘c8 and White is winning.

2c) 19...♖h7! 20 ♗xd5 (20 dxc5 ♗xf3 21 ♕xf3 ♖b8 is fine for Black) 20...exd5 21 ♕g4+ and now:

2c1) 21...♔h8 22 ♕g6 ♗g7 23 ♘f7+ ♔g8 24 ♘xh6+ ♔h8 25 ♕c6 gives White a clear advantage.

2c2) 21...♗g7 22 ♖f7 ♘xe5 23 dxe5 ♕xe5 24 ♕g6 ♕g5 25 ♕e6 ♗d4+ 26 ♔h1 ♕e5 27 ♕g6+ ♖g7 28 ♖xg7+ ♕xg7 29 ♕e6+ ♔h7 30 ♕xd5 may be slightly better for White.

2c3) 21...♖g7! is safest. After 22 ♕h3 ♖h7 White seems to have nothing better than to repeat moves.

18   ♘d6   ♖b8

At this stage White thought a long time, and made an imaginative but incorrect choice.

19   b4?

This is the wrong move. Kramnik reasons that Black's only way to free himself is to play ...c5, so he attempts to clamp down on this move. It is certainly an unexpected move, but in fact it allows Black to slip out of the net. In a situation where one has a strong bind, it is often hard to decide between slowly trying to increase the pressure and cashing in with immediate action. Here White should have chosen the latter course.

Perhaps the main defect of the text-move is that it doesn't succeed in its main ambition. Black can often play ...c5 despite White's pawn grip, since the activation of the light-squared bishop is usually worth more than a pawn. Moreover, if White meets ...c5 by bxc5 then Black obtains connected passed pawns, while White's pawn-chain e5-d4-c5 can be blockaded on the light squares.

The correct choice was 19 axb5! cxb5 (if 19...axb5, then 20 ♖a7 is good for White) 20 ♘xb7 ♖xb7 21 ♖xa6 ♖b6 (21...♘b6 22 ♖f6) 22 ♖xb6 ♘xb6 23 ♖f6 with a very unpleasant position for Black, since White obtains a third pawn for the piece and acquires two connected passed pawns in the centre of the board. The game Ward-Grabliauskas, Copenhagen 1998, played shortly after Kramnik-Anand, tested this assessment. Black was crushed after 23...♕d8 (23...♔h8 24 ♗xe6! ♗g7 25 ♖g6 leaves Black badly tied up) 24 ♗xe6+ ♔h8 25 ♕f3 (25 ♕g4 is also good) 25...♗g7 26 ♖f4 h5 27 h4 ♗h6 28 ♖f5 ♕xd4+ 29 ♔h2 ♕d8 30 ♖xh5 ♘d7 31 ♕d1 ♕e8 32 ♗xd7 ♖xd7 33 ♖xh6+ ♔g7 34 ♖d6 1-0. This line is a good example of how the addition of a4 and ...a6 helps White.

19   ...   h5!

This bid for space is essential. If White manages to play ♗h5, then Black will be virtually paralysed. Of course, 19...cxb3 is bad since 20 ♕xb3 wins the e6-pawn.

20   ♗h3

White keeps his bishop trained on the weak e6-pawn. After 20 ♗xh5 ♕g5, followed by ...♗xd6, much of White's pressure disappears, while 20 ♗f3 h4 gives Black a little freedom.

20   ...   ♗h6

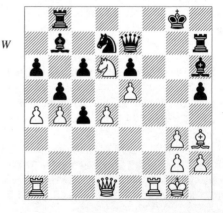

At last, one of Black's bishops shows signs of life. This is definitely a step in the right direction, but accurate play is still necessary.

21 ♔h1

Preventing ...♗e3+, and therefore threatening to take on h5.

21 ... ♗g5

Defending h5, and taking the f4- and f6-squares away from the f1-rook. Now that f6 is defended, Black might be able to disentangle his position further by ...♘f8, incidentally providing much-needed support for the e6-pawn.

22 ♕c2

This is White's idea; he intends to zigzag his queen to e4 by alternately threatening ♕g6+ and ♕xh5. After 22 ♖a3 c5! 23 dxc5 (23 ♘xb7 is met by 23...cxb4, while 23 bxc5 ♗d5 secures the e6-pawn, after which Black's connected passed pawns become very strong) 23...♗d5 24 axb5 axb5 25 ♗f5 ♖g7 26 ♖a7 ♖f8 Black is much better.

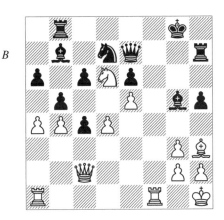

22 ... ♖g7

Black stops the check on g6. 22...♘f8 is also playable; for example, 23 ♖a3 (23 ♖f2 ♗e3 24 ♖f6 ♗xd4 gives White nothing, while 23 axb5 axb5 24 ♖a7 c5! 25 ♖xb7 ♖xb7 26 ♘xb7 ♖f7! favours Black) 23...c5 24 dxc5 ♗d5 25 axb5 axb5 26 ♖a6. However, Anand did not like to block f8, because he intends to offer the exchange of rooks by ...♖f8.

23 ♕e2

Now White attacks the h5-pawn.

23 ... ♗a8!

The strongest move. Black frees his rook to move to f8, and preserves his bishop ready for the eventual breakout with ...c5. This is in fact

the last passive move Black plays in the game. Move by move, the circumstances for a breakout have been gradually improving – Black has organized his kingside pieces and activated his dark-squared bishop, while White has made scant progress. 23...♖h7 is also playable, although less strong than the text-move since, if nothing else, White can simply repeat moves.

24 ♕xh5

White gets another pawn for the piece.

24 ... ♖f8

The natural move, but White has what appears to be an awkward reply.

25 ♘e4

This looks very unpleasant, because there is a nasty threat of 26 ♘xg5 ♖xg5 27 ♕h6 (27 ♗xe6+ is also possible), when the e6-pawn falls with disastrous consequences. Since the g5-bishop is almost trapped, it seems hard to counter this threat.

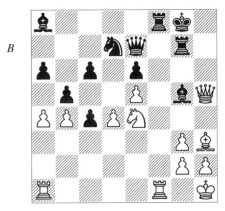

25 ... c5!!

A brilliant idea, the point of which is revealed next move. Black cannot play 25...♗e3 as 26 ♖xf8+ ♔xf8 27 ♕h8+ wins at once.

26 ♘xg5

White, of course, snaps off the bishop.

26 ... ♗d5!

Remarkable. Black simply ignores the fact that White has taken a piece and focuses on the real priority: supporting the crucial e6-pawn. 26...♖xg5 is bad as 27 ♗xe6+ ♔g7 28 ♕h4 leaves Black in a deadly pin, and White wins after 28...cxd4 29 ♗xd7 ♖xf1+ 30 ♖xf1 ♖xe5 ♕xe5 31 ♗e6!.

After the text-move, Black is genuinely threatening to take the knight. White decides simply to retreat it, but then Black acquires two connected passed pawns on the queenside.

27   ♘f3?!

This passive move is hopeless, but the alternatives all leave Black with a clear advantage: 27 ♗xe6+ (27 ♖xf8+ ♘xf8 28 ♗xe6+ ♘xe6 29 ♘xe6 ♕xe6 is also very good for Black) 27...♗xe6 28 ♖xf8+ (28 ♘xe6 ♕xe6 29 bxc5 b4) 28...♘xf8 29 ♘e4 ♖h7 30 ♕d1 (30 ♕e2 cxd4 31 ♘f6+ ♔h8 and again Black comes out on top) 30...♖xh2+! 31 ♔xh2 ♕h7+ 32 ♔g1 ♕xe4 33 bxc5 ♗d5 34 ♕d2 ♘e6 and Black should win.

27   ...   cxb4

The material balance has shifted so that instead of being a piece down, White is now a pawn up. However, everything else has changed in Black's favour. All his pieces are now on active squares, he has two well-advanced connected passed pawns and White's pieces (especially his queen and the h3-bishop) are out of play.

28   axb5   axb5

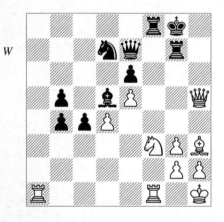

29   ♘h4

Hoping to play ♘g6, but this threat is easily countered.

29   ...   ♕g5!

If the queens are exchanged then, thanks to his offside minor pieces, White has no hope of halting the pawns. Thus, White has to duck the exchange, costing more time.

30   ♖xf8+   ♘xf8
31   ♕e8   ♖f7

Stopping ♖f1 and leaving White without a major threat in sight.

32   ♘f3

32 ♕xb5 b3 is also losing for White.

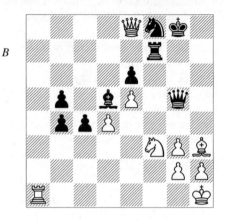

32   ...   ♕g6

By now there are several routes to victory, such as 32...♕e3 33 ♗g4 b3 34 ♗h5 ♖xf3 or 32...♕h6 33 ♗g4 c3. The text-move threatens 33...♖xf3, so White must move his queen yet again.

33   ♕xb5   b3
34   ♖f1

Or 34 ♕b4 ♖b7 and wins.

34   ...   ♕d3
35   ♔g1   ♕e3+
36   ♔h1   c3

Avoiding the last trap: 36...♖b7?? 37 ♗xe6+!.

37   ♗xe6

Desperation.

37   ...   ♗xe6
38   d5   ♖xf3!
39   gxf3

39 ♖xf3 c2 40 ♕f1 ♕xf3 41 gxf3 b2 is also dead lost for White.

39   ...   ♗h3
40   ♕c4   ♗xf1
41   ♕g4+   ♔h7
42   e6   ♘g6

0-1

This was an unusually complicated game. Starting with a double-edged opening, Kramnik soon had the chance to sacrifice a piece for a very dangerous attack. Objectively speaking, Black was in trouble. However, Anand made sure that Kramnik never had a straightforward win. Perhaps Kramnik was hoping for too much from the position, because he turned down some promising lines and tried to set up a complete bind. However, there was still room for Anand to wriggle and slowly, bit by bit, Black started to free his position. Kramnik's attack was still not dead, however, and it required an imaginative piece sacrifice by Anand before he could definitely take over the initiative. By this stage, White's attack had evaporated and the rest was slaughter.

The lessons here are:

1) In an ultra-sharp opening, it only takes one slip to end up in serious trouble.

2) Totally unexpected moves can have a great psychological impact on the opponent. However, it helps if they are also good.

3) If you have extra material in return for strong pressure, you should consider returning the material to free your position and take over the initiative.

4) Never give up.

2.3 Positional Play

If the position is quiet, and there are no tactics or attacks in progress, then the players have to think positionally. The long-term features of the position, such as the pawn-structure, assume a greater importance and both players have to evolve strategic plans which may reach far into the future. Acquiring positional skills is a lengthy process, because a lot depends on experience, but the following twelve games should provide an insight into some of the most important topics of positional chess.

We start with pawn-structure. There are many types of pawn weakness, such as doubled pawns, isolated pawns, and so on. These are usually long-term features of the position, and they are very often accepted in return for some asset, such as active pieces. Game 16 deals with the interplay between piece activity and pawn weaknesses. Another long-term asset is a space advantage, which we consider in Game 17.

Next comes a group of positional features which depend on the pawn-structure, but which are most often exploited by pieces. An *outpost* is a dominant square on which a piece can settle without being driven away by enemy pawns. Outposts usually arise on the fifth or sixth ranks. Game 18 deals with the creation and exploitation of outposts. Control of an open file can be a significant advantage, as in Game 19. A *weak colour complex* is a network of weak squares, all of the same colour. While this is clearly a function of pawn-structure, the weak squares themselves are almost always occupied by pieces. Game 20 is an excellent example of this.

Game 21 deals with the queenside attack and, in particular, the minority attack. These motifs, which are positionally based, do not really fit my definition of attack given on page 38, but since terms such as 'minority attack' are so well established, I will also use the word 'attack'. Readers should understand, however, that these are very different animals from the type of attack considered in section 2.1.

Game 22 discusses the advantage of the two bishops, and shows how such an advantage can be a long-term worry for the opponent. The dark side of the bishop is revealed in Game 23, which shows how a *bad bishop* (that is, one whose action is limited by friendly pawns) can be a fatal handicap.

Many modern openings lead to a blocked centre, with all the action taking place on the flanks. In such situations, it is important to understand how to handle pawn-chains. This is the topic of Game 24.

The next two games contrast the advantages and disadvantages of an isolated d-pawn, a feature which can arise from a wide range of popular openings. The dark side of the pawn is the danger that it will become a static weakness without any redeeming factors. This is what happens in Game 25. By contrast, Game 26 portrays a brighter picture in which the dynamic possibilities offered by the pawn are dominant. Which of these two scenarios actually happens depends on the skill of the players.

Finally, we come to the subject of *positional sacrifices*, i.e. sacrifices for long-term objectives. Such sacrifices are often very hard to judge, but can be extremely effective. Game 27 provides an example.

Bad Pawn-Structure

Textbooks usually devote a great deal of space to pawn weaknesses, perhaps because it is one of the few areas of middlegame play that can be treated systematically. Doubled pawns, isolated pawns, backward pawns, hanging pawns and so on are treated one by one. Usually the examples chosen to illustrate the exploitation of these weaknesses show a simple technical procedure leading to a win. One soon gains the impression that inflicting an isolated pawn on the opponent is tantamount to a decisive advantage. As we all know, real life is not like that. The writers of such textbooks want to make a clear-cut point, and usually select games in which the defender rolls on his back and practically asks for the *coup de grâce* to be administered. In practice, matters are usually less clear for two reasons.

Firstly, most opponents are not so generous as to accept a pawn weakness without any compensation. Normally, there is a trade involved: a weak pawn in return for active piece-play, a lead in development or some other transient advantage. Then you have to work to nullify this advantage before you can consider exploiting the weak pawns. One thing is operating in your favour: most pawn weaknesses are more or less permanent, so the burden is on your opponent to prove his compensation, whereas all you have to do is counter his plans, exchange a few pieces and reach a more simplified position where the pawn weaknesses become the dominant feature of the position.

Secondly, even if you succeed in nullifying your opponent's compensation, it may not in fact prove so easy to win the game. Once again, some writers of textbooks often employ a little sleight of hand. They choose a position in which, say, Black has an isolated pawn and show how White wins. Very often, however, the position chosen is one in which White has some other advantages in addition to the enemy pawn weakness (e.g. Black has a bad bishop, or some other weak pawns). Without really mentioning these other advantages they blame Black's defeat solely on his weak pawn. Before the 1974 Karpov-Korchnoi Candidates Final match, Karpov, as White, had won several games with a line in the French in which Black gets an isolated d-pawn (1 e4 e6 2 d4 d5 3 ♘d2 c5 4 exd5 exd5 5 ♘gf3 ♘c6 6 ♗b5). He almost made this line look like a forced win for White. In the match itself he repeatedly reached the same type of position and repeatedly failed to win. Korchnoi showed that the reason Karpov had won the earlier games was because he was stronger than his opponents, and not because the position was inherently bad. Thus you shouldn't count on a win just because of a structural advantage – good defence counts for a lot. Similarly, if you are the player with the weakness, don't give up or become depressed. Even Kasparov doesn't find it easy to win such positions without allowing some counterchances, as we shall now see.

Game 16

G. Kasparov – I. Sokolov

Olympiad, Erevan 1996

Scotch Opening

1	e4	e5
2	♘f3	♘c6

For comments on the moves up to here, see Game 7.

3	d4

This move introduces the Scotch Opening. While 3 d4 might appear a logical move, in a way White is scaling down his ambitions by playing it. Ideally, White would like to have two pawns abreast on d4 and e4. In the Ruy Lopez (see Game 7), White manages to achieve this by playing c3 and only then d4. Then ...exd4 can be met by cxd4, and White keeps his ideal pawn-centre. The defect is that in order to achieve his ambition, White has to spend quite a lot of time (♗b5-a4-b3, and advancing his pawn to h3). The Scotch operates on a different philosophy. White gives up his aspiration to form an ideal pawn-centre, and simply concentrates of getting his pieces out. For many decades, this opening was considered a rather harmless sideline in comparison to the Ruy Lopez, but then Garry Kasparov started to play it with success, and now it has been subjected to a far more detailed examination. Although the theoretical status of the Scotch is satisfactory for Black, this game shows that it can be an effective weapon.

> **3 ... exd4**

It is a kind of triumph for Black to force White to recapture with a piece on d4.

> **4 ♘xd4**

4 c3 is the so-called Göring Gambit. Black can obtain a satisfactory position by declining it with 4...d5 or 4...♘f6, but there is also little wrong with accepting it. In view of the wide range of good lines for Black, it has fallen into disuse.

> **4 ... ♘f6**

This is one of Black's two main lines in the Scotch. The other is 4...♗c5, when White has the choice between 5 ♗e3 ♕f6 6 c3, supporting his central knight, and 5 ♘xc6, doubling Black's pawns at the cost of allowing Black active piece-play.

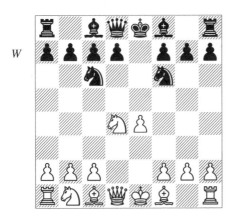

W

> **5 ♘xc6**

It is this move that has formed the basis for Kasparov's handling of the Scotch. Although it had been played before, Kasparov infused it with many new ideas. While the theoretical position is still satisfactory for Black, this game (amongst others) shows that it is not easy to handle Black's position in practice. White's idea is simple but ambitious. He at once inflicts doubled pawns on Black, and indeed these doubled pawns form the central theme of this whole game. However, in chess one can rarely get something for nothing. The price of inflicting this pawn weakness is that White will fall behind in development. The big question is whether White can consolidate his position, catch up with his development and set about exploiting the weak pawns. The alternative, 5 ♘c3, is thought insufficiently challenging; after 5...♗b4 current theory suggests that Black has no real problems.

> **5 ... bxc6**

Black's hopes rest on his piece activity, so he should not allow the exchange of queens by 5...dxc6 (which would also allow White to deprive Black of the right to castle).

> **6 e5**

This is the critical move, and the only one to justify the previous exchange. After 6 ♗d3 d5 Black can develop with ease, and White will almost certainly have to exchange on d5 at some stage, relieving Black of his doubled pawns.

> **6 ... ♕e7**

This more or less forces White to play ♕e2, after which the development of White's kingside is impeded. It can be argued that Black's kingside development is similarly obstructed, so he hasn't gained anything, but the concrete variations seem to indicate that White suffers slightly more than Black. The immediate 6...♘d5 is less effective, as after 7 ♗d3 d6 8 exd6 Black faces a typical dilemma. If he takes back with the bishop, he can develop without difficulty, but he has permanently weak pawns on the queenside. If he plays 8...cxd6, then his pawn weaknesses are less serious, but it is harder for him to activate his dark-squared bishop. In both cases, White can claim some advantage. However, 6...♘e4 is a playable alternative to the text-move.

> **7 ♕e2**

White is obliged to play this (see Game 13 for a similar manoeuvre) because after 7 f4, for example, Black can play 7...d6 rather than move his knight.

> **7 ... ♘d5**

The knight has to move, but unlike Game 13, it has a more active square available than g8!

> **8 c4**

The battle between White's better structure and Black's piece activity begins in earnest. White's main aim is to keep Black's activity under control while he develops his pieces. Black's knight is well placed on the central square d5, and White cannot easily complete his development while the knight stands ready to hop to b4 or f4 at a moment's notice. White therefore tries to kick the knight away, in order to know where it is going and if possible to sideline it completely.

8   ...   ♗a6

Black is not giving anything away and plays to maintain the knight on d5. However, this is a fairly committal move. If Black's scheme fails and the knight must eventually retreat to b6, then White will be able to secure the c4-pawn with b3, locking the a6-bishop and b6-knight out of play. Moreover, the slightly precarious position of the knight on d5 gives White some tactical opportunities (see the note to Black's 9th move, for example). For this reason, some players prefer 8...♘b6, because if White then plays b3, Black's a-pawn is still free and he can soften up White's queenside with ...a5-a4.

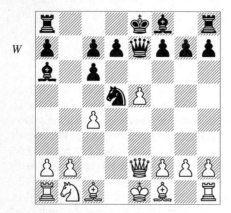

9   g3

Questions of move-order are important at this point. White's ideal plan of development is b3 and ♗b2 on the queenside, to secure the e5-pawn and lock the a6-bishop out, and g3 and ♗g2 on the kingside, to prepare castling. Obviously, this is all rather slow and gives Black plenty of time to complete his own development. It also raises the question as to whether White should start with 9 b3 or 9 g3. Kasparov has played both moves, so we cannot obtain any

guidance from the Master. After 9 b3, White has the extra option of meeting 9...g6 with 10 f4 (rather than 10 g3), but on the other hand Black has quite a few options against 9 b3 (9...g5 and 9...♕h4, for example) that don't exist against 9 g3.

9   ...   g6

The most solid move; Black simply gets on with his development. Given that White is unable to support the e5-pawn with ♗b2, it is tempting to challenge it by 9...f6, but this move is a mistake on account of 10 e6! dxe6 11 ♗g2 ♕d7 12 0-0 ♘b6 13 b3 and, at the cost of a pawn, White has secured a number of positional assets. Black's queenside minor pieces are definitely shut out, the c6-pawn is weak and exposed, and White can easily complete his development. Together, these factors are more relevant than the material, and so White has the advantage. Play might continue 13...0-0-0 14 ♘c3 ♗c5 15 ♖d1 ♗d4 16 ♗e3 e5 17 a4, when White has a strong initiative. This is a case in which it is even worth White sacrificing a pawn to stabilize the position and gain the time he needs to start exploiting Black's pawn weaknesses.

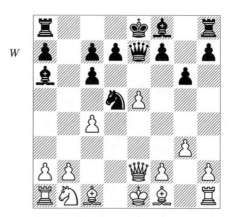

10   b3

In view of the imminent ...♗g7, White must make ready to defend his e5-pawn.

10   ...   ♗g7
11 · ♗b2   0-0

Both sides continue with their development with the key question still unresolved: will Black find a way to exploit his lead in development and active pieces before White consolidates?

12 &g2

Now White is ready to castle.

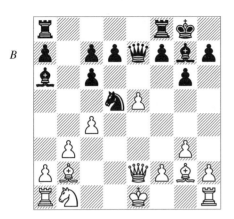

12 ... &fe8?!

Black must choose which rook to move to e8, and this certainly looks the more natural of the two. However, it is inaccurate for a very subtle reason. After 12...&ae8 13 0-0 Black, just as in the game, has the choice between:

1) 13...&b6 14 &e1 f6 (this move makes use of the position of the rook on f8) 15 &e3 (15 e6 &d6 is also unclear) 15...&e6 with chances for both sides.

2) 13...&xe5 14 &xe5 &xe5 15 &xe5 &xe5 16 cxd5 &xf1 17 &xf1 cxd5 18 &c3 c6. This ending is hard to assess. From the material point of view, Black has nothing to complain about, but he is handicapped by the immobile mass of pawns on the c- and d-files. However, it isn't easy for White to make progress and although the practical results are rather in White's favour, I suspect that the endgame should be a draw.

13 0-0

A key moment. Black must decide whether to liquidate to an ending by taking on e5.

13 ... &b6

13...&xe5 14 &xe5 &xe5 15 &xe5 &xe5 16 cxd5 &xf1 17 &xf1 cxd5 is very similar to the corresponding ending after 12...&ae8. However, White has one extra possibility here which did not exist in the note to Black's 12th move, namely 18 f4! &e3 19 &xd5. Now this gains a tempo by attacking a8, so Black has no time to respond with ...&d3 and ...&d1+, which would leave White completely tied up. After 19...&ae8 20 &d2 &d3 (20...&e2 21 &d1 &xh2 22 &g2

looks promising for White) 21 &e4 &g7 22 &c4 &f3+ 23 &f2 White has a definite advantage.

In the game, Black avoids the ending, but then he has to find another plan. The idea of playing ...f6 is far less promising when there is no rook on f8, so Black goes for a completely different plan, that of attacking the c4-pawn by ...d5. This plan is superficially tempting, because if it succeeds Black will have activated his queenside minor pieces at a stroke. However, Kasparov demonstrates that White can interfere with the clean execution of Black's plan, in which case the weakening of c6 caused by ...d5 becomes significant.

14 &e1

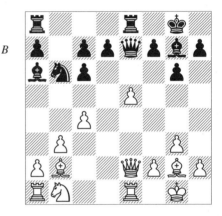

14 ... d5

In this position, White can meet 14...f6 by 15 f4, maintaining the e5-pawn. Then, for example, 15...fxe5 16 fxe5 &c5+ 17 &h1 &e7 (17...&xe5 18 &xe5 d6 19 &c3 &xe5 20 &e4 &a5 21 &b2 gives White good compensation for the pawn; note that, with the rook on f8 instead of a8, Black would have 17...&f2 here) 18 &d2 &ae8 19 &e4 gives White the advantage. Summing up, it doesn't matter whether Black wants to go for the ending or not – he is always better off playing 12...&ae8 rather than 12...&fe8.

15 &c2!

An excellent move. White spends a tempo freeing himself from the awkward pins along the a6-e2 and e8-e2 lines. At first, it looks risky to move the queen again, but Kasparov has accurately calculated that Black cannot use the time to any great effect. Now White will only need two moves to complete his development.

15 ♘d2 ♖ad8 is inferior as White no longer has a good square for his queen. 15 ♕d2 is playable but perhaps slightly less accurate than the text-move. White gains the advantage after 15...♕e6 16 cxd5 (16 ♕a5? ♗xc4 17 bxc4 ♘xc4 18 ♕c3 ♖ab8 is very good for Black) 16...cxd5 17 ♕a5 ♗b7 18 ♘d2 or 15...♗xc4 16 bxc4 ♘xc4 17 ♕c2 ♘xb2 18 ♕xb2 ♗xe5 19 ♘c3, in the latter case because the piece is worth more than Black's immobile pawn-mass on the c- and d-files. However, the simple 15...♗b7 is less clear. Then Black is threatening to take on c4 and after 16 cxd5 cxd5 he is able to force through ...c5.

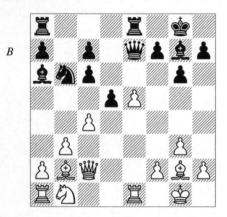

15   ...   ♖ad8

The tactical justification behind White's previous move is that 15...dxc4 loses an exchange to 16 ♗xc6. Although the text-move fails to equalize, other moves are no better:

1) 15...♗b7 16 ♘d2 allows White to complete his development.

2) 15...♕c5 16 ♕d2 threatens to trap the queen by ♗a3, and so Black has nothing better than 16...♕e7, which leaves White a tempo up over the note to his 15th move.

3) 15...♘d7 16 cxd5 (16 ♘d2 also gives White an edge) and now:

3a) 16...♘xe5 17 ♘d2 (17...♕b4 18 ♖e4 also favours White) 17...♗d3 18 ♕c1 ♕b4 19 ♖e3! (19 dxc6 ♕b6 is unclear) 19...♗f5 20 ♕e1 cxd5 21 ♘c4! ♕xe1+ 22 ♖axe1 dxc4 23 ♗xa8 ♖xa8 24 ♗xe5 gives White a clear advantage.

3b) 16...cxd5 17 ♘d2! (after 17 ♗xd5 ♘xe5 18 ♗xe5 ♖ad8 19 ♗c6 ♗xe5 20 ♗xe8 ♕f6 21 ♖xe5 ♕xe5 22 ♗xf7+ ♔xf7 23 ♘c3 the weak

light squares around the white king provide Black with sufficient compensation for the pawn) 17...♗b7 18 ♕xc7 ♘xe5 19 ♖ac1 and White has a small but permanent advantage thanks to Black's isolated d-pawn.

The text-move completes Black's development, whereas White still has to bring his queenside pieces into play. The next couple of moves are critical; if Black cannot achieve anything concrete within this short span of time, then he will be in trouble.

16   ♘d2   ♕c5

The best move, stepping up the pressure against c4. After 16...dxc4 17 ♗xc6 ♖f8 18 ♖ad1 White retains an edge as his e5-pawn is secure, Black's queenside pawns are broken and there is a continual danger of ♘e4-f6+.

17   ♖ac1

Defending the queen, and so threatening to reach a favourable ending by playing cxd5.

17   ...   d4?

Black changes his plan, and abandons the pressure against c4 in the hope of making something of his passed pawn and attack on the e5-pawn. However, in view of his out-of-play queenside minor pieces, coupled with the exposed c6-pawn, this is doomed to failure – indeed, the passed d-pawn only turns out to be an additional weakness. However, it is hard to criticize this move too harshly, as the truth is that Black did not have a really satisfactory move:

1) 17...♖e7 is strongly met by the surprising 18 ♘b1! (threatening ♗a3) 18...♖e6 19 ♕d2 (by controlling d4, White threatens to trap the queen by ♗a3) 19...♕e7 20 ♗h3 and White wins material.

2) 17...dxc4 18 bxc4 (18 ♘e4 ♕b4 19 ♗c3 ♕a3 is perhaps less clear) 18...♗xe5 (18...♖e6 19 ♘e4 and now 19...♕xc4 20 ♘c5 wins for White, while 19...♕e7 20 ♗h3 ♖xe5 21 ♗xe5 ♕xe5 22 ♖cd1 gives White a clear advantage) 19 ♘b3 ♕xc4 20 ♗xe5 ♖xe5 21 ♖xe5 ♕xc2 22 ♖xc2 ♖d1+ 23 ♗f1 ♗xf1 24 ♖c1 ♖xc1 25 ♘xc1 and White has a clear endgame advantage as the doubled and isolated c-pawns do not compensate for the extra exchange. This line is an example of how weak pawns can be a curse throughout the game. If Black had two healthy pawns for the exchange, then he wouldn't be in danger of losing, but as it is, he can only look forward to grim defence.

18   ♘f3

Defending the e5-pawn, and preparing to besiege Black's d-pawn by ♕d2, ♖cd1, etc.

18   ...   d3

If 18...♗xe5?, then 19 b4! wins a piece. After 18...♗c8 White can gain a clear advantage by 19 ♗xd4 (19 ♕d2 is another possibility, transposing to the game after 19...d3) 19...♖xd4 20 b4 ♕xc4 21 ♕b2 ♖e4 22 ♖xc4 ♘xc4 23 ♕c1 ♖xe1+ 24 ♕xe1 ♘xe5 25 ♘xe5 ♖xe5 26 ♕d2 and again Black's weak pawns tip the balance strongly in White's favour.

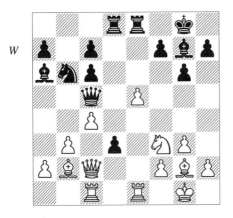

W

19   ♕d2?!

19 ♕c3 ♗c8 20 ♖cd1 ♗f5 21 h3 h5 22 ♘h4 would have been even more effective, since Black cannot defend the advanced d-pawn for long; for example, 22...♗c8 23 ♖xd3 ♖xd3 24 ♕xd3 ♗xe5? 25 ♘xg6 and White wins. Sometimes it is possible to fight on after losing a pawn, but not here, since Black still has his doubled c-pawns to contend with.

19   ...   ♗c8

The only hope for defending the pawn is to transfer the bishop to f5.

20   h3

White has a wide range of promising lines. Many players would have gone for Black's queen with 20 ♗d4 ♖xd4 21 b4 ♕xc4 22 ♖xc4 ♖xc4 but Kasparov prefers to continue his attempts to encircle the d3-pawn.

20   ...   h5

After 20...♗f5, 21 g4 picks up the pawn.

21   ♖cd1   ♗f5

22   e6?

Up to here, Kasparov has played instructively and well. Now, however, instead of simply winning a pawn, he goes in for a tactical liquidation which leads to an ending that is not so easy to win. It was both simpler and stronger to play, for example, 22 ♗c3 ♘c8 23 ♘h4 ♘e7 24 ♗b4 ♕d4 25 ♗f1 or 22 ♘h4 ♗e6 23 ♗c3 ♘c8 24 ♕e3, when Black is hardly able to avoid losing a pawn.

The rest of the game is also instructive, but the lesson is different. It proves that you should never give up, even against the world's strongest player.

22   ...   ♖xe6

After 22...♗xb2 23 exf7+ ♔xf7 24 ♕xb2, Black has an exposed king to add to his worries about his pawns. The alternative 22...fxe6 23 ♗xg7 ♔xg7 24 ♕c3+ ♔g8 25 ♘e5 leaves Black temporarily a pawn up, but with c6, d3 and g6 all weak, and with g4 coming, Black will be doing well to restrict his losses to just two pawns!

23   ♖xe6   ♗xe6

Not 23...fxe6? 24 ♗xg7 ♔xg7 25 ♕g5 ♕f8 (or else g4 wins a piece because of the pin along the fifth rank) 26 g4 hxg4 27 hxg4 and the bishop is lost in any case, as 27...♗e4 is met by 28 ♕e5+.

24   ♗xg7   ♔xg7

25   ♕c3+   ♔g8

25...f6 26 ♖xd3 leads to a position similar to the game.

26   ♖xd3   ♖xd3

27   ♕xd3

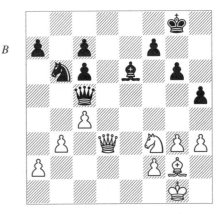

B

The position has been considerably simplified, but Black's weak pawns remain. Pawn weaknesses vary in severity according to two main factors: whether there is any possibility of liquidating the weakness, and how easy the weakness is to attack. As an example of the first factor, a backward pawn may not be a real weakness at all if it is impossible to stop the pawn advancing abreast of another pawn. The relevance of the second factor is clear: a weakness that cannot be attacked may have little practical importance.

In the current situation, Black's weaknesses come out badly. There is absolutely no hope of liquidating the doubled pawns, and the threats of ♕d8+ and ♘d4 make it clear that White will have no trouble at all bringing his pieces to bear on the weak pawns. Indeed, at first sight, White's threats will win a pawn immediately, but Sokolov finds an ingenious defence which keeps him in the game.

27 ... ♘d7!

This move fends off the immediate threats and sets a neat trap. I suspect that Kasparov would not have gone in for the liquidation if he had seen this defence.

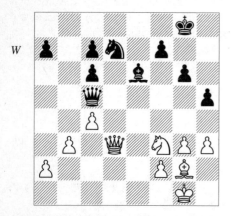

W

28 ♕c3?!

The obvious 28 ♘d4? is met by the surprise tactic 28...♗xh3! 29 b4 (not 29 ♗xh3 ♘e5 followed by 30...♕xd4) 29...♕b6 30 ♘xc6 ♗xg2 31 ♘e7+ ♔f8 32 ♕xd7 ♗f3! and there is no mate. Thus White cannot win a pawn by force, and Black has greatly improved his position by finally bringing his offside knight back into the game. 28 ♕e4! would probably have been stronger, centralizing his queen. After 28...♘f8 29 ♘d4 ♕a3 30 ♕c2 c5 31 ♘c6, for example, Black's position is miserable.

The text-move shifts the queen out of harm's way, and so genuinely threatens ♘d4.

28 ... ♗f5

Best. After 28...♘f8 29 ♘e5 ♗d7 30 b4 ♕d6 31 c5 ♕d1+ 32 ♔h2 ♕e2 33 ♕d4 ♗e6 34 a4 the c6-pawn cannot be saved. If 28...♕a3, then 29 ♘d4 ♕xa2 30 ♘xe6 fxe6 31 ♗xc6 ♘f8 leaves Black with a very unpleasant position.

29 ♘d4 ♕e5

Now Black is able to occupy the centre with his own queen – another change in Black's favour.

30 ♕d2

Threatening ♘xc6, so the reply is virtually forced.

30 ... c5
31 ♘xf5

White decides to play for the win of a pawn. This is by no means a forced win, but it requires accurate play by Black and was a good practical chance in view of Sokolov's time-trouble.

31 ... ♕xf5
32 ♕a5

White's queen attacks all three weak pawns on the queenside; it is inevitable that one of them will be lost. The only question is whether Black can drum up any counterplay on the kingside with his queen and knight.

32 ... ♘e5

Again best. 32...♕b1+ 33 ♔h2 ♕b2 34 ♕xc7 wins for White.

33 ♕xa7

33 ♕xc7 ♘d3 34 f4 is also dangerous, but Black can hang on by 34...♔g7 35 ♕e7 (35 ♕a5?! h4 36 ♕c3+ f6 37 ♗f1 ♘b4 gives Black good counterplay; 35 ♕d8 is met by 35...♘c1) 35...♕e6 36 ♕xe6 fxe6 37 a3 a5 38 ♗e4 ♘c1 39 ♗c2 ♘e2+ 40 ♔f2 ♘d4 41 ♗d1 and it is not clear if White can win.

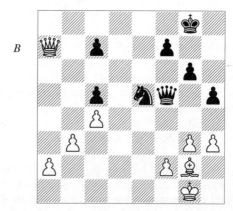

B

33	...	h4?

This time-trouble blunder allows White's queen to return to the centre, after which Black's counterplay is dead and the a-pawn will decide the game. 33...♘d3 would still have offered reasonable chances of survival. After 34 f4 Black has:

1) 34...h4?! 35 ♕a8+ ♔g7 36 ♕e4 ♕xe4 (after 36...hxg3 37 ♕xf5 gxf5 38 a4 White wins easily) 37 ♗xe4 ♘c1 38 a4 ♘xb3 39 gxh4 and the extra pawn coupled with the outside a-pawn is decisive. The win is lengthy but not difficult: 39...f5 40 ♗f3 ♘a5 41 ♗e2 ♔h6 42 ♔f2 ♘c6 43 ♔e3 ♘a5 44 ♔d3 ♘c6 45 ♔c3 ♘a5 46 ♗f3 (now Black is in zugzwang and must allow White to liquidate his doubled pawn with h5) 46...♔g7 47 h5 gxh5 48 ♗xh5 ♔h6 49 ♗f3 ♔g6 50 ♗e2 ♔h6 51 ♔d3 (the king begins the trek back to the kingside) 51...♔g6 52 ♔e3 ♔h6 53 ♔f2 ♔g6 54 ♔g3 ♔h6 55 h4 ♔g6 56 h5+ ♔h6 57 ♔h4 ♘b3 58 ♗d3 ♘a5 59 ♗xf5 ♘xc4 60 ♗e6 and White finally wins.

2) 34...♘c1! and now:

2a) 35 ♕xc7? ♘e2+ 36 ♔h2 (36 ♔f2 ♕c2 is also not clear) 36...♕d3 37 f5 ♕e3 38 h4 gxf5 39 ♕d8+ ♔h7 (39...♔g7? loses to 40 ♕g5+ ♕xg5 41 hxg5 ♘c1 42 a4 ♘xb3 43 ♔h3) 40 ♕g5 ♕g1+ 41 ♔h3 ♕f2! 42 ♕xh5+ ♔g7 43 ♕g5+ ♔h7 with a draw by repetition.

2b) 35 ♕b8+ ♔g7 36 ♕xc7 ♘xa2! (now 36...♘e2+ 37 ♔f2 is winning for White since he has a check on e5) and although White has an extra pawn, Black has good drawing prospects.

34	♕a8+	♔g7
35	♕e4	

Now it's all over because White keeps his passed a-pawn.

35	...	♕f6

35...♕xe4 36 ♗xe4 also wins easily.

36	♕xh4	1-0

This game falls into two phases. In the first, Kasparov adopted an ambitious plan to inflict pawn weaknesses on his opponent, even at the cost of falling behind in development. When Sokolov committed a slight inaccuracy in the opening (12...♖fe8?!), Kasparov started to gain control of the game. A further error on move 17 left Black with a clutch of weak pawns to nurse, and some offside pieces to boot. Rather surprisingly, Kasparov failed to finish the game cleanly, instead liquidating to an ending. Perhaps he expected the win to be a simple technical task, but just at this moment Sokolov started to defend with great ingenuity. In the second phase, Sokolov managed to bring his offside pieces back into play, which meant that he had only his weak pawns to contend with. However, very accurate defence was still required and just when it appeared that he might reach a draw, Sokolov made one further error and the game was abruptly over.

The lessons here are:

1) Pawn weaknesses tend to be long-term features of the position. If your opponent has weak pawns, you usually need not hurry to exploit them.

2) Falling behind in development can be dangerous, unless you are sure your opponent cannot exploit it.

3) If you can administer a lethal blow, do so even if it means a little calculation.

4) Exploiting a single pawn weakness is not easy unless one also has some other advantage.

Space Advantage

In general, it is an advantage to control more space. The reason is that it is easier to manoeuvre pieces in a wide-open area than a confined one. In particular, it is easier to switch pieces from one area of the board to another. Thus, a space advantage is most effective when there are weaknesses in the opposing position, especially if the weaknesses are well separated. The side with more space can switch the attack from one weakness to another, while his more restricted opponent cannot respond with the same speed.

Despite the above, attitudes to space advantages have changed in the past few decades. It is now recognized that if the side with less space has a solid position, it may be very difficult to exploit the space advantage. Indeed, the side with more space must take care not to become over-extended and vulnerable to a sudden counter-attack. This principle is nowhere more evident than in the 'Hedge-hog' opening system, which arises in the following game.

Game 17
A. Karpov – Z. Ribli
Olympiad, Dubai 1986
English Opening, Hedgehog System

1   c4

This is the first game in the book to feature 1 c4, a move which is called the English Opening. Like the Réti Opening, 1 ♘f3 (see Game 1), it serves a useful purpose while not making any great commitment. Playing c4 stakes out a claim in the centre, and restrains Black from playing an immediate ...d5, since this would involve the exchange of his central d-pawn for White's less central c-pawn. At the same time, White leaves his central pawns unmoved while he waits to see how Black intends to respond.

1   ...   c5

This symmetrical reply mimics White's strategy. Black has a wide range of alternatives, ranging from the fairly committal 1...e5, through 1...e6, 1...c6, 1...d6 and 1...g6 to the flexible 1...♘f6 and 1...c5 (as played).

2   ♘f3

No matter what happens in the centre, the white knights will almost certainly be best placed at c3 and f3, so White preserves maximum flexibility by bringing them out first.

2   ...   ♘f6

Black again preserves the symmetry.

3   ♘c3

Again, White keeps his options open. He may play d4 at some stage, which allows the exchange of his central d-pawn for Black's less central c-pawn, but in compensation White would create free play for his pieces. The logic here is rather similar to that behind 3 d4 in the Sicilian (see Game 8); while the exchange of pawns leaves Black with a central majority, White's greater control of space and active pieces are just as important.

3   ...   e6

Black breaks the symmetry. 3...♘c6 is also playable, when White has to choose between 4 d4, 4 g3 and 4 e3. As with most symmetrical openings, Black can maintain his imitation for

a certain time, but at some point (usually when the central pawns come into contact) he will be unable to do so for tactical reasons. Then Black has to come up with a satisfactory way to break the symmetry or fall into a bad position. Symmetrical openings are usually fairly solid, but they can be risky because it is easy to fall into a passive position. In this game, Ribli breaks the symmetry early on.

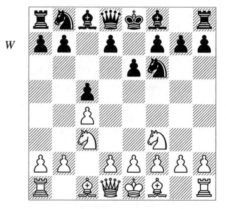

W

4   g3

After 4 e3, symmetry might well be restored, but since Black has chosen to develop his f8-bishop along the f8-a3 diagonal, Karpov takes the chance to develop his f1-bishop along the other diagonal.

4   ...   b6

The most popular and logical move. Once Black has played ...e6, it will be hard to develop his c8-bishop along the c8-h3 diagonal, so b7 is its obvious destination. However, once White's bishop is on g2, ...b6 may not be playable so Black makes sure his bishop is developed before White can exert pressure on his queenside.

5   ♗g2   ♗b7

A useful side-effect of Black's bishop development is that White's e4 is prevented.

6   0-0

At some stage, White would like to play d4, but then he has to decide how to meet ...cxd4. Taking back with the queen is possible, but the queen is clearly rather exposed on d4. Ideally, White would like to recapture on d4 with the knight but the problem with ♘xd4 is that it allows Black to exchange bishops on g2. White is playing for a space advantage, and a key principle is that the side with the space advantage should avoid piece exchanges. The reason is that the side with little space will always have problems with pieces stepping on each other's toes, and the congestion is worse when there are more pieces crammed into a small space. One possibility for White is to play ♖e1 followed by e4, and only then d4 and ♘xd4, since the bishop exchange has been prevented.

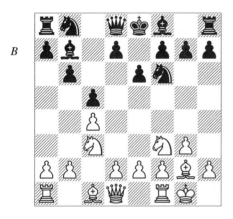

B

6   ...   d6

Black is heading for a so-called 'Hedgehog' position, which is characterized by the row of pawns along the third rank at a6, b6, d6 and e6. The most precise move-order to reach this position is to some extent a matter of taste, as the moves ...a6, ...d6 and ....♗e7 will all occur at some stage. However, 6...♗e7 may be the most accurate, since after 7 ♖e1 Black retains the option of crossing White's plan by playing 7...d5.

The immediate 6...d5 7 cxd5 ♘xd5 8 ♘xd5 ♗xd5 9 d4 favours White, as the position is opening at a time when he is considerably ahead in development.

7   d4

Karpov does not try to exploit Black's move-order by playing 7 ♖e1, and heads straight for a standard Hedgehog position.

7   ...   cxd4
8   ♕xd4

The exposed position of the queen is a lesser evil than allowing Black to free his position by exchanging light-squared bishops.

8   ...   a6

This will be necessary sooner or later, or else Black's d6-pawn will come under intolerable pressure after, for example, ♖d1 and ♘b5.

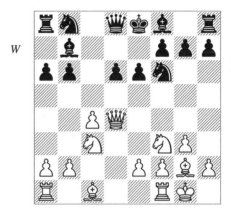

W

9   ♖d1

The quick build-up along the d-file forces Black to take care, or else he may lose his d6-pawn to b3 and ♗a3.

9   ...   ♗e7

Getting ready to castle.

10   b3

Even if White doesn't manage to exploit the d6-pawn with ♗a3, the b2-square will still be an effective post for the bishop.

10   ...   ♘bd7

It might seem odd not to exploit the white queen's exposed position by 10...♘c6, but after 11 ♕f4 Black has real problems countering White's build-up against d6 by ♗a3, ♖d2 and ♖ad1. With the knight on d7, this plan can be met by ...♘c5.

11   e4

White consolidates his grip on the centre and makes sure that Black cannot free himself by playing ...d5. A second point is that White might organize a quick breakthrough by e5.

11   ...   ♕c8

This interesting idea had only been played a handful of times before the present game, but has since become very popular. Black's immediate concern is to counter the threat of a breakthrough by ♗a3 followed by e5. 11...0-0, for example, allows 12 ♗a3 ♘c5 13 e5 dxe5 14 ♕xd8 ♜fxd8 15 ♘xe5 ♗xg2 16 ♚xg2 with a rather unpleasant ending for Black. The c6-square is weak, the knight on c5 is awkwardly pinned, and in the longer term, White's queen-side majority might prove a useful factor. 11...♕b8 is reasonable, but even here 12 ♗a3 ♘c5 13 e5 dxe5 14 ♕xe5 ♘cd7 15 ♕xb8+ ♜xb8 16 ♗b2 is not completely equal – White preserves a slight edge. The text-move aims for an improved version of this line should White adopt the same plan.

12   ♗b2

White abandons the idea of a central break-through and contents himself with simply de-veloping his remaining pieces. After 12 ♗a3 ♘c5 13 e5 dxe5 14 ♘xe5 (White is unable to play 14 ♕xe5? because of the tactical point 14...♘cd7 winning a piece – this does not work with Black's queen on b8 – and therefore has to content himself with the less dangerous knight capture) 14...♗xg2 15 ♚xg2 ♕b7+ 16 ♚g1 0-0 the position is equal. The fact that the queens are not exchanged makes a big difference. The weakness of c6 is irrelevant, the c5-knight is not pinned, and with queens on the board White's queenside majority is unlikely to be an important factor.

12   ...   0-0

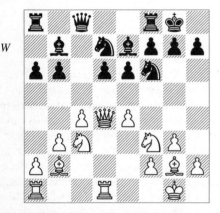

This position is typical for Hedgehog set-ups. White controls four ranks and Black three, and there is a no-man's-land of one rank which is inaccessible to White's pieces because all the squares are controlled by Black's 'hedgehog' pawns on the third rank. At one time, a position

such as this would have been assessed as highly favourable for White, but now we know better. Although a space advantage is a positive factor, it is not an end in itself – one still has to find a way to make progress.

White's problem in the diagram position is that Black's position is without weaknesses. The d6-pawn is a potential weakness, but it is very easy to defend by ...♕c7, ...♜fd8 and if necessary ...♘c5. There are no obvious pawn breakthroughs by White, except for e5, but nor-mally this leads only to exchanges. Therefore, White must manoeuvre slowly, in the hope of making progress somewhere or another. One idea might be a kingside pawn advance with h3 and g4-g5. However, this is very weakening and after Black replies with ...♜fd8 and ...♘e8 it isn't clear that White has achieved anything other than to expose his own king.

On the other hand, once Black has com-pleted his development by ...♕c7, ...♜fd8 and ...♜ac8, it isn't clear what *he* can achieve. Black would like to force through a liberating move such as ...b5 or ...d5, but unless White is care-less this won't be possible. Thus games with the Hedgehog tend to be slow manoeuvring struggles, with both sides taking care not to create any weakness. Positions of this type cer-tainly suit Karpov, and he puts his talent to good use in this game. Objectively speaking, White has only the faintest edge. Perhaps his only advantage is that if White plays solidly, there is nothing at all Black can do, whereas White has some chances to undertake a positive plan even against good defence by Black.

13   ♘d2

White has various possible plans, and Kar-pov typically goes for one involving little risk. This move supports the pawns on e4 and c4, and by defending c4 opens up the possibility of queenside expansion by a3 and b4. In the long run, White could then hope for a4-a5 followed by an exchange on b6, with a weak a6-pawn as the ultimate prize. Another idea would be 13 ♜ac1 ♜e8 14 ♕e3 ♕c7 15 ♘d4, which places both white knights on useful squares. Then White might aim for a slow-motion attack on the kingside with f4, h3 and g4, etc. However, as noted above, such a plan is not without its risks.

13   ...   ♕c7

Black is content to bring his a8-rook into play.

14   ♖ac1

White develops his last piece.

14   ...   ♖ac8

15   h3

For the moment White wants to keep Black guessing about his eventual plan, so he plays this little tidying-up move. It prevents an attack by ...♘g4 in case White plays ♕e3, while at the same time Black is left to wonder if this might not be intended to support a later g4.

15   ...   ♖fe8

Black also completes his development.

16   a3

White prepares b4. This move slightly weakens b3, but the knight on d2 secures this square against an attack by ...♘c5.

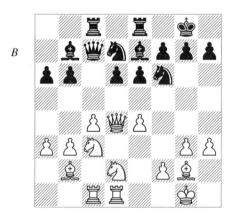

16   ...   ♕b8

Black is also doing his best to remain flexible. He might follow up this move by either ...♗a8, aiming to play ...b5, or ...♕a8 to exert more pressure against e4.

17   b4

At last, White makes a definite commitment. He gains more space on the queenside and keeps a black knight out of c5, but at the cost of weakening the c4-pawn. At the moment White is still a long way from creating a definite threat on the queenside, but the lurking danger of a4-a5 is a constant worry for Black.

17   ...   ♖ed8

As is usual in the Hedgehog, both sides manoeuvre, trying to anticipate the opponent. Black puts his rook opposite the white queen 'just in case'.

18   ♕e3

White would like to support a4-a5 with ♘b3, but at the moment 18 ♘b3 ♘e5 would more or less force the knight to return to d2. Therefore, White first locates his queen on the safer square e2 before contemplating ♘b3.

18   ...   ♗a8

18...♘e5 is unwise; after 19 ♕xb6 ♖xc4 (19...♘xc4 20 ♘xc4 ♖xc4 21 e5 wins material) 20 f4 ♖c6 21 ♕d4 ♘ed7 22 ♘b3 followed by ♘a5 White is slightly better.

The text-move threatens 19...b5.

19   ♕e2

There is still no real threat to play ♘b3, since Black can again reply ...♘e5. White would first have to play f4 in order to continue with this plan, but every pawn advance creates a potential weakness, and at the moment White is not ready for this.

19   ...   ♘e8

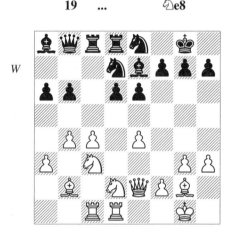

Black toys with the idea of playing ...♗f6.

20   ♘f1

The idea behind this move is the possible transfer of the knight to e3, where it again covers c4 but is otherwise more actively placed. Although this would make a4-a5 harder to achieve, with his knights so well placed White might again consider playing on the kingside. This sort of manoeuvring game, in which White toys first with this idea and then with that one, is very unpleasant to play against. Black must constantly be on the alert to counter attempts by White to make progress, while he has few active possibilities himself. The position itself does not significantly favour White, but this type of game is one which nobody played better than Karpov in his heyday. Of course, such lei-surely manoeuvres are only possible because Black is unable to improve his position.

20   ...   ♗b7

Black spots the defect in White's ♘e3 plan, namely that it weakens the e4-pawn. Therefore he prepares ...♕a8 and ...♘ef6.

21   ♔h2

Karpov does not want to commit himself to putting the knight on e3, so he again tidies up his position. If he eventually plays f4, it will be useful to have his king off the a7-g1 diagonal.

21   ...   ♘ef6

Now the pressure against e4 definitely rules out ♘e3.

22   ♘d2

So Karpov abandons that plan, and plays his knight back to d2.

22   ...   ♘e8

Ribli is content to have forced Karpov to retract his plan, and puts his knight back on e8.

23   ♖e1

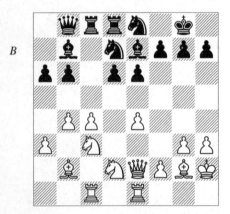

B

White introduces a new idea: he wants to play ♘b3, meeting ...♘e5 by ♘d1. Then he will either support the c4-pawn with ♘e3, or simply kick Black's knight away by f4.

23   ...   ♗a8

Black waits, but 23...♖c7 might be slightly more accurate, as Black can then build up against c4 more rapidly. In this case, the plan with ♘b3 would not be viable, and White would have to try something else.

24   ♘b3

White is slowly moving in the right direction on the queenside.

24   ...   ♗g5

Attempting to pressurize c4 by 24...♘e5 25 ♘d1 ♕c7 is not very effective. After 26 ♘e3 Black cannot step up the pressure any further, hence White will be able to drive the knight away by f4.

The text-move aims to induce f4, perhaps on the basis that this would be one pawn advance too many and would lead to the over-extension of White's position. It is often quite hard to judge whether such an advance is space-gaining and therefore favourable for White, or weakening and therefore favourable for Black. The same comment applies to many pawn advances, but it is especially relevant to cases in which the side pushing the pawn has already made a number of other pawn advances. This steady gain of space may eventually squeeze the opponent to death, or it may open up the possibility for counterplay – everything depends on the level of piece support for the pawn advances. Here White's forces are well coordinated and can take on the additional burden created by the new pawn advance.

25   ♖c2

The move-order doesn't matter very much. Karpov plays ♖c2 before f4, but he could also have reversed the order of these two moves. The battle over the next few moves revolves around the c4-pawn. If White can maintain the pawn while keeping his knight on b3, then he will have made progress, but if his knight has to retreat to d2 then Black will have foiled another attempt by White to achieve something.

25   ...   ♖c7

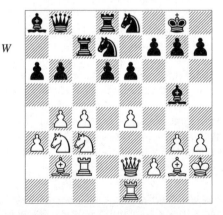

W

Rather late in the day, Black decides to double rooks.

26	f4

This is essential if White is to double rooks.

26	...	♗f6
27	♖ec1	♖dc8

After this, White is forced to move his knight from c3.

28	♘d1

Now the exchange of dark-squared bishops is more or less inevitable. This favours Black in one respect, since the exchange of a pair of minor pieces should favour the player with less space. On the other hand, the d6-pawn was quite economically defended by the e7-bishop, and now Black will have to tie up one of his other pieces in its defence.

28	...	♗b7

Black foresees that one of his knights will occupy f6 once the bishops are exchanged. This will provide him with ready-made pressure against e4, which he can now augment by ...♕a8.

28...b5 was the alternative, but with White's knight already on b3 it is less attractive. After 29 ♘a5 ♗xb2 30 ♘xb2 Black has the problem that an exchange on c4 would bring a white knight into an excellent position to attack the d6-pawn.

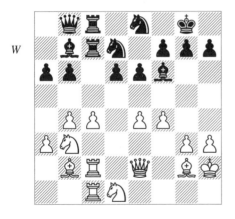

29	♕d3

The queen eyes the potentially weak d6-pawn.

29	...	♗xb2
30	♘xb2

Now that White has c4 securely defended, Black's main task should be to rearrange his rooks so that d6 is defended, thereby releasing the knight from e8.

30	...	♕a8
31	♘d1

The knight must be ready to meet ...♘df6 by ♘f2.

31	...	a5?

Up to this point, Black has not made any mistakes, and White's space advantage has not conferred any real advantage, because there simply haven't been any targets to attack. Now, however, Black suddenly loses patience and voluntarily removes one of the 'spines' of the Hedgehog. The result is a serious weakness at b5. The correct continuation was 31...♖d8, so as to defend the d6-pawn with the rook. In this case, Black's position would be without weaknesses, and White would find it hard to make progress.

32	♘d4

The d1-knight cannot go to b5, because of the weakness of c4, but the other knight can arrive there with no less effect. Now the d6-pawn is a genuine target and White's space advantage has something to bite on.

32	...	♖d8

To support d6 and provide a retreat for the other rook. 32...♗a6 is bad in view of 33 e5 d5 34 ♘e3 ♕b8 35 b5 dxc4 36 ♘xc4 with a nice pair of weak squares to jump into at c6 and d6.

33	♘b5

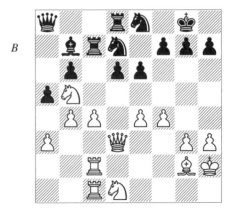

33	...	♖cc8
34	♘dc3

Having forced Black to undouble, the pressure against c4 is relieved, and the other knight can lend a hand. Black's clumsy rook manoeuvres are typical of the problems caused by lack of space. Note that 34 ♘xd6? ♘df6 35 e5

♗xg2 36 ♖xg2 ♘xd6 37 exd6 ♘e4 38 d7 ♖c7 is fine for Black.

34   ...   ♕b8

Reinforcement for d6.

35   ♖d1

Black is no longer able to mount any counterattack against c4, since both ...♘e5 and ...♕c7 are ruled out. Therefore, White is free to switch his rooks to the d-file to step up the attack on d6.

35   ...   ♘df6

Black has now manoeuvred his pieces into the best possible defensive positions and can only sit and wait to see how White intends to make progress.

36   ♖cd2   h6

This move relieves any back-rank worries and might prove useful if White tries to expand on the kingside by g4-g5.

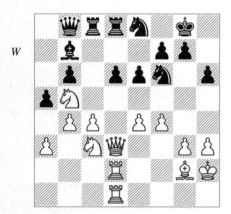

37   ♕e2

With the time-control approaching, neither side undertakes any positive action. White could win material by 37 e5 dxe5 38 ♕xd8 but after 38...♗xg2 39 ♕d3 ♗a8 the situation would not be at all clear. Black has one pawn for the exchange, and his active bishop is well placed to generate threats against White's rather exposed king.

37   ...   ♗a8?!

38   ♔g1?!

In time-trouble, both players miss the strong possibility 38 bxa5! bxa5 39 ♖b2 ♗b7 40 e5 dxe5 41 ♗xb7 ♕xb7 42 ♘d6, when White wins material.

38   ...   ♗c6

39   ♔h2   e5

Waiting passively was not very satisfactory; for example, 39...♗a8 40 bxa5 bxa5 41 ♖b2 winning as in the note to White's 38th move, or 39...axb4 40 axb4 ♗a8 41 ♖a2, when the open a-file provides White with another method of tormenting Black. Therefore Black makes a move in the centre, and cuts out the possibility of White playing e5. The defect is that this advance makes it easier for White to gain further space on the kingside.

40   f5

Now White has the obvious plan of g4 followed by h4 and g5, pushing Black back on the kingside.

40   ...   ♕a8

41   g4

Not 41 ♘xd6 ♘xd6 42 ♖xd6 ♖xd6 43 ♖xd6 axb4 44 axb4 ♕a3, when Black regains the pawn.

41   ...   ♕b8

42   h4   ♕b7

Black takes some action against White's kingside advance. The queen is to be transferred to e7, where it casts a glance towards both the b4-pawn and the g5-square.

43   ♗f3

Again, it would be wrong to grab the d6-pawn. After 43 ♘xd6 ♘xd6 44 ♖xd6 ♖xd6 45 ♖xd6 ♕e7 46 ♕d1 ♘e8 White's pawns are suddenly dropping off.

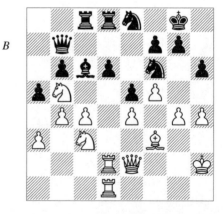

43   ...   ♕e7

This is the best square for the queen. Black intends to meet g5 by ...♘h7, when White will have trouble maintaining the advanced pawn on g5.

44   ♔g3?!

Karpov is content just to play positionally, but this allows Black a chance to break out from his passive position, based on tactical chances provided by the position of the king at g3. 44 ♔g2 would have been sounder, retaining White's advantage.

44   ...   axb4

It is undoubtedly correct to take advantage of the chance to break out, but in fact it is not so easy for White to win even if Black defends passively (and if White had played 44 ♔g2, then Black would have been forced to adopt this option). After 44...♗a8 45 ♖h1 ♗c6, for example, 46 ♖dd1 (46 g5 ♘h7 is unclear) 46...axb4 47 axb4 d5 48 cxd5 ♗xb5 49 ♘xb5 ♕xb4 50 g5 ♖c4! 51 gxf6 ♕xb5 52 ♖c1 ♖dc8 53 ♖xc4 ♕xc4 54 ♕xc4 ♖xc4 55 fxg7 b5 is unclear, as White's bishop is seriously restricted by his own pawns. White's problem is that it is not easy to prepare g5 without allowing Black to break out under more favourable circumstances than in the game. Of course, White would still have a clear advantage, but Black would not be lost.

45   axb4   d5!

This was the point behind Black's previous move.

46   cxd5

46 exd5 ♗xb5 47 ♘xb5 ♘d6 48 ♘xd6 ♕xd6 attacks b4 and threatens ...e4+.

46   ...   ♗xb5
47   ♘xb5

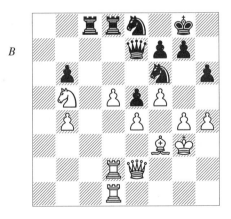

47   ...   ♕xb4?

It is natural to restore material equality, but in fact it was more important to blockade White's dangerous d-pawn by 47...♘d6!. The idea is to play on a pawn down, but with a good

knight against a very bad bishop. Then Black has good drawing chances, e.g. 48 ♘xd6 (48 ♖a1 ♘xb5 49 ♕xb5 ♖c3 gives Black unpleasant counterplay – this is another case in which the white king is poorly placed on g3) 48...♕xd6 (48...♖xd6 49 ♖c2 is very good for White) 49 g5 (49 ♕b5 ♖c3 50 ♖d3 ♖c2 51 ♖1d2 ♖c1 is also not clear) 49...♘h7 50 ♕e3 hxg5 51 hxg5 ♕xb4 and White is not able to exploit the h-file as in the game.

48   g5

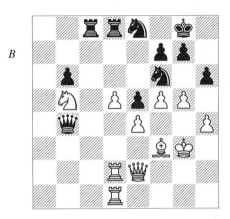

White tries to kick the black knight to an inferior square.

48   ...   hxg5

Opening the h-file is asking for trouble, but the alternatives are also unsatisfactory:

1) 48...♘h7 49 d6 ♖c5 50 ♖b2 ♕c4 51 ♕xc4 ♖xc4 and Black's passively placed pieces give White the chance to win by 52 d7 ♘c7 53 ♘d6 ♖d4 54 ♖xd4 exd4 55 ♗h5! ♖xd7 56 ♗xf7+ ♔f8 57 g6 ♘f6 58 e5, etc.

2) 48...♖c4 would have put up more of a fight:

2a) 49 gxf6 ♕xb5 50 ♖c2 (50 fxg7 ♕c5) 50...♖c5 (50...♖dc8 51 ♖xc4 ♖xc4 52 d6 ♘xf6 53 d7 wins for White) 51 ♕xb5 ♖xb5 52 fxg7 ♔xg7 is comfortable for Black.

2b) 49 ♖b2! ♘xe4+ 50 ♗xe4 (50 ♔g2 ♕a4 favours Black) 50...♖xe4 51 ♖xb4 ♖xe2 52 d6 is very good for White despite the minus pawn: 52...♖c2 (52...♖d7 53 ♖c4!) 53 d7 ♘c7 54 ♘a7 ♘a8 (the alternative 54...b5 55 ♖d6 is also very good for White) 55 ♘c8 hxg5 56 hxg5 f6 57 gxf6 gxf6 58 ♖g4+ with a large advantage for White.

49   hxg5   ♘h7

49...♖c4 gives White the pleasant choice between 50 ♖b2 ♘xe4+ 51 ♗xe4 ♖xe4 52 ♖xb4
♖xe2 53 d6, as in the note to Black's 48th move,
and 50 gxf6 ♕xb5 51 fxg7 ♘xg7 (51...♔xg7
52 ♕e3 gives White a winning attack) 52 ♕h2
f6 53 ♖h1, when White's attack is too strong.

50   d6!

Now there will be no blockade of the d-
pawn, and Black's queen cannot return to the
kingside. Black has no time to take on g5, because White threatens 51 d7.

50   ...   ♖c5

51   ♖b2

51 ♕h2 ♖xb5 52 ♖h1 (52 ♕xh7+ ♔xh7 53
♖h1+ ♔g8 54 ♖dh2 allows Black to escape by
54...♕e1+) also wins: 52...♖xd6 53 ♕xh7+ ♔f8
54 f6 ♘xf6 (54...gxf6 55 g6! fxg6 56 ♕a7 and
Black cannot meet the threat of ♖h8#) 55 gxf6
gxf6 56 ♖xd6 ♖xd6 57 ♖d1 ♕c7 58 ♗h5 and
there is no defence to 59 ♖d8+. However, the
text-move is even more effective.

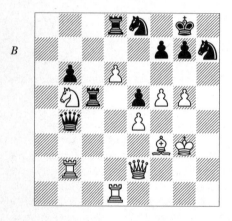

51   ...   ♕c4

51...♕a5 52 ♖h1 ♘xd6 53 ♘xd6 ♖xd6 54
♖a2 is also decisive.

52   ♕h2

This works now that Black no longer has the
...♕e1+ defence.

52   ...   ♖xb5

Ribli generously allows a neat finish.

53   ♕xh7+!

Forcing mate in a further four moves.

53   ...   ♔xh7

54   ♖h2+   ♔g8

55   ♖dh1   f6

Or 55...g6 56 ♖h8+ ♔g7 57 ♖1h7#.

56   ♖h8+   1-0

It is mate next move.

This was a typical 'Hedgehog' game, with
both sides manoeuvring slowly around, looking
for an opportunity to undertake some concrete
action. For a long time, the balance was preserved, until Black voluntarily weakened his
position with 31...a5, giving White the opportunity to mount serious pressure against the d6-
pawn. This, coupled with the possibility of a
general kingside pawn advance by White, made
Black's position very awkward. Although there
were a few inaccuracies later, Karpov was able
to round off the game with an attractive finish.

The lessons here are:

1) A space advantage usually confers an
advantage, but this advantage is minimized if
there are no weaknesses to attack.

2) 'Hedgehog' positions require a great deal
of patience by both players. Impetuous moves
are liable to be punished severely.

3) Even quite cramped positions offer scope
for resourceful defence.

4) Playing positionally for several hours can
make it easy to overlook tactics when they do
arise – a trap into which Karpov does not fall.

Outpost

What is an outpost? There is no generally accepted definition, but an outpost is normally considered to be a square in enemy territory where it is possible to establish a piece without it being easily
dislodged.

If we take each element of this in turn, it's important that the square be somewhere inconvenient
for the opponent, and that normally means in his half of the board. In practice, outposts usually
arise on the fifth or sixth rank. Secondly, it should actually be possible to get a piece to the outpost,
otherwise the outpost is of little practical significance. However, this doesn't necessarily mean that
the outpost needs to be occupied straight away; it could represent a lurking danger for the future

even if immediate occupation is impossible. The final part, that the occupying piece cannot easily be dislodged, very often means that the opponent can no longer defend the square concerned with a pawn. Thus, the square in front of a backward pawn is usually an outpost.

The two pieces that most often occupy outposts are the knight and the rook. A knight that is firmly established on the fifth rank is normally a serious problem for the opponent; one that settles down on the sixth rank may decide the game by itself. Rooks are perhaps less ideally suited to occupying outposts because they can be chased away by minor pieces. However, if the minor pieces have all been exchanged or are unable to attack the rook, then a rook taking up residence on the sixth rank is also very strong. Needless to say, outposts occupied by rooks frequently arise on open files.

Outposts play an important role in chess and many positional manoeuvres have the creation of an outpost as their ultimate objective. The following game is an excellent example of the systematic exploitation of an outpost.

Game 18

J. Piket – I. Smirin

Interzonal tournament, Biel 1993

King's Indian Defence, Classical Variation

1	d4	♘f6
2	c4	g6
3	♘c3	♗g7
4	e4	d6

For comments on the moves up to here, see Game 14.

| 5 | ♘f3 |

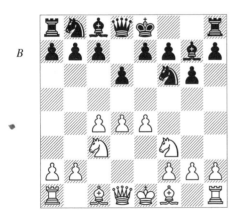

B

Instead of 5 f3, the Sämisch Variation (see Game 14), Piket prefers the straightforward development of his king's knight – the so-called Classical Variation. This is perhaps White's most natural system against the King's Indian. He just develops his kingside pieces to their most obvious squares by ♘f3 and ♗e2, and then castles. White's further course of action will depend on how Black responds. Although White's plan may seem unpretentious, it is one of the most challenging responses to the King's Indian.

| 5 | ... | 0-0 |

Black castles in preparation for action in the centre.

| 6 | ♗e2 |

Continuing his plan.

| 6 | ... | e5 |

This is the most common continuation, although several other moves have been tried. The text-move is Black's most natural counter, exerting pressure on the d4-pawn and trying to force White to commit himself to either d5 or dxe5.

| 7 | 0-0 |

White usually tries to keep his pawn on d4 for as long as possible, so as to keep Black guessing about whether White will open or close the centre. White cannot win a pawn by 7 dxe5 dxe5 8 ♕xd8 ♖xd8 9 ♘xe5 because Black can reply 9...♘xe4 10 ♘xe4 ♗xe5.

| 7 | ... | ♘a6 |

By far the most common move here is 7...♘c6, stepping up the pressure on d4. Then White is forced either to support the pawn by 8 ♗e3, or to push it forward by 8 d5, whereupon Black replies 8...♘e7. However, some players prefer not to incur the loss of time inherent in moving the queen's knight twice and therefore develop the b8-knight to d7 or a6. The advantage is that Black saves time if White plays d5, but the drawback is that it exerts less immediate pressure on White's centre and so White has no reason to commit his d-pawn straight away.

8   &e3

White's plan is simply to continue his development and support his centre. This is one natural method; another one is 8 &e1 followed by 9 &f1.

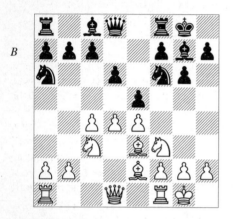

8   ...   &g4

There is not a wide range of constructive moves for Black here. After 8...c6, for example, White plays 9 d5, when the possibility of White opening the centre with dxc6 makes it hard for Black to prepare ...f5 effectively (for further remarks on this position, see the note to White's 9th move in Game 24). Therefore, Black usually plays the text-move, almost by a process of elimination. The idea is to disturb White's smooth development.

9   &g5

The most awkward reply, as Black has no ideal answer to the attack on his queen. If he plays ...f6, then the bishop has to retreat, but it also leaves the g4-knight rather stranded. This knight would then have to retreat to h6 and possibly f7, which would be quite solid but would not help Black to develop any real activity.

9   ...   &e8

This is the most natural choice, leaving f6 free for the retreat of the g4-knight. Thanks to the knight on a6, Black need not worry about his c7-pawn being exposed to attack by &d5.

10   dxe5

It is a good idea to make this exchange now, because White will have to play it in the next few moves in any case and there can be tactical problems if White delays it. After 10 h3 h6 11 &c1 (11 &d2 is not possible at all owing to 11...exd4), for example, Black does not retreat his knight to f6, but plays 11...exd4 12 &xd4 &f6, when White's e-pawn is under attack and Black has made good use of the position of his queen.

10   ...   dxe5

10...h6 is a possible alternative, although after 11 &d2 Black may not have anything better than to transpose to the game by 11...dxe5 12 h3 &f6. 11...&xe5 is perhaps possible, but after 12 &d4 c6 13 &e3, followed by &d2, White can develop his pieces comfortably and eventually push the black knight back by f4.

11   h3

11 &d2 is an interesting and quite promising alternative; White saves a tempo by missing out h3, at the cost of committing his knight rather early.

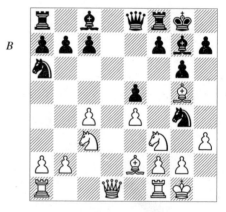

11   ...   h6

It is interesting to note that after 11...&f6 12 &e3 we reach the same position as in the game, except that Black's pawn is on h7 and not h6. Most black-players have preferred the pawn to be on h6, probably because it is useful to keep the white knight out of g5 (in case of ...&e6, for example).

12   &d2

In the King's Indian, control of the dark squares is very important and White must be careful to keep his dark-squared bishop. Were it to be exchanged, then squares such as d4 and f4 would become very weak. Therefore, White must retreat his bishop. It doesn't make any difference whether the bishop goes to c1 or d2, since it will soon return to e3 to support White's queenside play.

| 12 | ... | ♘f6 |
| 13 | ♗e3 | |

This flexible move serves a second useful purpose in that Black's a6-knight is kept out of c5, at least for the moment.

The opening phase is more or less over, and it is time for both players to decide on a plan for the middlegame. One of Black's main problems is the offside knight on a6; indeed, White is already threatening to embarrass it by 14 c5. Black's first step must be to take some action regarding this knight. It is possible to ignore White's threat and try to develop some counterplay elsewhere, in which case Black will probably play 13...♘h5. However, more likely Black will try to rescue the knight from its current position. There are three possible methods for activating the knight. The first is to play ...c6 and ...♘c7-e6, the second is to continue ...♘d7, followed by ...♘ac5-e6, and the third is to continue ...♕e7, again followed by ...♘c5-e6. All these plans involve a knight transfer to e6, which helps Black because there is a potential weak spot at d4, a square which White can no longer control with a pawn. At the moment, however, White has d4 well defended and it will not be easy for Black to jump in there. A big question for Black is whether he should adopt a plan with ...c6, or try to avoid this move. Playing ...c6 keeps White's pieces out of d5, but it creates a new weakness at d6, which White might exploit by c5 and ♘d2-c4-d6, for example.

White's plan involves restricting Black's counterplay as much as possible, while gradually expanding on the queenside. Once he has pushed his pawns to b4 and c5, he will be able to activate his light-squared bishop at c4 and may occupy the outpost at d5 (or, if Black has played ...c6, at d6).

| 13 | ... | ♘d7 |

Smirin goes for the second of the three plans mentioned above.

| 14 | a3 | |

At the moment both b4 and c5 are prevented, so White's queenside pawn advance has to start with this modest move.

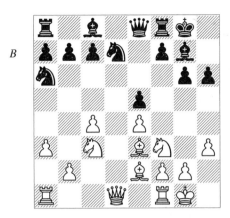

B

| 14 | ... | f5?! |

Although this move has been played a number of times, I do not like it. Of course, ...f5 is an integral part of Black's play in many lines of the King's Indian, but here the situation is a little unusual. First of all, the d-file is open, and if White plays b4 and c5, the a2-g8 diagonal will also become open. In view of these open lines, Black must be wary about weakening himself with ...f5, especially as his development is quite poor. Secondly, by not taking the opportunity to play ...♘ac5, he allows White to seal the a6-knight out by b4. Then the only route back for the knight is by ...c6 and ...♘c7-e6. This, of course, weakens d6 and it is this weak square which forms the key battleground for most of the game. In my view, 14...♘ac5 is a better chance; for example, 15 ♘b5 (15 b4 gives White a safe edge) 15...♕d8 16 ♕c2 a6 17 ♘c3 ♘e6 and White undoubtedly has some advantage, but Black is still in the game. For example, the obvious 18 ♕d2 may be met by the interesting pawn sacrifice 18...♘dc5!? 19 ♗xh6 ♕xd2 20 ♗xd2 ♘d4 21 ♖ae1 ♘cb3 with enough compensation for the pawn.

| 15 | b4 | |

White is only too happy to restrict the a6-knight.

| 15 | ... | c6 |

This move is inevitable sooner or later, or else the a6-knight will remain sidelined permanently.

| 16 | c5 | |

The expansion continues. In addition to gaining space, this move has two particular benefits for White. Firstly, it allows the light-squared bishop to enter the game at c4, and secondly it secures d6 as a possible outpost for White's pieces.

16   ...   f4

Black will never be able to counter White's strategic assets on the queenside by passive play, so he must aim for kingside activity. 16...♘f6 is bad because of 17 exf5 gxf5 18 ♕d6; hence the text-move, which gives Black the possibility of a general pawn advance on the kingside. Whether he will ever find the time for such an advance is, of course, another matter.

17   ♗c1

The bishop has to retreat, and c1 is the natural square – it avoids blocking the d-file, and the bishop can be repositioned on b2, where it bears down on the vulnerable e5-pawn.

17   ...   ♔h7

17...g5 is certainly possible, but it does not change the general structure of the position. After 18 ♘d2 ♘c7 19 ♘c4 ♘f6 20 ♗b2 White has some advantage.

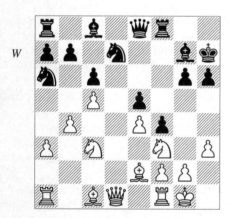

18   ♗b2!

The start of an excellent plan which allows White to exploit the weakness of d6 while at the same time restricting Black's kingside counterplay. The idea is to attack e5 with bishop and knight, thereby preventing ...♘f6, which is an essential ingredient for any kingside attack by Black. It will then be the c3-knight that heads for d6. Note that White is not interested in taking the wayward knight on a6 since he has a good, active square for his light-squared bishop on c4.

18   ...   ♘c7

The knight heads for d4.

19   ♘b1!

This is the key move. Once Black has played ...c6, this piece isn't doing very much on c3, so it is only natural to re-route the unemployed knight to d6. The f3-knight is well placed where it is, tying Black down to e5.

19   ...   ♘e6

There is little Black can do to prevent White's knight tour, so he at least aims for the modest success of occupying d4.

20   ♘bd2

Only two moves to go!

20   ...   ♘d4

21   ♘c4

The simplest continuation. Black's pleasure at reaching d4 turns out to be short-lived, since the triple attack on the knight forces him to exchange his only well-placed piece. 21 ♘xd4 exd4 is wrong, since it liberates the g7-bishop and gives Black the e5-square. Then 22 ♘f3? would be a blunder since 22...d3! 23 ♗xg7 dxe2 wins a piece.

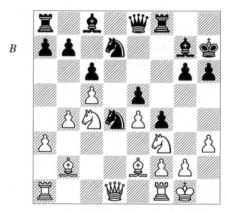

21   ...   ♘xe2+

21...♘xf3+ 22 ♗xf3 ♕e6 23 ♕e2 ♖d8 24 ♖ad1 is also very good for White, as Black has nothing to compensate for White's better development, control of the d-file and outpost at d6. Any attempt to avoid exchanging the knight is doomed to failure, because if the position is opened Black's lack of development will prove fatal; for example, 21...♕e7 22 ♘xd4 exd4 23 ♗xd4 ♕xe4 24 ♗xg7 ♔xg7 25 ♘d6 ♕e7 26 ♗g4 and White wins material.

22   ♕xe2

If Black does nothing, then White can increase the pressure in his own time. For example, he might double on the d-file, occupy d6 or step up the pressure on e5 by ♗c3 and ♕b2 (or all three!).

22   ...   b6

Black therefore tries to loosen White's grip on d6, and at the same time frees his c8-bishop to move to a6.

23   ♘d6

A good time for this move, as now Black will have to play ...a5 to release his bishop.

23   ...   ♕e6?!

Here the queen is exposed to attack from a white rook arriving on d6. 23...♕e7 was a better defence. Of course, White retains a clear advantage but there is no knockout blow – 24 ♖fd1, 24 ♕c4 and 24 ♖ac1 are all answered by 24...a5.

24   ♖fd1!

White continues with great energy. He is willing to let the c5-pawn go if he can activate his rooks with gain of tempo. 24 ♖ac1?! a5 offers Black more chances for counterplay.

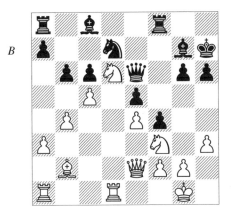

B

24   ...   bxc5

With the queen on e6, 24...a5 is less promising; for example, 25 ♘xc8 ♖fxc8 26 ♖d6 ♕e7 (26...♕e8 27 ♖ad1 ♖c7 28 ♕d3 ♖aa7 29 cxb6 ♘xb6 30 ♕b3 gives White extremely strong threats, such as 31 ♘xe5 ♗xe5 32 ♖d8) 27 ♖ad1 ♖c7 28 cxb6 ♘xb6 29 b5 ♖ac8 30 ♗a1! a4 (30...♘a4 loses to 31 bxc6) 31 ♕d3 leaves Black totally paralysed.

25   ♖ac1

Now White is threatening to cement his bind with 26 bxc5, so Black's reply is virtually forced.

25   ...   cxb4

26   ♖xc6

Here there was a choice of good moves, as 26 axb4 is also very strong. After 26...♘b8 (if Black allows ♖xc6, then White will have a similar position to that in the game, but with a pawn more) 27 ♖c5 ♘a6 28 ♖a5 (now e5 will fall) 28...♘xb4 29 ♗xe5 ♗xe5 30 ♖xe5 Black's position is a total wreck.

26   ...   bxa3

Or 26...a5 27 ♕b5 (threatening to capture twice on c8, winning Black's knight) 27...♘b8 (27...♕b3 28 ♖d2 ♘f6 29 ♖c7, followed by taking on e5, gives White decisive threats on the long dark-square diagonal) 28 ♖c7 ♘a6 29 ♖xg7+ ♔xg7 30 ♗xe5+ ♔h7 (30...♔g8 loses to 31 ♘xc8 ♖axc8 32 ♖d6) 31 ♘xc8 ♖axc8 32 ♖d6 and White wins.

27   ♗xa3

The bishop is deflected away from its attack on the e5-pawn, but now it settles on an equally dangerous diagonal. The immediate threat is 28 ♕c2, winning material. Black is a pawn up but this is of no help. White's tremendous piece activity, based on the dominating knight on d6, is far more important. In fact, White's position is so overwhelming that he has a number of ways to win, but the method chosen is both convincing and attractive.

27   ...   ♖d8

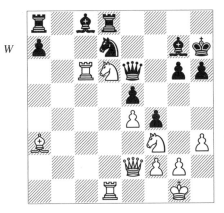

W

28   ♖dc1!

More accurate than 28 ♕c2, when Black can limp on by 28...♘b6 and White cannot move his knight because of the capture on d1.

28   ...   ♕g8

The queen must move, and there are only two squares which do not lead to an instant disaster. However, after 28...♕b3 29 ♖6c3 Black must play 29...♕g8 in any case, whereupon 30 ♖c7 transposes to the game.

29   ♖c7

The immediate 29 ♕b5 is also very strong.

29   ...   a5

Still hoping to develop his bishop at a6. White wins after 29...♘b6 30 ♘xe5 ♕e6 31 ♘df7, while 29...a6 30 ♕c2 ♗f8 31 ♕c6 ♗xd6 32 ♗xd6 leads to a catastrophic material loss for Black.

30   ♕b5

30 ♖1c6, with total paralysis, is also good. The text-move, which threatens 31 ♕c6 or simply 31 ♘xc8, sets up a nice combination.

30   ...   ♗a6

30...♖b8 loses to 31 ♕xa5.

31   ♕xd7!

An attractive finish. White sacrifices his queen to maximize the activity of his pieces.

31   ...   ♖xd7

32   ♖xd7

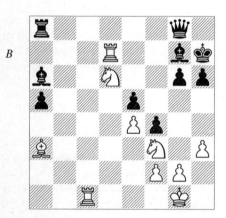

Threatening to double rooks on the seventh rank.

32   ...   ♖d8

There is no defence, e.g.:

1) 32...♖b8 33 ♖cc7 (threatening 34 ♘xe5) 33...♔h8 34 ♘h4 ♔h7 35 ♘df5! and White wins.

2) 32...♗e2 33 ♖cc7 ♗xf3 34 ♗b2 ♖d8 (or 34...♔h8 35 ♘f7+ ♔h7 36 ♘xe5 ♖b8 37 ♘g4) 35 ♗xe5 ♖xd7 36 ♖xd7 ♗e2 37 ♘e8! wins for White.

3) 32...♕b3 33 ♖cc7 ♖g8 (33...♕xa3 34 ♖xg7+ ♔h8 35 ♖h7+ ♔g8 36 ♖cg7+ ♔f8 37 ♖xg6) 34 ♘e8 ♕xa3 (34...♖xe8 35 ♖xg7+ ♔h8 36 ♖h7+ ♔g8 37 ♖cg7#, or 34...♔h8 35 ♘xe5

with a total collapse) 35 ♘f6+ ♔h8 36 ♘h4! with a quick mate.

33   ♖e7

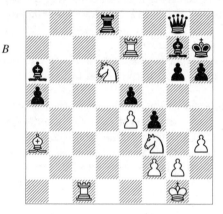

Black cannot oppose rooks any longer.

33   ...   ♗e2

Black also doesn't last long after 33...♖xd6 34 ♗xd6 ♔h8 35 ♖cc7 ♗f6 36 ♖f7.

34   ♘xe5

Of course, White does not allow Black to exchange one of his attacking pieces.

34   ...   ♕a2

35   ♖cc7   ♖g8

36   ♘e8!   1-0

In anticipation of 36...♕a1+ 37 ♔h2 ♔h8 38 ♘f6 ♕xe5 39 ♖xg7! (the most brutal finish) 39...f3+ 40 g3 ♖xg7 41 ♖c8+ mating.

Black adopted a combative opening line, but White reacted soundly, not launching an early attack but contenting himself with a small positional advantage. After Black's inaccurate 14th move, he was left with a choice of evils: either to see his a6-knight sidelined, or to weaken the d6-square and give White the opportunity to create an outpost. The game followed the latter course and White had to decide which piece would best occupy the outpost. This was a key moment, and thanks to Piket's accurate continuation White had soon established a ferocious positional bind. There remained only the exploitation of White's advantages, which Piket conducted with great energy.

The lessons here are:

1) One piece stuck permanently offside may be enough to lose the game.

2) While exploiting a positional advantage, it is also important to keep the opponent's counterplay under control.

3) Establishing an outpost on the sixth rank can be decisive. Such an outpost is especially effective if it can be occupied by a knight, but a rook can also prove lethal.

4) Even with a large positional advantage, the game does not win itself. Imagination may still be required to finish the opponent off.

Open File

The activity of any type of piece is affected by the pawn-structure. Bishops like open positions, and are less effective if there are many pawns on the board, especially if they are on the same coloured squares as the bishop. Rooks too are strongly influenced by the pawn-structure. They need open lines, especially open files, to gain their maximum activity. The problem is that an open file can usually be equally well exploited by either player, so deciding to open a file can be a far-reaching decision, which can end in one of three ways. One or other of the players can gain undisputed mastery of the file, or the result can simply be a liquidation of all the rooks along the open file. Once total control of a file has been established, it may very well be permanent. For example, suppose all the minor pieces have been exchanged and White has tripled his queen and rooks on the open d-file. Then the other player can only contest the file if he can manage to get his king, queen and both rooks controlling d8, whereupon a rook can be played to d8. Clearly, this is unlikely to be feasible. The following game demonstrates how control of an open file can impose a total stranglehold on the enemy position.

Game 19

N. Short – J. Timman

Tilburg 1991

Alekhine Defence, Modern Variation

1	e4	♘f6
2	e5	♘d5
3	d4	d6

For comments on the moves up to here, see Game 4.

4 ♘f3

This move is less aggressive than 4 c4 ♘b6 5 f4, as played in Game 4, but it is in many ways more natural. Instead of staking out a huge claim in the centre, White contents himself with his current pawn-centre, and hastens to support it with his other pieces. This straightforward plan is the most popular line against the Alekhine Defence, and is also one of the most awkward for Black. It is interesting to note that in many openings the most dangerous line is based on natural developing moves.

4 ... g6

This is already a key decision for Black. An alternative is to play 4...♗g4 5 ♗e2 e6, developing the dark-squared bishop to e7 rather than

g7. The text-move looks more active, since on g7 the bishop will exert pressure against White's central pawns. The danger is that if White can maintain his pawn-centre, Black's dark-squared bishop will be locked out of play.

5 ♗c4

Now White does not want to develop this bishop to e2, since he will need the e-file clear in order to support his e5-pawn. Therefore this move, which develops the bishop to an active diagonal with gain of time, is perfectly natural.

5 ... ♘b6

5...c6 is playable but slightly passive. It is rarely seen today, perhaps because 6 0-0 ♗g7 7 exd6 ♕xd6 8 ♘bd2 gives White a slight advantage with no risk.

6 ♗b3

During the next phase of the game, White sometimes plays a4, when Black usually replies ...a5, while Black sometimes plays ...a5, when White usually replies a4. This might seem odd, as if the insertion of a4 and ...a5 favours Black, why should White play a4, and vice versa? However, nobody really knows who benefits from including a4 and ...a5, so somehow or another these moves usually get played. My own, very personal, view is that White slightly benefits from having a4 and ...a5 inserted, but I am sure you could find another grandmaster who holds the opposite view.

6   ...   &g7

Black just continues his development. If instead 6...a5, White replies 7 a4.

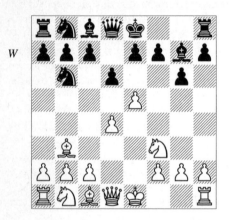

7   ♕e2

There are several possibilities for White here, but this is perhaps the most solid. At one time, the aggressive 7 ♘g5 was the most popular move, but it fell out of favour when it became clear that Black could fend off the immediate attack. White may play 7 a4, but at this moment it allows Black to enter unclear complications by means of 7...dxe5 8 a5 ♘6d7 and now:

1) 9 dxe5 ♘xe5 10 ♕xd8+ ♔xd8 11 ♘xe5 ♗xe5 12 0-0 gives White fair compensation for the pawn.

2) 9 ♕e2!? is an interesting idea, since now ♗xf7+ is a serious threat. If 9...exd4, then 10 ♗xf7+ ♔f8 (10...♔xf7 11 ♘g5+ wins Black's queen) 11 0-0 favours White. 9...♘c6 is probably the critical line; after 10 ♗xf7+ ♔xf7 11 ♘g5+ ♔e8 12 ♕c4 ♘f6 13 ♕f7+ ♔d7 14 dxe5 ♘h5 15 e6+ ♔d6 the position is extremely unclear.

3) 9 ♗xf7+ ♔xf7 10 ♘g5+ ♔g8 11 ♘e6 ♕e8 12 ♘xc7 ♕d8 13 ♘xa8 exd4 is also very unclear.

7   ...   ♘c6

Black steps up the pressure against d4 and e5. The immediate battle revolves around the e5-pawn. If White can maintain it, then he will have chances of shutting the g7-bishop out of the game, but if White is forced to play exd6 or e6 then Black will be at least equal.

8   0-0

White must castle here, because he needs to have ♖e1 available to defend the e5-pawn.

8   ...   0-0

Now that Black has castled, he is threatening 9...♗g4, which would definitely force White to concede the battle of e5. Hence, White's next move is almost forced. Note that Black could not have played ...♗g4 before castling, as White would have replied ♗xf7+ followed by ♘g5+.

9   h3

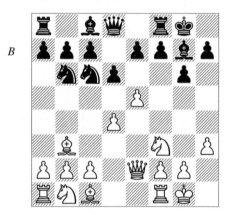

In fact, Black has no further shots to fire in the battle over e5, so this part of the struggle has ended in victory for White. However, Black can take some consolation in the fact that he has forced White to spend a tempo on the non-developing move h3, which gives him a free move to tackle the problem of generating counterplay.

9   ...   a5

Black decides to insert ...a5. As mentioned above, it is very hard to say whether this is a good idea. The main alternative (and one possible reason for not playing ...a5 earlier) is 9...♘a5. However, even here White can retain an edge by 10 ♘c3 ♘xb3 11 axb3 since White's absolutely secure centre and space advantage is more important than Black's possession of the two bishops.

10   a4

This is clearly the best move. If White plays 10 a3?, then after 10...a4 11 ♗a2 dxe5 12 dxe5 ♘d4 13 ♘xd4 ♕xd4 14 ♖e1 ♖a5 White will be in trouble over his e5-pawn. 10 c3 a4 11 ♗c2 ♗e6 is also poor, since not only does Black gain space on the queenside, but White's b1-knight is deprived of its best square, c3.

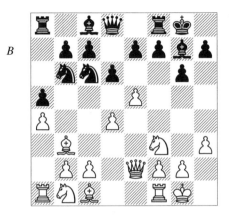

B

10   ...   dxe5

This is another critical long-term decision, the merit of which is hard to assess. Black opens the d-file in order to exchange some minor pieces, but in the long term it may well be that White is better placed to exploit the open file.

There is certainly a case for closing the centre by 10...♗f5 11 ♘c3 d5. It will take White a long time to reposition his b3-bishop on an active square, which Black might be able to use to create counterplay elsewhere. On the other hand, releasing the pressure against e5 leaves White's space advantage absolutely secure.

11   dxe5   ♘d4

This is the point behind Black's last move. After anything else, White seizes the d-file by ♖d1 with a clear advantage.

12   ♘xd4   ♕xd4
13   ♖e1

This move is necessary to defend e5. For the moment, Black's pieces look quite active, but this is a purely temporary state of affairs. If White is given a little time, then by ♘c3, ♗g5 and ♖ad1 he will take over the initiative and drive Black into passivity. However, it isn't so easy to counteract White's plan of natural development, and although Black has tried at least seven different moves in this position, none of

them appears to bring complete equality. Having said that, some of them come nearer to equality than others! As a matter of curiosity, this position can also arise from the Modern Defence (by, for example, 1 e4 g6 2 d4 ♗g7 3 ♘f3 d6 4 ♗c4 ♘f6 5 ♕e2 0-0 6 e5 dxe5 7 dxe5 ♘d5 8 h3 ♘b6 9 ♗b3 ♘c6 10 0-0 ♘d4 11 ♘xd4 ♕xd4 12 ♖e1 a5 13 a4).

13   ...   e6?!

This is not the most testing move. Although it prevents a breakthrough by e6, it blocks in the c8-bishop and, more seriously, weakens the dark squares on Black's kingside. 13...♘d7 is also bad in view of 14 e6!, while 13...♗e6 14 ♗xe6 fxe6 15 ♘d2 ♖f5 16 ♘f3 ♕c4 17 b3 ♕xe2 18 ♖xe2 is a depressing ending for Black, who has no compensation for his various weak pawns. 13...♗d7 is probably the best chance. Black exerts pressure against a4, and at the same time prepares to activate the bishop by ...♗c6. After 14 ♘c3 ♗c6 15 ♘b5 ♗xb5 16 ♕xb5 c6 17 ♕e2 ♘d5 White perhaps has a faint edge, but Black's position is solid and the exchange of a pair of minor pieces has relieved the problems caused by his lack of space.

14   ♘d2

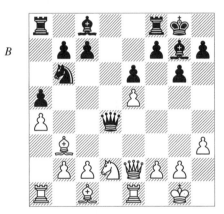

B

14   ...   ♘d5?!

This second slip leaves Black in a precarious situation. He intends to play ...b6 and then develop his c8-bishop, but this move is too slow and gives White a free hand to build up a dangerous initiative on the kingside. The c8-bishop should have been developed straight away by 14...♗d7. After 15 c3 ♕c5 16 ♘f3 ♗c6 17 ♗e3 ♕e7 18 ♗g5 ♕c5 19 ♘d4 White has an edge, but Black is still in the game. This was actually the continuation of an earlier game by Nigel Short (Short-Hennigan, British Championship, Swansea 1987).

15   ♘f3

Gaining time on the queen and securing the e5-pawn.

15   ...   ♕c5

Black cannot retain control of e4, because 15...♕b4 is met by 16 ♗d2.

16   ♕e4!

Suddenly Black's kingside is in danger. It requires only three moves (♕h4, ♗h6 and ♘g5) for White to develop a crushing kingside attack, and so Black has no time for the calm development of his light-squared bishop. Instead, he is obliged to take immediate panic measures to avoid being mated.

16   ...   ♕b4

Black offers a pawn to prevent the transfer of White's queen to h4. 16...b6? is impossible because of 17 c4, while 16...♗d7 17 ♕h4 favours White after 17...♕b4 18 ♖e4 or 17...h5 18 ♗g5.

17   ♗c4!

This is an excellent move. White is not deflected by the prospect of winning a pawn with 17 ♗xd5 exd5 18 ♕xd5 ♗e6, when Black would have reasonable drawing chances in view of his good development and active bishops.

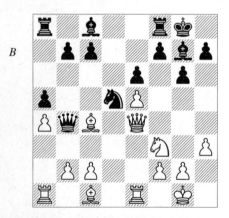

17   ...   ♘b6

Black is forced to continue actively; otherwise White first dislodges the enemy queen by ♗d2, and then returns to his original plan of ♕h4, etc. Note that the attempt to escape tactically by 17...♖d8 18 ♗d2 ♕xb2? fails to 19 ♖eb1 ♘c3 20 ♕h4.

18   b3!

White plays another very good move. He wants to continue with his attack, and doesn't care if his queenside pawns are shattered in the process. It is moves such as this that distinguish 'killer' players from those who, despite being technically just as proficient, are less successful in practice. It would have been quite reasonable to play 18 ♗d3, which gives White a modest advantage in perfect safety. However, Black, by dint of careful defence, might well manage to draw the resulting position. The text-move aims for a much larger advantage, but of course there is a risk involved in allowing ...♘xc4. If White's kingside pressure fails to materialize, he might have cause to regret his decision. In the end it all comes down to judgement, but players who have good judgement, and have the courage to back it up on the board, usually end up scoring more points.

18   ...   ♘xc4

19   bxc4

Threatening ♗a3, so Black decides to move his rook.

19   ...   ♖e8

19...♖d8 20 ♗g5 ♖d7 21 ♖ed1 is similar to the game – Black is short of moves while White can gradually improve his position by ♕h4, ♗h6 (or ♗f6) and ♘g5 (possibly followed by ♘e4).

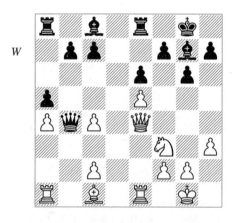

20   ♖d1

Although White has the potential for a dangerous attack on the kingside, it is not so strong as to deliver mate by force. White can play ♕h4 and ♗h6, for example, but Black defends by ...♕f8 and White's attack can only proceed rather slowly. In view of this long time-scale,

White has to take Black's potential counterplay into account. The text-move makes it much harder for Black to bring his pieces into play, as ...♗d7 is prevented and so Black must find some other way to develop his queenside pieces. As we shall see, it is a combination of White's kingside pressure and control of the open d-file that causes so many problems for Black.

20 ... ♕c5

Since ...♗d7 is impossible, Black has to try to arrange ...b6 in order to get his bishop out. At the moment this is not possible either, not only because the a8-rook is hanging, but also because ...b6 allows White to trap the queen by ♗a3. Thus, in order to play ...b6, Black will have to move his queen in any case – Timman chooses to do it straight away.

21 ♕h4

White presses ahead on the kingside.

21 ... b6

The c8-bishop glimpses the light of day. 21...♗xe5?? is impossible because 22 ♗a3 or 22 ♗e3 wins a piece.

22 ♗e3

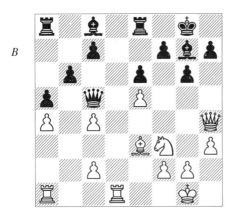

22 ... ♕c6!

Black aims to obstruct White's attack by setting up a battery on the long diagonal. The alternative was passive defence by 22...♕f8, but then White breaks through by 23 ♘g5 h6 24 ♘e4 and now:

1) 24...♗b7 25 ♘f6+ ♗xf6 26 exf6 h5 (or 26...♔h7 27 ♖d7) 27 c5! bxc5 28 ♕g5 e5 29 ♖d7 ♖ac8 30 ♖e7 with a decisive advantage for White.

2) 24...g5 25 ♗xg5! hxg5 26 ♕xg5 ♔h8 (26...♕e7 27 ♘f6+ ♔f8 28 ♖d4 followed by

♖g4 or ♖h4 wins for White, while 26...♔h7 27 ♖d4! followed by ♘f6+ leads to a quick mate) 27 ♕h5+ ♗h6 (27...♔g8 loses after 28 ♘f6+ ♗xf6 29 exf6 followed a rook-switch) 28 ♘f6 (threatening ♘xe8) 28...♗b7 29 ♘g4 ♔h7 30 ♖d7 and White wins.

23 ♗h6

Now that Black's queen cannot retreat to f8, this move becomes much stronger.

23 ... ♗h8

Just as in Game 10, Black retreats into the corner to preserve his fianchettoed bishop. Other moves are worse:

1) 23...♗xh6? is met by 24 ♕xh6 (threatening ♘g5) 24...♗b7 25 ♖d4 followed by ♖h4, when Black cannot defend h7.

2) 23...♗b7 24 ♗xg7 ♔xg7 25 ♖d4 is very good for White. Black cannot oppose rooks, so White can improve his position by ♖ad1 and ♖d7.

24 ♖d8

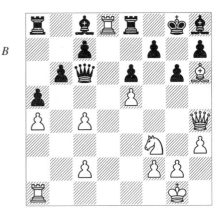

This move is the start of a manoeuvre designed to force Black to play ...♗g7. The immediate threat is 25 ♘d4.

24 ... ♗b7?

Even quite bad positions usually contain some defensive chances; the defender's task is to stay alert so as to seize any chance that comes along. Here Black misses his last chance to defend. He should have played 24...♗d7 25 ♘d4 ♖axd8 26 ♘xc6 ♗xc6, since the disappearance of White's knight relieves much of the kingside pressure. It is often hard to win ♕ vs ♖+♗ positions unless there are weak pawns for the queen to attack, and here Black's pawn-structure is solid. Moreover, White's weakened queenside pawns now work against him, since he cannot activate his rook without jettisoning the a-pawn, when Black's own a-pawn would offer considerable counterplay.

25   Îad1

Now White obtains a total grip on the d-file. The immediate threat is 26 ♕e7.

25   ...   ♗g7

After 25...♗xe5, 26 ♕e7 followed by ♖xa8 and ♖d8 wins, while 25...♕xa4 loses to 26 ♕e7 ♗xf3 27 gxf3 ♕c6 28 ♗g5!, when there is no defence to the threat of ♖1d7 (but not 28 ♖1d7? at once due to 28...♕xd7). After the text-move, 26 ♕e7 can be met by 26...♗xh6.

26   ♖8d7!

This threatens to win by 27 ♗xg7 ♔xg7 28 ♕f6+. Note that 26 ♗xg7? lets Black off the hook: 26...♖axd8 (26...♖exd8? 27 ♖xd8+ ♖xd8 28 ♕f6! ♖d1+ 29 ♔h2 mates) 27 ♕f6 (27 ♖xd8 ♔xg7 defends) 27...♖xd1+ 28 ♔h2 ♕c5 29 ♗h6 ♕f8! and Black has the advantage.

26   ...   ♖f8

Black is reduced to this passive defence. Other moves lose:

1) 26...♗xh6 27 ♕xh6 threatens 28 ♖xf7!, and if 27...♖f8 then 28 ♖1d4 followed by ♖h4 wins.

2) 26...♕e4 27 ♖xf7! ♗h8 28 ♗f4! g5 29 ♕h5 gxf4 30 ♖xc7 ♗xe5 31 ♖dd7 wins easily.

3) 26...♗xe5 also runs into 27 ♖xf7!.

27   ♗xg7

White has achieved as much as he can in the current situation and now exchanges bishops.

27   ...   ♔xg7

28   ♖1d4

Now Black has to worry that one day this rook might switch to g4 or h4.

28   ...   ♖ae8

Black hopes to be able to play ...♗c8 one day. The immediate 28...♗c8 loses to 29 ♕f6+ ♔g8 30 ♖xf7!.

29   ♕f6+   ♔g8

White obviously has a tremendous grip based mainly on his control of the open file. The position demonstrates two typical features of this control. The first is that it denies the opponent counterplay. If Black could oppose rooks then he would be able to liquidate the pressure, but he can never achieve this. The second is the ability of the rooks to operate sideways while remaining in control of the file. This is clearly

most effective when a rook is established on the seventh rank, but a rook can also switch along the third or fourth ranks to take part in a kingside attack.

After the text-move, Black threatens to dislodge the rook by ...♗c8.

30   h4

This meets the threat as now 30...♗c8 loses to 31 h5 gxh5 32 ♖g4+! hxg4 33 ♖d4 with a quick mate.

30   ...   h5

Therefore this is forced: Black must prevent the further advance of White's h-pawn. Despite White's bind, the question remains as to how White is going to win. Although his queen and rooks are superbly posted, he is handicapped by the fact that his knight is pinned against the mate on g2. Continuing this logic leaves the white king as the only piece that can be used to strengthen the attack. With hindsight, therefore, it is possible to say that White's next move is completely logical. Nevertheless, it is a brilliant idea and certainly deserves the praise that has been heaped upon it.

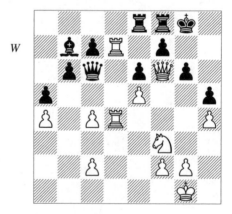

31   ♔h2!!

With the lethal threat of marching the king straight to h6. Remarkably, there is little Black can do to prevent this.

31   ...   ♖c8

After this passive move, White's plan succeeds admirably. 31...♗c8 would have made White work harder to win. After 32 g4! (now that Black's bishop has abandoned the long diagonal, this move is possible) Black can try:

1) 32...♗xd7 33 gxh5 ♕xf3 (33...gxh5 34 ♕g5+ and 33...♔h7 34 ♘g5+ ♔h6 35 ♘xf7+

both lead to mate) 34 ♕xf3 ♗xa4 35 ♕f6 ♔h7 36 h6! ♔xh6 37 h5 with a decisive attack.

2) 32...♗b7 33 ♖d3 ♕e4 (33...hxg4 loses to 34 h5) 34 gxh5 ♕f5 35 ♘g5! ♕xf6 (35...gxh5 36 ♖g3) 36 exf6 and White wins.

3) 32...♕xd7 33 ♖xd7 ♗xd7 34 gxh5 gxh5 35 ♕g5+ ♔h7 36 ♕xh5+ ♔g7 37 ♘g5 mates.

4) 32...hxg4 33 ♘g5! g3+ (33...♗b7 34 f3!, 33...♕xd7 34 ♖xd7 ♗xd7 35 h5 and 33...♗xd7 34 h5! g3+ 35 fxg3 ♗xa4 36 h6 ♕xc2+ 37 ♖d2 ♕xd2+ 38 ♔h3 are all decisive) 34 ♔xg3! (after 34 fxg3 ♗b7 35 ♘e4 ♕xa4 there is no clear-cut continuation to the attack) 34...♗xd7 (34...♕xd7 35 ♖xd7 ♗xd7 36 h5 mates) 35 ♔h2!! (Speelman suggested this amazing move; 35 h5 ♕h1 defends) 35...♕xa4 (35...♖e7 loses to 36 h5 gxh5 37 ♖h4) 36 h5 gxh5 37 ♖h4 followed by ♖xh5 and mate.

	32	♔g3	♖ce8

Black awaits his fate.

	33	♔f4	♗c8
	34	♔g5	

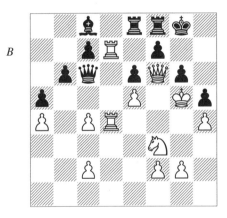

1-0

After 34...♔h7 35 ♖xf7+ ♖xf7 36 ♕xf7+ ♔h8 37 ♔h6 White mates in two more moves.

Timman took on a rather doubtful opening, which was made worse by an inaccurate 13th move. This allowed Short, who played the whole game with great energy, to develop a dangerous kingside initiative. Along the way, White gained control of the d-file and used this to force Black gradually into an utterly passive position. When Timman missed his last chance on move 24, White's grip grew tighter. Short was able to establish one rook on the seventh rank, where it further increased the pressure on Black's king position. Finally, Black was in such desperate straits that even a small addition to the pressure would cause his position to collapse. However, all White's pieces were occupied keeping the bind in place – all, that is, except for the king, which marched from the security of the castled position to finish his opposite number off personally. This is a classic game.

The lessons here are:

1) Opening a file is a major decision. Make sure that it is you and not your opponent who stands to benefit.

2) If there is only one open file, controlling it usually confers a large advantage.

3) Even very unpromising positions often contain defensive chances – if you can spot them.

4) Don't forget the king! It happens very rarely, but occasionally the king can play an active role in the middlegame. A precondition for this is that the opponent is more or less paralysed.

Weak Colour Complex

One often reads about a 'weak colour complex' in chess literature. It sounds like something to do with psychoanalysis, but in fact it is quite a simple chess concept. A 'weak colour complex' is basically a collection of weak squares of the same colour. Such complexes often arise when pawn-chains are present (see Game 24 for more about pawn-chains). If, for example, Black has pawns on a7, b7, d5, e6, g7 and h7 then the dark squares around the central pawns may become generally weak. If White has pawns on d4 and e5 this may not matter because the squares that might become weak are sealed off and cannot be occupied by White's pieces. However, if White has knights on d4 and e5, then the weakness of the dark squares is quite obvious. Pawn-formations that potentially create a weak colour complex thus require special attention. In the above example Black may be able to cover the potentially weak squares at d4 and e5, for example with a queen on b6, knight on c6 and bishop on d6 (this can happen in the French Defence). If White cannot occupy the potentially weak squares, then in fact they may not be weak at all.

Thus the ability to use pieces to cover the potential weak spots between the pawns is critical and, as we shall see in the following game, it can be worth some material to deprive the opponent of this possibility.

Game 20

G. Kasparov – A. Shirov

Horgen 1994

Sicilian Defence, Sveshnikov Variation

| 1 | e4 | c5 |
| 2 | ♘f3 | |

For comments on the moves up to here, see Game 8.

| 2 | ... | e6 |

In earlier games, we have seen examples of 2...♘c6 and 2...d6. The move 2...e6 is another possibility for Black which gives priority to freeing the dark-squared bishop. While this move can lead to a transposition into other Sicilian lines, there are a number of independent variations.

| 3 | d4 | |

Just as after 2...♘c6 and 2...d6, this immediate advance is White's most active continuation.

| 3 | ... | cxd4 |
| 4 | ♘xd4 | |

The pawn exchange has left Black with a central pawn-majority, but White can develop his pieces quickly.

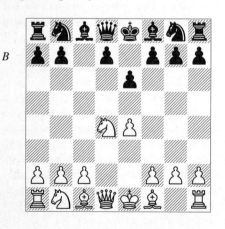

| 4 | ... | ♘f6 |

After this move, play is likely to transpose into one of the main Sicilian systems. The two major lines which are specific to the 2...e6 move-order are 4...♘c6 (the Taimanov Variation) and 4...a6 (the Kan Variation).

| 5 | ♘c3 | ♘c6 |

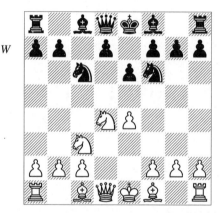

The opening of this game shows how confusing move-order questions can be. Black is trying to reach the position arising in the game after 8 ♗g5. There are two different move-orders arriving at the same position:

A) 1 e4 c5 2 ♘f3 ♘c6 3 d4 cxd4 4 ♘xd4 ♘f6 5 ♘c3 e5 6 ♘db5 d6 7 ♗g5.

B) 1 e4 c5 2 ♘f3 e6 3 d4 cxd4 4 ♘xd4 ♘f6 5 ♘c3 ♘c6 6 ♘db5 d6 7 ♗f4 e5 8 ♗g5.

You will notice that the second move-order is one move longer, a fact which is very awkward for authors of opening books! It is also worth mentioning that some database programs have a 'search position' facility that does not correctly find positions with a different move numbering. In this case, it is quite easy to overlook key games in the database unless one does two searches.

Obviously, the above lines are not forced and in both cases White has a number of opportunities to deviate. Which move-order Black selects depends on which of White's alternatives he wishes to prevent. Here is a list of the key differences:

Disadvantages of move-order A:

A1) White can play 3 ♗b5.

A2) White can play 7 ♘d5 or 7 a4.

Disadvantages of move-order B:

B1) White can play 6 ♘xc6 bxc6 7 e5.

B2) Black may not succeed in completely avoiding the lines with ♗b5, since White can play 3 ♘c3 and if Black still wants to aim for his target position, then he must continue 3...♘c6, allowing 4 ♗b5. It is true that with this move-order White's options are restricted (for example, he cannot play c3 any more) but equally Black is limited by being committed to ...e6 (whereas after 1 e4 c5 2 ♘f3 ♘c6 3 ♗b5, for example, Black might prefer to play 3...g6).

When deciding on the best move-order, a player must consider not only objective factors but also which lines are more to his taste.

In this game, Black opts for move-order B (while in Game 23, he prefers move-order A).

6   ♘db5

This is the most common move, targeting the weak square at d6. However, the line 6 ♘xc6 bxc6 7 e5 ♘d5 8 ♘e4 is a major alternative and is quite irritating for Black, as the positions resulting are quite different from the ones he is aiming for.

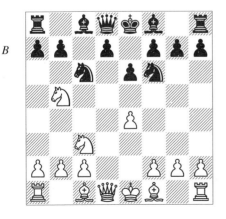

6   ...   d6

Black has an alternative in 6...♗b4, but after 7 a3 Black is more or less forced to take on c3, which gives White the two bishops at little cost.

7   ♗f4

This is the logical follow-up to White's previous move. He aims to force ...e5, when the d5-square will become weak.

7   ...   e5

Forced, as 7...♘e5 is strongly met by 8 ♕d4.

8   ♗g5

Here the bishop stands ready to eliminate the f6-knight, thus increasing White's grip on d5.

8   ...   a6

Black's compensation for the weak d5-square is the possibility to drive White's knight to the edge of the board. Black must take advantage of it right away, as White is threatening 9 ♘d5.

9   ♘a3

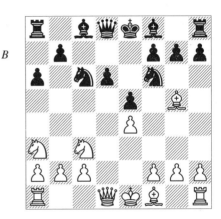

This misplaced knight is one of the cornerstones of Black's play. Thanks to Black's ...e5, the d5-square is a weakness in his position, but dynamic factors can offer compensation for a static weakness. In this case, the offside knight on a3 must come back into the game, which gives Black time to develop his counterplay.

9   ...   b5

This whole line is usually referred to as the Sveshnikov Variation, after the Soviet grandmaster who popularized it in the 1970s. Sveshnikov's move 9...b5 was really the key to the revitalization of this system. Previously, Black tended to play either 9...d5, a pawn sacrifice which is not really sound, or 9...♗e6, which allows the offside knight to return to the centre by ♘c4 and ♘e3.

10   ♘d5

This is one of the two main methods of dealing with Black's threat to win a piece by 10...b4. The other is 10 ♗xf6, for which see Game 23.

10   ...   ♗e7

Thanks to White's delay in exchanging on f6, Black is able to avoid the doubled f-pawns by this move. 10...♗e6 is wrong, because after 11 ♗xf6 gxf6 12 c3 f5 13 exf5 ♗xf5 Black has wasted a tempo with his bishop (compared to the standard line 10 ♗xf6 gxf6 11 c3 f5 12 exf5 ♗xf5) and so White has the strong possibility 14 ♕f3!, when the extra move c3 prevents the reply ...♘d4.

The text-move unpins the f6-knight and so threatens both 11...♘xe4 and the favourable liquidation 11...♘xd5 12 ♕xd5 ♗b7.

11   ♗xf6

Now White takes the knight.

11   ...   ♗xf6

Here 11...gxf6 is wrong, as the bishop is not well placed on e7 in the resulting position (it should be on g7).

12   c3

By exchanging the f6-knight, White has consolidated the position of his knight on d5. It is not easy for Black to break White's grip on d5, for two reasons. The first is that the other knight can lend support by ♘c2-e3 and the second is that the obvious challenge to d5, namely ...♘e7, allows White to double Black's pawns by playing ♘xf6+, without Black obtaining the two bishops as compensation.

The text-move aims to bring the offside knight on a3 back into the game via ♘c2.

12   ...   ♗b7

This interesting move became quite popular during the 1990s. Black aims to mount a direct challenge to the d5-square using the b7-bishop and c6-knight. The usual plan is ...♘b8-d7, ...♗g5 and ...♘f6. The bishop on g5 stands ready to eliminate White's other knight (after ♘c2 and ♘ce3), while Black's remaining minor pieces converge on the d5-square. In principle, this is a very effective plan, which might well lead to White having to recapture on d5 with his e-pawn. However, being forced to make such a capture is almost always a sign that Black's strategy has been a success. White wants d5 occupied by one of his pieces, not an immobile pawn, and the transfer of the pawn from e4

to d5 also gives Black the opportunity to develop active play by ...f5 and ...e4. The defect with Black's plan is, of course, that it takes four moves to position his pieces on their ideal squares and this gives White the opportunity to undertake some active play of his own.

12...0-0 13 ♘c2 is the most common continuation, when Black has the choice between 13...♗g5 and 13...♖b8. Each of these has its disadvantages. One problem with 13...♖b8 is that White can reply 14 h4, preventing the activation of the bishop at g5. On the other hand, 13...♗g5 has the defect that after 14 a4 Black is obliged to play 14...bxa4, which frees c4 for White's light-squared bishop and leaves Black's a-pawn weak.

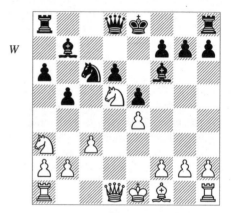

W

13   ♘c2

A multi-purpose move. The knight returns to the centre, moves into position to support its colleague by ♘ce3, and frees the a-pawn to break open Black's queenside pawn-structure by a4.

13   ...   ♘b8

Although this move is a continuation of the plan mentioned in the note to Black's 12th move, it does look slightly odd to put the knight back on its original square. Why not, for example, play 13...♗g5 and then 14...♘e7, reaching the same type of position, but saving two moves? The answer is that 13...♗g5 14 a4 bxa4 15 ♖xa4 ♘e7 doesn't really achieve Black's objective of breaking White's grip on d5, because after 16 ♗c4 White is ready to keep recapturing with pieces on d5. As we shall see, the knight is much better placed on d7 to prevent White from reinforcing d5, partly because a later ...♘f6 also attacks the e4-pawn, but also because Black has various options to harass a rook on a4 by ...♘b6 or ...♘c5.

14 a4

As explained above, White must take quick action to disrupt the execution of Black's plan. This move exposes Black's a-pawn to attack, and gains access to the c4-square.

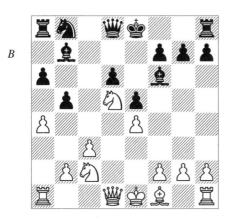

B

14 ... bxa4

Forced, as Black has no reasonable method of defending b5.

15 ♖xa4

There is no reason not to recapture the pawn immediately. The only real alternative is 15 ♘ce3, aiming to take on a4 with the queen. However, after 15...♘d7 16 ♕xa4 0-0 17 ♕c2 (17 ♗c4 ♗g5 knocks away the props supporting d5) 17...♗g5 White is unable to maintain his grip on d5.

15 ... ♘d7

This is a more flexible move than castling, since Black will definitely play ...♘d7 sooner or later.

16 ♖b4

Kasparov immediately puts the question to Black's bishop. This is a more dynamic move than 16 ♘ce3, which causes Black fewer problems after 16...0-0.

16 ... ♘c5?!

The obvious reply, defending the bishop and preparing to chase away White's rook by ...0-0 and ...a5. However, after White's amazing reply Black is forced on the defensive. The devastating example offered by this game has put other players off repeating Shirov's move and recent games have concentrated on 16...♖b8, when 17

♗c4 0-0 18 0-0 ♗g5 19 ♕e2 leaves White with a very slight advantage.

16...♗c6?! is wrong; after 17 ♖c4 ♗xd5 (the alternative 17...♖c8 18 ♘cb4 is also very good for White) 18 ♕xd5 0-0 (18...♘b6 19 ♕c6+ ♔e7 20 ♖b4 gives White a near-decisive advantage) 19 ♖c6 White will win a pawn for inadequate compensation.

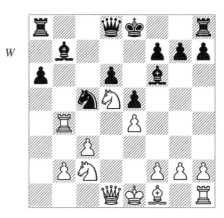

W

17 ♖xb7!!

An extraordinary idea. White gives up a whole exchange in order to obtain a stranglehold on the light squares. It is worth taking some time to look at the play so far, so as to understand the justification for this remarkable sacrifice. Judged by the classic criteria for good opening play, White's strategy has been about as far from the textbook as it is possible to imagine:

'Castle as quickly as you can': here White's king is still in the centre, and indeed he still requires two moves to castle.

'Don't move the same piece twice in the opening': White has moved his knights a total of seven times.

'Develop your rooks to the central files': White has developed his queen's rook like a beginner, to a4 and b4, and to cap this manoeuvre off he has given it up for a bishop!

In fact, if you had gone down to your local chess club and seen someone playing like this with White, then you would probably have laughed. However, White is one of the greatest players (some would say *the* greatest) of all time, so presumably there must some reason behind his play. Kasparov's logic is based on two closely related factors: the light squares and the d5-square. Black's opening involves establishing his central pawns on dark squares; this inevitably results in a weakening of the light squares. In cases such as this, where one player's pawns are fixed on squares of one colour, it is important for that player to retain some control over the squares of the opposite colour. In some cases, this can be achieved using pawns; for example, if Black had a pawn on c6 then he would control d5 and the fact that his central pawns were on dark squares would be irrelevant. Where, as here, there are no pawns to do the job, then it must be done by pieces.

The key piece is very often the bishop that controls the squares of the opposite colour to the pawns. While this bishop remains on the board, the possibility of fighting for the squares not controlled by the pawns exists. If this bishop is missing, then the player can only fall back on his knights, but unless these are already well-posted, it can take time to manoeuvre them into effective positions.

How do these general considerations apply to the game under discussion? The d6-e5 pawn-chain leaves Black's light squares generally weak, but the d5 outpost has particular significance. A knight established there will control several squares in Black's position and exert a powerful influence on the game. We have already seen in the above notes how many lines revolve around the battle for d5. Thus the answer to the apparent paradox represented by Kasparov's play is that he recognized the critical nature of the struggle for d5, and was prepared to assign the highest priority to it – even to the extent of sacrificing the exchange.

Now more pieces of the jigsaw fall into place. White has not yet castled because Black's plan of fighting for d5 demanded immediate attention; there was simply no time for quiet development by, for example, ♗e2 and 0-0. A further point is that White would really like to develop his f1-bishop to c4, where it controls d5, and so Kasparov is prepared to wait until he has played a4 before developing this bishop, so that it has a chance to occupy its optimum square without loss of time. The second point, about the odd development of White's rook, is based on the same idea. White has greater ambitions for his a1-rook than simply to develop it to d1; this rook is to be used to eliminate Black's important

light-squared bishop. The third point, about White's repeated knight moves, is again a question of priorities. White may have moved his knights seven times, but now they are ideally posted to control d5 – in any case, Black has nothing to boast about as he has moved his own queen's knight four times.

In other words, White's moves form a seamless whole; they may appear odd individually, but when examined together they represent an ambitious plan to obtain a complete grip on the light squares. Of course, the importance of controlling d5 in this type of Sicilian pawn-structure is well-known, but before this game I think few grandmasters would have been prepared to give up a whole exchange to cement control of d5.

One of the main differences between a strong player and a truly great one is that the latter is able to go beyond what is generally known and accepted to discover new ideas and principles. If successful, these are then incorporated into the general body of chess theory and become more familiar as time passes – to such an extent that what appeared extraordinary when played for the first time may elicit only a yawn when played a few years later. Of course, the same thing happens in virtually every area of human endeavour.

This game provides an excellent example of a theme I mentioned in the Introduction – that much top-class chess is incomprehensible when viewed in terms of the principles formulated in contemporary textbooks. Whereas chess has advanced greatly in the last half-century, much of the instructional material has not kept up with these advances. It is impossible to explain White's play in this game in terms of the old ideas: 'rooks belong in the centre', 'don't move the same piece twice in the opening', and so on. In order to make sense, the game has to be viewed in modern terms: White's play is founded on the creation of a strategic plan and the single-minded execution of that plan, based on the specific requirements of the position.

| 17 | ... | ♘xb7 |
| 18 | b4 | |

A key move. The only black piece which is capable of fighting for the central light squares is the knight, which could return to play via ...♘c5-e6-c7, for example. This move cuts out that plan. In order to activate his knight, Black will have to move his queen and then play ...♘d8-e6, but this is not so easy to achieve since there is no good square for the queen.

Objectively speaking, White probably has only a very slight advantage, but in practical play it is desirable to possess the initiative. Black has trouble finding a constructive plan whereas White's options are much clearer.

18   ...   ♗g5

Since Black cannot activate his other pieces easily, he at least moves his bishop to a better square. The immediate 18...♕c8 19 ♘ce3 ♘d8 leaves d6 too weak: after 20 ♘c4 ♕c6 21 b5! axb5 22 ♘xe5 White wins material. 18...0-0 19 ♘ce3 is similar to the game.

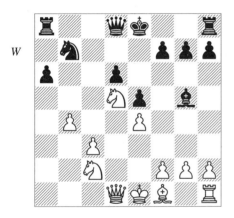

19   ♘a3

The knight cannot now be activated via e3, so it reaches c4 by an alternative route. In fact, the c4-square is a good outpost for both the f1-bishop and the c2-knight, but obviously both pieces cannot stand on the same square. It makes sense for the knight to take precedence since whereas the bishop has an alternative fairly good square (d3), the knight is doing very little on c2 or a3.

19   ...   0-0
20   ♘c4

There is still little danger of Black undertaking anything active, so White is taking no risk in leaving his king in the centre.

20   ...   a5

Black plays consistently to activate what pieces he can. This move will open up the a-file and bring the a8-rook into play. The alternative is 20...f5, aiming for counterplay via a different route. However, after 21 ♗d3 f4 (21...fxe4 22 ♗xe4 is worse as the bishop radiates power from e4) 22 ♕g4 a5 23 0-0 axb4 24 cxb4 f3 25 g3 Black has not solved his problems; for example, 25...♔h8 26 ♖d1 ♗h6 27 ♗f1 followed by ♖d3 and ♖xf3.

21   ♗d3

Thanks to White's grip on the light squares, Black's counterplay is very limited. Therefore, this is a good time for White to complete his development. 21 ♘cb6 has little point as Black can just reply 21...♖a7.

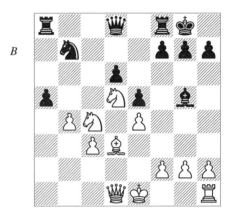

21   ...   axb4
22   cxb4

It is up to Black to find some way of activating his passively-placed pieces.

22   ...   ♕b8

Shirov decides to concentrate on play along the a-file, by ...♕b8, ...♖a2, ...♕a7 and perhaps ultimately ...♖a8. This plan is satisfactory if followed up correctly, but 22...♖b8 is perhaps the most solid idea. Black eliminates the fork at b6, and so prepares ...♕d7 followed by ...♘d8-e6. After 23 h4 ♗h6 24 ♕g4 ♔h8 25 0-0 ♕c8 the position is unclear.

Other possibilities are less effective. 22...♗h6 (22...♖a2 23 0-0 ♕a8 24 ♘cb6 ♕a3 25 ♗c4 ♖d2 26 ♕g4 favours White) 23 0-0 ♕h4 (after 23...♕g5 24 g3 Black has no obvious plan, as 24...♘d8 loses to 25 h4) tries to activate the queen on the kingside, but White can continue 24 g3 ♕h3 25 ♗e2 ♗g5 (otherwise Black has to surrender material) 26 ♗g4 ♕h6 27 ♘db6 ♖a2 28 h4 with a good position; e.g., 28...♗d2 (or 28...♗xh4 29 gxh4 ♕xh4 30 ♕f3 and White retains his grip) 29 ♕b3 ♖a6 30 ♖d1.

23   h4

Now Black is forced to make a critical decision. Should he keep the bishop on the c1-h6 diagonal, or should he drop it back to d8?

The alternatives 23 ♘cb6 ♖a2 24 ♘d7 ♕a7 and 23 0-0 ♘d8 24 ♘cb6 ♖a7 favour Black.

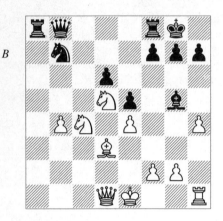

23   ...   ♗h6?

The wrong choice. The bishop certainly appears to be more active on h6, where it controls the squares d2 and c1, but in fact Black would have done better to retreat. 23...♗d8! intends ...♗c7 followed by ...♘d8, and covers b6 so that a white knight cannot jump there without being exchanged. White can continue 24 g3 ♗c7 (24...♕a7 25 0-0 ♕d4 26 ♕b3 followed by ♖d1 expels the queen) 25 0-0 ♘d8 26 b5 (26 ♕g4 ♔h8 does little to change the situation) 26...♘e6 27 b6 ♗d8 with an unclear position. White has managed to push his pawn to b6, but in compensation Black has activated his knight. After the text-move, White gains the upper hand.

24   ♘cb6

With the bishop on h6, this move can be played with impunity.

24   ...   ♖a2

Note that although Black has a theoretically 'bad' bishop, the bishop is actually relatively active on h6. It is not the inactivity of his bishop that dooms him, it is the amazing activity of White's minor pieces on the light squares. It is true that weak colour complexes and bad bishops often go hand-in-hand, but in this case the weak squares are the primary factors in Black's downfall. We will examine bad bishops more closely in Game 23.

25   0-0

Stronger than 25 ♘d7? ♕a7 26 0-0 ♖a8!, when a subsequent ...♖a1 will force exchanges.

25   ...   ♖d2

This permits a powerful reply, but other moves were also fairly uninviting:

1) 25...♕a7 26 ♗c4 ♖d2 27 ♕h5 ♘d8 28 ♘f6+ ♔h8 29 ♘bd7 ♖e8 30 ♘xe8 (30 ♗xf7 ♘xf7 31 ♕xf7 ♖a8 32 ♘e8 ♕a2 is less clear) 30...♕xd7 31 ♘f6 ♕c7 32 b5 with an advantage to White; for example, 32...♕xc4? fails to 33 ♕f5 gxf6 34 ♕xf6+ ♔g8 35 ♕xh6 followed by ♕g5+, giving White a near-decisive advantage.

2) 25...♕e8 26 ♗c4 ♖a7 27 ♘c8 ♖a3 28 ♘ce7+ ♔h8 29 ♘f5 (notice how the white knights hop around, making use of all the weakened light squares) 29...♕e6 30 ♘de3 ♕g6 31 h5 ♕g5 32 ♗d5 ♘d8 33 b5 and Black's coordination is so poor that he will have trouble stopping the b-pawn.

26   ♕f3?!

A slip. White could have played the simple but strong 26 ♕b1!, threatening to trap the rook with ♘c4. There isn't much Black can do to stop this; for example, 26...♕d8 (26...♕a7 27 ♘c4 ♖a2 28 ♘c3 will also pick up the exchange) 27 g3 (27 ♘c4 ♖xd3 28 ♕xd3 ♕xh4 is less clear) and Black will have to surrender the exchange. This would leave a situation of material equality, but with most of White's positional advantage intact.

26   ...   ♕a7

26...♕e8 is strongly met by 27 ♖a1! followed by ♘c4 (but not 27 ♗a6? ♘d8 28 ♘c4 ♖d4 29 ♘xd6 ♕e6 and Black wins).

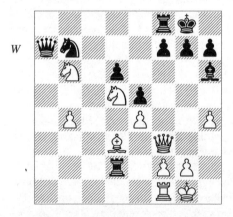

27   ♘d7?!

Another slip. White could still have retained strong pressure by continuing 27 ♗b5 ♘d8 (27...♖c2 28 ♘d7 ♖a8 29 ♘e7+ ♔h8 30 ♕xf7 ♕a2 31 ♘d5 gives White a clear advantage) 28 ♘d7 ♘e6 29 ♘e7+ (29 ♘xf8 ♔xf8 30 ♕c3 g6 31 ♕c6 is also good for White) 29...♔h8 30 ♘xf8 ♕xe7 31 ♘xe6 ♕xe6 (31...fxe6 32 ♖a1 g6 33 ♗c4 is very unpleasant for Black) 32 ♗c6 with good winning chances despite the opposite-coloured bishops.

| 27 | ... | ♘d8? |

Black returns the exchange, but this does not solve his problems since White retains a strong initiative. The alternatives are:

1) 27...♕a3? 28 ♘e7+ ♔h8 29 ♘xf8 ♖xd3 30 ♕xf7 and White wins.

2) 27...♘c5? 28 bxc5 ♕xd7 29 c6 ♕a7 30 c7 ♕c5 31 ♖b1 ♖a2 32 ♖b8 ♖a8 33 ♖xa8 ♖xa8 34 ♕f5 is winning for White.

3) 27...♖d8?! 28 ♘e7+ ♔h8 29 ♕xf7 ♕a8 (29...g6 30 ♘f6 ♗g7 31 ♕xg6 forces mate; 29...♖xd3 loses to 30 ♘f8) 30 ♗b5 and White has a very good position.

4) 27...♖a8! (the only move; White can force a draw but he has no clear route to the advantage):

4a) 28 ♘7b6?! ♕a3 favours Black slightly.

4b) 28 ♘e7+ ♔h8 29 ♕xf7 ♖xd3 30 ♘f8 ♕a2! 31 ♕f5 g6 32 ♘exg6+ hxg6 33 ♕f6+ ♗g7 (33...♔g8 34 ♘e6 ♔h7 35 ♕e7+ is a draw) 34 ♘xg6+ ♔h7 35 ♕f5 ♕d2 36 ♘xe5+ is also drawn.

4c) 28 ♗b5 ♘d8 29 ♕f5 is unclear.

4d) 28 ♗c4 ♘d8 (28...♖e8? loses to 29 ♘5f6+) 29 ♕f5 (29 ♘5b6 ♖b8 30 ♘xb8 ♕xb6 is unclear) 29...g6 30 ♕f6 ♗g7 31 ♕xd6 ♔h8 and Black is hanging on.

| 28 | ♘xf8 | ♔xf8 |
| 29 | b5 | |

White's advantages are decisive: his pieces are more active, Black's king is in danger, the b-pawn is very dangerous and to cap it all Black still has crippling light-squared weaknesses.

| 29 | ... | ♕a3 |

Black struggles to generate counterplay. Alternatives are no better:

1) 29...♘e6 30 b6 ♕a3 (30...♕b8 loses to 31 ♖a1) 31 b7 ♕b3 (31...♖b2 32 ♗b5! ♕a7 33 ♕a3 is decisive) 32 ♘c7 ♘d4 (32...♘xc7 33 ♗c4 finishes Black) 33 ♕g4 ♕xb7 34 ♕d7 ♕b8 35 ♖b1 and there is no defence.

2) 29...♕d4 30 ♗e2 (threatening 31 ♕a3 and 31 ♕f5! ♖xe2 32 ♕d7) 30...♕a7 (or 30...♘e6 31 ♖c1) 31 b6 ♕a8 32 ♕f5 ♖xe2 33 ♕xh7 f6 34 ♕h8+ ♔f7 35 ♘c7 ♕c6 36 ♕xd8 and wins.

| 30 | ♕f5! |

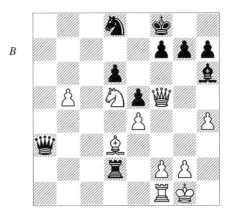

B

Again, a key move involves occupation of a light square. White sacrifices the bishop and plays for a direct attack.

| 30 | ... | ♔e8 |

Black cannot accept, as 30...♖xd3 loses to 31 ♕d7 g6 32 ♕xd8+ ♔g7 33 b6.

| 31 | ♗c4 | ♖c2 |

31...♕c5 (31...♕a4 32 ♕c8) 32 ♕xh7 ♔d7 33 ♕f5+ ♔e8 34 ♗b3 ♖b2 35 ♗d1 wins.

| 32 | ♕xh7! | ♖xc4 |

32...♕c5 loses to 33 ♗b3 ♖b2 34 ♕g8+ ♔d7 35 ♗d1.

33	♕g8+	♔d7
34	♘b6+	♔e7
35	♘xc4	♕c5

35...♕b4 is also met by 36 ♖a1.

| 36 | ♖a1 | ♕d4 |

36...♕xc4 37 ♖a7+ ♔f6 38 ♕xd8+ ♔g6 39 ♕xd6+ f6 40 ♕c6 is winning for White.

| 37 | ♖a3 | ♗c1 |
| 38 | ♘e3 | 1-0 |

This was an exceptionally creative game by Kasparov. An amazing exchange sacrifice was followed by a gradual build-up of pressure on the numerous weak light squares. It was difficult for Black to find a plan to free himself, and the error on move 23 was quite understandable. There were a few inaccuracies in the following moves, but a further mistake by Shirov on move 28 sealed his fate.

The lessons here are:

1) Squares which are weak relative to the central pawn-structure need to be covered by pieces.

2) If this is not possible, then the weakness can become serious.

3) The defender has to remain alert for any inaccuracy of the part of the attacker. Here Shirov had a momentary chance, but he let it pass by.

4) Learning when you can break the 'rules' is part of chess improvement.

The Queenside Attack

An attack does not have to be directed at the enemy king – it is quite possible to launch an attack on the opposite flank. Here we will use the term 'queenside attack' to indicate such an attack, since the enemy king is most often on the kingside. Of course, if the enemy king has castled queenside, then all the comments we make here apply with 'kingside' and 'queenside' reversed. Certainly, the immediate object of a queenside attack cannot be mate, but that does not mean that a queenside attack is any less dangerous than one directed at the king. The object of the attack is usually to open some lines and penetrate into the enemy position. Along the way, any enemy pawns left on the queenside will be vulnerable to attack, so material gain may also be an objective. Once the pieces have entered the opposing fortress, they can switch sideways along the seventh and eighth ranks, and then the queenside attack may turn into an attack on the king. This idea is, of course, most effective if the attacker's rooks have managed to penetrate.

If you are lucky, the defender will not have been able to generate much counterplay while all this has been going on. However, more likely he will try to launch a counterattack on the opposite wing. Such counterattacks should be treated with great respect; whereas a queenside attack is only a means to an end, a counterattack directed against the king can, if it is successful, decide the game at a stroke. Because of this disparity, a player conducting a queenside attack should keep a watchful eye on the other side of the board.

It is rare for a queenside attack to be conducted with pieces alone. Usually at least one pawn must be advanced in order to open some lines.

When should you launch a queenside attack? This often depends on the pawn-structure. Typical indicators for launching a queenside attack are:

1) Space advantage on the queenside. If White has pawns on d5 and e4 facing black pawns on d6 and e5, then White's space advantage is more significant on the queenside, and his chances to open a file with c4-c5 may be quite good.

2) Enemy pawn weaknesses on the queenside.

3) Where a 'minority attack' is possible.

This last point is one of the main themes of the following game.

Game 21

A. Yermolinsky – L. Christiansen

US Championship, Salt Lake City 1999
Queen's Gambit Declined, Exchange Variation

	1	d4	♘f6

For comments on the moves up to here, see Game 13.

	2	♘f3

In previous games in this book starting 1 d4 ♘f6, White played 2 c4, but the text-move is equally viable. Move-order choices are often determined by which openings the particular player wants to get into, and which he wants to avoid. If, for example, White is happy to enter the Orthodox Queen's Gambit Declined (1 d4 ♘f6 2 c4 e6 3 ♘c3 d5 4 ♘f3) but wants to avoid the Budapest Gambit (1 d4 ♘f6 2 c4 e5), then he might prefer 2 ♘f3 to 2 c4. Of course, you cannot keep every option open – all moves are committal to some extent. In playing the knight to f3, for example, White rules out certain lines against the King's Indian (e.g. the Sämisch – see Game 14). If White's normal response to the King's Indian is one of these lines, then he should have a reserve option in place should Black continue 2...g6. Thus questions of move-order depend on the repertoire of the particular player concerned and his opponent – perhaps even on how he feels on the day the game is played!

2   ...   e6

No King's Indian, at any rate.

3   c4

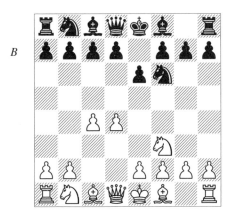

This position is more often reached via the move-order 1 d4 ♘f6 2 c4 e6 3 ♘f3.

3   ...   d5

Black decides to go in for the Queen's Gambit. The main alternatives are 3...♗b4+, the Bogo-Indian Defence, and 3...b6, the Queen's Indian Defence.

4   ♘c3

The most natural and flexible move. White develops his knight to its most natural square, at the same time exerting pressure on Black's strongpoint in the centre at d5. We have now transposed into Game 15.

4   ...   ♘bd7

In Game 15, Black played 4...c6, the Semi-Slav Defence. Christiansen prefers a developing move which steers the game into the Orthodox Queen's Gambit Declined, an opening which has been popular for more than a century.

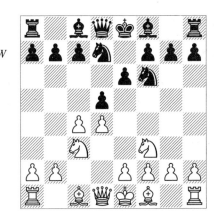

5   cxd5

Although this opening has been around for a long time, that does not mean that there have been no developments in the past 100 years. On the contrary, there has been a gradual shift in opinion as regards the correct method of handling this type of position for White. At one time, White would almost invariably play ♗g5, e3 and then, assuming Black plays ...♗e7 and ...0-0, some combination of ♖c1, ♕c2 and ♗d3. It was held that White should avoid taking on d5, as the reply ...exd5 would free the c8-bishop, which was thought to be Black's problem piece in the Orthodox Queen's Gambit Declined.

Gradually opinion has shifted, with white-players taking on d5 earlier and earlier. It turns out that it is not so easy for Black to find a good square for his c8-bishop. When White's knight is on f3, he often plays h3 to prevent ...♗g4, while White's bishop on d3 prevents Black playing his own bishop to f5. Thus Black is usually reduced to ...♗e6, which is not a sparklingly active square. The exchange on d5 also stabilizes the pawn-structure, which makes it easier for White to focus on his main plan – an attack on the queenside. I should add here that in cases where White has not played ♘f3, there is a second plan he can adopt, namely e3, ♗d3, ♘ge2 and 0-0 followed eventually by central expansion with f3 and e4. This plan leads to an entirely different type of position, but it need not concern us here as White gave up the option of this plan as early as move two.

5   ...   exd5

Black maintains his strongpoint in the centre. 5...♘xd5 6 e4 would give White a central advantage without any compensation.

6   ♗g5

In order to develop his light-squared bishop, White must play e3, so the other bishop should be developed first to avoid it being blocked in. It is quite possible to develop the bishop to f4, but the text-move is most popular.

6   ...   c6

White was threatening to take on d5 (the trick 7 ♘xd5 ♘xd5 8 ♗xd8 ♗b4+ doesn't work here because White can reply 9 ♘d2). Black could have prevented this threat by 6...♗e7, but he will probably have to play ...c6 sooner or later to secure his d5-pawn.

7   e3

White prepares to complete his kingside development.

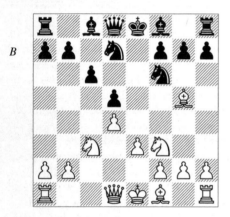

7   ...   ♗e7

Black does likewise.

8   ♕c2

White's next two moves are probably going to be ♕c2 and ♗d3 in any case, so White chooses the order that keeps Black's options to a minimum. After 8 ♗d3, Black can play 8...♘e4.

8   ...   0-0

Now, however, 8...♘e4 loses a pawn for insufficient compensation after 9 ♘xe4 dxe4 10 ♕xe4 ♕a5+ 11 ♔d1.

9   ♗d3

Exerting pressure along the b1-h7 diagonal. Black will be reluctant to play ...h6, because his plan for developing kingside play includes ...♖e8 and ...♘f8-g6. With the pawn on h6, it isn't possible to play ...♘g6.

9   ...   ♖e8

A natural developing move, which also frees his slightly congested mass of minor pieces.

10   0-0

The most common move, but it is not the only possibility. White can sharpen the struggle by playing 10 0-0-0 or 10 h3 followed soon by 0-0-0. Then we would have a situation of castling on opposite wings; both sides would play to attack the enemy king, Black by advancing his a- and b-pawns and White by pushing his g- and h-pawns.

10   ...   ♘f8

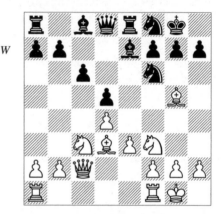

The pawn-structure determines the basic plans for both sides. White's ambitions lie on the queenside, where he will conduct the famous 'minority attack'. The idea is to play b4-b5 (possibly supported by a4). If Black takes on b5, he is left with a weak d5-pawn; if he allows White to take on c6, then he must either recapture with a piece, when d5 is again weak, or with a pawn, when he has a backward pawn on c6. In many ways, the ideal response for Black is to meet b5 by ...c5. This often results in an isolated d-pawn for Black, but this may not be a high price to pay in return for the time White has spent advancing his queenside pawns. However, Black cannot guarantee to be able to meet b5 by ...c5 – it depends on the specifics of the position.

Black, on the other hand, will try to generate play on the kingside. White's castled position is unweakened, and he has some defensive minor pieces on that side of the board, so progress will not be easy. However, Black should at least try to create enough play to ensure that White still has to keep an eye on the kingside and therefore cannot operate with complete freedom on the other flank. The above scenario is perhaps the most typical, but it is important for both players not be hamstrung by preconceived notions about their correct plan. If Black decentralizes his pieces, for example, White can change tack and play for a central break with e4.

11   h3

This is one of those little moves which is quite hard to explain, because there is no single reason for playing it – it is based on a combination of small factors. Of course White would like to deny the c8-bishop any good squares, but there is no immediate threat to play ...♗g4, because White can reply ♘e5. However, it is quite likely that h3 will be necessary sooner or later, so it is unlikely to be a waste of time. Secondly, the main alternative is 11 ♖ab1, preparing b4, but White still harbours a hope that he might be able to play b4 without the preparatory ♖ab1, in which case playing h3 first saves a tempo. As we shall see, whether White can get away with this depends on Black's reply. Thirdly, White stops the f6-knight moving to g4. This is relevant if White plays ♘e5 at some stage. Indeed, the best reply to the immediate 11 ♘e5 is 11...♘g4!. Finally, White creates a bolt-hole for his bishop on h2. In many cases White would like to keep his dark-squared bishop, meeting ...♘e4 (for example) by ♗f4. Then having h2 free is very useful. In any case, 11 h3 is the currently fashionable move, although several other moves have been tried. Note that the immediate 11 ♗xf6 ♗xf6 12 b4 (trying to save a tempo by missing out ♖ab1) is met by 12...♗g4, when the knight has to retreat to the relatively passive square d2.

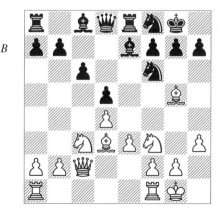

11   ...   ♗e6

Black has tried a number of different responses:

1) 11...♘h5 12 ♗xe7 ♖xe7 13 ♖fe1 and White is preparing for action in the centre, while Black must still recall his offside knight back from h5.

2) 11...♘g6 12 ♗xf6 (12 ♘e5 is also promising) 12...♗xf6 13 b4 gives White an edge, as Black can no longer play ...♗g4.

3) 11...♘e4 12 ♗f4! is awkward for Black, in view of the triple attack on e4. Neither 12...♘xc3 13 bxc3 nor 12...f5 13 ♘e5 equalizes for Black.

4) 11...g6 is one of Black's better responses. The idea is to play ...♘e6, without losing a pawn to ♗xf6 followed by ♗xh7+.

The text-move is also quite solid. Black just develops a piece, and otherwise keeps his options open. If White now plays 12 ♗xf6 ♗xf6 13 b4, then after 13...♖c8 Black is in time to meet 14 b5 with 14...c5. The position of the bishop on e6 is also useful if White plays 12 ♖ab1, since after 12...♘e4! Black does not lose a pawn to 13 ♗xe7 ♖xe7 14 ♘xe4, because the a2-pawn is hanging.

12   ♖fe1!?

An interesting and flexible move. White has tried quite a range of other moves, but this seems as good as any of them. It also has the advantage of being unexpected (so far as I can tell, it was only played once in grandmaster chess before the current game). I have already mentioned why 12 ♖ab1 is inferior, so if White wants to prepare b4 he has to play 12 a3, but then Black can reply 12...♘6d7 13 ♗f4 ♘b6 aiming for the potentially weak square on c4 should White push his b-pawn. The text-move prepares to counter the ...♘6d7-b6 plan, which decentralizes the black knight, with the central push e4.

12   ...   ♖c8

12...♘e4? loses a pawn to 13 ♗xe7 ♕xe7 14 ♗xe4 dxe4 15 ♕xe4, while 12...♘6d7 13 ♗f4 ♘b6 (13...♘g6 14 ♗h2 makes use of the h2-square) 14 e4 dxe4 15 ♗xe4 gives White active piece-play. In particular, 15...♘g6 is bad because of 16 ♗xg6 hxg6 17 ♖xe6 fxe6 18 ♕xg6 with excellent play for the exchange.

The move played is mainly defensive. It aims to meet b4-b5 by ...c5, but otherwise the rook is not especially well placed on c8.

13   a3

White has played as many flexible moves as he can, and now turns his attention toward the traditional minority attack plan.

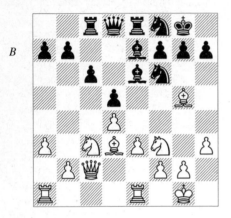

13   ...   ♘g6?!

The knight on f8 wasn't going anywhere else, so this move is natural. Having said that, the knight doesn't have many possible destinations from g6 either! One of Black's problems in this line is that the correct organization of his minor pieces is not at all obvious, while White's ideas are far more clear-cut. In my view, since Black doesn't really know where his minor pieces belong, he should have left them where they were for the moment and played 13...a5, obstructing White's queenside expansion, at least temporarily.

Note that 13...c5 14 dxc5 ♖xc5 15 ♘d4 gives White a safe advantage. There is a big difference between playing ...c5 when White's queenside pawns are still at home and playing it after b4-b5. In the latter case, White has wasted time and his advanced queenside pawns can easily become weak.

14   b4

This is the natural follow-up to White's previous move, even though 15 b5 is not a threat, because of the reply 15...c5. In fact, it is still not clear whether White will play on the queenside (for example, by ♘a4-c5) or in the centre with ♖ad1 and e4. Keeping your opponent guessing is always a good idea.

14   ...   a5

Black doesn't have many constructive moves; for example, 14...♗d6 15 e4!? dxe4 16 ♘xe4 ♗e7 17 ♘c5 forces 17...♗xc5 18 dxc5, when

White, with his two bishops and more active pieces, stands very well.

15   ♘a4!?

An interesting move. The obvious continuation would be 15 ♖ab1 but White would prefer not to play ♖ab1 for two reasons. Firstly, it consumes a tempo and secondly, if Black opens the a-file by exchanging on b4, then the rook may well be better placed on a1. However, White had a safe and effective alternative in 15 ♗xf6 ♗xf6 16 ♘a4. Then:

1) 16...axb4 17 axb4 ♖a8 (17...b6 18 ♗a6 ♖c7 19 ♘xb6 ♗e7 20 ♖eb1 favours White) 18 ♘c5 ♖xa1 19 ♖xa1 b6 20 ♘xe6 ♖xe6 21 ♗f5 ♖d6 22 ♖a7 followed by ♕a2 or ♕a4, with strong positional pressure.

2) 16...♘f8 17 ♘c5 b6 18 ♘xe6 fxe6 19 bxa5 bxa5 (19...c5 is awkwardly met by 20 ♗a6) 20 ♖ac1 and again White has a positional plus. Black cannot liquidate his backward c-pawn with 20...c5 21 dxc5 ♗e7 because 22 ♗b5 ♖xc5 23 ♕a4 wins material.

With the text-move, White tries to save a tempo by transferring his knight to c5 at once, even at the cost of offering his b-pawn.

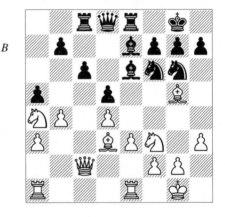

15   ...   ♘e4?!

Black trusts White's calculations and turns down the offered pawn, but now he falls into a very passive position. Black would have had reasonable chances to save the game if he had simply lopped off the b-pawn by 15...axb4!?. Then:

1) 16 axb4 ♗xb4 (16...♘e4 17 ♗xe7 ♖xe7 18 ♘c5 f5 19 ♖a7 is good for White) 17 ♖eb1 ♕e7 18 ♕b2 ♗d6 (18...c5 19 dxc5 ♗xc5 20 ♗xf6 gxf6 transposes to line '2') 19 ♕xb7 ♖c7

20 ♕b6 h6 21 ♗xf6 ♕xf6 22 ♗e2 ♗f5 is not very clear.

2) 16 ♗xf6 gxf6 17 axb4 ♗xb4 18 ♖eb1 ♕e7 19 ♕b2 c5 20 dxc5 ♗xc5 21 ♕xb7 (after 21 ♘xc5 ♖xc5 White cannot regain the pawn by 22 ♕xb7?? because of 22...♖c1+) 21...♘e5 (21...♗a7 22 ♕b2 should be good for White) 22 ♗e2 (22 ♘xe5 fxe5 23 ♘xc5 ♖xc5 doesn't offer White much) 22...♗a7 and White has only a slight advantage. However, the prospect of defending a position in which Black has only a long period of arduous defence in view would have put many players off, even if objectively it was the right choice.

16   ♗xe7

Now Black is left with his problem bishop, which still shows little sign of generating any activity.

16   ...   ♖xe7

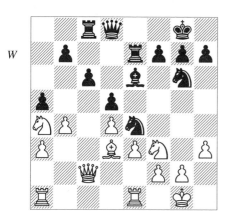

17   ♘c5

An excellent square for the knight, exerting pressure against both b7 and the e4-knight. Black can hardly take on c5, because after the reply bxc5 he has a backward pawn on an open file.

17   ...   f5

Securing the knight at e4 for the moment, but imprisoning the e6-bishop. The alternative is 17...♗f5, but then 18 ♘g5 (18 ♘d2 ♘xc5 19 ♗xf5 ♘e6 20 ♘b3 also offers White some advantage) 18...axb4 (18...♘xg5 19 ♗xf5 ♖a8 20 f4! b6 21 ♘d3 ♘e4 22 ♘e5 ♘xe5 23 dxe5 is very good for White) 19 axb4 ♕e8 20 ♗xe4 ♗xe4 (20...dxe4 21 f3) 21 ♘gxe4 dxe4 22 ♖a7 ♖b8 23 ♖ea1 offers White considerable pressure.

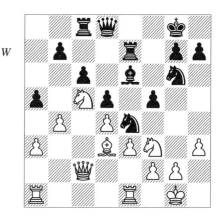

18   bxa5!

This excellent move shows flexibility of thought. White abandons the traditional minority attack plan because in this position he sees that he can force his a3-pawn forward to a5. This will leave Black with a weak and backward b-pawn on a half-open file. On the kingside, it is hard for Black to get going because his pieces are inactive and White's pressure against e4 restricts his freedom.

18   ...   ♕xa5
19   ♖eb1

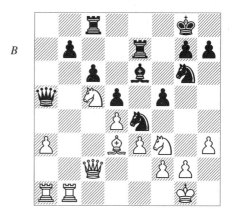

19   ...   ♕a7?!

This is rather a concession: Black voluntarily retreats his queen and thereby allows the a-pawn a free run up to a5. The alternatives are:

1) 19...♘xc5? 20 dxc5 is positionally very bad for Black, as in addition to his other assets White now has the d4-square for his knight.

2) 19...b6 20 ♘xe6 ♖xe6 21 ♖b5! ♕a6 22 ♖c1 ♖f8 23 ♖xd5 ♕xa3 24 ♖d7 with a near-decisive advantage in view of Black's numerous

weak pawns and White's excellent piece activity.

3) 19...♖cc7 20 ♖b4 (threatening 21 ♖a4) 20...b5 (if Black retreats his queen, then a4-a5 as in the game) 21 ♖bb1, with a4 to come, leaves Black much worse. If he tries 21...♕a8, with the idea of meeting 22 a4 by 22...♖a7, then White wins a pawn by 22 ♘xe6 ♖xe6 23 ♖xb5.

4) 19...♖b8 is probably the toughest defence. White continues 20 a4, followed by ♘b3 and a5, reaching a similar type of position to that in the game, but at least Black would have gained some time.

20   a4   ♖f8

Black is hoping to generate some kingside counterplay by ...f4. 20...b6 21 ♘xe6 ♖xe6 22 ♕b3 ♖b8 23 a5 b5 24 ♖c1 ♕a6 25 ♕b4 is also very unpleasant for Black.

21   a5   ♗c8

Thanks to the pressure against e4 and Black's offside queen, he still isn't ready to play ...f4. In any case, it is far too late since White's queenside attack is close to breaking through. If 21...♘xc5 22 dxc5 ♗c8, then 23 ♘d4 ♖ef7 24 a6 and White crashes through even more quickly.

22   ♖b6!

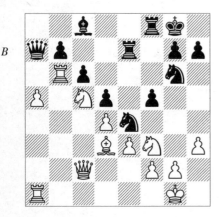

Intending to put the queen behind the rook and then play a6.

22   ...   h6

There is nothing Black can do. A typical line would be 22...♔h8 (trying to avoid the pin along the a2-g8 diagonal which occurs in the game) 23 ♕b1 ♘xc5 24 dxc5 ♖f6 25 a6 bxa6 26 ♗xa6 ♗xa6 27 ♖axa6 ♕d7 28 ♖a8+ ♘f8 29 ♖bb8 ♔g8 30 ♘g5! (leading up to an attractive

finish) 30...h6 31 ♖d8 ♕c7 32 ♖xf8+! ♖xf8 33 ♕xf5 and mates.

23   ♕b3

White prepares a6, while at the same time preventing ...f4 because then the e4-knight would be hanging.

23   ...   ♔h7
24   a6!

The queenside attack has arrived. Black is lost.

24   ...   ♘xc5

After 24...f4 25 ♖e1 fxe3 (25...♘xc5 26 dxc5 fxe3 27 ♕b1 exf2+ 28 ♔xf2 is winning for White) 26 ♖xe3 bxa6 (or 26...♘xc5 27 dxc5 ♖xe3 28 fxe3 bxa6 29 ♕c2 winning the pinned knight) 27 ♘xe4 dxe4 28 ♗xe4 ♗f5 29 ♗xf5 ♖xf5 30 ♖xc6 White has a straightforward win – he is a pawn up and Black's position is in total disarray.

25   dxc5   ♖f6
26   ♘d4   ♘e5

This allows a tactical finish, but even 26...♖ef7 27 ♕c2 is hopeless; for example, 27...bxa6 (27...f4 28 exf4) 28 ♖xc6 ♖xc6 29 ♘xc6 ♕c7 30 ♘d4 ♕e5 31 c6 ♖c7 32 ♕b1, threatening a6 and f5, and Black is dead lost.

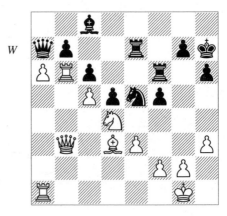

27   ♗xf5+!

Suddenly White strikes on the kingside as well.

27   ...   ♗xf5

27...♖xf5 28 ♕b1 attacks f5 and, by defending the a1-rook, threatens axb7.

28   ♘xf5   ♖xf5
29   ♕b1   1-0

The same principle. The twin threats ensure a large material gain.

Yermolinsky is an expert on handling the white side of the Orthodox Queen's Gambit, and it shows. His opening play was full of little finesses (such as 12 ♖fe1) to make life awkward for his opponent. For a time, he kept open the possibility of both a minority attack and play in the centre, and Christiansen found it hard to find a constructive plan which could cope with both these eventualities. When White definitely decided for queenside play, the odds were already stacked somewhat in his favour – Black's rook on c8 was inactive and his position could not easily be reorganized to generate kingside counterplay. After Black turned down White's b-pawn at move 15, he quickly ran into trouble. Yermolinsky pressed his queenside attack home with great vigour, and even managed to end with a tactical flourish on the kingside.

The lessons here are:

1) One of White's most dangerous plans with the Orthodox Queen's Gambit pawn-structure is the minority attack on the queenside.

2) However, flexibility is important. A queenside attack is much less committal than one conducted against the king and it is possible to change direction if circumstances warrant it.

3) A queenside attack is usually combined with efforts to restrict the enemy counterplay.

4) A queenside attack is a powerful weapon – it should not be underestimated.

The Two Bishops

Two bishops, operating in concert, are usually worth more than a bishop and a knight or two knights – this is what is meant by 'the advantage of the two bishops'. Of course, if the two bishops are pointing directly at the enemy king, one can well understand that the king might be in danger, but even when there are no immediate threats, the two bishops often confer a nagging advantage. Factors that tend to accentuate this advantage include:

1) An open position. Bishops are generally superior to knights in open positions, so this should come as no surprise.

2) A lack of outposts for the knight. If there are no stable squares for the knight, then it may end up being pushed away to the edge of the board, further reducing its activity. A special case of this arises when the centre is totally devoid of pawns, denying the knight any central support point.

3) Potentially weak pawns on both wings. The bishops are effective at targeting both wings simultaneously, while the knight can only hop laboriously from flank to flank.

The factors that reduce the advantage of the two bishops are really just the converse of the three points mentioned above.

In the following game, White uses the power of the two bishops to torture Black into submission.

Game 22
M. Gurevich – N. Miezis
Bonn 1996
Budapest Gambit

1	d4	♘f6
2	c4	

For comments on the moves up to here, see Game 13.

2	...	e5

This is the Budapest Gambit, an attempt to seize the initiative by sacrificing a pawn. If White hangs on to the pawn, then Black does indeed obtain some compensation (although whether it is really sufficient is a matter for debate). The main problem with this gambit, and the reason why it is not more popular, is that White can simply return the pawn and thereby obtain the advantage of the two bishops.

3	dxe5

The only test is to accept.

3	...	♞g4

This is the most common continuation, in which Black plays simply to regain the pawn. The alternative is 3...♞e4, a risky idea which aims for active piece-play at the cost of not regaining the gambit pawn.

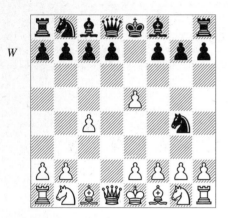

4	♝f4

The main line against the Budapest involves playing ♞f3 and ♝f4, but White's precise choice of move-order depends on which lines he wishes to avoid. The sequence 4 ♞f3 ♞c6 5 ♝f4 transposes to the game, but this allows Black the option of 4...♝c5 5 e3 ♞c6, regaining the e5-pawn without conceding the two bishops. True, this line is thought good for White on account of his grip on d5, but Gurevich probably reasons that as it costs little to prevent it, he might as well do so. The only possible drawback to the 4 ♝f4 move-order is that it allows two possible sidelines by Black. The first is 4...♝b4+ 5 ♞d2 d6 (5...♞c6 6 ♞f3 again transposes to the game), but then 6 exd6 ♛f6 7 ♞h3 is thought to favour White. The other idea is 4...g5 5 ♝g3 ♝g7 6 ♞f3 ♞c6, but then 7 h4! is very promising. As with many move-order questions, there is little objective reason for preferring one option over another – it all depends on which lines one wants to avoid.

4	...	♞c6

Black decides simply to head into the main line of the Budapest.

5	♞f3

White must put up a fight for the e5-pawn, in order to extract some sort of concession from Black.

5	...	♝b4+

Black must now devote himself to regaining the pawn, otherwise he will be left without compensation.

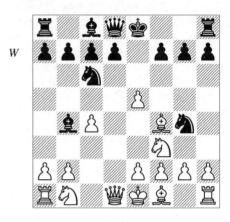

6	♞bd2

This is the most solid continuation. White can keep his extra pawn by playing 6 ♞c3 ♛e7 7 ♛d5, but Black obtains fair compensation after 7...f6 8 exf6 ♞xf6 9 ♛d3 d6 10 e3 (10 g3 is also possible) 10...0-0. In this position, Black has a significant lead in development, his remaining pieces can easily come into play and his pressure along the e- and f-files makes it awkward for White to undertake any positive action. It is hard to say whether this is really enough for the pawn, and with few high-class examples to work from, any assessment will be partly a matter of guesswork.

6	...	♛e7

Now White is unable to keep the e5-pawn.

7	a3

It is more accurate to play a3 sooner rather than later, as it virtually forces Black to part with his dark-squared bishop. The alternative is 7 e3 ♞gxe5 8 ♞xe5 ♞xe5 9 ♝e2 (White can still play 9 a3 here, transposing to the game, but further delay is unwise) 9...0-0 10 0-0, but then Black has the option of 10...a5! 11 a3 ♝c5, when he keeps his bishop.

7	...	♞cxe5

A little trick; Black threatens 8...♞d3# and so White has no time to take the bishop.

8	♞xe5	♞xe5
9	e3	

Stopping the mate and putting the question to the b4-bishop.

9	...	♝xd2+

There is nothing better. 9...♗d6 is bad for Black in view of 10 ♘e4! (10 ♗e2 ♘d3+ 11 ♗xd3 ♗xf4 is unclear) 10...♘xc4 11 ♘xd6+ ♘xd6 12 ♖c1 ♔d8 (otherwise White regains the pawn, while retaining the two bishops and a vastly superior pawn-structure) 13 ♕d4 ♘e8 14 ♗b5 with an enormous initiative for the pawn. The rarely-adopted 9...♗c5 is perhaps playable, although White can retain some advantage by 10 ♘b3 (10 b4 ♗d4! 11 ♖a2 d6 12 ♗e2 0-0 13 0-0 ♗b6 is only marginally better for White) 10...d6 11 ♘xc5 dxc5 12 ♕h5 ♘g6 13 ♗g3, when he can take comfort in his two bishops.

10	♕xd2	0-0?!

After this inaccuracy, White can obtain a clear positional advantage. Black should have played 10...d6 in order to inhibit the advance c5. I do not want to go too deeply into questions of opening theory, but it is worth noting that White cannot hope for more than a slight advantage after 10...d6. His main ideas are based on trying to play c5 in any case:

1) 11 c5 (this is clearly critical, but Black can accept the offer) 11...dxc5 (after any other move, Black ends up with the same poor position as in the game) 12 ♕d5 ♘g6 13 ♗b5+ c6! 14 ♗xc6+ bxc6 15 ♕xc6+ ♕d7 and Black obtains sufficient compensation for the sacrificed exchange.

2) 11 ♕c3 (definitely threatening c5) 11...f6 (by supporting the e5-square, Black once again prevents c5) 12 ♗e2 b6 13 0-0 0-0 14 b4 c5 with an unclear position. White has the two bishops, but Black's e5-knight is well placed and his light-squared bishop will be active on the long diagonal.

3) 11 ♖c1 b6 12 c5 bxc5 13 ♗xe5 ♕xe5 14 ♗b5+ ♔f8 with an unclear position. White has enough compensation for the pawn but possibly not more.

The above lines make it clear that achieving c5 is a key target for White. Why is this move so important? The basic reason lies in White's possession of the two bishops. They are at their best in an open position in which both bishops have plenty of scope. While the pawn is on c4, it is not easy for White to activate his light-squared bishop; it is blocked in by the c4-pawn and it cannot be developed to f3 since Black's knight is controlling that square. However, once White

has played c5 this bishop has much more scope, and the two bishops then have excellent chances of becoming a major force in the game. It is also relevant that the move c5 weakens Black's support for his e5-knight. A knight occupying a firm post in the centre is usually a match for a bishop, but once the knight gets driven away towards the edge of the board, the bishop is usually far superior. Thus Black's ability to maintain his knight on e5 is important, and anything White can do to undermine the knight is helpful.

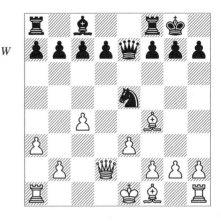

W

11	c5!

White must make the most of his opportunity. After the less accurate 11 ♗e2 d6 12 0-0 b6 13 ♕c3 ♗b7 Black can consolidate his position, when White's chances of gaining an advantage are much reduced. Note that this is a case in which White is fully justified in postponing castling while he gets on with more important business. Black's poor development means that there is no risk involved in keeping the king in the centre for a few moves.

11	...	♖e8

Black is unable to avoid a significant positional disadvantage:

1) 11...♕xc5 12 ♖c1 ♕d6 13 ♕xd6 cxd6 14 ♖d1 (14 ♗e2 followed by 0-0 and ♖fd1 is also good) 14...♖e8 15 ♖xd6 b6 16 ♗e2 and White is better since he has the two bishops, while Black has an isolated and rather backward d-pawn.

2) 11...b6?! 12 ♕d5 ♘c6 13 ♗xc7 is very good for White.

3) 11...d6 12 cxd6 cxd6 13 ♗e2 is similar to the game.

12   &Xc1   d6

12...b6 13 cxb6 cxb6 14 &Wd5 &Nc6 15 &Be2 does not change the situation; White has two active bishops and Black has an isolated pawn. 12...c6 13 &Wd4 f6 14 &Be2 is unpleasant for Black since he can hardly free himself on the queenside.

13   cxd6   cxd6

Black has better chances of consolidating with queens on the board. After 13...&Wxd6?! 14 &Wxd6 cxd6 White has the choice between exerting positional pressure by 15 &Xc7 and grabbing a pawn straight away by 15 &Xd1 &Bf5 16 &Xxd6 &Xac8 17 &Bb5!, although in the latter case White has to allow opposite-coloured bishops after 17...&Xe6 18 &Xxe6 &Bxe6 19 &Kd2 &Nc4+ 20 &Bxc4 &Xxc4.

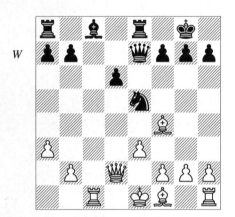

14   &Be2

White has achieved his positional aim and now catches up on his kingside development.

14   ...   &Be6
15   0-0   &Xac8?!

An ingenious defence, offering a pawn for some counterplay. Although it is not totally correct, I cannot criticize the move harshly, because Black's position is inferior after any move; for example, 15...&Xad8 16 &Bb5 &Xf8 (16...&Bd7 17 &Xc7) 17 &Wd4 b6 18 &Xc3 and Black has weakened his queenside pawns, while White can gain control of the open c-file.

16   &Wd4

After 16 &Wb4 &Xc5 17 &Xfd1 b6 followed by ...&Xec8 Black is in a good position to contest the c-file. However, the move played looks very strong since it attacks both e5 and a7.

16   ...   &Nc6

This is the point of Black's play: he offers the d6-pawn in order to gain counterplay. In positions where the defender's position is crippled by a weak pawn, he should always be alert for a chance to offer this pawn in order to stir up trouble. It is often better to be a pawn down with some compensation than to have material equality with serious weaknesses. This particular case is a marginal example, since it is by no means clear that White couldn't have taken the pawn.

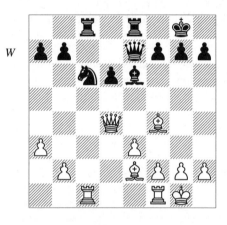

17   &Wd2?

Gurevich decides to play safe and refuse the pawn. This is a typical practical decision since it would take considerable time to verify that it was really safe to take on d6, whereas repeating the position is a decision that can be taken quickly. However, in this case it would probably have been objectively better to take the pawn, as with accurate play White can consolidate his material advantage. 17 &Wxd6! and now:

1) 17...&Wxd6 18 &Bxd6 &Xed8 19 &Xfd1 &Nd4 (19...&Bb3 20 &Xd3 &Nd4 21 &Xxc8 &Nxe2+ 22 &Kf1 &Xxc8 23 &Xxb3 and White will be two pawns up) 20 exd4 &Xxc1 21 &Xxc1 &Xxd6 22 &Xc7 &Xxd4 23 &Xxb7 leaves White a clear pawn up.

2) 17...&Wf6 (this attacks b2 and threatens 18...&Xed8) 18 &Wd3! (Black can be happy with his position after 18 &Wc5 &Wxb2 since he has exchanged his weak d6-pawn for the healthy pawn on b2; 18 &Wd2?! &Xed8 is unpleasant for White as 19 &Wc3? runs into 19...&Nd4, when White loses material) with another branch:

2a) 18...&Xcd8 19 &Wb5! (19 &Wc3 &Wxc3 20 bxc3 &Xd2 21 &Bf3 &Na5 gives Black a little counterplay against the weak queenside pawns)

19...♘d4 20 exd4 ♕xf4 21 ♕xb7 ♗d5 22 ♕b5 and White will keep an extra pawn.

2b) 18...♕xb2 19 ♖b1 ♕a2 20 ♖xb7 ♘a5 21 ♖c7 (this is the key move, as otherwise Black could continue 21...♗c4) 21...♘c4 22 ♖c1 ♖xc7 23 ♗xc7 ♘xa3 24 ♗e5 and Black is in considerable difficulties owing to his offside pieces; for example, 24...♘c4 25 ♗d4 and White will win the a-pawn. The resulting position, with White having the two bishops and an extra kingside pawn, will be very uncomfortable for Black.

> **17   ...   ♘e5**

Black simply repeats. 17...d5 is inferior because Black gives up one of his main assets – the secure square e5 for his knight.

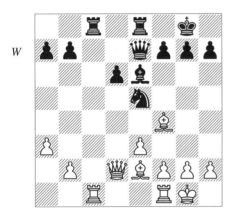

> **18   ♖xc8**

White decides to exchange all the rooks and try to exploit his advantage in the more simplified position that results. White retains some advantage with this plan, but far less than if he had taken the d6-pawn.

> **18   ...   ♖xc8**

White has two positional advantages: the two bishops, and Black's weak d-pawn. Despite this, the game is far from won. In most textbooks, you will find examples in which such advantages rapidly prove decisive. Readers who only study such examples will then wonder why it proves so difficult to win similar positions in their own games. Indeed, if Black were to make a couple of inferior moves here, he would probably soon lose the game. However, what makes this game so instructive is that Black puts up a determined resistance for a long time. This provides us with an object lesson in

how to defend unpleasant positions, and how to overcome the obstacles placed in one's path by the defender.

> **19   ♖c1**

19 ♕d4 is no longer effective as 19...♖c2 gives Black counterplay.

> **19   ...   ♖c7**

Black does not want to exchange immediately, as this would leave White in control of the c-file. He cannot really prevent this in the end, as White can continue ♖c3 and ♕c2, but at least he makes it as hard for White as possible.

> **20   ♖c3**

Doubling the major pieces will more or less force Black to take on c3.

> **20   ...   f6**

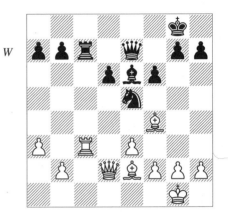

Reinforcing the important e5-knight, and thereby ruling out forks based on attacking e5 (such as ♕d4, as White played earlier).

> **21   e4**

White has to come up with a concrete plan for achieving progress. As has already been mentioned, the secure e5-knight is one of Black's main assets because it restricts the activity of White's dark-squared bishop. Therefore, White decides to circumvent the knight by repositioning his bishop on the g1-a7 diagonal, where it attacks Black's queenside pawns.

> **21   ...   a6**

Anticipating White's attack by ♗e3.

> **22   ♗e3   b5**

Black would like to use the c4-square, and the secure outpost this move provides is probably more important than the slight weakening of the queenside pawns. Note that 22...♘c4?? loses a piece to 23 ♕c1, followed by b3.

23 ♕c1

Black cannot avoid the exchange of rooks.

23 ... ♖xc3

24 ♕xc3

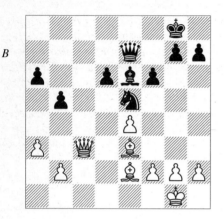

24 ... ♕b7

Black is content to play passively for the moment, but this gives White the chance to consolidate his position. However, active play, although more complicated, probably also does not completely equalize: 24...♘c4 25 ♗d4 (25 ♗c1 ♗f7 26 b3 is wrong owing to 26...♕xe4 27 ♗f1 ♕e5!) 25...♗f7 26 f3! (26 b3 ♘xa3 27 ♗d3 ♕e6 28 ♕a5 b4 29 ♕d8+ ♗e8 is unclear) 26...d5 and although Black liquidates his d-pawn, White retains some advantage by 27 b3 ♘d6 (27...♘xa3? loses material to 28 ♗c5 ♕c7 29 exd5 ♗xd5 30 ♕e3) 28 ♗c5 and now:

1) 28...♕e6 29 ♗xd6 (29 ♕d2 ♘b7 30 exd5 ♕xd5 31 ♕xd5 ♗xd5 is a draw) 29...♕xd6 30 ♕c8+ ♕f8 31 ♕xa6 dxe4 32 b4 exf3 33 gxf3 and Black faces the loss of his b5-pawn.

2) 28...dxe4 29 ♕b4 exf3 30 ♗xf3 a5 31 ♕xa5 ♕e5 32 ♗xd6 ♕d4+ (32...♕xd6 33 ♕a8+ ♕f8 34 ♕xf8+ ♔xf8 35 a4 and White has an advantage due to his outside passed pawn; the point of the intermediary check becomes clear later) 33 ♔f1 ♕xd6 34 ♕xb5 (34 ♕a8+ ♕f8 35 ♕xf8+ ♔xf8 36 a4 b4 is safe for Black; thanks to the position of the white king on f1, 37 a5 ♗xb3 38 a6 may be met by 38...♗c4+ 39 ♗e2 ♗d5) 34...♕xa3 35 ♕b8+ ♕f8 36 ♕xf8+ ♔xf8 37 b4 and White has just an edge.

25 f3 ♗c4

25...d5 is similar to the game. 25...♘c4 26 ♗d4 is slightly better for White than the previous note, since he has already played f3.

26 ♗d1

White must keep his two bishops, otherwise he has nothing.

26 ... ♗e6

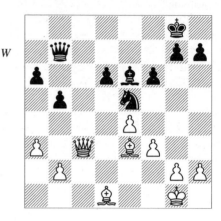

For the moment Black is not sure how to proceed; in particular, he cannot decide whether to play ...d5 or not. Of course, it is desirable for him to liquidate his isolated pawn, but on the other hand every exchange of pawns opens the position further and accentuates the power of the two bishops. This is a typical phenomenon when one side has the two bishops – it may not be their immediate power which is dangerous, but the latent power they may exert as the position becomes more simplified.

27 ♗d4

White is also toying with different ideas; this move doesn't actually threaten anything, but it does remove the bishop from attack after a possible ...♘c4.

27 ... ♘c6

Black decides to kick the bishop back.

28 ♗f2 ♕d7

28...♘e5 29 h3 would be similar to the game.

29 h3

White's plan is to gain space by f4 and ♗f3, denying Black's knight any central square. Now that White shows clear signs of an ability to make progress, Black decides to play ...d5.

29 ... d5

30 exd5 ♗xd5

30...♕xd5 31 ♗c2 threatens ♗e4, and if Black goes for an exchange of queens by playing 31...♕c4 then an ending similar to that in the game arises.

31 ♗c2!

An excellent move; White intends to attack h7 with ♕d3. After the more or less forced reply ...g6, Black's dark squares on the kingside will be weakened and the power of White's dark-squared bishop will be enhanced.

31	...	♕e6
32	♕d3	g6
33	♕e3	

Having softened Black up slightly, White decides to offer the exchange of queens.

| 33 | ... | ♕xe3 |

Since the ending turns out to be unpleasant for Black, the question arises as to whether Black should have avoided the exchange of queens. However, it is not so easy to achieve this aim; for example, 33...♘e5 34 f4 ♘c4 35 ♕xe6+ ♗xe6 36 ♗d4 is rather similar to the game, while after 33...♕d7 34 ♕b6 ♕c8 35 h4 the possibility of h5 is a further worry for Black.

| 34 | ♗xe3 | |

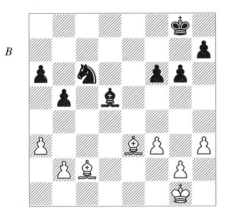

It would be easy to dismiss this position as simply a draw, since the pawn-structure is fairly symmetrical, but in fact White has genuine winning chances. The two bishops are certainly better than a bishop and a knight in this relatively open position, and in addition Black's knight lacks any stable outpost. However, the most important factor is that Black's pawn-structure has been slightly weakened on both wings. Take the kingside, for example. The pawn on f6 can be attacked by the dark-squared bishop, leaving Black the choice of having one piece constantly tied down to defending it, or of pushing it by ...f5. The problem with this latter choice is that it opens up a path for the white king to penetrate into the kingside via the dark

squares. The situation on the queenside also poses a potential danger for Black: his pawns are already fairly far advanced and on light squares, so again there is the possibility of a white king invasion.

It would therefore be quite wrong to dismiss the position as a dead draw. It may well be that objectively speaking the result should be a draw. However, a protracted period of accurate defence is required for Black to achieve this result, so White is fully justified in pressing on. The advantage of bishop against knight is often underestimated; the remainder of this game will show how White can play to exploit his advantage.

| 34 | ... | ♗f7 |
| 35 | ♔f2 | ♔e6 |

Both sides bring their kings to the centre.

| 36 | ♗b6 | |

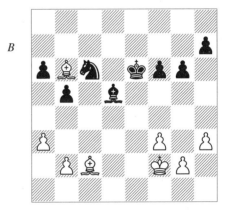

White clears the way for his king to advance to e3. In a position with the king on e3 and the dark-squared bishop on g3, Black's knight would be tied down to preventing ♔d4-c5 by White.

| 36 | ... | f5?! |

It is a critical decision whether to play this move or not, but I think that Black jumped the wrong way. Offering the white king an entry route via f4, g5 and h6 is a major concession, which should certainly not have been made voluntarily. Black should simply wait by 36...♔d6 37 ♔e3 ♔e6, leaving the burden on White to make progress. One idea is 38 h4, intending to break up Black's kingside pawns by h5. Black might have to meet h5 by ...f5 in any case, but at least the possible exchange on g6 would reduce the number of pawns on the kingside. If Black plays 36...♞e5, then 37 ♝d4 ♞c6 38 ♝c3 followed by ♚e3 and h4 is similar.

37   ♝e3!

Perhaps Black had not foreseen this switchback. Other moves are less effective; for example, the obvious 37 ♚e3?! (after 37 g4?!, 37...f4 not only keeps the king out, but also enables Black to target f3 with ...♞e5) is met by 37...g5, when Black gains a measure of dark-square control on the kingside. If Black can play ...f4+ then White's king will be shut out of the kingside, but attempts to prevent this move do not work: 38 f4 (38 g3 ♞e5 attacks f3 and threatens ...♞c4+) 38...♝xg2 39 fxg5 ♝xh3 40 ♝b3+ ♚d6 (40...♞e5 41 ♝c7#) 41 ♝g8, for example, backfires in view of 41...♞e7, when White cannot take the pawn on h7.

The strength of the move played is that it fixes Black's kingside pawns and therefore prevents him from repairing the dark-squared weaknesses created by ...f5. Black now has the constant worry of an invasion by the white king.

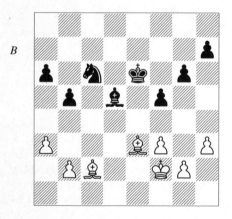

B

37   ...   ♝c4

37...♞e5 is a reasonable alternative, since the plan of transferring the knight to c4 makes it harder for White to activate his pieces. White may continue 38 ♚g3 ♞c4 39 ♝c1 (39 ♝d4 g5 40 h4 f4+ is fine for Black) 39...♚e5 40 h4 ♝f7 41 h5, and now:

1) 41...gxh5 (tempting, but now White has a clear target on the kingside) 42 b3 ♞b6 (after 42...♞a5 43 ♝b2+ ♚e6 44 ♚f4 ♝g6 45 ♝c3 ♞c6 46 b4 ♞e7 47 ♝b3+ ♞d5+ 48 ♚g5 ♚d6 49 ♝d4 Black's position remains uncomfortable) 43 ♚h4 ♞d5 44 ♚g5 h6+ 45 ♚xh6 f4 46

♝b2+ ♚e6 47 b4 ♞e3 48 ♝b3+ ♚e7 49 ♝xf7 ♚xf7 50 ♚xh5 ♞xg2 51 ♚g4 ♚e6 52 ♝c1 ♚e5 53 ♚g5 and now Black is in zugzwang and must lose his f-pawn.

2) After 41...♝f6! 42 ♚h4 ♝d5 it is not easy for White to make progress since b3 is met by ...♞a5, when the b3-pawn comes under fire.

38   g4!?

The immediate 38 ♚g3 is met by 38...♝f1, when White cannot advance his king further. Hence, White decides first to push the g-pawn and only then to play ♚g3.

38   ...   ♞e5

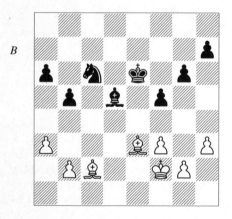

W

Black immediately takes steps to attack the f3-pawn, which is now deprived of support.

39   ♚g3   ♝e2

The alternatives are:

1) 39...♝d5 40 gxf5+ gxf5 41 ♚f4 ♞g6+ 42 ♚g5 f4 43 ♝xf4 ♝xf3 44 ♝f5+ ♚d5 45 ♝c8 is unpleasant for Black.

2) 39...♝d3!? is a reasonable defensive plan. After 40 ♝d1 ♞c4 41 ♝c1 ♞d6 (41...♞b6 42 ♚f4 ♞d5+ 43 ♚g5 favours White) 42 ♚f4 it is not easy for White to make progress since ♚g5 may be met by ...♞f7+.

3) 39...fxg4 is a logical move, because Black avoids the possible breaking-up of his kingside pawns by gxf5+. After 40 hxg4 (40 fxg4 ♚d5 41 ♚f4 ♞d3+ 42 ♚g5 ♞xb2 43 ♚h6 ♝d3 44 ♝xd3 ♞xd3 45 ♚xh7 ♞e5 should be enough to draw) 40...♝d3 41 ♝d1 Black's active pieces make progress difficult.

As we can see, at this stage Black still has a choice of reasonable plans to obstruct White's progress. However, his tiny inaccuracies in the last few moves before the time-control have a cumulative effect, with the result that the safe path starts to become very narrow.

40   ♔f4

Attacking the f5-pawn. If White exchanges first, then 40 gxf5+ gxf5 41 ♔f4 ♗d3 42 ♗d1 ♗f1 43 ♗d4 ♘g6+ (only possible because of the exchange on f5) 44 ♔g5 ♗xh3 45 ♗b3+ ♔d6 46 ♗g8 ♘e5 offers White at most a slight advantage.

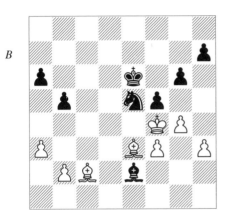

B

40   ...   ♗d3?!

Not 40...♘xf3? 41 gxf5+ gxf5? 42 ♗xf5+ followed by ♗g4 and White wins. However, 40...♘d3+ is a better defence; after 41 ♔g5 fxg4 42 fxg4 we transpose to the note to Black's 39th move, in which Black has excellent drawing chances.

41   ♗d1

Again, White must keep his two bishops to retain any winning chances.

41   ...   ♗f1

Threatening both the h-pawn and ...♘d3+.

42   ♗d4

Gaining time by attacking the knight.

42   ...   ♘c6?!

This allows White to break up Black's kingside pawns. Alternatives:

1) The tactical try 42...fxg4? fails to 43 ♗xe5 gxh3 44 ♗b3+ ♗c4 45 ♗xc4+ bxc4 46 ♔e4, when the h3-pawn is stopped.

2) 42...♘d3+ 43 ♔e3 (43 ♔g5 ♗xh3 44 gxf5+ ♗xf5 is fine for Black) 43...♘e5 is a better defence. After 44 h4 fxg4 45 fxg4 Black has avoided the breaking-up of his kingside pawns, although he must still worry about ♔f4-g5.

43   gxf5+   gxf5

44   ♗g7

Suddenly it turns out that Black cannot take the h3-pawn for tactical reasons, and the result is that Black has no compensation for the shattering of his kingside pawns, which leaves him with two weaknesses instead of one.

44   ...   ♘e7

If 44...♗xh3, then 45 ♗e2! (threatening 46 ♔g3) 45...♗g2 46 ♔g3 ♗h1 47 ♔h2 and the bishop is trapped.

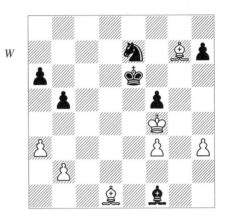

W

The text-move supports the f5-pawn; this will be necessary sooner or later because White is threatening ♗b3+ followed by ♗c2, forcing the knight back to e7.

45   ♔g3?!

White adopts a safety-first approach, but it was better to push the h-pawn straight away: 45 h4 ♘d5+ 46 ♔g5 ♘e3 (forcing the exchange of a pair of bishops, but it is too late to do much good) 47 ♗b3+ ♗c4 48 ♗xc4+ ♘xc4 (48...bxc4 49 ♗c3 followed by h5 and ♔h6 is also very good for White) 49 ♔h6 and White wins the h-pawn.

45   ...   ♘g6?!

Black aims to control f4 and h4, and so stop White's king advancing. However, after White plays h4, Black will face an awkward choice: to allow the knight to driven away by h5, or to play ...h5 himself, when the h-pawn will be more exposed to attack. 45...♘d5 was a more active continuation; after 46 f4 (46 ♔h4 ♘f4 draws) 46...♗d3 47 ♗e5 ♘e3 48 ♗f3 ♘c4 49 ♗c3 ♘d6 50 ♔h4 ♘e4 51 ♗e5 ♗f1 Black's pieces work together well, since the knight controls g5 while the bishop attacks the h-pawn and so prevents ♔h5.

46 h4 ♝c4

46...h5? is certainly not possible straight-away, as it loses a pawn to 47 f4.

47 ♝c2

47 h5 is also possible, but after 47...♘e7 White should not play 48 ♔f4? ♘d5+ 49 ♔g3 ♘e3, which costs him at least a pawn, but 48 ♝c2 ♘d5 49 ♔h4 with good winning chances.

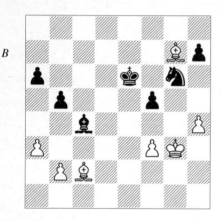

B

47 ... ♝e2

Black decides to allow h5. 47...h5 is no better in view of 48 ♝h6 ♝e2 (48...♔e5 49 f4+ fol-lowed by ♝d1 wins a pawn; 48...♝d5 49 f4 is similar) 49 ♝e3!, when Black is in zugzwang. A knight move allows ♔f4, 49...♔e5 50 ♝g5 ♔e6 51 ♔f2 ♝c4 52 f4 and ♝d1 wins a pawn, while 49...♝c4 50 ♝d1 ♘e5 51 ♝d4 ♘c6 52 ♝c3 is followed by either f4 or ♔f4.

48 h5 ♘e5

48...♘e7 49 ♔f4 ♘d5+ 50 ♔g5 ♘e3 51 ♝b1 is also very bad for Black since 51...♝xf3? loses a piece to 52 ♔f4.

49 ♔f4 ♝d3

The only move, because 49...♘d3+ 50 ♔e3 ♘c1 51 ♔d2 costs Black a piece.

50 ♝d1

Once again, White ducks the exchange of bishops.

50 ... ♘c4

51 ♝c3 ♘d6

51...a5 is ingenious, the idea being to an-swer ♔g5-h6 with ...a4 and ...♘e3 trapping the bishop on d1. However, after 52 a4! b4 53 ♝h8 White again threatens ♔g5 and there seems lit-tle Black can do about it.

The text-move aims to keep White's king out by meeting ♔g5 with ...♘f7+.

52 ♔e3

A typical situation has arisen for positions in which one side is defending passively. If Black makes the correct reply, White has the option of repeating the position, but if Black makes the wrong choice, then White can win fairly easily. The defender is in an unenviable position; he has to make the right choice again and again, while the attacker risks nothing. This is espe-cially difficult at the end of a long and tiring game and in practice the laws of probability usually catch up with the defender, and he even-tually makes a fatal slip.

52 ... ♝c4?

Black decides to abandon the b1-h7 diago-nal, but now White is definitely winning. Black should have played 52...♝b1, maintaining the status quo. Then 53 ♔d4 is tempting, heading for the queenside pawns, but after 53...♘c4 54 ♔c5 ♝d3 White's king has to go a very long way round to attack the pawns. Therefore, White should adopt a different plan, possibly based on a preliminary a4 and axb5 to increase the effect of a subsequent ♔d4-c5.

53 ♝c2

The bishop settles on an ideal diagonal exert-ing pressure on the weak f5-pawn. The imme-diate threat is ♔f4 followed by ♝b4.

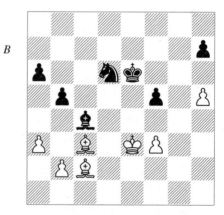

B

53 ... ♝f1

Black aims to defend the f5-pawn from h3, but this is a journey into oblivion for Black's bishop. Other moves:

1) 53...♝d5 54 ♔f4 followed by ♝b4 wins the f5-pawn.

2) 53...♘c8 54 ♔f4 ♘e7 55 ♔g5 ♝d5 is the toughest defence, when White has to take care:

2a) 56 ♗b4 ♗xf3 57 ♗xe7 ♔xe7 58 ♗xf5 is tempting, but Black can save the game by 58...h6+! 59 ♔xh6 ♗f6 60 ♗g6 a5! 61 ♔h7 (61 b4 axb4 62 axb4 ♔e5 draws as Black can give up his bishop for the h-pawn) 61...b4 62 h6 bxa3 63 bxa3 ♗d5 and the white king can never escape from the corner.

2b) 56 ♗d1! ♗c4 57 ♔h6 ♘d5 58 ♔xh7 ♘xc3 (58...♘e3 59 ♔g7 and the pawn slips through) 59 bxc3 ♔f6 is another attempt to imprison White's king in the corner, but it doesn't work here: 60 f4! ♗f7 61 h6 ♗c4 62 ♗f3 ♗e6 63 ♗b7 a5 64 ♗c6 ♗c4 65 ♗d7, followed by ♗xf5, winning. If Black simply jettisons the f5-pawn, then White wins by playing f5 and manoeuvring the bishop to e6.

54 ♔f4 ♗h3
55 ♗d3

This little move causes Black's defence to collapse. There is no reasonable way to meet the threat of ♔g3, trapping the bishop.

55 ... ♗g2

The only move to avoid immediate loss of a piece.

56 ♗b4

56 ♔g3 ♗h1 57 ♗e2 is also decisive. The text-move intends h6 followed by ♗xd6, winning both kingside pawns.

56 ... h6

Black tries to save one of his kingside pawns.

57 ♔g3 ♗h1
58 ♗e2

58 ♗xd6 ♔xd6 59 ♗xf5 followed by ♗g4 and ♔h2 was simpler, but it makes no difference to the result.

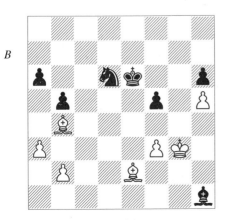

58 ... f4+

Or else ♔h2 wins a piece.

59 ♔xf4

59 ♔h2 ♘f5 60 ♗d1 ♘g3 61 ♗e1 is also good enough.

59 ... ♘f5

Or else ♔g3-h2 wins the bishop after all. However, Black's fate will not be long delayed because he cannot maintain his knight on the f5-square.

60 ♗c3

Intending ♗d1-b3+.

60 ... ♘e7
61 ♔g3

The king moves in to round up the cornered bishop.

61 ... ♘d5
62 ♗d2

Apparently White enjoys prolonging the agony!

62 ... ♘f6
63 ♔h2 ♘xh5
64 ♗d1

Not, of course, 64 ♔xh1?? ♘g3+.

1-0

Black finally loses his trapped bishop.

Readers may well argue that I have overstated the power of the two bishops – after all, the above analysis shows how Black could have improved his defence at various moments. However, the point is not at which stage the position actually became winning for White, but rather that, starting from a roughly symmetrical position, White was able to create so many problems for Black – so many, indeed, that Black was soon on the slippery slope to defeat.

The lessons here are:

1) The advantage of the two bishops is often a significant asset, especially in open positions.

2) This advantage is long-term, and may require considerable patience to be fully exploited.

3) If your opponent offers a pawn, it is worth looking closely at taking it – a casual 'that looks a bit risky' isn't good enough.

4) Defending an inferior ending for several hours is a very tough job, and in practice it is very easy for the defender to lose his way through time shortage or exhaustion.

Bad Bishop

'Good' and 'bad' bishops are a favourite topic for writers of chess books. What does 'good' and 'bad' mean in this context? The usual definition is that a 'bad' bishop is one that is impeded by friendly pawns, while a 'good' bishop is one that is not so impeded. A 'bad' bishop is inferior for two reasons. Firstly, it is itself inactive, often merely duplicating the work of the pawns blocking it in. Secondly, the squares of the other colour are usually left weak, because the bishop and pawns are incapable of defending them.

Although the 'bad' bishop is an important concept, it is important not to become obsessed with 'bad' bishops – in many positions, the concept of 'good' and 'bad' bishops is not especially relevant. Take the position after 1 e4 d6 2 d4 ♘f6 3 ♘c3 g6 4 ♘f3 ♗g7 5 ♗e2 0-0 6 0-0 c6, for example. In this case, it makes no sense to try to find White's 'bad' bishop – both bishops are about equally active, and neither is really being impeded by friendly pawns. Now take the position after 1 e4 g6 2 d4 ♗g7 3 ♘c3 c6 4 f4 d5 5 e5 h5 6 ♗e3. In this case, it is reasonable to say that the e3-bishop is 'bad' – both forward diagonals are blocked by friendly pawns. There are two key points relating to this example:

1) The pawns with respect to which the bishop is 'bad' are in the centre. If you are measuring 'badness', then centre pawns are far more important than flank pawns.

2) The pawns in question are unlikely to move in the near future, as the centre is blocked. Temporary 'badness' may not be 'bad' at all; if the obstructing pawn can later move out of the way, then the bishop can regain its full power.

Thus, in most cases of practical importance, a 'bad' bishop is one *that is on the same colour as a friendly central pawn-chain*. Even in this case, there are many exceptions; for example, the bishop may be outside the pawn-chain – if White has pawns on c4, d5 and e4, and Black has pawns on c5, d6, and e5 then a black bishop on e7 might be badly placed, but one on d4 usually would not be. Even if the bishop is behind the pawn-chain, one has to look to the future. In the King's Indian, Black's g7-bishop is often 'bad' with respect to the central pawn-chain on d6 and e5, but Black intends to loosen up the centre with ...f5, and then his 'bad' bishop may suddenly became very powerful. Of course, there are also many cases in which Black's 'bad' King's Indian bishop lives down to its name.

In the following game, the battle revolves around Black's attempts to activate his 'bad' dark-squared bishop.

Game 23

M. Stean – G. Sax

Las Palmas 1978

Sicilian Defence, Sveshnikov Variation

1	e4	c5
2	♘f3	♘c6
3	d4	cxd4
4	♘xd4	♘f6
5	♘c3	

For comments on the moves up to here, see Game 12.

| 5 | ... | e5 |

This move leads into the Sveshnikov Variation. We have already discussed the similar

Kalashnikov Variation in Game 9, and some of the comments made there also apply in this case. However, there are also significant differences. The move 5...e5 has been played for a long time – indeed Emanuel Lasker played it in his 1910 World Championship match against Schlechter. However, its appearances were very infrequent and it was only in the 1970s that this line began to attract a real following. The modern handling of this system, which depends on the sidelining of White's knight on a3, is due very largely to Soviet grandmaster Evgeny Sveshnikov.

Pushing the pawn to e5 has both advantages and disadvantages. The main advantage is the gain of time. White's knight is chased from the centre of the board and in the most critical line ends up stuck on a3. The disadvantage, which would be enough to make most classical masters blanch, is that the d5-square is weakened and Black's d-pawn is rendered backward. However, modern masters are more open-minded about positional defects, and this line is now regarded as an entirely respectable opening. The list of top players who have used it is quite impressive: Kramnik, Topalov, Gelfand, Adams and Khalifman are but a few. Recently, even that paragon of positional respectability, Ulf Andersson, has started playing it, which shows that 5...e5 is now in the mainstream of positional thinking.

For a more detailed discussion of move-orders in this opening, see Game 20.

6 ♘db5

This is the only dangerous move. After 6 ♘f5, Black has the tactical possibility 6...d5!, while other knight moves allow Black to develop his dark-squared bishop outside the pawn-chain, when he has a comfortable position.

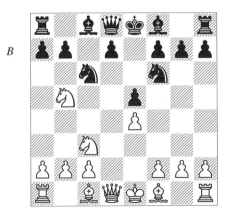

6 ... d6

Black should not allow ♘d6+, as then he would have to part with a bishop. In the resulting fairly open position, the two bishops would be a significant factor.

7 ♗g5

Although this is not the only possibility, it is the most popular and critical. White prepares to eliminate the f6-knight, thereby emphasizing his control of d5. There are two other important lines. The first is 7 ♘d5 ♘xd5 8 exd5 ♘b8, which leads to a totally different type of position. The backward d-pawn has disappeared, and White's hopes for the future rest on his queenside space advantage. However, by playing ...0-0, ...f5 and ...♘d7, Black can develop enough activity on the kingside to offset White's queenside prospects. The second is 7 a4, which aims to prevent Black from gaining space by ...a6 and ...b5. This is a very laudable objective, but to spend a whole tempo on it is perhaps too much. After 7...a6 8 ♘a3 ♗g4!?, for example, Black has satisfactory play.

After the text-move, we have transposed into Game 20.

7	...	a6
8	♘a3	b5
9	♗xf6	

This is one of White's two main lines. The other is the quieter 9 ♘d5 (see Game 20).

9 ... gxf6

Black has to accept doubled pawns, because 9...♕xf6 10 ♘d5 ♕d8 fails to the tactical point 11 c4 b4 (11...bxc4 12 ♘xc4 is very good for White as there is a nasty threat of 13 ♕a4) 12 ♕a4 ♗d7 13 ♘b5! axb5 14 ♕xa8 ♕xa8 15 ♘c7+ ♔d8 16 ♘xa8 and the knight emerges via b6.

10 ♘d5

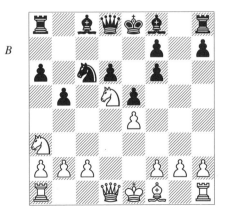

Forced, as Black was threatening 10...b4. It is time to take stock of the opening so far. The most obvious feature of the diagram is indeed the knight on d5, which is not going to be shifted easily (10...♘e7?? allows mate in one!). Classic textbooks are full of examples in which White establishes a knight on d5 in the Sicilian, and goes on to win comfortably. However, the examples chosen are often those in which Black has other disadvantages (for example, his only minor piece is a dark-squared bishop) or in which Black plays with the dynamism of a soggy tea bag. Limp play can lose virtually any position, so these examples do not paint a realistic picture of such positions. In the diagram Black has the additional problem posed by his shattered kingside, so a player brought up on the chess 'classics' would probably feel that Black should simply resign to avoid an undignified end.

In fact, of course, matters are not that simple, or else players such as Kramnik would not be happy to take on the black side. A number of points operate in Black's favour:

1) the knight on a3 will take time to re-enter the game, for example by c3, ♘c2 and ♘ce3.

2) Black has the two bishops; if the position could be opened up, these bishops would become very powerful.

3) Black can liquidate his doubled pawn by ...f5, and after the exchange of e4- and f5-pawns, he can play ...f5 again, thereby gaining a certain degree of central control. In this respect, the doubled pawns are actually an asset.

4) Black can still fight for the d5-square, for example by ...♗g7 and only then ...♘e7. His dream would be to play ...♘e7 to exchange knights, ...f5 and ...fxe4 to liquidate White's only central pawn and then ...d5 and ...f5 (again) to create a massive centre. Believe it or not, this sometimes happens!

While it is right to mention these points, those classical textbooks are not entirely wrong – they just lack balance. The danger of White establishing a death-grip based on the d5-knight is very real, and it only requires a small slip by Black for this fate to befall him (the current game is a case in point). The Sveshnikov is a sharp opening line that offers winning chances for both sides – which is, of course, one reason why it is so popular.

10 ...   f5

Black has two main systems at this point. The text-move gives priority to exerting pressure on

e4 while the alternative, 10...♗g7 11 ♗d3 ♘e7, lays emphasis on challenging d5.

11   ♗d3

This is one of many continuations for White here. Perhaps the most common line these days is 11 exf5 ♗xf5 12 c3 ♗g7 (the move-order 11 c3 ♗g7 12 exf5 ♗xf5 is also possible; Black cannot play 11...fxe4? in this line because then 12 ♗xb5! axb5 13 ♘xb5 is strong) 13 ♘c2, followed by 14 ♘ce3. Then White will develop his bishop, either to d3 or to g2, and castle. Other ideas are the sacrifices 11 ♗xb5 and 11 ♘xb5 (the former unclear, the latter almost certainly unsound), 11 c4 and 11 g3 – quite a range, in fact!

11   ...   ♗e6

White was threatening to take on f5, so this is more or less forced.

12   ♕h5

This is one of two main lines for White, although it is rarely seen these days for reasons explained in the following note. The alternative is 12 0-0, which Black usually counters by 12...♗xd5 13 exd5 ♘e7. Then the problems associated with the d5-square have disappeared, and the struggle centres on whether Black's pawn-mass on the e- and f-files is strong or weak.

The text-move is tempting, since if Black castles kingside then White's queen is in a position to create threats against the enemy king.

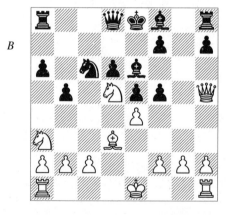

12   ...   ♗g7

For many years, this was virtually the only move played. However, in the 1980s some doubts began to appear as to whether it was genuinely satisfactory for Black. Suddenly, the whole Sveshnikov appeared to be under threat. Then along came **12...♖g8** to save it. This is the current preference, and indeed it appears so effective that few players care to try 12 ♕h5 any more. We will look at one practical example of this move, which should help to counterbalance any impression the main game might create that those old textbooks were right after all! **13 c3** (White decides to jettison the g2-pawn; 13 g3 is the main alternative, but then 13...♖g5 14 ♕xh7 ♗xd5 15 exd5 ♘e7 is satisfactory for Black) **13...♖xg2 14 ♕f3** (this regains the pawn) **14...♖g4 15 exf5 ♗xd5 16 ♕xd5 ♘e7 17 ♕b7** (a critical position; White has a grip on the light squares, but now Black starts to play his own trumps) **17...♗h6** (preventing castling) **18 f6** (ambitious but risky; 18 ♘c2 is safer) **18...♘g8!** (this retreating move is very strong; for a few moments Black's position looks precarious, but once the f6-pawn disappears it becomes clear that he is in control) **19 ♗e4?** (White should have played 19 ♖d1 ♘xf6 20 ♗e2 ♖e4 21 ♔f1, with an unclear position) **19...♖b8 20 ♕c6+ ♔f8**.

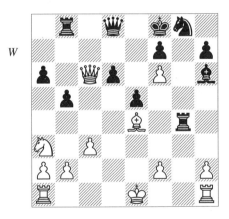

W

Suddenly everything is going wrong for White. The f6-pawn is falling, and his own king will be the more exposed; note how irrelevant White's control of d5 has become. **21 ♖d1 ♕xf6 22 ♔f1** (22 ♖xd6 fails to 22...♖xe4+) **22...♖d8** (22...♖f4 23 ♖xd6 ♖xf2+ 24 ♔e1 ♕f4 was perhaps even stronger) **23 ♘c2 ♘e7 24 ♕c7 ♘g6** (Black is a pawn up with an attack) **25 ♗b7 e4 26 ♖e1? ♕f3!** (an attractive conclusion) **27 ♕xd8+ ♔g7 28 ♘d4** (28 ♘e3 ♗xe3 29 ♖xe3 ♕d1+ 30 ♖e1 ♕d3+ 31 ♖e2 ♘f4 and 28 ♕xd6 ♕xh1+ 29 ♔e2 ♕f3+ 30

♔f1 ♘f4 also lead to a quick mate) **28...♕h3+ 0-1** Am.Rodriguez-Timoshenko, Ubeda 1998. It is mate next move.

13 0-0

Simple development is the best answer.

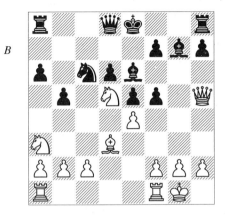

B

13 ... f4

Black's problem is that 13...0-0 fails to 14 exf5 ♗xd5 15 f6, so the text-move is a necessary preliminary to castling. It has some advantages in that Black gains space on the kingside, which might eventually lead to an attack there, and prevents the manoeuvre ♘c2-e3. However, it does surrender one of the main motivations for playing ...f5 in the first place: to exert pressure on e4. It is true that Black has another f-pawn with which he can try to undermine e4, but it is not so easy to arrange ...f5 in favourable circumstances. We can also see the beginnings of what will turn out to be a major problem for Black later on – his g7-bishop is starting to become bad. The chain of pawns d6-e5-f4 significantly restricts the bishop, and unless Black can force through ...f5, the bishop may remain inactive for the rest of the game.

14 c4

The strongest move. White opens up more space on the queenside, helping to activate both the a3-knight and the d3-bishop.

14 ... bxc4

14...b4 15 ♘c2 a5 might seem more logical, in that it denies White's minor pieces access to c4. However, White can continue with the awkward 16 g3. Then, if 16...fxg3 17 hxg3, White's knight gains access to e3 and White can also continue with ♔g2 and ♖h1, with a dangerous attack (assuming that Black will castle kingside

– and where else is his king going?). Black can delay ...fxg3, but he will probably have to play it sooner or later; for example, after 16...0-0 17 ♔h1 further delay in taking on g3 will only invite White to play gxf4 followed by ♖g1, with a strong attack.

15 ♗xc4

15 ♘xc4 is also playable, but the text-move looks best as the tactical possibilities along the a2-g8 diagonal will make it harder for Black to play ...f5.

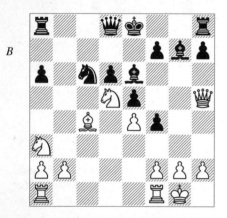

15 ... 0-0

Black's king is now relatively safe, but his strategic aims are largely unfulfilled. He hasn't dislodged White from either d5 or e4. Note how these targets are linked to the question of the g7-bishop. If White's blockade in the centre is broken, Black will probably be able to play ...e4 at some stage and activate his dark-squared bishop, but otherwise it will be very hard to get the g7-bishop into play.

16 ♖ac1

Putting a rook on an open file is rarely bad. Here White is also setting up potential tactics against the undefended c6-knight.

16 ... ♖b8

This looks most natural – Black brings his rook out with gain of tempo. 16...f5 is bad in view of 17 ♖c3 ♘a5 (17...fxe4 18 ♖h3 h6 19 ♕g6 ♘d4 20 ♖xh6 ♖f7 21 ♘c2! ♘xc2 22 ♕xe6 and White wins) 18 ♖h3 ♘xc4 (18...h6 loses to 19 ♕g6!) 19 ♕xh7+ ♔f7 20 ♕h5+ ♔g8 21 ♘xc4 fxe4 22 ♕h7+ ♔f7 23 ♖h6 and again White wins.

16...♘e7 can be met by 17 ♘c7 ♕xc7 18 ♗xe6 ♕b7 19 ♗b3, utilizing the tactical point

19...♕xe4? 20 ♗c2 to liquidate Black's light-squared bishop, leaving him with only the crippled bishop on g7. After 19...♖ad8 20 ♖fd1, Black cannot play 20...d5 21 exd5 ♘xd5 due to 22 ♕f3.

17 b3

Now Black faces similar problems as on the previous move.

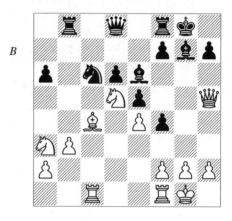

17 ... ♗xd5?

Conceding his light-squared bishop is a serious error, even though Black thereby wins a pawn. 17...f5 may be met by 18 ♖c3, which is very similar to the analysis of 16...f5, and 18 ♘xf4 ♗xc4 19 ♖xc4 exf4 20 ♖xc6 is a good alternative now that the b2-pawn isn't attacked.

17...♕d7 is the best chance. Black defends both the loose c6-knight and the e6-bishop, reducing White's tactical opportunities. After 18 ♖fd1 White retains some advantage, but Black is still in the game. Note that 18...♗g4 is bad owing to 19 ♕g5 ♔h8 20 ♘f6.

18 ♗xd5

Not 18 exd5? ♘e7, when White's own bishop has become rather bad, thanks to the pawn on d5, while Black now has no trouble activating his bishop by ...f5 and ...e4.

18 ... ♘b4

This is Black's idea. He threatens to exchange on d5, after which he can again activate his bishop with ...e4, and at the same time attacks the a2-pawn.

18...♘d4 is no better since 19 ♘c2 gives White a large advantage. If Black now exchanges knights, we reach an opposite-coloured bishop position that is far from drawn – in fact, it is virtually winning for White. Black's bishop is permanently bad, since there is no longer any chance of lifting the central blockade, while White's bishop is extremely powerful. The f7-square is very weak, amongst Black's many other problems.

19   ♖fd1!

Of Black's two threats, the positional threat of taking on d5 is far more serious than the attack on White's largely irrelevant a-pawn. Stean quite rightly ignores the latter threat.

19   ...   ♘xa2

Black has nothing better than to execute his 'threat'. After 19...♘xd5 20 ♖xd5, followed by ♘c4 and ♖cd1, Black will be completely tied down to the defence of d6; for example, 20...♕f6 21 ♘c4 ♖fd8 22 ♖cd1 ♗f8. Now one way to win is 23 ♖a5 ♖a8 24 ♘b6 ♖a7 25 ♘d5 ♕h6 26 ♕xh6 ♗xh6 27 ♖c1 f3 28 ♖c6 picking up the a6-pawn, when the two connected queenside pawns will decide. Even being able to play ...f3 doesn't help Black's poor bishop, since the white knight is totally dominant.

20   ♖c6

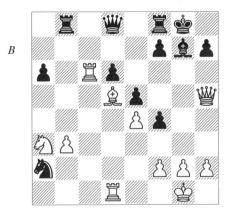

Having an extra pawn is scant consolation for Black, as he is unlikely to enjoy it for very long. White threatens both 21 ♖xd6 and 21 ♘c4.

20   ...   ♖b6?!

Black goes down without a fight. 20...♕e7 was the only way to keep the game going, but White retains a clear advantage in any case after 21 ♘c4 (21 ♖xd6? is a mistake as after 21...♘c3 we see that White has trapped himself in a nasty pin along the f8-a3 diagonal; in any case, White really wants to take the d6-pawn with his knight, so that it can move on to f5) and now:

1) 21...♘b4 22 ♖xd6 ♘xd5 23 ♖6xd5 ♖xb3 24 ♘d6! (much better than taking on e5, which risks activating Black's bishop) 24...h6 25 h4! (preventing ...♕g5) 25...♖fb8 26 ♘f5 ♕f8 27 ♕g4 (threatening 28 ♖d8) 27...♖b1 28 ♘xh6+ ♔h7 29 ♘f5 with a winning position for White, Wolff-Bronstein, Wijk aan Zee 1992.

2) 21...♘c3 22 ♘xd6! (an excellent exchange sacrifice) 22...♘xd1 23 ♕xd1 ♔h8 24 ♕g4 and White's total domination of the light squares and very active pieces provide excellent compensation for the exchange. Black is in considerable difficulties, e.g.:

2a) 24...♗f6 25 g3 fxg3 26 hxg3 ♖g8 27 ♕f5! is very strong; for example, 27...♖g6 28 ♘xf7+ ♔g7 29 ♖d6 and the rook penetrates to d7.

2b) 24...♕a7 25 h3 (preventing any back-rank trickery) 25...a5 26 ♕h5 a4 27 ♘xf7+ ♖xf7 28 ♗xf7 a3 (28...axb3 29 ♗xb3 gives White an extra pawn and a large positional advantage) 29 ♗g6 ♗f6 (29...h6 30 ♗f7 threatening 31 ♖xh6+ wins for White, as does 29...♗h6 30 ♗f5 a2 31 ♖xh6 a1♕+ 32 ♔h2) 30 ♖a6 ♕c7 31 ♖xf6 a2 32 ♖a6.

21   ♖xb6   ♕xb6

The exchange of rooks hasn't helped Black, as the white knight can now reach f5 by force.

22   ♘c4   ♕c7

As good or bad as any other square.

23   ♘xd6   ♘c3

The knight attempts to hop back into the game, but it is far too late.

24   ♘f5

Threatening 25 ♕g5, so Black has no time to take the rook.

24   ...   ♔h8

Or 24...♘xd5 25 exd5 (at this late stage the possible activation of the g7-bishop makes little difference, since the d-pawn stands ready to decide the game; of course, taking with the rook would also win, but more slowly) 25...♗f6 26 d6 ♕d7 (26...♕c2 27 d7 ♔h8 28 ♘h6 ♕g6 29 ♕xg6 fxg6 30 d8♕ ♗xd8 31 ♖xd8 is winning for White) and now White can win with a neat manoeuvre: 27 ♘h6+ ♔h8 (27...♔g7 loses to 28 ♘g4) 28 ♘g4 ♕e6 29 ♕h6 ♗g7 30 ♕xe6 fxe6 31 d7 ♖d8 32 ♖c1 ♖xd7 33 ♖c8+ ♗f8 34 ♖xf8+ ♔g7 35 ♖g8+! with a clear extra piece. The final finesse was necessary as otherwise White would lose his rook!

25   ♖d3   ♘xd5

25...♕a5 26 h3 ♘xd5 27 ♖xd5 doesn't make any difference, since 27...♕e1+ 28 ♔h2 ♕xf2 loses to 29 ♕g5 ♖g8 30 ♖d8.

26   ♖xd5

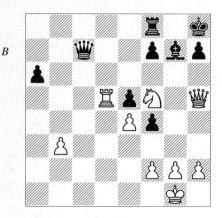

B

Black is dead lost, and all because of his bad bishop. The diagram shows the two characteristic features of 'bad bishop' positions, firstly that the bishop itself is condemned to miserable passivity, and secondly that the squares of the opposite colour to the bishop are riddled with weaknesses.

26   ...   f6

Seeing Black put another pawn on a dark square is just the icing on the cake, so far as White is concerned. Of course, by this stage it makes no difference. 26...♖c8 27 h3 followed by ♔h2 and ♕d1 is similar to the game, while 26...♖d8 27 h3 also makes no difference – giving White a passed d-pawn would only accelerate the end.

27   h3

Safety-first. Black cannot do anything, so White can afford to spend a tempo on this precaution.

27   ...   ♖g8
28   ♕d1   1-0

In view of the coming ♖d7, Black preferred not to see any move. The finish might have been 28...♕b8 29 ♖d7 ♕e8 (at least this sets a small trap) 30 ♕d6 (after 30 ♘xg7 ♕g6 Black could limp on) 30...a5 31 ♕c7 ♕f8 (31...♕g6 32 ♘e7) 32 ♖f7 and Black loses material.

Many lines of the Sveshnikov Sicilian revolve around White's light-squared blockade in the centre, with the squares e4 and d5 being a key battleground. In this game, Black made a grave error of judgement when he conceded this battle for the sake of a pawn. In such a double-edged opening, small errors can have serious consequences and so it proved here. White not only regained the pawn in short order, but he also established a crushing positional bind. With Black's bishop reduced to the status of a pawn, White was effectively a piece up and the end was not long in coming.

The lessons here are:

1) A 'bad' bishop is a serious handicap if there is no prospect of activating it in the future.

2) A considerable positional advantage is often worth more than a pawn.

3) A knight established on a fifth-rank outpost is usually very strong.

4) If you play very double-edged openings, you may score some notable victories but you have to accept the odd disaster.

Pawn-Chain Play

The pawn is the only chess unit that captures in a different way from its normal move. This gives rise to the curious situation that two pawns can immobilize each other. For example, with a white pawn on e4 and a black pawn on e5, the e4-pawn cannot make a non-capturing move because the e5-pawn is in the way. With any other chess unit, the e4-pawn could simply take the e5-pawn, but because the pawn's capturing direction is diagonal and not straight ahead, the e4-pawn has no moves.

There may well be more than one pair of immobilized pawns; for example, White may have pawns on f3, e4 and d5, and Black on f4, e5 and d6. When pairs of immobilized pawns link up diagonally like this, we speak of a *pawn-chain*. If the centre is occupied by immobile pawns, we speak of a *blocked centre*.

Many popular opening systems can give rise to a blocked centre (e.g. Ruy Lopez, French, Caro-Kann, King's Indian). Understanding pawn-chains is essential to the correct handling of these openings. In rare cases the centre might be smashed open by a sacrifice, but more often a blocked centre means that most of the action takes place on the flanks. In many cases, the pawn-structure determines that the players should attack on opposite flanks and then the position can become very tense, as in the following game.

Game 24

P. San Segundo – V. Topalov

Madrid 1996

King's Indian Defence, Classical Variation

1	d4	♘f6
2	♘f3	g6
3	c4	♗g7
4	♘c3	0-0
5	e4	d6
6	♗e2	e5

For comments on the moves up to here, see Game 18.

7   ♗e3

An interesting alternative to 7 0-0, which we saw in Game 18. White delays castling, instead preferring to develop his bishop to a natural square where it supports the centre. This has certain advantages; in some lines, White plays an early ♘d2, and then it is useful that the dark-squared bishop has already been developed.

On the minus side, the bishop is committed to a particular square rather early, and it is vulnerable to attack by ...♘g4.

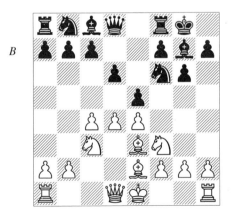

B

7   ...   c6

This is a flexible but not especially fashionable reply. The main variation has always been

7...♘g4, immediately exploiting the bishop's position. Play generally continues 8 ♗g5 f6 9 ♗h4 (9 ♗c1 is also sometimes played) 9...♘c6 10 d5 ♘e7 11 ♘d2 ♘h6 and the game proceeds along typical King's Indian lines, with White playing for c5 (often supported by f3 and ♗f2), while Black advances on the kingside.

One of the points behind 7 ♗e3 is revealed after the common but inaccurate move 7...♘c6. White continues 8 d5 ♘e7 9 ♘d2 and, thanks to the early development of the bishop at e3, he is well-prepared for an early c5. After 9...♘e8, White can play 10 c5 at once, while 9...♘d7 10 b4 only delays it slightly. Finally, if Black continues 9...c5, White plays a move that appears odd at first sight: 10 g4. His plan is to block Black's kingside play before turning his attention to the queenside. After 10...♘e8 11 h4 f5 12 f3, Black is in an awkward situation. If he plays ...f4, then his kingside play is dead, giving White total freedom on the opposite wing. On the other hand, if he leaves the pawn on f5, then White will play ♕c2, opening up the possibility of playing on the kingside himself, by gxf5, followed by 0-0-0 and ♖dg1. The line with 7...♘c6 is best avoided by Black.

Black has a number of other playable options; for example, 7...exd4 8 ♘xd4 ♖e8 9 f3 c6, aiming to play a quick ...d5, or 7...h6, an odd-looking move which aims to play ...♘g4 without allowing the reply ♗g5. 7...♘a6 is also popular, and often transposes to the line discussed in Game 18.

The main advantage of the text-move is that it does not commit a piece. Black might still go for ...exd4 or he might play ...♘g4. Alternatively, he could just continue his development with ...♘bd7 or ...♘a6. However, I doubt that 7...c6 is as strong as the more common continuations. If White plays d5 at some stage, the move ...c6 may actually hinder Black, since he must continually take into account the possibility of White playing dxc6. In particular, it is hard for Black to prepare ...f5 effectively.

8   d5

A natural reply for the reasons mentioned in the previous note. 8 0-0 is also quite good, since if Black plays 8...exd4 White can reply 9 ♗xd4! ♖e8 10 ♕c2 followed by developing his rooks to the centre, with at least a slight advantage. Note that 9 ♗xd4 was only possible as Black's ...c6 deprived him of the possibility of ...♘c6, attacking the bishop.

8   ...   ♘a6

Black simply continues his development. After 8...♘g4 9 ♗g5 f6 10 ♗h4 the position resembles that arising after 7...♘g4, but here Black is committed to the not necessarily ideal move ...c6, so White should be slightly better.

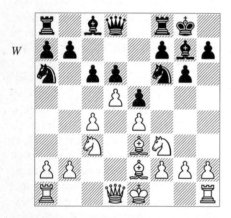

9   ♘d2?!

This makes life easy for Black. Now that the d-file is blocked, Black need not worry about dxc6, and so he is better able to prepare ...f5. The best move is 9 0-0 and in fact we have already mentioned this position in the note to Black's 8th move in Game 18. After 9...♘g4 (Black is no longer able to prepare ...f5, since 9...♘e8 fails to 10 dxc6 bxc6 11 c5) 10 ♗g5 f6 11 ♗h4 Black should try 11...c5 or 11...h5, although in either case White is slightly better. As an example of the tactical problems created by ...c6, suppose Black plays 11...♘h6. Then White has the strong reply 12 c5! ♘xc5 (12...dxc5 13

♗xa6 bxa6 14 dxc6 is also good for White) 13 b4 and White is clearly better after 13...♘d7 14 dxc6 or 13...♘a6 14 ♗xa6 bxa6 15 dxc6.

9   ...   ♘e8

Thanks to White's previous move, Black can prepare ...f5 without difficulty.

10   0-0

10 a3 f5 11 f3 ♗h6! is a typical trick. Black's bishop is 'bad' with respect to his central pawn-chain, so it is desirable to exchange it for White's good bishop. This applies particularly in the current position because White has weakened his dark squares by playing f3 – if his dark-squared bishop disappears, these squares will be very vulnerable. Since 12 ♗xh6 ♕h4+ 13 g3 ♕xh6 favours Black, White should try 12 ♗f2. However, Black has activated his dark-squared bishop with gain of time and after 12...♕g5 13 ♘f1 c5 he is at least equal.

10 g4 is a similar idea to that mentioned in the note to Black's 7th move, but here it is bad for two reasons. Firstly it is too slow, and secondly it is ineffective when Black has not yet played ...c5, because Black can open the c-file and deny White's king a safe refuge on the queenside. For example, after 10...cxd5 11 cxd5 f5 12 exf5 (12 f3 is impossible here owing to 12...fxg4 13 fxg4 ♕h4+) 12...gxf5 13 gxf5 ♗xf5 White's position is crumbling.

10   ...   f5

Threatening 11...f4.

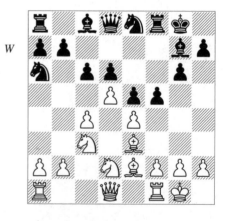

11   f3

While this move is not really a mistake, it doesn't present Black with any particular difficulties. 11 exf5!? would have been a more challenging alternative. As usual in the King's

Indian, it is better to meet exf5 with ...gxf5 rather than a piece recapture. This is sometimes presented as an absolute rule, but in fact there are a fair number of exceptions. If Black can contest the e4-square then it may be reasonable to take on f5 with a bishop, while if there is a knight on e7, it may sometimes be good to play ...♘xf5 followed by ...♘d4. Here there is no doubt that 11...♗xf5 is bad, as after 12 ♘de4 ♘f6 13 f3 White has a firm grip on e4. Thus Black should play 11...gxf5 12 f4 (the main reason why Black might be reluctant to play ...gxf5 is the possibility of f4; if White can fix the enemy pawn on f5 then, in a curious reversal of fortunes, Black's light-squared bishop may become 'bad') and now:

1) 12...exf4 13 ♖xf4! (13 ♗xf4 ♕b6+ 14 ♔h1 ♕xb2 favours Black) 13...♗h6 (13...♗e5 14 ♖f1 and Black suffers from his weak f-pawn and poor development) 14 ♖f3 ♗xe3+ 15 ♖xe3 looks favourable for White. He has good development and Black's kingside is weakened. Note that Black cannot win material by 15...♕b6 (15...♘f6 16 dxc6 bxc6 17 ♘b3 also favours White) 16 ♘f1 f4 because of 17 ♘a4.

2) 12...e4 may be better. This type of rigid pawn-structure is usually slightly better for White, but here White's pieces are not especially well placed so Black has fair equalizing chances.

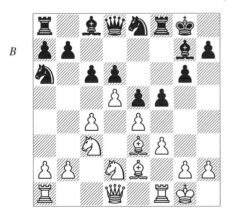

11   ...   f4

Black decides to close the position. 11...♘f6 is a playable alternative.

12   ♗f2   c5

Black intends playing on the kingside, and therefore he should slow White down as much

as possible on the other side of the board. This is best done by closing the queenside as well. If, for example, Black plays 12...♘f6, then 13 dxc6 bxc6 14 a3 followed by b4-b5 would allow White to open the position on the queenside relatively quickly.

13   a3

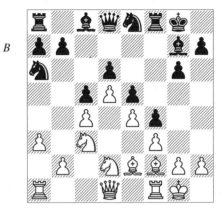

A typical position with pawn-chains has arisen. The centre is blocked, and is likely to remain so indefinitely (indeed, the pawns on the d- and e-files remain where they are until the end of the game). Thus, the only active play can take place on the flanks.

The pawn-structure indicates that White should play on the queenside, and Black on the kingside. Why? Because Black has a space advantage on the kingside, which makes it easier for his attacking pieces to operate on that side of the board, and harder for White to bring defensive pieces to useful positions. White's pawn-chain, on the other hand, points diagonally forward to the queenside, and the advanced d5-pawn guarantees him a space advantage on that side of the board. In the subsequent play, White can easily start his attack, as the c5-pawn can be quickly put under pressure by playing b4. Black's attack is slower, but has the advantage that it is aimed at White's king, so when it does finally arrive, it is likely to create the more serious threats.

Should the players attack with pieces or pawns? It is obvious that White cannot achieve anything by pieces alone – he must open some lines using his pawns before he can make real progress. In Black's case it is perhaps more difficult to say, because he could try to play ...g5,

...♖f6-h6 and put his queen on h5. However, this takes six moves and White could counter it in only two: ♖e1 and ♘f1. Then Black would have to try a breakthrough with ...♘f6 and ...g4. However, there are various problems with this. Firstly, even after all this, it still isn't mate, as White plays fxg4 followed by h3. Secondly, it takes eight moves altogether. Taking away the two white moves, this gives White six free moves on the queenside, during which time he could do quite a lot of damage.

A second point, to which we will return in the note Black's 14th move, is that if Black plays ...g5 before ...h5 (as this plan necessitates) then White may be able to reply g4. Therefore, on balance, Black should also attack with pawns. White's pawn attack will, to begin with, operate against c5, the only available target, but if Black supports this with ...b6, White could contemplate attacking that pawn with a4-a5. Black will try to force through ...g5-g4. This gives him several options: he may simply leave the pawn at g4 and funnel his pieces in behind it (for example, queen to g5 and rook to g6), he may open the g-file with ...gxf3, or he may play ...g3 to create some holes in White's kingside. Note that ...gxf3 has the defect that it activates White's pieces on the kingside.

The principle is often put forward that one should 'attack the base of the pawn-chain'. Like many chess principles, it is sometimes good advice, sometimes bad advice, and sometimes not really applicable at all. In this case, for example, the base of Black's pawn-chain lies at d6 and is unreachable – White has to be content to attack the point he can reach.

The text-move prepares b4.

13   ...   b6

As with all positions with slow-motion pawn advances on opposite wings, the players have to give thought not only to furthering their own attack, but also to defending against the opponent's. For the moment, Black's strategy on the queenside is clear – he must strive to retain a pawn on c5. If Black is ever forced to play ...cxb4, then he will be in trouble. After the reply axb4, the a-file and the g1-a7 diagonal will be opened, and a breakthrough by c5 (the base of the pawn-chain at last!) will be on the way. His knight at a6 is well posted to support c5, but almost certainly further defence will be needed

(e.g. after b4 and ♘b3). Thus, Black decides to reinforce the key square straight away.

14   b4!?

White is prepared to offer a pawn to induce Black to give up his key defensive point at c5.

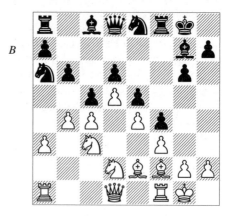

14   ...   h5

Black declines the offer and spends the tempo on the kingside. After 14...cxb4 15 axb4 ♘xb4 16 ♕b1 ♘a6 (not 16...a5? 17 ♘a2 ♘xa2 18 ♖xa2, when White will win back the pawn at b6, after which he will be well-placed for a further breakthrough with c5 – and all before Black has made the first move on the kingside) 17 ♘b5 ♖f7 18 ♘b3 the position is unclear. White has greatly accelerated his play on the queenside and is now ready to double or even triple his major pieces on the a-file. On the other hand, Black does have a pawn.

14...g5 is less accurate. First of all, Black denies himself the possibility of ...♗f6-h4, and secondly White might reply 15 g4. This might seem a very odd move, given the well-known principle that you should not touch your pawns on the side where you are being attacked. However, while this one of the better chess principles (see Game 12), there are certainly exceptions to it. Two are relatively common. The first exception arises when the defender has the chance to block the pawns on the side where he is under attack. The second exception occurs if the defender has to fight for space. It may be that he is so short of space where he is being attacked that it is not feasible to bring any pieces to defensive positions. Then it may be necessary to move a pawn to create room, for example to open the second rank and allow a lateral defence. 15 g4 depends on a combination of these two factors. If Black does not take on g3, then the kingside pawn-structure becomes rather blocked. White meets ...h5 by h3, and although Black can open the h-file, an attack conducted on so narrow a front stands little chance of succeeding. On the other hand, after 15...fxg3 16 hxg3 White has gained more space on the kingside. His plan is ♔g2, ♖h1 and ♗e3, effectively bringing Black's attack to a halt. Of course, Black can interpolate 16...♗h3 17 ♖e1, but the bishop cannot stay on h3 for long, since White can play ♔h2 or ♗f1, so this does not change the situation.

15   bxc5

Thanks to the position of the knight on a6, it is hard for White to make progress without this exchange. He would like to play a4-a5, but his b4-pawn is too weak for this to be possible. White could play b5 and then a4-a5, but then he could only attack along the a-file, which is too narrow an attacking avenue.

15   ...   ♞xc5

An excellent decision. 15...dxc5 is clearly bad because it gives White a ready-made target to hit with a4-a5. 15...bxc5 is also doubtful, because after 16 ♕a4 the a6-knight has no real future. At the moment it is a liability, because Black needs to defend it with his bishop, but even if it moves to c7, it is hard to see where it is going next. Meanwhile, White has few problems making progress on the queenside, by some combination of ♖ab1, ♞b5 and especially ♞b3-a5-c6.

The text-move leads to the exchange of the awkwardly placed a6-knight.

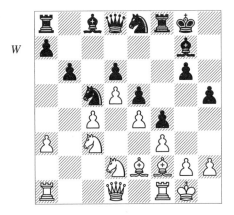

16   a4?

This tempting move, which aims to attack the b6-pawn with a5, is in fact a subtle error, which Topalov is quick to exploit. 16 ♞b3 g5 17 ♞xc5 bxc5 was the best continuation, but now we can see that Black's 15th move has had a positive effect on his position. He is no longer handicapped by the a6-knight, while White is missing the knight that could have ended up on c6. In this case, the position would be equal, with the outcome of the kingside vs queenside struggle yet to be determined.

16   ...   a5!

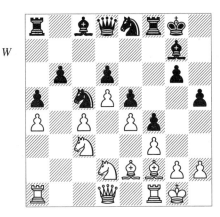

Here we see another counter-example to the principle that one should not move pawns on the side where one is being attacked. Since, moreover, this move leaves a hole on b5 and makes the b-pawn backward, it needs some explanation. The basic idea behind the text-move is to block the queenside. The move ♞b5 achieves nothing by itself, nor is an attack against the b6-pawn likely to be any real inconvenience for Black – the pawn is simply too easy to defend. Therefore, White will probably have to take the knight on c5 in order to make progress. Black will play ...bxc5, and the pawn-structure on the queenside is more or less symmetrical. White will, of course, have his b5-square, but in compensation Black has the b4-square, which he can occupy by ...♞c7-a6-b4. That will be an end to any activity on the queenside, and any subsequent play will take place on the kingside, where Black is better.

17   ♖a3

It is quite hard to see what this move is for, although of course the general structure of the position remains the same virtually whatever

White plays. After 17 ♘b3 ♘c7 18 ♘xc5 bxc5 19 ♘b5 ♘a6 Black is well on the way to b4.

| 17 | ... | ♗f6 |

In view of White's lacklustre 17th move, Black feels safe in inching forward on the kingside. This move is flexible. Black might play for the thematic ...g5-g4, or he might play ...♗h4, either forcing the weakening g3 or exchanging his 'bad' bishop. Even if Black eventually decides to go for ...g5-g4, the move ...♗f6 will not be wasted as it allows Black to switch a rook to g7, where it supports the g-pawn. If possible, it is a good idea to keep your opponent guessing about your intentions.

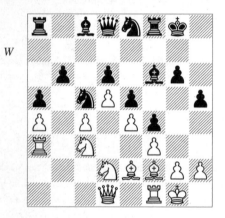

W

| 18 | ♘b3 |

White realizes that he cannot get anywhere without eliminating the c5-knight. Of course, he does not want to take it with his 'good' dark-squared bishop, so the d2-knight is assigned the duty of removing it.

| 18 | ... | ♖f7 |

18...♘c7 is just as good, heading immediately for b4. The text-move is another useful step forwards on the kingside – the rook is heading for g7.

| 19 | ♔h1 |

White foresees a time when play will only take place on the kingside, and realizes that if he defends there passively, then sooner or later Black will find a way to break through. Hence, he decides to fight for space on the kingside by means of the advance g3.

The alternative is 19 ♘xc5 bxc5 20 ♖b3 ♘c7 when Black is, as usual, heading for b4. The only way White can disturb this is by the reckless 21 ♖b6 ♘a6 22 ♖c6 ♘b4 23 ♘b5 but

Black need not take the exchange immediately. Instead, he can play 23...♖d7 followed by ...♗b7, and then White's rook is in real trouble.

| 19 | ... | ♘c7 |

The knight is heading for b4.

| 20 | ♘xc5 | bxc5 |
| 21 | ♖g1 |

White is preparing to play g3, which is probably the best practical chance. If he just waits, Black can take all the time he needs to build up. For example, Black could put his rooks on g7 and h7, and only then go for ...g5-g4.

| 21 | ... | ♘a6 |
| 22 | g3 | ♖g7 |

Meeting the threat of gxf4.

| 23 | ♔g2 |

White decides on the rather desperate measure of playing his king to the queenside. 23 gxf4 exf4 is no help, since Black plays ...♗e5 and then quietly prepares ...g5-g4.

| 23 | ... | ♖aa7 |

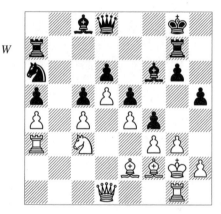

W

Black prepares to switch his other rook to the kingside.

| 24 | ♔f1 | ♘b4 |

The culmination of Black's play. The queenside is totally blocked and he is free to proceed on the kingside, where the pawn-structure favours him.

| 25 | ♔e1 |

A long and weary trek lies ahead for the white king.

| 25 | ... | ♖af7 |
| 26 | ♘b5 |

If White tries to block the kingside by 26 g4, then Black wins after 26...hxg4 27 fxg4 ♗h4 28 ♘b5 ♗xf2+ 29 ♔xf2 ♕h4+, and now:

1) 30 ♔g2 f3+! 31 ♗xf3 (31 ♖xf3 ♗xg4 32 ♖g3 ♗h3+ 33 ♔h1 ♖f2 is winning for Black) 31...♗xg4 32 ♘xd6 ♖f6 33 ♘e8 ♖xf3 34 ♖xf3 ♗xf3+ 35 ♕xf3 ♖f7 36 ♕e3 ♘d3! and White is lost.

2) 30 ♔f1 f3 31 ♗xf3 ♗xg4 32 ♘xd6 (32 ♖g3 loses after 32...♗xf3 33 ♖axf3 ♕xh2) 32...♕h3+ 33 ♔f2 ♖f8 and Black's attack is too strong; for example, 34 ♖g3 (34 ♖e3 ♖d7 followed by ...♖df7) 34...♕xh2+ 35 ♖g2 ♕h5 36 ♖b3 ♖xf3+ 37 ♖xf3 ♕h4+ 38 ♔e3 (or 38 ♖gg3 ♖d7 39 ♘b5 ♗xf3 40 ♕xf3 ♖f7) 38...♗xf3 39 ♕xf3 ♕e1+ 40 ♕e2 ♕c3+ 41 ♔f2 ♘d3+ winning.

| **26** | **...** | **fxg3!** |

It's time for Black to make inroads on the kingside. If he allows White's king to proceed any further to the queenside, White might be able to play g4 at some stage.

| **27** | **hxg3** | |

27 ♗xg3 ♗g5 is also very bad for White.

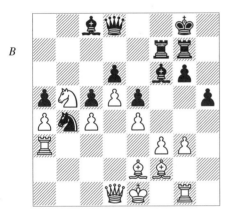

| **27** | **...** | **h4** |

The exchange of Black's h-pawn for White's g-pawn will not only leave White with a backward pawn on f3, but it will also lead to the exchange of dark-squared bishops within a few moves. This makes the f4-square into an outpost for Black's pieces and a jumping-off point for further penetration into White's position. It is interesting to note how the white knight on b5 is virtually irrelevant to the action, whereas the one on b4 proves a considerable help to Black.

| **28** | **♔d2** | |

28 g4 ♗g5 followed by ...♕f6 and ...♖h7 is even worse for White, since he has the passed h-pawn to contend with.

| **28** | **...** | **hxg3** |
| **29** | **♖xg3** | |

Trying to flee with the king by 29 ♗xg3 ♗g5+ 30 ♔c3 (30 ♔e1 ♕f6 is also bad) is no help: 30...♗e3 31 ♖h1 ♗d4+ (as mentioned in Game 23, a theoretically 'bad' bishop outside the pawn-chain may not be bad at all) 32 ♔b3 (32 ♘xd4 loses to 32...cxd4+ 33 ♔b3 ♖b7) 32...♕g5 33 ♗e1 (33 ♘xd4 cxd4 34 ♗e1 ♖b7 35 ♗xb4 ♖xb4+ 36 ♔a2 ♖gb7 is winning for Black) 33...♕e3+ 34 ♘c3 ♖b7 35 ♗d2 ♘xd5+ 36 ♔c2 ♘xc3! (an attractive combination) 37 ♗xe3 ♖b2+ 38 ♔d3 ♘xd1 39 ♗xd1 d5! gives Black a winning position.

| **29** | **...** | **♗h4** |

Black exchanges his 'bad' bishop.

| **30** | **♖g2** | **♗xf2** |
| **31** | **♖xf2** | **♕g5+** |

Since 32 ♔c3 loses to 32...♕e3+, White must either return with his king or self-pin his rook.

| **32** | **♖e3** | |

Here is a sample line if White avoids the pin: 32 ♔e1 ♖f6 (simplest; there is no need to sacrifice the d6-pawn) 33 ♕d2 ♕h4 34 ♗f1 ♖gf7 35 ♗g2 g5 36 ♔d1 g4 37 ♖f1 (or 37 ♔c1 g3 38 ♖f1 ♖h7 and the rook will soon penetrate to h2) 37...gxf3 38 ♗xf3 ♗g4 39 ♕g2 ♕g5! (cutting off the white king's escape-route) 40 ♕g3 ♔f8 41 ♖b3 (White can only wait) 41...♗xf3+ 42 ♖fxf3 ♕xg3 43 ♖xg3 ♖f1+ (now there is a nice finish) 44 ♔d2 ♖7f2+ 45 ♔e3 ♘c2+ 46 ♔d3 ♖d1+ 47 ♔c3 ♘d4 and Black wins.

| **32** | **...** | **♖f6** |

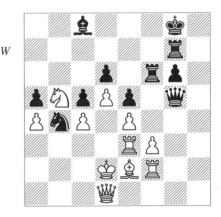

Intending ...♕f4, ...g5 and ...♖h6 with eventual penetration to h2. Black's positional advantage is sufficient to win in the long run.

33   ♖h2

White puts up a fight. This intends ♕h1 with counterplay.

33   ...   ♖h7

Black does not mind exchanging rooks, although he should certainly keep the queens on because much of his advantage depends on his threats against the white king.

34   ♖xh7   ♔xh7

35   ♗f1

35 ♕h1+ ♔g7 36 ♗d1 ♕f4 followed by ...g5 and ...♖h6-h2 wins much as in the game.

35   ...   ♕f4

White is virtually paralysed.

36   ♘c3

The knight never achieved much on b5 and now it returns to the defence. However, even with the knight's assistance White cannot hope to hang on.

36   ...   ♗d7

Black is in no particular hurry, so he reminds White that the a4-pawn is vulnerable.

37   ♗g2

If White attempts to expel the queen by 37 ♘e2, then after 37...♕h2 38 ♖c3 ♔g8! he is helpless (playing 38...♕f2 39 ♕e1 ♖xf3? immediately doesn't work because of 40 ♖xf3 ♕xf3 41 ♕h4+).

37   ...   ♔g7

The plan is ...♕g5, ...♖f4-h4 and ...♕f4, followed by ...♖h2. White is almost powerless to prevent this.

38   ♕g1

Black wins after 38 ♕h1 ♘c2.

38   ...   ♕g5

39   ♕f2   ♖f4

40   ♗f1   ♖h4

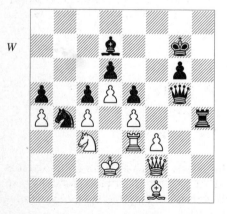

W

41   ♗e2

Or 41 ♘b5 ♕f4 42 ♕g1 ♖h2+ 43 ♗e2 (43 ♔d1 loses to 43...♖a2) 43...♕h4 (threatening 44...♖h1) 44 ♕e1 ♕xe1+ 45 ♔xe1 ♘c2+ 46 ♔d2 ♘xe3 47 ♔xe3 ♗xb5 48 cxb5 ♔f6 with a simple win; for example, 49 b6 (49 ♔d2 ♔e7 50 ♔e3 ♔d7 51 ♔d2 c4!) 49...♖h8 50 b7 ♖b8 51 ♗a6 ♔g5 52 ♔e2 ♔f4 53 ♔f2 g5 followed by ...g4.

41   ...   ♕f4

42   ♕g1

42 ♘b5 ♖h2 43 ♕g1 ♕h4 transposes to the previous note.

42   ...   ♕h6

42...♖h3 followed by ...♕h4 is also very good.

43   ♗d1

43 ♘b5 ♖h1 44 ♕f2 ♖b1 45 ♘xd6 ♕h1 is decisive.

43   ...   ♖h3

The alternative 43...♖h1 leads to a neat win after 44 ♕g3 ♘a2! 45 ♘xa2 ♖xd1+ 46 ♔xd1 ♕xe3 47 ♔c2 ♗xa4+ 48 ♔b2 ♕b3+ 49 ♔a1 ♕d1+ 50 ♔b2 ♕c2+ 51 ♔a1 ♗b3 with a quick mate.

44   ♕e1

44 ♘e2 ♖h1 45 ♕f2 transposes to the game.

44   ...   ♖h2+

45   ♘e2

45 ♗e2 ♘c2 is winning for Black.

45   ...   ♖h1

46   ♕f2   ♗e8

46...♘d3 47 ♔xd3 ♖xd1+ 48 ♔c3 ♕h1 also wins, but the text-move puts White in zugzwang – a rare occurrence in the middlegame.

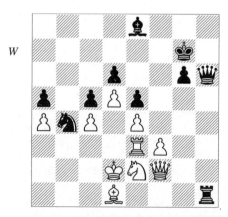

W

47   ♗b3

Let's list the moves: 47 ♔c1 ♘d3+; 47 ♔c3 ♖xd1; a knight move loses the queen to ...♖h2; 47 ♕g2 (or ♕g3) 47...♖xd1+; 47 f4 ♖h2 48 ♕g1 exf4 49 ♖f3 ♕h4 followed by ...g5 and ...♗h5. The move played is the only other possibility.

    47   **...**   **♖b1**
    48   **f4**

48 ♗d1 ♗d7 is again zugzwang. Black wins after 49 f4 (49 ♗c2 ♖b2 or 49 ♕g1 ♗xa4) 49...exf4 (or 49...♕h1 50 ♕g1 ♕xg1 51 ♘xg1 exf4) 50 ♕xf4 ♕h1 51 ♘c3 ♖b2+ 52 ♔c1 ♖c2+ 53 ♔b1 ♖xc3 54 ♖xc3 ♕xd1+.

    48   **...**   **♕h1**
               0-1

It didn't take much for San Segundo to lose this game, and he was unlucky to be facing a Topalov on such good form. White handled the opening in a slightly passive manner; he appeared content to play merely satisfactory moves rather than taking the battle to his opponent. Against a counter-attacking opening such as the King's Indian, this is usually an unwise policy. A slight slip by White at move 9 and a rather innocuous choice at move 11 left Black with a comfortable position. The resulting struggle was between Black's kingside attack and White's queenside play. Topalov handled the position cleverly, keeping his options open as long as possible. White made a definite error on move 16, allowing Topalov to block the queenside. Although it was a long time getting under way, Topalov's kingside attack presented a serious threat in view of White's lack of counterplay. San Segundo tried to flee with his king to the other side of the board, but there was no escaping the fundamental defects of his position and Topalov wrapped the game up very nicely.

The lessons here are:

1) Attacking the base of a pawn-chain may be the best course, but this is not an absolute rule and there are many exceptions.

2) As well as furthering one's own attack, it is essential to make a plan for defending against the enemy advance.

3) Care must be taken to ensure that the opponent cannot block the pawn-structure where one's attack is taking place.

4) It is unusual for a zugzwang to arise in the middlegame, but on occasion it can be the quickest way to win.

Exploiting the Isolated d-Pawn

This is the first of two games devoted to the isolated d-pawn. While this may seem a rather specialized subject, whole books have been devoted to the pros and cons of the isolated d-pawn. Isolated d-pawns can arise from a wide range of openings, and such positions share many common features, so they are worth looking at in more detail. This subject is also a good demonstration of the fact that many chess features have both good and bad sides; the skill lies in maximizing the advantages and minimizing the disadvantages.

    The weak side of the isolated d-pawn comes first, as it is the more obvious aspect – the d-pawn is, after all, isolated and therefore potentially weak since it cannot be defended by another pawn.

    In the following game, Karpov gives a textbook demonstration of current thinking about how to play against an isolated d-pawn.

Game 25

G. Kamsky – A. Karpov

FIDE World Championship match (game 4), Elista 1996

Caro-Kann Defence, Panov-Botvinnik Attack

    1   **e4**
For comments on 1 e4, see Game 3.
    1   **...**   **c6**

This move, the Caro-Kann Defence, may appear illogical in that it takes away the best square from the c8-knight on the very first move.

Yet it has been played by World Champions, and is generally regarded as one of the most solid defences to 1 e4. Black's plan is to challenge White's e4-pawn by 2...d5. If White takes on d5, Black is ready to reply ...cxd5, gaining a central majority and avoiding the exposure of his queen that would result from ...♛xd5. Black's strategy is similar to that in the French Defence (1 e4 e6 2 d4 d5 – see Game 6). The advantage of the Caro-Kann over the French is that the c8-h3 diagonal is left open for the development of Black's light-squared bishop. In some lines, for example the popular variations 2 d4 d5 3 e5 and 2 d4 d5 3 ♘c3 dxe4 4 ♘xe4, the bishop can be developed to f5. It is true that the c6-square is blocked, but the knight can always be developed to d7 if necessary.

2   d4

The most natural reply. White forms an ideal centre, although he will not be able to maintain it.

2   ...   d5

The logical consequence of Black's first move.

3   exd5

This point is the first main parting of the ways in the Caro-Kann, as White has the choice between three popular continuations. The first is the text-move, the second is 3 e5 and the third is 3 ♘c3 (or 3 ♘d2) 3...dxe4 4 ♘xe4. The ambitious 3 e5 gains space and closes the position, but unlike the corresponding situation in the French, here Black can still develop his light-squared bishop to f5. 3 ♘c3 (or 3 ♘d2) 3...dxe4 4 ♘xe4 is perhaps the 'main line' of the Caro-Kann. Both Black's main responses, 4...♘d7 and 4...♗f5, have amassed a huge body of theory.

3   ...   cxd5

Taking with the queen would render the move ...c6 totally pointless.

4   c4

The text-move is called the Panov-Botvinnik Attack, and aims for rapid piece development at the cost of an isolated d-pawn.

4   ...   ♘f6

The knight emerges on its most natural square.

5   ♘c3

White exerts pressure on d5, with the aim of inducing Black to play ...e6.

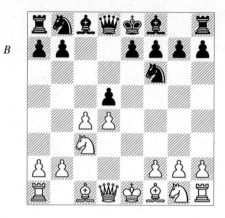

B

5   ...   e6

This is the most solid option. 5...g6 is effectively a pawn sacrifice, as after 6 ♕b3 ♗g7 (6...dxc4 7 ♗xc4 awkwardly attacks f7) 7 cxd5 Black cannot immediately regain the pawn. However, Black gets fair compensation for the pawn and it is easy for White to become tied down to the defence of the d5-pawn, only to lose it in the end anyway.

The other main line, 5...♘c6, aims for flexible development. Black might still play ...e6, or he might meet 6 ♘f3 by 6...♗g4.

6   ♘f3

Natural development.

6   ...   ♗b4

6...♗e7 is also possible, but the text-move is more combative.

7   cxd5

White wants to continue his development by moving his f1-bishop and castling, but 7 ♗e2 and 7 ♗d3 can both be met by 7...dxc4, when White loses a tempo. Therefore, White prefers to take on d5 himself, so that he can develop his bishop to its optimum square d3 without loss of tempo.

7   ...   ♘xd5

7...exd5 is also playable, although after 8 ♗d3 0-0 9 0-0 White retains a slight advantage. After the text-move, White must first spend a tempo defending c3.

8   ♗d2

8 ♕c2 is perhaps the most natural move, because when the bishop comes to d3 White will have a ready-made threat against Black's kingside. However, it runs into a tactical problem after 8...♘c6 9 ♗d3 ♗a5! (9...♘xc3 10 bxc3 ♘xd4 11 ♘xd4 ♕xd4 gives White a dangerous

attack after 12 ♗b5+ ♔e7 13 0-0 ♕xc3 14
♕a4) 10 a3 (White must meet the threat of
...♘db4) and now Black may be able to take the
pawn, viz. 10...♘xc3 11 bxc3 ♘xd4 12 ♘xd4
♕xd4 13 ♗b5+ ♗d7 (this would be impossible
without a3 and ...♗a5 inserted, as White could
win a piece by ♗xd7+ followed by ♕a4+) 14
0-0 ♕d5. Alternatively, the simple 10...♗b6,
exerting immediate pressure on the isolated
pawn, is safe and satisfactory for Black.

In view of these problems with 8 ♕c2, Kamsky prefers to meet the threat to c3 with the
text-move, which has the slight defect that on
d2 the bishop blocks the queen's defence of the
d4-pawn.

8   ...   ♘c6

Black continues his development.

9   ♗d3

The bishop arrives on its best square, where
it has a clear line of sight to Black's kingside.

9   ...   ♗e7

This bishop has done its duty in inducing
♗d2, and now returns to the kingside, which is
looking rather bare of defensive minor pieces.

10   0-0   0-0

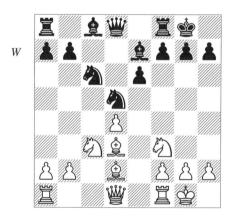

We have reached a typical position with an
isolated d-pawn. Such positions, which are normally referred to as 'IQP positions', can arise
from a wide range of openings, such as the
Caro-Kann (as here), Nimzo-Indian, Queen's
Gambit Accepted and 2 c3 Sicilian. They therefore have an importance that extends beyond
the theory of a specific opening.

The isolated d-pawn has both strengths and
weaknesses. The weaknesses are perhaps more
obvious – it is indeed an isolated pawn and

must be defended by pieces rather than pawns.
One can easily imagine a situation in which
White ends up with his pieces tied down to the
defence of the pawn, while Black can do very
much as he pleases – indeed, something like
this happens in the current game.

However, the pawn has its plus side. It is on
the fourth rank, so White controls more space
than Black. Moreover, White has a lead in development since all his minor pieces are in play
while Black still has to develop his c8-bishop.
White must put these advantages to use before
Black catches up with his development, and the
usual method is to create threats against Black's
kingside.

One unusual feature in the diagram is the position of White's bishop on d2. When the bishop
is on c1, White often adopts the plan of a3, ♗c2
and ♕d3, to force ...g6, when the dark-squared
bishop can go to h6 directly. Black's cunning
manoeuvre with ...♗b4 and ...♗e7 has lured the
bishop to d2, preventing ♕d3 and so blocking
this manoeuvre. White therefore adopts another
plan, which takes advantage of the fact that the
free move ♗d2 allows White to develop his
rooks without loss of time.

If White's plan is to create kingside threats,
what should Black be doing? His main objectives are:

1) To pay attention to White's kingside play
– nothing else matters if he gets mated!

2) To aim for piece exchanges. As the material thins out, the danger to Black's kingside
lessens, which frees him to manoeuvre against
the isolated pawn.

3) He should keep a watchful eye on the
d5-square. If the isolated pawn is able to advance, it may do a lot of damage.

This third point is one of the main themes of
the game. At one time, keeping an eye on d5
meant planting a knight there and not moving
it, and this is the advice you will find in many
older textbooks. However, it is now appreciated
that this is not always the best strategy – it is
solid, but it makes it awkward for Black to conduct any active manoeuvres. An increasingly
common trend is to attack the d-pawn directly,
while making sure that the advance d4-d5 is
never favourable. In the current game, Karpov
conducts this more ambitious but potentially
double-edged strategy to perfection.

11   ♕e2

11 a3 ♗f6 12 ♕c2 is an alternative plan, but it is not especially effective with the queen and bishop this way round. Here Black can play 12...h6, which is less weakening than ...g6 since it does not give the dark-squared bishop a square at h6. If White could now swap his bishop and queen around, then Black would be in trouble, but this takes too long. The modest text-move aims simply to bring the rooks to the centre. It also involves a pawn sacrifice, but few players have summoned up the courage to accept it.

11   ...   ♘f6

After 11...♘db4 12 ♗e4 ♘xd4 13 ♘xd4 ♕xd4 14 ♖fd1, White clearly has a dangerous initiative for the pawn. Black will lose further time with his queen, and White's control of the d-file and pressure along the diagonal from e4 to a8 makes it hard for Black to develop his queenside. While it is not so clear that White has the advantage, such positions are hard to play in practice and black-players have in general avoided taking the pawn.

The text-move genuinely threatens the d-pawn, so White has to take some action.

12   ♘e4

This frees the c3-square for the bishop and so indirectly defends the d-pawn.

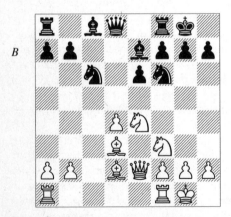

12   ...   ♕b6!

This is Karpov's improvement over 12...♗d7, which was played in the second game of the same match. That game continued 13 ♖ad1 ♖c8 (13...♕b6 14 ♘e5!? is slightly better for White – compared to the note to White's 14th move, the more useful move ♖ad1 is substituted

for a3) 14 ♖fe1 ♘d5 15 ♘c3. Here Black hasn't solved the problem of developing his queen and light-squared bishop, while White has all his pieces in play. White did in fact win by a direct attack.

12...♘xd4 is far too risky; after 13 ♘xd4 ♕xd4 14 ♗c3 ♕d8 15 ♘xf6+ ♗xf6 (15...gxf6 16 ♕g4+ ♔h8 17 ♕e4 wins Black's queen) 16 ♖ad1 ♕e7 17 ♕e4 g6 18 ♗b4 White wins the exchange.

The text-move is most accurate. White has to deal with the threat to the b2-pawn and this not only costs time but also makes it more awkward to develop the a1-rook.

13   a3

White prevents the capture on b2 but of course this move costs a tempo.

13   ...   ♗d7

13...♕xb2? loses to 14 ♖fb1 ♘xd4 15 ♘xf6+ ♗xf6 16 ♕e4 ♘xf3+ 17 gxf3 winning Black's queen.

After the text-move, the main difference from 12...♗d7 is seen. White can't develop his rooks in the most natural way (to d1 and e1), because 14 ♖ad1 drops a pawn to 14...♕xb2.

14   ♖fd1

14 ♘e5!? is an interesting alternative, which demands an accurate reply:

1) 14...♘xd4? 15 ♘xf6+ ♗xf6 (15...gxf6 16 ♕g4+ ♔h8 17 ♗h6 mates, e.g. 17...♖g8 18 ♘xf7#) 16 ♕e4 and Black loses the bishop on d7.

2) 14...♕xd4? 15 ♗c3 ♕d5 16 ♘xf6+ ♗xf6 (16...gxf6 loses to 17 ♕g4+ ♔h8 18 ♕h5) 17 ♖ad1 ♗xe5 18 ♗xh7+ ♔xh7 19 ♖xd5 exd5 20 ♗xe5 wins the queen for a rook and a knight.

3) 14...♖fd8? 15 ♘xf6+ ♗xf6 16 ♗xh7+ ♔f8 (16...♔xh7 17 ♕h5+ ♔g8 18 ♕xf7+ ♔h8 19 ♘xd7 and White wins a pawn) 17 ♗c3 g6 18 ♕f3 ♔g7 19 ♘g4 ♗xd4 20 ♕f4! with a large advantage for White.

4) 14...♖ad8 15 ♘c4 and now:

4a) 15...♕xd4? 16 ♗c3 ♕d5 17 ♘e3 ♕b3 (17...♘d4 loses a piece to 18 ♕d1) 18 ♗c2 ♕b6 19 ♘xf6+ ♗xf6 20 ♕d3 ♖fe8 21 ♕xh7+ ♔f8 22 ♖ae1 with a decisive attack.

4b) 15...♕c7 16 ♘xf6+ ♗xf6 17 ♕e4 g6 18 ♗f4 is slightly better for White because Black's queen is uncomfortably placed.

5) 14...♗e8! is the correct reply, when White suddenly faces problems with his d-pawn. For

example, after 15 ♘xf6+ ♗xf6 16 ♕e4 g6 17 ♗h6 ♗g7 18 ♗xg7 ♔xg7 the d4-pawn is under attack. Black may even be slightly better.

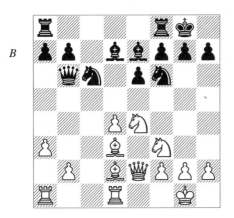

14   ...   ♖ad8

Black is content to continue his development, since it is too dangerous to take either of the pawns on offer:

1) 14...♘xd4? 15 ♘xd4 ♕xd4 16 ♗c3 ♕a4 17 b3! ♕c6 (17...♕xb3 loses to 18 ♘xf6+ ♗xf6 19 ♕e4) 18 ♘xf6+ ♗xf6 19 ♗xf6 gxf6 20 ♖ac1 ♕b6 21 ♗xh7+ ♔xh7 22 ♕h5+ ♔g7 23 ♕g4+ ♔h7 24 ♖c3 mating.

2) 14...♕xb2? 15 ♘xf6+ gxf6 (15...♗xf6 16 ♕e4 g6 17 ♖db1 traps the queen) 16 ♖db1 ♘xd4 17 ♗xh7+ ♔g7 18 ♕e3 wins Black's queen.

Karpov apparently preferred to play his queen's rook to d8 in order to leave the other rook to defend the kingside, in particular the f7-square. While in some positions this might be essential, here it just seems to be the normal Karpov caution. Objectively speaking, 14...♖fd8 15 ♘xf6+ ♗xf6 16 ♕e4 g6 17 ♕f4 ♗g7 18 ♗c3 ♗e8 also seems perfectly playable.

15 ,   ♘xf6+?!

Up to here, all White's moves have been perfectly natural, but over the next couple of moves, White's active play evaporates and he is left with nothing to compensate for the weakness of the d-pawn. Here 15 b4!? was a better chance. White threatens ♘c5, so Black is more or less forced to exchange on e4, which saves White time: 15...♘xe4 16 ♕xe4 f5 (16...g6 17 ♗h6 ♖fe8 18 ♕f4 is slightly better for White) 17 ♕e3 ♗f6 18 ♗c3 ♘e7 19 ♗c4 ♔h8 20 ♖ac1 may give White an infinitesimal advantage.

15   ...   ♗xf6
16   ♕e4   g6
17   ♗e3?!

The text-move threatens both 18 d5 and, even more strongly, 18 ♕f4 followed by 19 d5. However, after Black's reply it can be seen as just a blow into thin air. White should have accepted that he has no chances for an advantage and played for a draw by 17 ♗h6 ♗g7 18 ♗xg7 ♔xg7 19 ♖d2.

17   ...   ♘e7!

A very effective reorganization of Black's forces. The c6-square is cleared for the d7-bishop, while the knight might go to d5 or f5, as appropriate.

18   ♘e5

After 18 ♕f4 ♘d5 19 ♕g3 ♕xb2 it is not clear what White has for the pawn, while 18 d5 is no longer effective as the black knight is not under attack. The reply 18...♕xb2 19 ♖ab1 ♕xa3 20 ♖xb7 exd5 21 ♕f4 ♕a4! forces the exchange of queens and Black keeps one of his extra pawns.

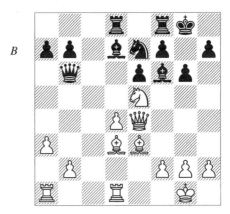

18   ...   ♘f5

This move is characteristic of the modern approach to tackling the isolated pawn. It would have been perfectly possible to play 18...♘d5, and the occupation of the blockading square may be thought of as the traditional method of playing against the isolated pawn. The only problem with this method is that it is essentially passive; the pawn is blockaded, but it is often not so easy to make progress. Black's plan is to exchange pieces and then eventually move from the blockade of the isolated pawn to a direct attack on it. However, if White avoids exchanges, it is quite easy for Black to end up with little to do (see Game 26). The modern approach is to cut out all the intermediate stages and go directly for the attack on the pawn, as Karpov does here. Obviously, there are dangers with this approach. The weakened control of the blockading square means there is a greater danger of the pawn lurching forward, and careful calculation may be necessary to see if this is dangerous.

Not every isolated pawn position is suitable for this modern approach; in many positions, the traditional method is more appropriate. However, it is important to be aware of the different methods of play against the isolated pawn, so as to choose the most suitable one for the position in front of you.

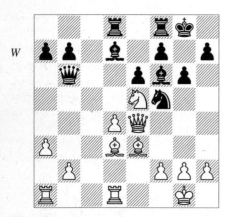

19   ♘c4

19 d5? ♘xe3 20 ♘xd7 ♖xd7 21 dxe6 ♘xd1 wins for Black, while 19 ♘xd7 ♖xd7 is very unpleasant for White. The pawns on d4 and b2 are both under fire, and Black can easily step up the pressure by ...♖fd8. Note how having the f5-knight ready to eliminate the e3-bishop at a moment's notice takes virtually all the sting out of the advance d5.

19   ...   ♕a6!

It looks odd the put the queen opposite the d3-bishop, but in fact White cannot exploit this arrangement. Black now threatens to activate his d7-bishop by ...♗c6 or ...♗b5.

19...♕b3 is also good enough for some advantage. For example, 20 ♘a5 and now:

1) 20...♕xb2 21 ♘xb7 (21 ♕xb7 ♕b6 22 ♕xb6 axb6 is also slightly better for Black) 21...♘xe3 22 fxe3 ♖c8 with a small advantage.

2) 20...♕a4 21 b4 b6 22 ♗c2 ♘d6! and the resulting liquidation only emphasizes the weakness of the d-pawn.

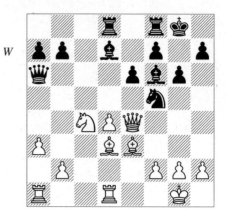

20   a4

20 ♘e5 is met by 20...♗b5 since Black is quite happy to exchange light-squared bishops. Then his remaining bishop would be quite active, whereas White's would be stuck on e3, doing little more than just defending the d4-pawn.

The text-move cuts out ...♗b5, and again hopes to cause some damage by moving the knight.

20   ...   ♗c6

21   ♕f4

White doesn't even threaten g4, because Black has the reply ...g5.

21   ...   ♗d5

So Black blockades the isolated pawn after all. His strategy has yielded several benefits:

1) All his minor pieces are on active squares. The f6-bishop and f5-knight are exerting direct pressure on the d4-pawn, while his remaining bishop is well posted on the blockading square. Note how this differs from the more traditional arrangement of knight on d5 and bishop on b7. That would be fine for the knight, but the bishop could only become active if the knight moved away.

2) White's position has become rather disorganized. In particular, his queen is not very well placed.

3) White still has to complete his development, but it is not so easy to bring the a1-rook into play as it must defend the a4-pawn.

The alternative 21...♗xd4 22 ♗xf5 ♕xc4 (22...♗xe3 23 ♘xe3 exf5 24 ♘xf5! ♖xd1+ 25

♖xd1 ♕xa4 26 ♘e7+ ♔g7 27 ♘f5+ and White escapes with a draw) 23 ♖xd4 ♖xd4 24 ♗xd4 exf5 wins a pawn, but it is not clear whether there are any realistic winning chances in view of the opposite-coloured bishops and Black's weak kingside.

22 ♘e5

All White can achieve with his discovered attack is to force the queen to move. 22 g4? g5! 23 ♕c7 ♖c8 would cost White material.

22 ... ♕b6

The two tempi Black has spent with his queen balance the two tempi White has consumed with his knight. However, the move a4 has not only cost White a further tempo, it has actually weakened his queenside. Thus the dance between the queen and the knight has left Black considerably ahead.

23 ♗xf5

This is a grim move to have to play, but there is little choice: 23 ♘g4 (after 23 g4? g5 Black wins material) 23...♗g7 24 ♖d2 defends b2, but leaves White's pieces in a horrible tangle. Black can exploit this by 24...♕b4, threatening 25...♘xe3 26 ♕xe3 (26 fxe3 leaves the d2-rook hanging) 26...♗xd4. Thus, White is forced to play 25 ♗xf5 exf5 with a position very similar to that which arises in the game.

23 ... exf5

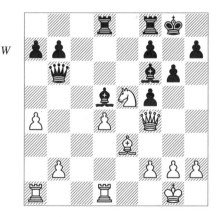

The exchange of White's more active bishop has given Black the further advantage of the two bishops. White will feel the lack of a light-squared bishop more and more as the game progresses, while Black's monster bishop on d5 can only grow in strength.

24 ♖d2

White has to look after his b-pawn.

24 ... ♗g7

White has no counterplay, so Black can take the time to tidy up his position. This move puts the bishop on a more secure square, and gives Black the option of kicking the knight away at a moment's notice by ...f6.

25 h4

Not so much to create counterplay, as to prevent Black from activating his kingside pawn-mass by ...h6, ...♕e6 and ...g5.

25 ... ♖fe8

Black completes his development. His advantage is close to being decisive, but the game will not win itself, especially against determined resistance. Black has to come up with a plan for actually improving his position.

26 ♕g3

White retreats his queen to counter the threat of ...f6 followed by ...♖e4.

26 ... ♖c8

Occupying the open file is perfectly natural, especially as White is unable to oppose rooks. At some stage Black should probably have taken time out to tidy up his position a bit more by ...h6 and ...♔h7. It might seem a long way off, but once Black starts penetrating into White's position with his rooks, it is useful not to have a weak back rank.

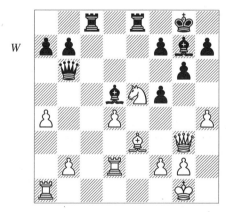

27 ♘d7

After 27 ♘d3, Black has a choice. He can either play 27...♖e4 28 ♘f4 ♕d8 with a similar position to the game, or enter favourable complications by 27...♗xd4!? 28 a5 ♖xe3! (not 28...♕f6? 29 ♘f4) 29 axb6 (29 fxe3 ♗xe3+ 30 ♔h1 ♕d4 31 ♖dd1 ♖c4! is winning for Black,

while 29 ♕f4 ♕e6 30 ♕xd4 ♖e4 31 ♕xa7 ♖g4
gives Black a large advantage) 29...♖xg3 30
♘f4 ♗xg2 31 bxa7 (31 ♖xd4 ♖g4 32 bxa7
♗e4+ 33 ♔f1 ♖xf4 transposes) 31...♗e4+ 32
♔f1 ♖g4 33 ♖xd4 ♖xf4 34 a8♕ (34 ♖ad1 ♔g7!
35 ♖d8 ♖c2 36 ♖1d2 ♖xd2 37 ♖xd2 ♖xh4 38
a8♕ {or else ...b6} 38...♗f3 and wins) 34...♖xa8
35 ♖xa8+ ♔g7, when Black will end up with
three pawns for the exchange.

27   ...   ♕c6

27...♕d8!? 28 ♘c5 b6 29 ♘d3 ♖e4 is perhaps slightly more effective, as it gains a tempo
over the game.

28   ♘c5

The knight has been manoeuvred to a new
post, but it can easily be dislodged.

28   ...   b6

29   ♘d3   ♕d7

The immediate 29...♖e4 30 ♖c1 ♕a8 31
♖xc8+ ♕xc8 32 ♕d6 allows some counterplay,
so Black quietly moves his queen off the c-file
in preparation for ...♖e4.

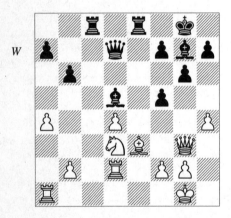

30   a5

If White returns his knight to e5 by 30 ♘e5,
then 30...♕b7 followed by ...h6 and ...♔h7
gradually improves Black's position. The text-
move aims to dislodge Black's pawn from b6
and thereby create a stable square for the knight
on c5.

30   ...   ♖e4

With the deadly threat of ...♖g4.

31   ♘f4

White has no time to exchange on b6, because 31 axb6 ♖g4 32 ♖xa7 ♕d8 33 ♕h3 (33
b7 loses after 33...♖xg3) 33...♕xb6 wins for
Black.

31   ...   b5

Black has the choice between allowing axb6,
when White has liquidated the weak a-pawn
and opened the a-file for his rook, and the text-
move, which avoids the exchange but gives
White a potential outpost for his pieces on c5.
Thanks to the possibility of ...♖g4, White's
knight is unlikely to be able to take advantage
of the weakness, but if White opposes rooks on
the c-file, then one of his rooks may be able to
utilize c5. Karpov's decision to allow the weakening of c5 is vindicated by the further course
of the game.

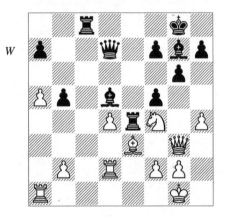

32   ♖dd1

Exchanging minor pieces by 32 ♘xd5 ♕xd5
does not help White. Black's queen has re-
placed his bishop on the dominant square d5,
and White has given up his only piece that was
showing a glimmer of activity. After 33 ♖ad1
b4 White faces a host of problems: his a-pawn
is weak, and Black has the slow but deadly plan
of ...h6, ...♔h7, ...b3 and ...♖c2.

The text-move opens up the possibility of
challenging rooks on the c-file.

32   ...   ♗c4

Black's problem is that he does not have an
obvious reply when White opposes rooks on
the c-file. He cannot contest the file while one
rook is on e4, but if he concedes the file, then a
white rook can occupy c5. Therefore, Karpov
decides to block the c-file so as to avoid the exchange of rooks, while at the same time controlling d3 to prevent the knight jumping to c5.
However, this move weakens Black's control of
d5 and so may allow White to play d5, releasing
his bishop. Karpov correctly judges that if this

happens, the activation of the g7-bishop on the long diagonal will compensate for the increased activity of White's bishop.

The alternatives are less clear; for example, the immediate 32...h6 gives White a chance to relieve some of the pressure by 33 ♘xd5 ♕xd5 34 ♖ac1 ♖xc1 35 ♖xc1 ♗xd4 36 ♕b8+ ♔g7 37 ♗xd4+ ♕xd4 38 ♕xb5, when the position is not especially clear even though Black can win a pawn. If 32...♗b3, then 33 ♖dc1 ♖xc1+ 34 ♖xc1 h6 35 ♘d3 ♗xd4 36 ♗xd4 ♖xd4 37 ♘c5 is also unclear.

33 ♖ac1

White should probably have tried to stir up some complications by 33 h5!? although Black retains a distinct advantage in any case. If 33 ♘d3, then 33...♗xd3 34 ♖xd3 ♕d5 is very good for Black.

33 ... h6

Black prevents h5 (in view of the reply ...g5) and at the same time creates a bolt-hole for his king on h7.

34 ♖c3

34 ♖c2 ♖c6 35 d5 ♗e5 would also be very good for Black.

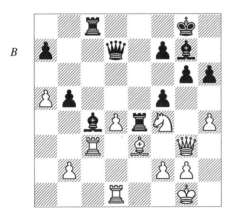

34 ... b4

Kicking the rook away and so preventing b3.

35 ♖c2

Threatening to double rooks.

35 ... ♖c6

36 ♖dc1

36 d5 is strongly met by 36...♗e5! with a large advantage after 37 ♖cd2 ♗d6 or 37 ♖d4!? ♖c7 38 ♖xe4 fxe4.

36 ... ♗b5

37 ♔h2

37 ♖xc6 ♗xc6 38 d5 (38 ♘d3 ♖g4 39 ♕b8+ ♔h7 is again very good for Black) 38...♗b7 is very bad for White, because 39 ♗xa7 fails to 39...♗xb2 followed by ...♗e5.

37 ... ♔h7

A useful precautionary move against a possible tempo-gaining back-rank check.

38 ♖xc6 ♗xc6

39 ♖c4

After 39 d5 ♗b7 40 b3 ♗e5 Black's pressure is unbearable, while 39 ♖c5 ♗xd4 40 ♗xd4 ♖xd4 gives Black a clear extra pawn.

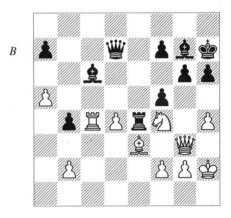

39 ... ♗f8!

A very strong move, defending the b4-pawn and threatening ...♗d6. The two bishops, operating on parallel diagonals, will exert tremendous pressure against White's kingside.

39...♗xd4 is wrong since after 40 ♗xd4 ♖xd4 41 ♕b3 ♖xc4 42 ♕xc4, the pawns on b4 and f7 are under fire, and it is by no means certain that Black can put his extra pawn to any use.

40 ♘d3?!

White makes a final effort to transfer his knight to a better square, but it allows a forced win. If he remains passive by 40 ♖c2, then 40...♗d6 41 ♔g1 ♗b7 followed by ...♕a4 penetrates decisively on the queenside. The bishops at d6 and b7 are ideally posted, both for attacking purposes and to prevent White's rook from making use of the c-file.

40 ... ♕e6?

This move, threatening not only the rook but also ...♖g4, preserves excellent winning chances, but Black misses an immediate win by 40...♕d5!:

1) 41 ♖c1 ♗d6 42 ♘e5 (or 42 f4 ♖xe3)
42...♗xe5 43 dxe5 ♖xh4+ 44 ♔g1 ♖g4 and
Black wins.

2) 41 ♖c2 ♖xh4+ 42 ♔g1 ♖g4 is again decisive.

3) 41 ♘e5 ♖xe5 42 ♖xc6 ♖xe3 is crushing.

Note that 40...♖g4? would be a serious error
due to 41 ♘e5!.

41　d5

This is the only chance. 41 ♖c1 (41 ♖c2 ♗d6
is similar, and clearer than 41...♖g4 42 ♖xc6
♕xc6 43 ♘e5) 41...♗d6 42 ♘f4 (42 ♘e5 ♗xe5
43 dxe5 ♖g4 and 42 ♗f4 ♖xf4 43 ♘xf4 ♕e4
win for Black) 42...♕d7 (42...♕e8 43 ♕f3 ♗a8
is also very good) 43 ♔g1 ♗b7 is basically the
same as the note to White's 40th move.

41　...　♗xd5

Not 41...♗d6?? 42 dxe6 ♗xg3+ 43 ♔xg3
♖xc4 44 exf7 ♔g7 45 ♗xh6+! ♔xf7 46 ♘e5+,
when White wins. 41...♕xd5? is also wrong,
because although 42 ♖xe4 fxe4 43 ♘e5 ♗d6
(43...♗b5 44 ♘g4 offers counterplay) 44 ♗f4
♗xe5 45 ♗xe5 ♕xa5 wins two pawns for Black,
the continuation 46 ♕f4 f5 47 ♗d4 ♕d5 48
♗e3 gives White dangerous threats.

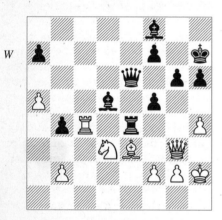

42　♖xe4

42 ♘c5 ♗d6 43 ♖xe4 ♗xg3+ 44 fxg3 ♕d6
45 ♖xb4 ♕e5 46 ♗f2 ♗c6 followed by ...♕d5
is winning for Black, while 42 ♘f4 ♗d6 doesn't
make White's life any easier, because 43 ♖xe4
♕xe4 gives Black an extra pawn and strong
pressure against White's kingside.

42　...　♗xe4

Better than blocking in the light-squared
bishop with 42...fxe4, when 43 ♘f4 ♕f5 44
♕h3 enables White to fight on.

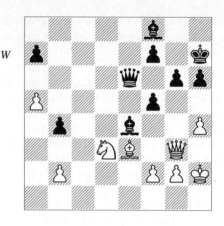

43　♗xa7?

This is a blunder that loses immediately –
White cannot afford to weaken the b8-h2 diagonal like this. The alternatives are:

1) 43 ♘f4 ♕e5 44 ♘h5 ♕h8! 45 ♘f4 ♕xb2
46 ♗xa7 ♕e5 and Black wins.

2) 43 ♘e5 ♗g7 44 f4 ♕a2 45 ♗xa7 ♕xb2
wins for Black, e.g. 46 ♘xf7 ♗xg2!.

3) 43 ♗c5 ♗g7 44 ♘f4 (44 ♘xb4 f4 45 ♕a3
♕c4 gives Black a winning attack based on
...♕f1, while 44 ♗d6 ♗xd3 45 ♕xd3 ♗e5+ 46
♗xe5 ♕xe5+ picks up the b2-pawn) 44...♕c4
45 ♗xa7 ♗xb2 should win. Exchanging the
pawns on b2 and a7 favours Black, because he
already covers the queening square of White's
a-pawn, whereas the passed b-pawn is almost
impossible to stop.

4) 43 ♘c5 was the best chance, but Black
should still win after 43...♕d5 44 ♘xe4 fxe4
(threatening 45...♗d6) and now:

4a) 45 ♗xa7?? loses to 45...♗d6 46 f4 exf3.

4b) 45 ♕h3 ♗g7! 46 ♗xa7 (46 b3 loses to
46...♕xb3 47 ♕d7 a6 48 h5 ♕e6) 46...♗xb2 is
winning for Black as White's pieces are abys-
mally posted to fight against Black's passed b-
pawn.

4c) 45 a6 ♕d3 46 h5 ♕xa6 47 hxg6+ ♕xg6
48 ♕xg6+ ♔xg6 49 ♗xa7 b3 gives Black a
winning bishop ending.

43　...　♗d6

Both 43...♕a6? and 43...♕d7? can be met by
44 ♗c5.

44　♘f4

44 f4 ♕d7! wins material, e.g. 45 ♗d4 ♗xd3
46 ♕xd3 ♗xf4+ followed by ...♗e5.

44　...　♕e5

45　♘h3?!

Losing a piece, but even after 45 ♗e3 ♕xb2 46 a6 b3 47 a7 ♕c3 the b-pawn runs home.

45	...	♕e7

0-1

Karpov unveiled an important opening novelty that reduced White's initiative. Rather than accept equality, Kamsky continued to play for the advantage but was soon in trouble. White was forced to concede the two bishops and in addition had serious light-square weaknesses – in fact, he had most of the positional disadvantages from this chapter rolled up in one game! Despite this, White put up fierce resistance, even causing Karpov to stumble. However, one

final error on move 43 proved too much for White's position, which promptly collapsed.

The lessons here are:

1) If there is no compensation, an isolated d-pawn is a serious weakness.

2) Control of the square in front of the isolated pawn is an important factor, but a direct attack on the pawn can also be awkward.

3) The owner of the isolated pawn should try to retain the bishop that controls the square in front of the pawn.

4) If the position is equal, it is better to accept the fact rather than start an unjustified aggressive action.

The Isolated d-Pawn Triumphs

As with many chess motifs, an isolated pawn typically has both positive and negative features. The pawn itself needs protecting, and the square in front it may be a safe haven for enemy pieces, but an isolated pawn frequently offers dynamic chances to its owner. In the following game, we once again look at the IQP, with the same player handling the white pieces. This time things go much better for him. Take a look at the diagram after White's 18th move in the game. In compensation for the weak pawn, White controls more space, his pieces are actively posted and he has some attacking chances on the kingside. Although it is not the case in this position, an isolated d4-pawn can often provide valuable support to a knight on e5.

One of Black's problems is that although he has a useful square on d5, just in front of the pawn, only one piece can occupy it at a time. While there are still many pieces on the board, this is a significant limitation. If one also takes into account the fact that Black's position is rather cramped, we can deduce one general principle: the owner of the isolated pawn usually prefers there to be many pieces on the board. His opponent, on the other hand, should seek exchanges with a view to reaching an ending in which only the negative side of the IQP is apparent.

A second principle is perhaps less obvious (but is more so if you look at the notes to the following game): the side with the IQP should retain the option of contesting the square in front of the pawn. The reason for this is that the attacking chances conferred by the IQP are hardly ever enough, by themselves, to force a breakthrough. The IQP owner normally has to tease his opponent in more than one area – usually this means having a fight over (in this case) d5. A direct attack is only likely to succeed once the defender has weakened his king position to deal with a problem in another area.

The following game shows how these ideas work out in practice.

Game 26
G. Kamsky – N. Short
PCA Candidates match (game 5), Linares 1994
Nimzo-Indian Defence, Rubinstein Variation

1	d4	♘f6
2	c4	

For comments on the moves up to here, see Game 13.

2   ...   e6

We have previously seen 2...g6 and 2...e5, but this is the first appearance of 2...e6 which, along with 2...g6, is one of the most common moves in this position. Black declares his intention to develop his dark-squared bishop along the f8-a3 diagonal, enabling rapid kingside castling. Depending on the next few moves, quite a wide range of different openings can arise.

3   ♘c3

White still hopes to be able to play e4, but Black has various ways to prevent this. For 3 ♘f3, see Game 21.

3   ...   ♗b4

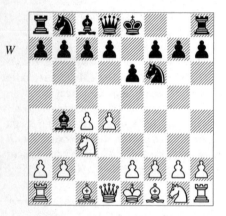

This is the Nimzo-Indian Defence, which is one of the most popular Queen's Pawn openings. It arises less often these days, mainly because it has such a good reputation that many players prefer to avoid it with 3 ♘f3. The idea behind 3...♗b4 is two-fold. First of all, Black is fighting for control of e4. By pinning the white knight, the immediate 4 e4 is prevented; if White shows signs of preparing it some other way, Black always has the counter ...b6 and ...♗b7 available. The second motivation is to double White's pawns by exchanging on c3. Ideally, Black would prefer White to waste a tempo on a3 before making this exchange, but there are some lines where Black plays it even without being provoked by the white a-pawn. These doubled pawns are a potential weakness, which Black might be able to exploit later on.

4   e3

There are basically three plans White can adopt. The first is for White simply to continue his development, leaving it up to Black whether to make the exchange on c3. The most common system with this plan involves e3, ♗d3 and ♘f3 by White, but 4 ♘f3 and 4 g3 also fall into this category.

The second general plan is to make Black take on c3 by playing 4 a3. In this line, White aims to build up a massive centre by f3 and e4, arguing that his attacking chances outweigh the damage to his pawn-structure. This plan is very committal and is not often played these days.

The third plan is to play to avoid the doubled pawns altogether. This is the basis behind one of the most popular systems for White, 4 ♕c2. White will play a3 and then recapture with the queen, gaining the two bishops without incurring any pawn weaknesses. The defect, of course, is that this costs time and Black obtains a lead in development to compensate for the bishop-pair. At the time of writing, it is impossible to predict who will win this argument as new ideas are being introduced all the time.

The text-move does not definitely commit White to one plan or another. He intends to start developing his kingside by ♗d3, and then he will decide whether to go for simple development with ♘f3, or try to avoid the doubled pawns with ♘e2. Of course, Black can take on c3 before White gets around to playing ♘e2, but this is likely to prove premature.

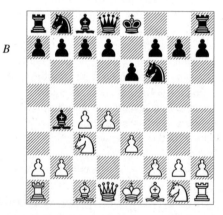

4   ...   c5

Black has quite a wide range of moves here. Other popular lines are 4...0-0 and 4...b6, the latter aiming for a better grip on e4. The text-move starts to stake out Black's claim in the centre, while leaving open the option of whether to play ...d6 or ...d5.

5   ♗d3

White begins to bring his kingside pieces out. Another possibility is 5 ♘e2, immediately denying Black the chance to double White's pawns. The obvious problem is that it interferes with White's natural kingside development.

5   ...   ♘c6

Black steps up the pressure against d4. This is a big decision-point for White.

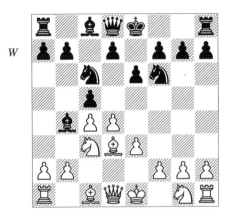

6   ♘e2

White decides that his priority is to avoid the doubled c-pawns. The defect is that e2 is a less active square for the knight than f3. After 6 ♘f3, Black usually continues 6...♗xc3+ 7 bxc3 d6 followed by ...e5. In this case the decision to play ...♗xc3+ without a3 is justified because Black can immediately set up a solid central pawn-structure on the dark squares. This tends to block the position, minimizing the danger from White's two bishops, and fixes the doubled c-pawn for possible later exploitation. It also works against White that his knight is on f3, because it blocks the move f4, which White might otherwise use to break up Black's pawn-centre.

6   ...   cxd4

Black must take action in the centre, for two reasons. First of all, White threatens a3, which would force Black to take on c3 in a position where it does not double White's pawns. Secondly, if Black ignores the centre, White can play 0-0 followed by d5, gaining space and time.

7   exd4   d5

This type of central pawn-structure can arise from many openings, but the position of the knight on e2 rather than f3 is unusual and adds a

new twist. From e2, there is no possibility of the knight occupying e5, but at least White avoids the immediate problems with the c3-knight which arise (after cxd5 ♘xd5) in, for example, the Caro-Kann (see Game 25).

8   cxd5

In such positions, it is often hard to decide whether to exchange on d5, or to leave Black to play ...dxc4. If White has already developed his bishop to d3, the former is normally better. The bishop is better placed on d3 than c4, and the exchange on d5 draws Black's knight away from f6, leaving the kingside a little bare. 8 0-0 dxc4 9 ♗xc4 0-0 gives Black an easier time.

8   ...   ♘xd5

This is by far the most common response. 8...♕xd5 9 0-0 ♕h5 leaves the queen somewhat misplaced, and after 10 ♘e4 ♘xe4 11 ♗xe4 0-0 12 ♕d3 ♗d6 13 ♘f4 White has a slight advantage. 8...exd5 9 0-0 0-0 is more solid, and the symmetrical pawn-structure renders it hard for White to make progress. However, even here 10 a3 ♗e7 11 f3 gives White an edge, since Black's light-squared bishop will be hard to activate, whereas all White's minor pieces are doing a useful job.

9   0-0

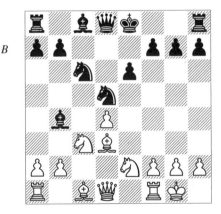

I have already described the general strategy of IQP positions in the previous game. The slightly unusual feature of White's knight being on e2 rather than f3 does not affect these general principles. White is aiming for play on the kingside, while Black can be content to defend and exchange pieces, because the long-term chances lie with him.

9   ...   ♗d6

An interesting idea. Black attempts to lure White's c3-knight to e4, believing that it will be worse placed there than at c3. The logic is that it is not only White's kingside threats but also his pressure against d5 that is annoying. If White forces Black to loosen his grip on d5, there is always the danger that the d-pawn will suddenly advance. By deflecting the knight to e4, Black at least hopes to avoid any problems at d5. However, White can argue that on e4 his knight is nearer Black's kingside and so may eventually play an effective part in the attack.

9...0-0 10 &c2 &e8 11 &d3 g6 is an alternative plan, intending ...&f8-g7.

10   &e4

This is the only challenging move. After 10 &xd5 exd5, White's advantage is infinitesimal.

10   ...   &e7

Black's dark-squared bishop is an important defensive piece, since after &c2 and &d3 Black will have to play ...g6, when he will need the bishop to cover the weak dark squares.

11   a3

White intends &c2 and &d3, so he must cut out a possible ...&cb4.

11   ...   0-0

12   &c2

White begins to line up against h7.

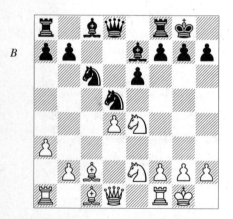

12   ...   &e8

Black adopts a plan for developing his remaining pieces which is characteristic for IQP positions. The main problem piece at the moment is the c8-bishop, but this can emerge via ...b6 and ...&b7. This frees the rook to occupy c8. Beyond that, Black's play depends on what White has done in the meantime.

However, Black has two alternative plans designed to exploit specific features of this position. The first is the simple 12...e5. This is only possible because there is no white knight on f3. Obviously, by liquidating the remaining central pawns Black is not playing for more than equality, but he has quite good chances of achieving that limited objective, as White's pieces are not active enough to take full advantage of the opening of the position. Playing ...e5 also solves the problem of the c8-bishop without loss of time.

The second idea is to continue 12...&c7 13 &d3 &d8. This makes use of the position of the knight on e4, which blocks the b1-h7 diagonal and so prevents White's bishop and queen battery from generating any instantly deadly threats. The advantage of this continuation is that the f8-rook is developed to d8, where it is much more active than on e8 (as in the game). In this variation the line-up of Black's rook and White's queen suggests that ...e5 might again be a possibility. This continuation does leave Black's queen on a slightly exposed square but there is no obvious way for White to exploit this. It is hard to say whether either of these plans is better than that chosen in the game.

13   &d3

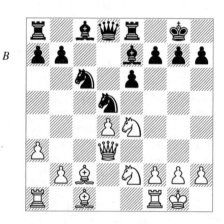

13   ...   g6

Perhaps Black could have got away with 13...b6 since 14 &d6 &xd6 15 &xh7+ &f8 16 &h8+ &e7 17 &xg7 &d7 is rather unclear, but I can understand that Short didn't want to play such a risky move. In any case, ...g6 will be necessary sooner or later, so there is little to be gained by taking a chance now.

14   &h6

Now that Black has played ...g6, the bishop can be developed to a good square without loss of time.

14   ...   b6

For the moment, White has no immediate threats and it will take him some time to build his attack up. Therefore, Black has the opportunity to complete his development.

15   ♖ad1

Taking stock, the position is objectively about equal, with White's dynamic possibilities balancing Black's solid position and hopes for a favourable liquidation. White cannot hope to break through by brute force so he should keep his pieces active, avoid exchanges and await events.

15   ...   ♗b7
16   ♖fe1

All these moves are perfectly natural. As usual with IQP positions, the d5-square is very important. Provided Black keeps a firm grip on it, White's attacking chances are restricted. However, if the grip should falter, White's attack would suddenly flare up.

16   ...   ♖c8

With this move Black completes his development.

17   ♗b3

White's bishop has done all it can on the b1-h7 diagonal in provoking ...g6, and now the bishop switches to another role – that of exerting pressure on d5. Moreover, if Black's grip on d5 does slip, the bishop will be well placed, either for a sacrificial breakthrough on e6, or in support of d5 by White.

17   ...   a6

Black's main problem is that once he has developed his a8-rook, it isn't easy to find a constructive plan that maintains his grip on d5. 17...♖c7!? is certainly playable; after 18 ♘2g3 (18 ♗xd5 exd5 19 ♘4c3 ♗f6 is equal) 18...♖d7 19 ♘h5 a very unclear position arises.

17...♘a5 18 ♗a2 ♘f6 is riskier. Admittedly, Black exchanges a pair of minor pieces, but his hold on d5 is weakened. After 19 ♘xf6+ ♗xf6 20 ♘f4 (20 b4 ♘c6 21 d5 ♘e5 gives White nothing because 22 dxe6? ♘xd3 23 exf7+ ♔h8 is unsound), the move 20...♗g5, consistently pursuing a policy of exchanges, runs into 21 ♘xe6!. Then:

1) 21...♖xe6 22 ♖xe6 ♗xh6 23 ♖xg6+ ♗g7 (23...hxg6 24 ♕xg6+ ♗g7 25 ♕xf7+ ♔h7 26 ♕f5+! ♔h6 27 ♗f7 mates) 24 ♖g4 favours White.

2) 21...fxe6 22 ♖xe6 ♖xe6 23 ♗xe6+ ♔h8 24 ♗xg5 ♕xg5 25 d5! ♘e5 26 ♗xc8 ♗xc8 is very good for White. His rook and two pawns are worth slightly more than Black's minor pieces, and in addition Black's king is exposed and his knight is offside.

The text-move is not bad. In some lines in which Black moves his knight from c6, the reply ♗a4 is annoying, so Black takes time out to make sure that ...b5 will be available in this case.

18   ♘2g3

It is probably not an immediate threat, but the idea of ♘h5-g7 is in the air.

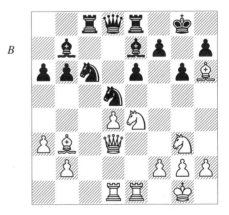

18   ...   ♘b8?!

This is a very artificial move. Black apparently intends to reorganize his pieces by playing ...♘d7, ...♖c7 and finally ...♕a8, freeing the e8-rook to move to d8 or c8. However, this plan is extremely slow. Black had a choice of reasonable alternatives:

1) 18...♗h4! is the simplest. This prevents ♘h5, because White's queen no longer has access to g3, and it prepares ...♘c6-e7-f5, expelling the dangerous bishop from h6. At no stage in this plan does Black's grip on d5 loosen.

2) 18...♘a5 19 ♗a2 f5 is a dynamic but slightly riskier plan. It goes against the grain to create a backward e-pawn, but there is no white knight in a position to jump into e5, so this weakening is not serious. It is also true that the a2-g8 diagonal is weakened, but so long as d5 remains firmly occupied, the a2-bishop will never get a glimpse of the new weakness. Modern players are often willing to incur pawn weaknesses if they can thereby achieve some dynamic aim and this is a case where such a decision would be justified. By playing ...f5 Black gains time and activates his pieces. After 20 ♘c3 ♗f6 21 ♘xd5 ♗xd5 22 ♗xd5 ♕xd5 23 ♕xa6 ♘c4, Black has excellent compensation for the pawn (which he will almost certainly win back in a move or two). The g3-knight, in particular, is now poorly placed.

19   ♕f3

It may be possible to play 19 ♘h5!? straight away. Then 19...♗h4 (19...f5 can be met by 20 ♘c3 ♗g5 21 ♘xd5 ♗xd5 22 ♗xd5 ♕xd5 23 ♗xg5 gxh5 24 ♕h3, winning) 20 ♘g7 (20 ♕f3 transposes to line '2' of the next note) 20...♖f8 21 ♕h3 ♕e7 is very unclear. White would clearly be taking on a big risk in playing his knight to g7, and so Kamsky preferred the text-move, which helps the attack along without taking unnecessary chances.

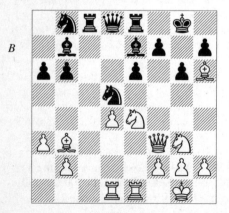

19   ...   ♖c7?!

Or:

1) 19...♘d7 20 ♘h5 b5 21 ♘f4 (after 21 ♘g7 ♖f8, White doesn't appears to have anything better than to repeat moves by 22 ♘h5) 21...♘7b6 (trying to maintain a grip on d5; 21...♘xf4 22 ♕xf4 is also slightly better for White) 22 ♘d3, followed by ♘e5 or ♘dc5, leaves White slightly better.

2) 19...♗h4 is probably still the correct move. Then 20 ♘h5 f5 (20...gxh5 21 ♕xh5 f5 22 ♗xd5 ♗xd5 23 ♘d6 ♕xd6 24 ♕xh4 is also unclear) 21 ♘g7 fxe4 22 ♕xe4 ♖e7 23 ♕xh4 ♖xg7 24 ♕xd8+ ♖xd8 25 ♗xg7 ♔xg7 26 ♖xe6 is unclear.

20   ♘h5!

White's attack suddenly starts to look dangerous. There is a threat of 21 ♗xd5 followed by 22 ♘hf6+.

20   ...   ♘d7

Of course 20...gxh5? loses to 21 ♕g3+ ♗g5 22 ♗xg5. In this position, 20...f5 is too loosening; after 21 ♘c3 Black cannot survive the weakness of the a2-g8 diagonal, e.g. 21...♗f8 (21...♘xc3? 22 ♗xe6+ ♔h8 23 ♗g7#) 22 ♗xd5 ♗xh6 23 ♗xb7 gxh5 24 ♕xh5 ♗g7 25 ♗d5! with a winning position for White.

The text-move is the only other way to counter White's threat.

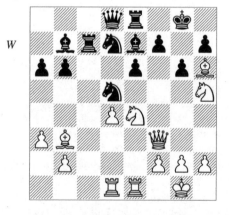

21   h4!

An excellent move. White introduces a new idea: ♘g5.

21   ...   ♘7f6?!

This leads to a rapid disaster, because Black's grip on d5 is weakened. There were no really satisfactory moves, but of course anything is better than an immediate forced loss. Here are the alternatives:

1) 21...♗xh4 loses to 22 ♘d6 ♖e7 23 ♖e4!.

2) 21...♕a8 22 ♗xd5 ♗xd5 (22...exd5 loses to 23 ♘ef6+) 23 ♘hf6+ ♘xf6 24 ♘xf6+ ♔h8 25 ♘xd5 ♕xd5 26 ♕xf7 is winning for White.

3) 21...f5 22 ♘c3 ♗f8 (22...♗xh4 23 ♘xd5 ♘f8 24 ♘hf4 exd5 25 ♖xe8 ♕xe8 26 ♘xd5 and White wins) 23 ♗g5 ♕a8 24 ♘xd5 ♗xd5 25 ♗xd5 exd5 26 ♖xe8 ♕xe8 27 ♗f4 ♖a7 (27...♖c2 28 ♕xd5+ ♕f7 29 ♕xd7 gxh5 30 ♕d8 wins) 28 ♕xd5+ ♕f7 29 ♕xf7+ ♔xf7 30 ♘g3 and White is a pawn up in the ending.

4) 21...♗a8 (21...b5 is very similar) 22 ♘g5 and now:

4a) 22...♘7f6 23 ♘g7 ♖f8 24 ♘7xe6 is winning for White.

4b) 22...♘5f6 23 ♘xf7! ♗xf3 24 ♘xd8 ♗xh5 (24...♗xd8 25 ♖xe6 and 24...♗d5 25 ♘xe6 are also hopeless for Black) 25 ♗xe6+ ♔h8 26 ♘f7+ ♔g8 27 ♘d6+ ♔h8 28 ♘xe8 ♘xe8 29 g4 wins material.

4c) 22...♗xg5 23 ♗xg5 with a final branch:

4c1) 23...f6 24 ♗h6 ♖e7 (24...♘c3 loses to 25 ♖xe6) 25 ♖xe6! ♖xe6 26 ♗xd5 ♗xd5 27 ♕xd5 ♖cc6 28 ♘f4 ♕e7 29 ♖e1 wins.

4c2) 23...♕c8 24 ♗h6 ♕d8 (24...♘e7? 25 ♕xf7+ mates next move) 25 ♕g3 and Black's weakened dark squares give White a clear plus.

22 ♘hxf6+ ♘xf6

This is forced, since 22...♗xf6 loses to 23 ♗xd5, but now White's d-pawn is unchained.

23 d5!

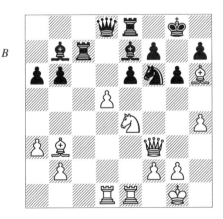

When the isolated pawn can advance with impunity, the result is very often a catastrophe as the pent-up energy behind the pawn is released.

The thematic combination initiated by this move utilizes all the key elements of White's attack: Black's weak back rank, the weakness of f6 (and g7) and the a2-g8 diagonal.

23 ... ♘xe4

Or 23...♘xd5 (23...exd5 24 ♘xf6+ ♗xf6 25 ♕xf6! mates, while 23...e5 loses material to 24 d6) 24 ♗xd5 ♗xd5 (24...exd5 25 ♘f6+ ♗xf6 26 ♕xf6 is again decisive) 25 ♖xd5! exd5 (25...♕xd5 loses to 26 ♘f6+ ♗xf6 27 ♕xf6) 26 ♘f6+ ♗xf6 (26...♔h8 27 ♘xe8 ♕xe8 28 ♕f6+ and mate next move) 27 ♖xe8+ ♕xe8 28 ♕xf6 and White wins.

24 dxe6

White has too many threats.

24 ... f5

Or 24...fxe6 25 ♗xe6+ ♔h8 26 ♕f7 ♗f6 27 ♖xd8 and White wins.

25 ♖xd8 ♖xd8
26 ♖d1 1-0

Black is way down on material and his king is still terribly exposed.

Many opening systems lead to IQP positions, including several lines of the Nimzo-Indian. Although the position arising in this game had some unusual features, the general principles applying to IQP positions were still valid. White successfully avoided exchanges, while making the first moves towards developing a kingside attack. For some time, the position remained in equilibrium, with Black's position sufficiently solid to hold off White's army. However, the balance was disturbed when Black adopted an incorrect plan on move 18. This and the following move gave White the opportunity to switch to a direct attack, which he conducted with great vigour. Black's forces became over-stretched and the climax came when Black released the blockade of the IQP, which promptly struck the decisive blow.

The lessons here are:

1) The first step in a kingside attack is often to force a pawn weakness.

2) The owner of the IQP should usually avoid piece exchanges.

3) It is important for both sides to bring pieces to bear on the square in front of the IQP.

4) Lifting the blockade of an IQP may allow it to advance with devastating effect.

Positional Sacrifices

It is easy to understand a sacrifice that has an immediate concrete result – it leads to mate, or to the recovery of the material with interest, for example. However, it is also possible to sacrifice material on a longer-term basis. In this case, the compensation usually consists of positional factors – for example, the creation of a permanent weakness in the enemy position, or the exposure of the enemy king in a way which can eventually be exploited. It is often hard to judge the soundness of such positional sacrifices, since both tactical and positional factors are involved. We have already seen a good example of a positional sacrifice in Game 20, where Kasparov sacrificed the exchange in order to create a network of weak light squares in his opponent's position.

Since the exploitation of positional advantages usually takes some time, positional sacrifices often occur in positions where the opponent has difficulty generating counterplay. The following game represents a marginal case.

Game 27

J. Lautier – A. Shirov

Interzonal tournament, Manila 1990

King's Indian Defence, Fianchetto Variation

	1	d4	♘f6
	2	♘f3	g6

For comments on the moves up to here, see Game 24.

3   g3

A solid move. Now that Black is committed to fianchettoing his king's bishop, White does likewise, counting on his extra move to give him the edge. As with all symmetrical lines, Black must take care not to carry on the mimicry for too long, as he might end up with a depressingly passive position. See also Game 17.

	3	...	♗g7
	4	♗g2	0-0

For the time being, both sides content themselves with natural developing moves, which will have to be played sooner or later in any case.

5   0-0

The symmetry continues, but now Black has completed his kingside development. Before he can bring his queenside pieces into play, he must decide how to react in the centre.

5   ...   d6

Shirov definitely decides to break the symmetry. The main alternative is 5...d5, when after 6 c4 it is risky for Black to play the symmetrical 6...c5. Instead, 6...dxc4 and 6...c6 are popular and solid options.

6   c4

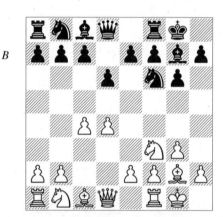

B

Now the game has transposed into the King's Indian Defence, Fianchetto Variation (so-called because White develops his bishop at g2). As in virtually all lines of the King's Indian, sharp play can result.

6   ...   ♘c6

This move may look a little odd, because it blocks the move ...c5, which is often a means of challenging White's centre in the Fianchetto King's Indian. Moreover, White can simply kick the knight away with d5. However, there is considerable logic behind Black's move and it is in fact the second most common in this position. Black's idea is to develop flexibly for the moment. He may decide to challenge in the centre with ...e5, or he may play on the queenside with ...a6, ...罝b8 and ...b5, aiming to exchange his b-pawn for White's more central c-pawn. In this latter case, any activity by Black in the centre will be delayed for several moves. Since White's set-up is based more on soundness than aggression, Black can afford the time for this rather leisurely plan of counterplay.

The main alternatives are 6...包bd7, followed by ...e5, 6...c6, aiming for piece-play with ...豐a5 and (probably) ...象e6, while 6...c5, directly attacking White's centre, is another major option. All these lines are perfectly playable and, objectively speaking, there is little to choose between them.

7   包c3

White simply continues his development, bringing his queen's knight out to its most natural square.

7   ...   a6

This is the most common move nowadays, as the plan of queenside activity is thought to be the best follow-up to ...包c6. The alternative 7...e5 8 d5 包e7 9 e4 should favour White. Play often develops into a traditional King's Indian queenside vs kingside battle, but White's fianchetto structure makes his kingside harder to attack than in similar lines with the bishop on e2.

8   h3

This flexible and useful little move prevents both ...包g4 and ...象g4. The former is significant if White develops his dark-squared bishop at e3, while the latter is important if White wants to play e4. The immediate 8 e4, for example, is inaccurate because of 8...象g4 9 h3 象xf3 10 象xf3 包d7 11 象e3 e5, when Black establishes a knight at d4. There are two other popular ideas for White. The first is the direct 8 d5 包a5 9 包d2 c5 10 豐c2, when Black aims to attack the c4-pawn with ...a6, ...罝b8 and ...b5. The second is 8 b3, which avoids spending a tempo on h3 because it isn't necessary if the bishop is developed on b2.

8   ...   象d7

This is a slightly unusual move. Black normally continues 8...罝b8, in order to play ...b5 as soon as possible. In this line he often leaves his bishop on c8 for some time since it is not yet

clear where it will be best placed. It is true that d7 is very often the bishop's destination, but Black need not commit it so soon.

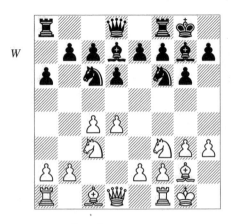

9   象g5

Lautier avoids the standard lines 9 e4 and 9 象e3, and finds a very unusual move. White's idea is to induce ...h6, and then retreat his bishop to e3. After a later 豐d2, Black will have to spend a tempo defending his h-pawn and White will have effectively gained a tempo over the line 9 象e3.

9   ...   h6

This is not the only possible move, but it is logical to drive the bishop away from its active position on g5.

10   象e3   罝b8

Black continues just as if the pawn were on h7. He intends ...b5, exchanging his b-pawn for the more central c4-pawn.

11   包d5

After 11 豐d2 Black can reply 11...堂h7 12 包d5 包e4 (12...b5 is also playable) 13 豐c2 f5 with a satisfactory position. If White continues sharply by 14 包h4!? e6 15 象xe4 fxe4 16 包f4, then 16...罝xf4! (16...g5? loses to 17 包xe6) 17 象xf4 g5 18 豐xe4+ 堂g8 19 d5 exd5 20 豐xd5+ 堂h7 leads to perpetual check.

11   ...   b5!?

A consistent and very combative move. Black does not mind having his pawns broken up if he can generate good piece activity. The quieter 11...e6 12 包xf6+ 豐xf6 13 豐d2 leaves White with a small but safe positional advantage after 13...堂h7 14 罝ac1 豐e7 15 d5 包e5 16 包d4 or 13...g5 14 罝ac1.

12   包xf6+

White accepts the offer to double Black's pawns. This exchange is virtually forced sooner or later, as White's d5-knight was being undermined.

12 ♕d2 was played in a later game Timman-Shirov, Donner Memorial, Amsterdam 1995. Black obtained a satisfactory position after 12...bxc4 13 ♘xf6+ exf6 14 ♗xh6 ♗xh6 15 ♕xh6 ♖xb2 16 ♘h4 ♘e7 and now Timman decided to force a draw by 17 ♗d5 ♘xd5 18 ♘xg6 fxg6 19 ♕xg6+ ♚h8 20 ♕h6+ with a repetition of moves.

12   ...   exf6

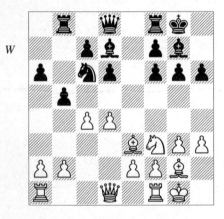

In this position the doubled pawns constitute a weakness, albeit a slight one. It is not so much that the pawns are weak in themselves; it is more that without an e-pawn Black will find it hard to challenge White's main central strongpoint, the d4-pawn. In compensation, the e-file is opened for Black's rook and Black gains a little time, since White has exchanged a knight that has made three moves for a knight that has only moved once.

13   cxb5

13 d5 ♘e7 14 c5 is over-aggressive; after 14...♘f5 Black stands well.

13   ...   ♖xb5

Again, Black prefers activity over structure. It might seem more solid to play 13...axb5 keeping his queenside pawns together. The problem is that after 14 d5 Black has no good reply. For example, after 14...♘e5 (14...♘e7 15 ♘d4 followed by ♖c1 also starts to exert pressure against Black's queenside) 15 ♘d2, followed by ♖c1, Black faces problems both with his queenside and with the almost trapped

knight on e5. Thus playing 13...axb5 doesn't really solve Black's problems on the queenside, and offers no piece activity in compensation.

14   ♕d2

14 ♕c1!? might be slightly more accurate. If Black plays 14...g5 (as in the game) then White can reply 15 ♘xg5 fxg5 16 ♗xc6 ♗xc6 17 ♕xc6 (17 a4 ♖b6 18 a5 ♖b4 19 ♕xc6 ♕c8 is unclear) 17...♖xb2 18 ♕xa6 ♕a8 19 ♕c4 with a slight advantage.

14   ...   g5

14...♚h7 is also possible, but Shirov prefers to reduce the activity of White's dark-squared bishop.

15   d5!

If White plays passively, then Black will continue ...♘e7-d5, occupying an excellent central square and preparing active play by ...f5. 15 ♖ac1 and 15 ♘e1, for example, are both met by 15...♘e7 with satisfactory play for Black.

15 a4 is a critical move. Then:

1) 15...♖b8 16 d5 ♘e7 (16...♘e5 17 ♖fc1 also gives White an edge) 17 ♘d4 leaves Black a little passively placed.

2) 15...♖b3! is more active. After 16 d5 ♘e5 17 ♖fc1 (17 ♘d4 ♘c4 18 ♕c2 ♘xe3 19 ♕xb3 ♘xf1 20 ♖xf1 f5 activates the dark-squared bishop with a satisfactory position for Black) 17...♕b8 Black has sufficient counterplay.

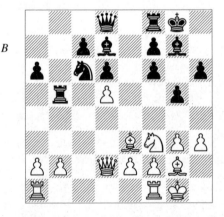

15   ...   ♘e7

15...♘e5 16 ♖ac1! (16 ♘d4?! ♘c4 17 ♕c3 ♘xe3 18 fxe3 f5 is fine for Black) 16...♘xf3+ 17 exf3 f5 18 b3 is uncomfortable for Black. White will play f4, when it is not clear what compensation Black has for his weak queenside pawns.

16   ♘d4

The natural follow-up. White has to move his knight in order to defend the d5-pawn, and after any other knight move Black achieves a good position with ...♘f5.

16   ...   ♖xd5!?

This sacrifice is the point behind Black's play. Passively retreating the rook by 16...♖b8 would be an admission of failure; White would obtain an advantage with the natural move 17 ♖ac1.

17   ♗xd5   ♘xd5

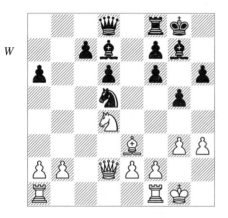

Black has given up the exchange in return for a pawn. His compensation is not in the form of an immediate attack against the king, or any particularly strong threats. It is of a long-term nature, and is primarily positional rather than tactical. Such sacrifices are usually called 'positional sacrifices', although there is of course no clear-cut dividing line between positional sacrifices and those aiming for shorter-term compensation. Looking at the diagram, what has Black gained in return for his (admittedly fairly modest) material deficit? Firstly, he has eliminated White's cramping central pawn, which both restrained his own c-pawn and created a possible outpost on c6. Secondly, he has removed White's light-squared bishop. This not only gives White the immediate problem of dealing with the h3-pawn, but also raises the possibility that the weak light squares around the white king might eventually enable Black to start a direct attack.

Despite these advantages, the game is far from plain sailing for Black. His main problem is the vulnerability of his c- and d-pawns to attack along the half-open files. White's rooks are well placed to swing into action, and Black could easily find himself facing strong pressure. Time is clearly an important factor here. If White has time to complete his development without Black having generated any active play, then Black will be forced back into a defensive posture. Therefore, both sides must try to make every tempo count. Objectively speaking, I believe that White has some advantage, but the resulting highly complex positions suit Shirov much better than Lautier, so while the balance of the position may still favour White, he is facing a tough challenge.

18   ♘f5!

Lautier also knows how to play for the initiative, and is willing to offer his h-pawn in order to speed his rooks onto the central files. The alternatives are:

1) 18 ♔h2 ♕a8 (18...♘xe3? 19 fxe3! ♕c8 20 g4 is bad, as White's grip on f5 prevents Black from activating his dark-squared bishop) 19 ♘c2 c5 keeps White's pieces out of d4, and affords Black good compensation. He can continue with ...♖e8, ...♗c6 and ...f5 (in some order) with plenty of activity, while White's minor pieces have little scope.

2) 18 g4 ♕c8 19 f3 (otherwise Black can at any rate force a draw by ...♗xg4) 19...♘xe3 20 ♕xe3 f5 and with two active bishops against a knight and a weakened white kingside, Black is at least equal.

18   ...   ♗xf5

Forced, because 18...♘xe3? 19 fxe3! sets up a blockade on f5.

19   ♕xd5   ♗xh3
20   ♖fd1

20 ♖fc1 is inferior. After 20...♗e6 21 ♕b7 f5 22 ♖xc7 ♗d5! 23 ♕xd5 (23 ♕a7 f4 24 ♗b6 ♕f6 gives Black dangerous threats, while after 23 ♕b6 f4 24 ♖d1 fxe3 25 ♖xd5 exf2+ 26 ♔xf2 ♕f6+ 27 ♔g2 ♕e6 28 ♖d2 ♕e4+ 29 ♔h2 ♗e5 White's kingside is looking exposed) 23...♕xc7 it is up to White to demonstrate full equality.

20   ...   ♖e8

Pinning the e3-bishop against the undefended e2-pawn.

21   ♖ac1

This natural move completes White's development. The alternative 21 ♖d2 f5 22 ♗d4

♗xd4 23 ♕xd4 ♕a8 24 f3 looks approximately equal.

21	...	f5

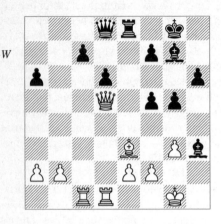

W

Once again, Black must act quickly or else White will converge on the weak c7-pawn. This move not only threatens the b2-pawn, but also starts a general pawn advance in the direction of White's king.

22   ♖d2

This move defends the e2- and b2-pawns in preparation for ♗d4, and with very accurate play should give White an advantage. However, White can also gain an advantage with the simpler 22 ♕c6. Then:

1) 22...f4 23 gxf4 gxf4 24 ♗xf4 ♗xb2 25 ♖c4 is inadequate as Black is unable to exploit White's slightly exposed king position. Note that 25...♖xe2? fails to 26 ♕f3.

2) 22...♖xe3!? 23 fxe3 ♕e7 is dubious here as White effectively has an extra tempo compared to the game. Although there are some traps to be negotiated, White should gain the advantage:

2a) 24 ♖d3 ♗xb2 25 ♖c2 (25 ♕xc7 ♕e4 is good for Black) 25...♗e5 26 ♕xc7 ♕f6 gives Black good play; for example, 27 ♕c8+ (27 ♔h2 g4 is similar) 27...♔g7 28 ♔h2 g4 29 ♖d5 (29 ♕e8? ♗xg3+! 30 ♔xg3 ♕a1 wins for Black) 29...h5 with a dangerous attack.

2b) 24 ♔f2! ♗e5 (24...♗xb2 25 ♕xc7 is very good for White) 25 ♖d3 (25 ♕xc7?? ♗xg3+ mates) leaves Black struggling for compensation; for example, 25...♕f6 (25...h5 26 ♕xc7 ♕f6 27 ♕d7 h4 28 gxh4 g4 29 ♖c8+ ♔g7 30 ♕d8 defends) 26 ♕e8+ ♔g7 27 ♖xc7 f4 28 exf4 gxf4 29 gxf4 ♕xf4+ 30 ♔e1 ♕f1+

31 ♔d2 ♗f4+ 32 ♖e3 and Black will end up the exchange for a pawn down.

3) 22...♗xb2 23 ♖c2 ♗e5 24 ♕xc7 and now:

3a) 24...♕a8 25 ♕c6 ♕xc6 (25...f4 26 gxf4 gxf4 27 ♕xa8 ♖xa8 28 ♗d4 is also slightly better for White) 26 ♖xc6 ♗xg3 27 ♗d4 and White has the better ending.

3b) 24...♕xc7 25 ♖xc7 ♗xg3 (25...f4 26 gxf4 gxf4 27 ♗d4 favours White) 26 ♖d3 ♗e5 27 ♗xg5 ♗g4 (27...hxg5 28 ♖xh3 and Black's a-pawn is liable to be lost within a few moves) 28 ♖e7 (28 ♗xh6 ♗xe2 29 ♖e3 ♗b5 30 ♖f3 ♔h7 31 ♗f4 ♔g6 is drawish) 28...♖c8 29 ♗xh6 ♗xe2 30 ♖h3 and White retains a slight advantage. It is true that Black has two pawns for the exchange, but his pawns are weak and isolated. White is better, but the general reduction in the number of pawns means that Black retains fair drawing chances.

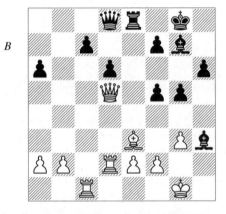

B

22	...	♖xe3!?

This second sacrifice ups the stakes. Black is willing to invest more material to increase his positional assets. Note that again the sacrifice does not lead to an immediate attack on the white king, so this could again be described as a 'positional' sacrifice. In this case, however, the possibility of an attack is closer than hitherto, since White's shattered pawns and the ominous presence of the h3-bishop pose an obvious danger to the king.

23	fxe3	♕e7
24	♔f2!	

Black has sufficient counterplay after the alternatives, e.g. 24 ♕d3 ♗e5 25 ♔h2 ♗g4 followed by ...h5, 24 e4 fxe4 25 e3 h5, 24 ♔h2 ♗g4, or 24 ♕f3 g4 25 ♕f2 c5 26 ♖cd1 ♗e5 27

♕xf5 ♗xg3 – in all cases Black has full compensation for the material. White's king remains very exposed and his rooks have, as yet, little scope.

The text-move is effective because it not only defends g3 and e3, but also prepares to evacuate the king to the queenside if Black's kingside threats become too dangerous.

24   ...   ♗e5

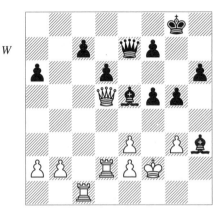

White's main problem is that there is little activity for his rooks. If he could penetrate with a rook to c7 and tie Black down to the defence of f7, then it would be hard for Black to proceed with his attack. Accurate play is necessary to achieve this.

25   ♖h1?

Up to here White has played simply and directly, but now makes a serious error under the pressure imposed by Black's sacrificial play. The alternatives provide a good illustration of the principles governing defence against a positional sacrifice:

1) 25 b4 gives White no advantage against accurate play, e.g.:

1a) 25...♗xg3+? 26 ♔xg3 ♕xe3+ 27 ♔h2 ♕f2+ 28 ♔h1 and White wins.

1b) 25...h5?! 26 ♖dc2 h4 (26...f4 27 gxf4 gxf4 28 ♖g1+ ♗g4 29 exf4 ♗xf4 30 ♔e1 also gives White a clear advantage) 27 gxh4 g4 (27...gxh4 loses after 28 ♖xc7 ♗g3+ 29 ♔g1 ♕xe3+ 30 ♔h1) 28 ♔e1 and the king escapes from the danger zone, when White is better.

1c) 25...g4! 26 ♖d3 (26 ♖dc2? ♗xg3+ 27 ♔xg3 ♕xe3+ 28 ♔h2 ♕f2+ 29 ♔h1 g3 wins for Black) 26...h5 gives Black enough counterplay.

2) 25 ♖d3 and now:

2a) 25...h5 with a further branch:

2a1) 26 ♕b7 h4 27 ♖xc7 ♗xg3+ 28 ♔g1 ♕e5 29 ♖xf7 (29 ♕d5 ♗f2+ 30 ♔h1 ♕xd5+ 31 ♖xd5 g4 looks dangerous for White after 32 ♖xd6 g3 33 ♖d1 ♗xe3 or 32 ♖xf5 g3 33 ♖g5+ ♔f8 34 ♖b7 ♗e6) 29...d5 30 ♖g7+ ♕xg7 31 ♕xd5+ ♔h7 32 ♕e6 draws.

2a2) 26 ♕a8+! ♔g7 27 ♕b7 looks promising for White, as the line of '2a1' would now lead to the f7-pawn being taken with check.

2b) 25...c5 26 ♖h1 g4 gives Black fair compensation.

3) 25 ♕d3 h5 26 ♖h1 and now 26...♗g4 is unclear, but Black should avoid 26...g4 27 ♕xf5 ♗xg3+ 28 ♔xg3 ♕xe3+ 29 ♔h4 ♕xd2 30 ♕g5+ ♕xg5+ 31 ♔xg5, which favours White.

So what is the correct move? When defending against a positional sacrifice, the key point is that the enemy attack arrives more slowly than after a direct sacrifice. Very often, part of the compensation for the material lies in the inability of the defender to make effective use of his extra material. In the current position, White's problem is that he cannot easily get his rooks into play – but that shouldn't have prevented him from trying!

4) 25 ♖dc2! (the best continuation) 25...c5 26 b4 (White must be prepared to return some material in order to activate his rooks) 26...g4 (trying to disrupt White's efforts by the threat of a sacrifice on g3) 27 ♖c3! (now that Black has sealed his light-squared bishop out of the game with ...g4, it is definitely worth giving up a rook for the dark-squared bishop; in particular, once an endgame is reached, it almost doesn't matter how many extra pawns Black has since he is playing without the bishop on h3) and now:

4a) 27...♗xc3 28 ♖xc3 cxb4 (28...♕f6 29 ♖d3 favours White) 29 ♖c6 h5 30 ♖xd6 and White stands very well.

4b) 27...h5 28 bxc5 h4 29 c6 hxg3+ 30 ♔g1 ♗xc3 31 ♖xc3 ♕c7 32 ♖b3 wins for White.

4c) 27...cxb4 28 ♖c7 ♕f6 29 ♖b7 f4 30 exf4 ♗xf4 31 ♖xf7 ♕xf7 32 ♕xf7+ ♔xf7 33 gxf4 h5 34 ♔g3 is a promising ending for White.

25   ...   ♗xg3+!

Suddenly the balance tips in Black's favour. One careless move and Shirov is in his element.

26   ♔xg3

After 26 ♔f3 g4+ 27 ♔xg3 ♛xe3+ 28 ♔h4
♛f2+ 29 ♔h5 ♛f4 30 ♔h4 (30 ♛a8+ ♔g7 31
♛d8 g3 mates quickly) 30...♛g5+! 31 ♔g3 f4+
32 ♔h2 ♛h4 White is defenceless.

26	...	♛xe3+
27	♛f3	

Not 27 ♔h2? ♛f2+ 28 ♔xh3 g4#.

27	...	♛xd2

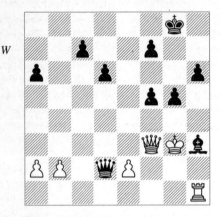

W

28	♛a8+

28 ♖xh3 is no better, e.g. 28...g4 29 ♛a8+
♔g7 and now:

1) 30 ♖h2 ♛e3+ 31 ♔h4 (31 ♔g2 ♛xe2+
transposes) 31...♛e7+ 32 ♔g3 ♛e5+ 33 ♔g2
♛xe2+ 34 ♔g1 ♛e1+ 35 ♔g2 f4 wins for
Black.

2) 30 ♖h5 ♛e1+ 31 ♔h2 ♛xe2+ 32 ♔g3 (32
♛g2 loses to 32...g3+) 32...♛e1+ 33 ♔g2 (33
♔h2 ♔g6 is also hopeless for White) 33...f4
and Black wins.

3) 30 ♖h1 ♛e3+ 31 ♔h2 ♛xe2+ 32 ♛g2
(32 ♔g3 ♛e3+ 33 ♔g2 f4 34 ♛xa6 ♛e4+ 35
♔g1 g3 is winning for Black, while 32 ♔g1 f4
33 ♛g2 ♛e1+ 34 ♛f1 ♛e4 35 ♖h5 ♔g6 36
♖h2 h5 is a familiar pattern) 32...♛e5+ 33 ♔g1
♔g6 and White is powerless to prevent ...h5
followed by ...f4, with a deadly tidal wave of
pawns. The material balance of five pawns
against a rook rarely occurs in practice. In this
case, the poor position of White's rook and the
security of Black's king are the deciding factors.

28	...	♔g7
29	♔xh3	

29 ♖xh3 g4 transposes to the previous note.

29	...	♛xe2

Also good is 29...g4+ 30 ♔h2 ♛xe2+ 31
♛g2, transposing into the note to White's 28th.

30	♛d5?!

This move should have lost at once, but there
was no satisfactory alternative, e.g.:

1) 30 ♛g2 g4+ 31 ♔h2 ♛e5+ 32 ♔g1 again
transposes to the note to White's 28th move,
which is very good for Black.

2) 30 ♛c6 ♛f2 31 ♛c3+ ♔g6 32 ♛g3
♛xb2, with six pawns for the rook, is certainly
very good for Black.

30	...	♔g6?!

30...♛f2 wins immediately.

31	♛d4?!

31 ♛g2 was again the only chance, although
after 31...g4+ 32 ♔h2 ♛e5+ 33 ♔g1 h5 White
has the same bad position as before, only this
time a tempo down.

31	...	f4

There is no longer any defence.

32	♖g1	f5
	0-1	

This was an amazing tactical struggle, in
which the players fought tooth and nail for the
initiative. Shirov's idea was highly creative, but
owing to the relatively open nature of the position, White had the chance to create counterplay and this cast doubt on Shirov's sacrifice.
Had White found the correct continuation at
move 25, then the game might have ended dif-
ferently. However, one should never underesti-
mate the practical side of chess. Whatever the
objective assessment of Shirov's idea, countering it over the board was fiendishly difficult.

The lessons here are:

1) Sacrifices can be made for long-term aims
as well as immediate ones.

2) When defending against a positional sacrifice, generating counterplay is critical. A
counter-sacrifice may be necessary to achieve
this.

3) If the enemy king is sufficiently exposed,
a queen plus a bunch of well-placed pawns can
be enough to provide a strong attack.

4) Once you have started along the sacrificial path, there is usually no turning back.

3 Endgame Themes

If the struggle has been more or less balanced in the middlegame, it will probably be decided in the endgame. Skill in endgame play is an important factor in practical success, and all the world champions (even Tal!) were expert endgame players. There are many books that give an encyclopaedic coverage of basic endgames, but in keeping with the theme of this book we will deal with general principles rather than specifics. Game 28 describes the importance of king activity in the endgame and shows how an active king can be enough to decide the game. Much endgame play is concerned with the creation and advance of passed pawns; Game 29 represents an excellent example of the power of passed pawns.

Finally, in Game 30 we show how a rook on the seventh rank can practically paralyse the opposing forces. Although there are only three games in this chapter, some of the games examined in earlier chapters also illustrate important themes relevant to the endgame.

The Active King

In the middlegame, the king is best kept secure behind a barricade of pawns, but as the endgame approaches, and the two armies thin out, the king becomes a more and more important factor. When there is no longer a danger of being mated (and you should be sure about this!), the king can emerge from its shelter and take an active part in operations – indeed it must, because in the endgame the king represents a significant fraction of one's army, and cannot be wasted.

The king is particularly effective if it can penetrate amongst the enemy pawns. A chain of pawns can be gobbled up by a rampant king in just a few moves, so an active king can pose a serious danger. Even if the king cannot actually invade the enemy position, the threat to do so may tie down one of the enemy pieces and so provide an advantage that can be exploited by other means.

In this game the position is virtually symmetrical except for one factor – Black's king is more active than White's. This advantage proves decisive.

Game 28
V. Smyslov – G. Sax
Tilburg 1979
Pirc Defence, Fianchetto Variation

	1	♘f3	♘f6

For comments on the moves up to here, see Game 11.

	2	g3	

This is one of the most flexible moves available in this position. White's aim is simply to complete his kingside development by ♗g2 and 0-0, while maintaining all his options in the centre.

	2	...	g6

Black is prepared to maintain the symmetry for the moment. We have already seen symmetrical openings in Games 17 and 27 and, as mentioned in those games, Black's main problem is deciding when to break the symmetry, as maintaining it for too long can prove dangerous.

	3	♗g2	♗g7
	4	0-0	0-0

Both sides have completed their basic kingside development, hence the responsibility for playing the first committal move in the centre falls to White.

5   d4

We have now transposed to Game 27.

5   ...   d6

Just as Shirov did, Sax decides to break the symmetry by pushing his d-pawn only one square.

6   ♘c3

Lautier played 6 c4, transposing to the King's Indian Defence, but Smyslov prefers a different and unusual path. The text-move aims to set up a 'two-abreast' centre by playing e4. Black may be reluctant to prevent this by ...d5, because this involves wasting a tempo. If White manages to play e4, the result will be a transposition to the Pirc Defence (1 e4 d6). The problem with this strategy is that the line of the Pirc that arises is not one which is considered especially favourable for White.

6   ...   ♘bd7

This is the most natural reply to White's plan; Black prepares his own counter-action in the centre with ...e5.

Despite the loss of tempo, 6...d5 is a playable alternative. It prevents e4, and now that White's knight is on c3, he cannot easily play c4. Thus White has little dynamic play in the centre, so Black has few problems completing his development with a satisfactory game.

7   e4

White continues with his plan.

7   ...   e5

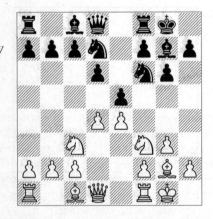

This position may also arise via the move-order 1 e4 d6 2 d4 ♘f6 3 ♘c3 g6 4 g3 ♗g7 5 ♗g2 0-0 6 ♘f3 ♘bd7 7 0-0 e5. Playing g3

against the Pirc Defence is a perfectly respectable system, but the development of the bishop at g2 is almost invariably associated with ♘ge2 rather than ♘f3. The reason is obvious enough: on e2 the knight does not block the g2-bishop and so White retains considerable pressure on d5. The combination of g3 and ♘f3 is not troublesome for Black.

8   dxe5?!

Many openings give rise to a central pawn-structure with d4, e4 against d6, e5 – perhaps the best-known example is the Closed Ruy Lopez. This type of structure inherently gives White a slight advantage, provided that he can maintain his 'two-abreast' pawn-centre. The reason is that White retains more options in the centre than Black – he might play dxe5, or he might close the centre with d5, or he might just leave the pawns where they are. Black has to take these options into account at every move, and this often restricts his own possibilities.

Black's central play is more limited. He can, of course, play ...exd4 but this surrenders his main strongpoint in the centre and leaves White with a space advantage. Black would like to play ...d5, but this is usually not possible for tactical reasons (it often loses a pawn).

These considerations are rather general, and may be overridden by the particular situation on the board, but the basic principle is clear – White is better off maintaining his pawn-centre as it is, unless he can gain a definite advantage by clarifying the situation. Indeed, in the Closed Ruy Lopez Black often goes to a great deal of trouble to exert pressure against e4 (see Game 7) to force White to commit himself in the centre. In the current position, there is no real reason for White to exchange so quickly on e5. This releases the tension in the centre and leads to a symmetrical pawn-structure offering White only minimal chances for the advantage. It would have been better for White to improve his position while leaving the centre fluid. Several moves were possible, for example 8 ♖e1 supporting the centre, 8 h3 preparing ♗e3 and 8 a4 gaining space on the queenside.

8   ...   dxe5

Now that the pawn-structure is symmetrical, White's only claim for an advantage is the slight lead in development he possesses by virtue of being White.

9   b3

With the aim of developing the bishop to a3. Although this may cause Black some temporary inconvenience, in the long run there is a danger that Black will exchange dark-squared bishops by ...♗f8, leaving White with only the inactive bishop on g2.

9   ...   b6

A combative plan. Black intends ...♗b7 to exert pressure against e4, exploiting the fact that the g2-bishop is not defending this pawn. It is also possible for Black to continue 9...♖e8 10 ♗a3 ♗f8, with a roughly level position.

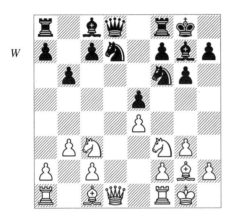

W

10   a4

White aims to gain space on the queenside, but this plan never comes to anything and pushing the a-pawn consumes a valuable development tempo. 10 ♗a3 ♖e8 11 ♕e2 would have been a more logical follow-up to White's previous play. After 11...♗f8 12 ♗xf8 ♘xf8 13 ♖ad1 ♕e7 14 ♘d5 ♘xd5 15 exd5 e4 16 ♘d4, White may still have an edge.

10   ...   ♗b7

Forcing White to attend to the e4-pawn.

11   ♘d2

This activates the g2-bishop, but White has lost time as a result of moving his king's knight twice.

11   ...   ♖e8

Anticipating White's ♗a3.

12   ♗a3   ♗f8

Black's g7-bishop is his less active one, because at the moment it is only staring at the e5-pawn, while the b7-bishop is exerting pressure on White's position. Therefore Black is quite happy to exchange dark-squared bishops.

13   ♗xf8

White has nothing better than to swap.

13   ...   ♘xf8

Thanks to White's lacklustre opening, Black has equalized – indeed, if it were Black's turn to move he could play ...♘e6, heading for d4, and claim to be slightly better owing to his more active bishop. However, it is White to move and he has time to inhibit Black's knight manoeuvre.

14   ♘c4

White's knight moves to a more active square, putting pressure on e5 and preparing queenside action with a5.

14   ...   ♘e6?

Black believes that he can play this thematic move despite White's attack on e5. However, it seems likely that this move was based on a tactical oversight by Black.

Straightforward development by 14...♕e7 and ...♖ad8 would leave the game equal.

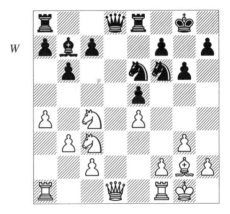

W

15   ♖e1?

White takes Black at his word and responds by supporting his e4-pawn. However, if he had simply taken the pawn then Black would have been struggling for compensation: 15 ♘xe5! and now:

1) 15...♘c5 16 ♘g4! ♘xg4 17 ♕xg4 ♕d2 18 ♘d5 and Black does not have enough for the pawn; for example, after 18...♗xd5 19 exd5 ♕xc2 20 d6 ♖ad8 21 dxc7 ♖c8 22 ♖ae1 ♘e6 23 ♗d5 Black cannot regain his pawn by 23...♘xc7 due to 24 ♖c1 and 25 ♗b7.

2) 15...♕d4 (according to Sax's notes, this was his intended reply, but it runs into a tactical riposte) 16 ♘d5! (the only other move is 16 ♕xd4, but then 16...♘xd4 17 ♘f3 ♘xf3+ 18

♗xf3 ♘xe4 leads to total equality) 16...♘xd5 (Black has no really satisfactory reply, since 16...♕xe5 loses to 17 f4 ♕b2 18 ♖b1) 17 exd5 ♕xe5 18 dxe6 ♖ad8 (this is relatively the best chance, as Black gets a little compensation for the pawn) 19 exf7+ ♔xf7 20 ♕g4 ♗xg2 21 ♔xg2 ♕c3 22 ♖ad1 ♖xd1 23 ♕xd1 and White has consolidated his extra pawn, although in view of the passive position of his pieces it is not certain that he can win.

| **15** | **...** | **♕d4** |

Or 15...♘d4 16 ♘b5 a6 17 ♘xd4 ♕xd4 18 ♕xd4 exd4 19 e5 ♗xg2 20 ♔xg2 ♘d5 21 ♖ad1 c5 with an equal ending. The text-move is more ambitious but somewhat double-edged.

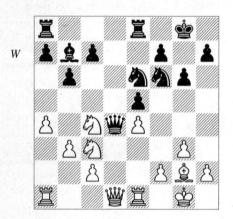

W

| **16** | **♘d5** |

16 ♕f3 ♔g7 17 ♖ad1 ♕c5 is fine for Black, so the text-move is the only one to trouble him.

| **16** | **...** | **♔g7** |

It looks risky to allow the king to be drawn out to f6, but in fact White cannot exploit this. 16...♘d7 is inferior as 17 c3 ♕xd1 18 ♖exd1 ♖ad8 19 b4 gives White the better ending – his knights occupy active squares and White has gained a lot of space on the queenside.

| **17** | **♕f3** |

Or 17 ♘xf6 ♔xf6 18 ♕f3+ ♔g7 19 ♖ad1 ♕c5 20 ♖d7 (if White doesn't do something active Black will just occupy d4 with his knight) 20...♖e7 21 ♖xe7 (21 ♘xe5 loses material after 21...♘g5 22 ♕f4 ♖xe5 23 h4 ♗c8) 21...♕xe7 and Black is safe as White cannot take the e-pawn: 22 ♘xe5? ♘d4 23 ♕f4 g5 and Black wins a piece.

Liquidating by 17 ♕xd4 ♘xd4 18 ♘xc7 ♘xc2 19 ♘xe8+ ♖xe8 20 ♘d6 ♖e7 21 ♖ac1

♘xe1 22 ♖xe1 ♖d7 23 ♘xb7 ♖xb7 should be a draw.

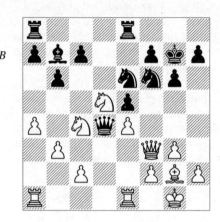

B

| **17** | **...** | **♗xd5** |

This liquidation forces an equal ending.

| **18** | **exd5** |

18 c3 is no better, although it forces Black to be accurate. He may try:

1) 18...♘g5 19 ♕xf6+ ♔xf6 20 cxd4 ♗xc4 21 bxc4 is slightly uncomfortable for Black, as White will take on e5 and then activate his bishop by f4 and e5.

2) 18...♕c5 19 exd5 e4 20 ♕e2 ♘xd5 21 b4 ♕e7 22 ♕xe4 ♖ad8 23 ♘e5 is again awkward for Black, owing to the weakness of the c6-square. Note that 23...♘xc3?? loses to 24 ♕c4.

3) 18...♗xe4! 19 ♕xf6+ ♔xf6 20 cxd4 ♗xg2 21 dxe5+ ♔e7 22 ♔xg2 ♘c5 23 ♖ab1 ♖ad8 and, if anything, Black has a slight edge as White's queenside pawns are a little vulnerable.

| **18** | **...** | **e4** |
| **19** | **♕d1** |

19 ♕e3 is marginally better. After the continuation 19...♕xd5 (19...♘xd5 20 ♕xe4 ♕xe4 21 ♗xe4 ♖ad8 22 ♔f1 is also dead equal) 20 ♗xe4 (20 ♖ad1 ♕h5 is perhaps slightly riskier for White as 21 ♗xe4 ♘xe4 22 ♕xe4 ♘g5 23 ♕d4+ ♔g8 favours Black; however, White probably has enough compensation for the pawn after 21 ♕c3!) 20...♕xe4 21 ♕xe4 ♘xe4 22 ♖xe4 the position is totally equal.

| **19** | **...** | **♘xd5** |

19...♕xd5 20 ♗xe4 ♕xd1 21 ♖axd1 ♘xe4 22 ♖xe4 ♖ad8 is completely equal. The text-move is better as it gives White more chance to go wrong.

20 &xe4

White has other possibilities, but it is hard to prevent Black retaining a microscopic edge:

1) 20 ♕xd4+ ♘xd4 21 &xe4 ♖ad8 is more clearly unfavourable for White, e.g. 22 &xd5 ♖xe1+ 23 ♖xe1 ♖xd5 24 ♖e7 ♖c5 and Black is definitely better.

2) 20 ♖xe4 ♕xd1+ 21 ♖xd1 ♘c3 22 ♖ee1 ♖ad8 23 ♖xd8 ♖xd8 is perhaps fractionally better for Black as his knights are quite actively posted.

20 ... ♖ad8

Black hopes to induce White to exchange on d4, bringing his knight to a good square with gain of time.

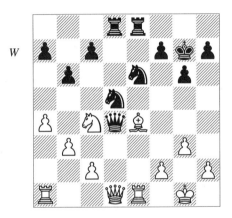

21 &xd5

21 ♕xd4+ ♘xd4 transposes into line '1' of the note to White's 20th move.

21 ... ♕xd5

21...♖xd5 22 ♕xd4+ ♖xd4 23 a5 b5 24 ♘e5 offers no chances for Black.

22 ♕xd5 ♖xd5

23 ♖ad1

With the rook on d5, 23 a5 b5 24 ♘e5? is impossible due to 24...♘d4, when Black wins. Therefore, White simply exchanges one pair of rooks.

23 ... ♖ed8

24 ♖xd5 ♖xd5

It is time to take stock. After a quick glance at the position, most players would evaluate it as 'dead drawn'. It is certainly true that the position is drawn, but it is perhaps not entirely dead. In fact, it doesn't take many inaccuracies by White to give Black concrete winning chances. White's main problem is the slight weakening

of his queenside pawns created by b3 and especially a4. If Black's knight settles on d4, then it will be hard to expel the knight, because the natural pawn thrust c3 will leave the b3-pawn hanging. Another factor that slightly favours Black is that his rook is better posted. It occupies an open file that is still some distance away from the kings. After ...♔f6 Black can move his knight without worrying about ♖e7, while White has no corresponding manoeuvre to free his own knight.

Obviously, these advantages are very slight and at this stage the game is still well within the bounds of a draw. However, chess history is full of cases in which planless play has lost 'dead drawn' positions. What is perhaps surprising is that it is the endgame virtuoso Smyslov who gradually slides downhill into a lost position. If there is a lesson to be learned from this, it is that even simplified endgame positions can be quite tricky, and one should not relax one's concentration for a moment, even when it seems that a loss is out of the question.

25 ♔g2

The first tiny slip. 25 ♔f1 was more accurate, because after 25...♔f6 26 ♘e3 ♖d2 White can continue 27 ♖e2. Then the exchange of rooks gives Black nothing at all, while after 27...♖d8 28 ♘g4+ ♔g7 29 ♘e5 it is hard to see how Black can make any progress as 29...♘d4 30 ♖d2 ♔f6 31 ♘f3 c5 is totally level.

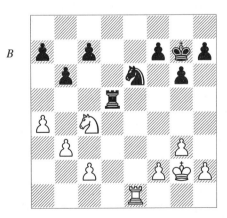

25 ... ♔f6

Black may be able to exert some degree of pressure using his rook and knight, but as so often in endgames, it is the activity of the king that is the deciding factor. At the moment, Black's king is scarcely more active than White's, but if the rooks are exchanged then there is a danger that Black's king will be able to make a run for White's queenside pawns. The main problem here is the move b3, which leaves the c3-square ripe for occupation by the enemy king.

26   ♘e3?

When in a slightly inferior position, one often faces an awkward choice: is it better just to wait, or should one take some positive action? The danger of waiting is that the opponent will find some way to improve his position gradually, so that in the end one is forced to take action in any case, but under less favourable circumstances than if this decision had been made right away. On the other hand, taking action may simply create further weaknesses and give the opponent options that did not exist before.

This type of decision is often far-reaching, since in either case it may be hard to switch to an alternative plan later on. From the psychological point of view, it is almost always easier to take action, but one should try to ensure that such a decision is backed up by an objective assessment of the position.

In this case, Smyslov decides to allow Black's rook onto White's second rank. True, White can always exchange this rook by playing ♖d1, but this leads to the type of position mentioned above, in which Black can play to attack White's queenside pawns with his king. In fact, I think that this was not the right decision. White could have corrected his inaccurate previous move with 26 ♔f1, or simply waited since Black has no concrete threats.

Note that the alternative active plan of 26 ♔f3 also fails to equalize because 26...♖d8 (26...♘d4+ would be wrong as after 27 ♔e4 ♘xc2 28 ♔xd5 ♘xe1 29 ♔c6 White has vastly the more active king and is certainly not worse) 27 ♖c1 ♘d4+ 28 ♔e4 a5 gives Black an edge; for example, 29 ♖d1 ♖e8+ 30 ♔d3 ♘f3 and now it is the weakness created by g3 which gives Black the opportunity to attack White's pawns.

26   ...   ♖d2

The rook exerts considerable pressure from here, and the only way to get rid of it is to offer the exchange of rooks by ♖d1.

27   ♘g4+?

White faces an unpleasant choice since he cannot now equalize:

1) 27 ♖d1 ♖xd1 28 ♘xd1 ♘d4 29 ♘e3 ♔e5 30 f3 (or else ...♔e4, when there will be no dislodging Black's pieces) 30...♔d6 31 ♔f2 ♔c5 32 f4 ♔b4 with the same type of position as in the game.

2) 27 ♖c1 may be relatively the best chance, intending to expel the rook by ♘c4. After 27...♘d4 28 ♘d5+ ♔e5 29 ♘xc7 ♘xc2 30 ♘b5 a6 31 ♘c3 ♘b4 (not 31...♔d4? 32 ♘b1 ♖e2 33 ♔f1), however, Black retains some advantage.

27   ...   ♔e7

Black's king has been driven away from f6, but now heads for the queenside and penetration via c5 and b4.

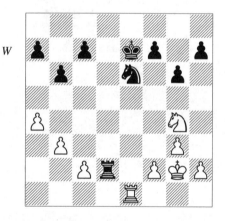

28   ♘e3

Forced.

28   ...   ♔d7

This is clearly not a position in which White can wait, as Black threatens to advance his king via the network of weak dark squares on the queenside. Therefore, White decides to exchange off the intruding rook.

29   ♖d1

29 ♖c1 ♘d4 leaves White virtually paralysed.

29   ...   ♖xd1
30   ♘xd1   ♘d4
31   ♘e3

Black's knight is amazingly effective since it ties down White's knight and immobilizes his queenside pawns. It is also extremely difficult to remove since even the option of ♔f1-e1-d2 is not immediately available, as this would cost

White his h-pawn after ...♘f3+. It is curious how the pawn moves White has made conspire against him to prevent any counterplay.

| 31 | ... | ♔d6 |

Heading for c3.

| 32 | h4 |

White must first move his h-pawn before he can play his king to f1 and e1.

32	...	♔c5
33	♔f1	♔b4
34	♔e1

34 ♘d5+ ♔a3 35 ♘xc7 ♘xc2 36 ♘b5+ ♔xb3 37 ♘xa7 ♔xa4 is hopeless for White. In addition to the extra outside passed pawn, Black's king is very active and White's knight is offside.

| 34 | ... | ♔c3 |

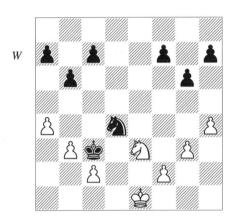

The king settles on its target square. White can defend against this immediate attack, but his forces are badly tied down in the process. This gives Black the time to launch an assault against White's kingside pawn-structure by ...f5-f4; when Black has created a further weakness on the kingside, his king is well placed to switch to the other side and take advantage of the new possibilities available on that side of the board.

| 35 | ♔d1 |

White still hopes to expel Black's king by ♔c1 followed by a knight check.

| 35 | ... | c6 |

Black rules out the more dangerous check on d5. 35...♔b2? is quite wrong as after 36 ♔d2 White's king becomes active.

| 36 | ♔c1 |

White now even threatens to win by 37 ♘d1+ and 38 c3+, so Black is forced to move

his knight, which in turn frees White's knight. Black obviously has a large advantage but there is not yet a forced win.

| 36 | ... | ♘f3 |

This position could be used as an object lesson concerning the weakness of the fianchettoed position once the bishop has disappeared. The moves b3 and g3 have created weaknesses which are occupied by Black's two remaining pieces. I realize that Black also fianchettoed both his bishops, but as I have mentioned earlier, weaknesses are only significant if they can be exploited. Thanks to Black's active pieces, in particular his king, White's weaknesses are serious while Black's play no part in the game.

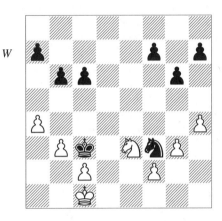

| 37 | ♘c4?! |

After this passive defence, Black wins without difficulty. 37 ♘d1+ was a better try, and after 37...♔d4 White can continue:

1) 38 ♔b2 f5 (intending ...f4 and ...fxg3 to create a new weakness at g3) 39 ♘e3 (just waiting by 39 ♔c1 doesn't help; Black wins by 39...f4 40 ♔b2 h5 41 ♔c1 fxg3 42 fxg3 g5 43 hxg5 ♘xg5 44 ♘f2 ♘e4 and the g3-pawn falls) 39...f4 40 ♘g4 (40 ♘d1 transposes to the previous bracket) 40...h5 41 ♘f6 ♔e5 42 ♘d7+ ♔f5 43 ♘f8 (43 ♘b8 fxg3 44 fxg3 ♘e5) 43...g5 44 hxg5 ♘xg5, followed by ...♘e4, with a winning position for Black.

2) 38 ♘e3! is the most resilient defence. Black then has a range of promising ideas, but no forced win. 38...b5 is one possibility; then 39 a5 ♔c3 followed by ...♔b4 should win a pawn, while allowing ...bxa4 leaves the a4-pawn weak. Thus 39 axb5 cxb5 40 ♔b2 a5 41 ♘d1 is best, with ♘c3 to come. The alternative

is 38...f5 39 h5 (this wasn't available after 38 ♔b2) 39...♔e4 40 hxg6 hxg6 when 41 ♔d1 or 41 ♘c4 gives White slender drawing chances, although Black retains a large advantage.

| 37 | ... | f5 |

In this position White cannot counter Black's plan to weaken White's kingside pawns by ...f4 and ...fxg3.

| 38 | ♘b2 | |

38 ♘e3 f4 39 ♘d1+ ♔d4 transposes to a variation given in note '1' to White's 37th move that is losing for White.

| 38 | ... | f4 |
| 39 | ♘c4 | |

This move costs a pawn, but the alternatives were no better. 39 ♘d3 also loses a pawn, to 39...fxg3 40 fxg3 ♘d4, while 39 ♘d1+ ♔d4 transposes as in the previous note.

| 39 | ... | ♘d4 |

Now the twin threats of ...♘xc2 and ...fxg3 followed by ...♘e2+ pick up a pawn.

| 40 | ♘e5 | |

White tries to activate his knight at least. 40 a5 b5 41 ♘e5 fxg3 42 fxg3 a6 is hopeless.

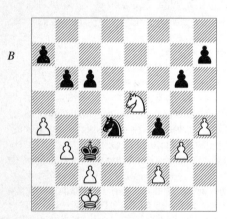

| 40 | ... | fxg3 |
| 41 | fxg3 | c5 |

Removing the c-pawn from attack and netting the c2-pawn.

| 42 | a5 | |

White is trying to exchange as many pawns as possible.

| 42 | ... | ♘xc2 |

42...bxa5 43 ♘d7 ♘xc2 44 ♘xc5 ♘d4 is also decisive.

| 43 | axb6 | axb6 |
| 44 | ♘d7 | |

Although White resolutely exchanges pawns, he cannot save the game. It is not only the fact that Black is a pawn up which decides matters; it is also the persistent advantage conferred by his excellent king position which makes the technical task simple.

| 44 | ... | ♘d4 |
| 45 | ♘xb6 | ♘e2+ |

45...♘xb3+ 46 ♔d1 ♘d4 is even easier, e.g. 47 ♘a4+ ♔b4 48 ♘b2 c4 or 47 ♘d7 c4 48 ♘f8 ♔b2.

| 46 | ♔d1 | ♘xg3 |

So Black ends up with an extra pawn on the kingside instead of the queenside, but it doesn't make any difference to the result.

| 47 | ♘d7 | ♔b4 |

47...♘f5 is met by 48 h5.

| 48 | ♔c2 | |

48 ♘f8 ♔xb3 49 ♘xh7 c4 promotes the pawn, so White has to defend b3.

| 48 | ... | ♘f5 |

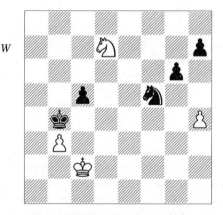

| 49 | ♘f8 | ♘xh4 |

Black must still take some care; for example, 49...♘d4+ 50 ♔b2 ♘xb3? allows White to escape by 51 ♘xh7 c4 52 ♘f8 c3+ 53 ♔b1! ♘d4 54 ♘xg6 ♔b3 55 ♘f4, when the knight comes back just in time.

| 50 | ♘xh7 | ♘f5 |

Taking aim at White's remaining pawn.

| 51 | ♘f6 | |

After 51 ♘f8 g5 the pawn speeds away.

| 51 | ... | ♘d4+ |
| 52 | ♔d3 | |

Or 52 ♔b2 ♘xb3 53 ♘d5+ ♔c4 54 ♘e3+ (54 ♘b6+ ♔b5 also retains both black pawns) 54...♔d3 55 ♘g4 (55 ♘d5 loses to 55...c4 56

♘f4+ ♔d2) 55...♘a5! (not 55...c4?? 56 ♘e5+, drawing) 56 ♘e5+ ♔d2 57 ♘xg6 c4 and White cannot halt the pawn.

52 ... ♔xb3

With two extra pawns, there is of course no hope for White.

53 ♘d7

After 53 ♔e4 ♘c6 54 ♔d5 the simplest win is 54...c4 55 ♘e4 c3 56 ♘c5+ ♔b4 57 ♘d3+ ♔b5 58 ♘c1 c2.

53 ... ♘e6

54 ♘e5 g5

0-1

White cannot stop both pawns.

In this game, the active black king, coupled with White's slight pawn weaknesses on both sides of the board, proved too much for White.

Curiously, White seemed almost unaware of the danger until it was too late. Nevertheless, Black played the endgame very well to make the most of his chances.

The lessons here are:

1) Take care in 'dead drawn' positions; it only takes a few errors for the position to be 'dead' rather than 'drawn'.

2) In the endgame, an active king can be a decisive advantage all by itself.

3) The danger posed by an active king is enhanced if there are pawn weaknesses in the enemy position.

4) I can only repeat the lesson from Game 22: if your opponent offers a pawn, it is worth looking closely at taking it – a casual 'that looks a bit risky' isn't good enough.

The Power of Passed Pawns

The advantage of a passed pawn is obvious – if it promotes, then the opponent will usually have to give up a piece for it. However, it is important to note that even if the passed pawn cannot promote by force, it usually still confers an advantage. The reason is that the opponent will have to keep a watchful eye on the pawn, and will probably have to assign one piece to keeping it under control, which is one less piece to take part in the rest of the battle.

As with all chess principles, this one comes with a number of provisos:

1) First of all, it must be possible to support the passed pawn – indeed, the level of support is just as important as the mere fact of possessing a passed pawn. A passed pawn that cannot be supported may simply be one that has strayed too far into enemy territory, only to be surrounded and captured. Also, a passed pawn may not be much of an advantage if all the pieces are tied to protecting it. Thus, the most useful passed pawns are the ones that can be economically supported, leaving most of the pieces to fight the rest of the battle. Best of all is for the passed pawn to be supported by another pawn, as in the following game. In this case, no pieces at all need be allocated to defending the pawn.

2) The danger posed by a passed pawn depends on how far advanced it is. A passed pawn on the second rank may not fill the opponent with terror, but one on the sixth rank probably will.

3) Passed pawns become more dangerous as the number of pieces on the board decreases. The reason is clear. If you have six pieces, and one of them has to keep an eye on a passed pawn, it may be an inconvenience but it is not a disaster. If have only one piece, and that is tied down by an enemy passed pawn, then that may be the end of the game.

4) A passed pawn which is securely blockaded and is no further advanced than the fifth rank may not be much of a danger. Suppose, for example, you have pawns on e4 and d5, and your opponent has a pawn on e5 and a knight on d6. If the blockading knight can't be shifted, then the passed pawn may be of no value. Indeed, if, for example, White has only a light-squared bishop it may even be a handicap.

If one passed pawn is dangerous, then two are even more so. This applies particularly when the two passed pawns are on adjacent files – these are called *connected passed pawns*. If they advance abreast of one another, then it may be difficult or impossible to blockade them, because a piece which blockades one pawn can be driven away by the other one. In the following game, Kramnik creates first one dangerous passed pawn and then a second, by which time it is all too much for Black.

Game 29

V. Kramnik – P. Svidler

Dortmund 1998

Grünfeld Defence, Exchange Variation

1	d4	♘f6
2	c4	g6
3	♘c3	

For comments on the moves up to here, see Game 14.

| 3 | ... | d5 |

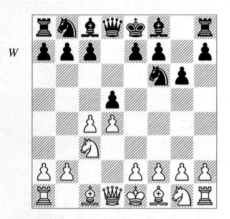

This move introduces the Grünfeld Defence. At first sight, playing ...d5 looks anti-positional, because it leads to the exchange of Black's central d-pawn for White's less central c-pawn. The upshot is that White gains a 2 to 1 preponderance of pawns in the centre. Indeed, if Black were to follow up passively and allow White to consolidate his grip in the centre, then the extra central pawn would be a key factor. However, Black has no intention of continuing passively. His main plan is to exert pressure on the pawn at d4, using the half-open d-file and the fianchettoed bishop on g7. In many lines Black plays ...c5 to enhance this pressure.

| 4 | cxd5 | |

White accepts the challenge straight away. There are a number of other lines in which the exchange of pawns is postponed. These include 4 ♘f3, 4 ♗f4, 4 ♗g5 and even the boring 4 e3.

| 4 | ... | ♘xd5 |

There is a big difference between the Grünfeld and the bad line 1 d4 ♘f6 2 c4 d5? 3 cxd5 ♘xd5 4 ♘f3. In this line Black is forced to retreat his knight when White plays e4, whereupon White consolidates his centre with ♘c3, gaining a clear advantage. In the Grünfeld, on the other hand, Black can meet e4 with ...♘xc3, avoiding any loss of time. This is such an important point that some players have even tried 5 ♘a4!? in the Grünfeld, in order to play e4 without allowing the exchange on c3. It is probably only a matter of time before someone plays 5 ♘b1!

| 5 | e4 | |

This is the consistent follow-up to White's previous move. He at once creates a 'two-abreast' pawn-centre.

| 5 | ... | ♘xc3 |
| 6 | bxc3 | |

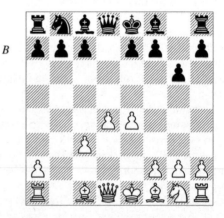

This is the fundamental position of what is called the Exchange Grünfeld. The battle will revolve around the strength or weakness of White's pawn-centre. Black's assault on d4 will be conducted by means of ...♗g7, ...c5 and ...♘c6. If White plays ♘f3, Black may well reply ...♗g4. Black's aim is to force White to move his d-pawn. If White can maintain his pawn on d4 permanently, without making a concession elsewhere, then he will usually gain some advantage.

If White does have to move the d-pawn, he will probably not play dxc5, even if it temporarily wins a pawn, since taking on c5 damages White's pawn-structure too much. Instead, White will normally play d5. Then a new struggle ensues. The advance of the d-pawn activates the g7-bishop, but if White's central pawns can push forward far enough, they can become dangerous in themselves.

6   ...   ♗g7

The first minor piece is brought to bear on d4.

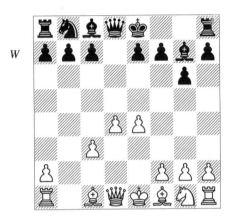

W

7   ♗c4

White has two main ways of handling this position. He can either try to keep the pawn on d4, or else he can prepare to play d5 when the pressure becomes too much. If White adopts the first option, the d4-pawn will need all the support White can muster, so he should avoid ♘f3, which allows ...♗g4 eliminating one defender. The knight will instead be developed to e2, where it is immune to the pin. White therefore develops his light-squared bishop first, to avoid it being blocked in. c4 is the most active square, and is obviously better than d3, which blocks the queen's support of d4.

7 ♗b5+ is possible, and this line is quite popular. The idea is that each of the possible interpositions interferes with Black's attack on d4. Clearly, playing a piece to d7 blocks the queen's attack, while if Black plays ...c6 then ...♘c6 is no longer possible. The defect is that

after 7...c6, Black has another method of undermining White's centre, namely ...b5-b4, and this enables Black to keep the game more or less in balance.

If White adopts the alternative plan of playing d5 at some moment, then he must do something about the attack on c3 and the pressure on the long diagonal. White can continue with systems based on ♘f3 and ♖b1, or ♗e3 and ♕d2, but we will not examine them in detail here.

7   ...   c5

The pressure starts to mount. White must defend d4.

8   ♘e2   ♘c6

Only eight moves, and already four black units are attacking d4.

9   ♗e3

The fourth defender moves into place.

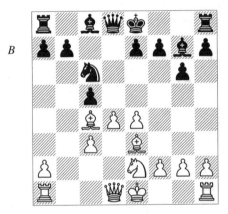

B

9   ...   cxd4

For the moment, Black's attack on d4 has come to a dead end, because there are no further pieces to bring to bear. Although White is the immediate victor in this struggle, Black can claim to have tied many of White's pieces down to defensive positions. The main question is how Black is going to proceed. The most common move is 9...0-0, when White usually plays 10 0-0 (although there is a case for 10 ♖c1 or even 10 h4!?). Then Black has two different ideas. The first is 10...♕c7, eyeing the undefended bishop on c4 and preparing ...♖d8 to help in the attack on d4. The second idea, which is more common these days, is 10...♗g4 11 f3 ♘a5 12 ♗d3 (12 ♗xf7+ is another popular variation) 12...cxd4 13 cxd4 ♗e6. Now Black threatens to play ...♘c4, so White has a choice between sacrificing the exchange by 14 d5, and sacrificing his a-pawn by 14 ♖c1. Neither of these lines is thought to give White a significant advantage.

The move played often transposes to one of the above variations, but in this game Black pursues an independent course.

10 cxd4 ♕a5+

This is Black's idea. He intends to disturb White's plan of development.

11 ♗d2

11 ♕d2 doesn't offer White much. After 11...0-0 White cannot castle, while 12 ♕xa5 ♘xa5 13 ♗d3 ♗e6 gives Black active piece-play.

11 ♔f1 may look odd, but it is a reasonable move. White's king is relatively safe on f1, while White intends to activate his rook by starting an attack with h4-h5. Kramnik prefers the less committal bishop retreat.

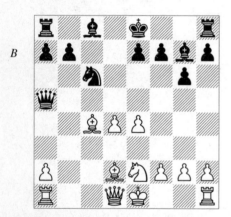

11 ... ♕d8

Black offers a repetition of moves, but if it were that simple to equalize, everybody would play the Grünfeld! The alternatives are:

1) 11...♕a3 (now White can simply sacrifice his d-pawn) 12 0-0 and now:

1a) 12...♘xd4? 13 ♘xd4 ♗xd4 14 ♗b4 ♕xb4 (after 14...♕b2, 15 ♖b1 traps the queen) 15 ♕xd4 and White wins due to the twin threats of 16 ♕xh8+ and 16 ♗xf7+.

1b) After 12...0-0 13 ♖b1 Black again cannot take the pawn: 13...♘xd4? 14 ♗b4 ♘xe2+ 15 ♕xe2 ♕a4 16 ♗b5 and his queen is trapped. Given that Black cannot accept the sacrifice, it is hard to see what he has achieved by playing his queen to a3.

2) 11...♕h5 12 d5 ♘e5 13 ♗b5+ ♗d7 14 ♗xd7+ ♘xd7 15 ♖c1 0-0 16 0-0 ♖fc8 17 f3 and White is better since the black queen is not serving any useful function on h5.

12 d5

Assuming that White does not want a draw, he has two plans, mirroring his choice earlier. One is to maintain the pawn on d4 by 12 ♗c3 0-0 13 0-0 ♗d7 14 ♕d2 and the second is to push the pawn to d5. Both plans are probably sufficient to give White an edge, but Kramnik's choice is the more energetic.

12 ... ♘e5

12...♗xa1? loses to 13 ♕xa1.

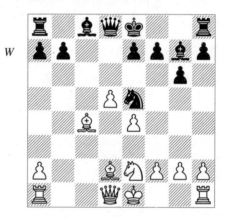

13 ♗c3

The diagram is typical of lines in which White plays d5 in the Exchange Grünfeld. White still has his central majority and if he can consolidate then he can expect to gain the advantage. One day he may be able to push Black's knight back by f4, and then roll forward in the centre by e5. However, before this can happen he must organize his position, which is not easy in the face of Black's active pieces. White's greater command of space leaves Black's position a little cramped – in particular, the c8-bishop has no obviously good square. Thus, White should avoid piece exchanges, if possible. It follows that 13 ♗b5+ ♗d7 14 ♗xd7+ ♕xd7 is wrong – Black is at least equal here. 13 ♖c1 0-0 14 0-0 ♘xc4 15 ♖xc4 e6 16 ♗c3 perhaps gives White a faint edge, but the general simplification of the position gives Black good defensive chances.

Kramnik's move gives White the best chance of keeping all the minor pieces on the board.

13 ... 0-0

Not, of course, 13...♘xc4 14 ♗xg7, when Black will never be able to castle.

14 ♗b3

Black must now act quickly, or White will gain a large advantage by 15 f4.

14 ... ♛b6

Black anticipates White castling and 'pins' the f2-pawn in advance. Simple development by 14...♗d7 is not enough. After 15 f4 ♘g4 16 ♗xg7 ♔xg7 17 ♕d4+ ♔g8 18 h3 ♕a5+ 19 ♘c3 ♖ac8 20 ♖c1 Black must retreat his knight, whereupon White castles, consolidating his massive central superiority.

15 f4!?

This move is far more challenging than 15 0-0 ♗g4, when Black escapes from most of his difficulties. Thanks to the pin on the f-pawn, White cannot play f3, and so Black can exchange his problem bishop. The pin also makes it more awkward for White to play f4, and thus Black gains further time to activate his pieces. After 16 ♔h1 (16 h3 ♗xe2 17 ♕xe2 ♖fc8 18 ♖ac1 a5 gives Black sufficient counterplay) 16...♖ac8!? 17 f3 ♗d7, 18 ♖b1 ♗b5 is level, while 18 f4 may be met by 18...♖xc3 19 ♘xc3 ♘g4 20 ♕f3 ♗xc3 21 ♕xc3 ♘f2+ 22 ♖xf2 ♕xf2 with equality.

15 ... ♘g4?!

A tempting but dubious move. Superficially, the knight is active on g4 but if Black is unable to maintain it there, it will have to drop back with considerable loss of time. 15...♘d7 is more solid. After 16 ♗xg7 ♔xg7 17 ♕d4+ ♕xd4 18 ♘xd4 ♘c5 19 ♗c2 f5 20 exf5 ♗xf5 21 ♘xf5+ gxf5 22 0-0 White has an edge but nothing more.

16 ♗d4!

This more or less forces the exchange of queens. In the resulting ending, White has excellent chances to support his pawn-centre. White should avoid 16 ♗xg7 ♕f2+ 17 ♔d2, when Black can take a draw with 17...♕e3+ or continue the game by 17...♔xg7 18 ♕g1 ♗d7, with unclear play.

16 ... ♕a5+

Or 16...♗xd4 17 ♕xd4 ♕xd4 (17...♕a5+ 18 ♘c3 ♗d7 19 h3 transposes into the note to Black's 14th move) 18 ♘xd4 and now:

1) 18...♘f6 19 e5 ♘e4 (19...♖xd5 loses to 20 ♗xd5 ♖d8 21 ♘b5 ♖xd5 22 ♘c7) 20 ♖c1

gives White a clear advantage. His pawn-centre is secure and in some lines he can penetrate to the seventh rank with his rook.

2) 18...♖d8 19 0-0 again favours White. If Black tries 19...e5 20 fxe5 ♘xe5 then White seizes the initiative by 21 ♘f3! ♘xf3+ (or 21...f6 22 ♘xe5 fxe5 23 ♖ac1) 22 ♖xf3, when f7 is in White's firing-line.

17 ♕d2 ♕xd2+

Otherwise Black gets a bad position along the lines of the note to Black's 14th move.

18 ♔xd2

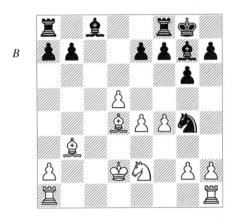

B

18 ... e5?

A serious error. Black hopes to solve his problems with the g4-knight by the use of force, but this just rebounds on him. The alternatives are:

1) 18...♘f6 19 e5 ♘e4+ 20 ♔e3 f5 21 ♖ac1 is winning for White.

2) 18...♗xd4 19 ♘xd4 ♖d8 20 h3 ♘f6 21 ♔e3 gives White a clear advantage. Black still doesn't have a good square for his bishop since if it goes to d7, White can play e5. Meanwhile, White is threatening to penetrate to c7 with a rook.

3) 18...♖d8 is relatively the best chance, although Black's position remains unpleasant after 19 h3 ♘f6 20 ♔e3; for example, 20...b6 (or 20...e6 21 d6) 21 ♖ac1 ♗a6 22 ♗xf6 ♗xf6 23 e5 ♗g7 24 ♖c7.

19 h3!

19 fxe5 is a mistake, since after 19...♘xe5 Black's firm grip on e5 keeps White's central pawns under restraint. The text-move both sacrifices a pawn and allows a liquidation to an opposite-coloured bishop position. Nevertheless,

it is a very strong move. The reason is that White is able to set up a chain of pawns lending firm support to a powerful passed pawn on d6. This passed pawn poses such a danger that the various factors in Black's favour are irrelevant.

19   ...   exd4

If 19...♘f6 20 fxe5 ♘xe4+, then 21 ♔e3 ♗f5 (21...f5 22 d6+ ♔h8 23 ♖ac1 gives White a large advantage due to his two connected passed pawns) 22 g4 ♗h6+ 23 ♘f4 ♘g3 24 ♖he1! ♗d3 25 ♔xd3 ♗xf4 26 d6 with a winning position for White.

20   hxg4

White's plan is simple – he will play e5 and d6, setting up an unbreakable pawn-chain. Thanks to the b3-bishop, Black will be unable to play ...f6, while ...g5 can simply be met by g3, so there will no way to dismantle White's pawn-structure.

20   ...   g5

Black does his best to attack the pawn-chain. 20...♗xg4 21 e5 ♗xe2 22 ♔xe2 is similar to the game, while after 20...d3 21 ♘c3 ♖e8 (21...♗xg4 22 ♔xd3 ♖ac8 23 ♖ac1 is very good for White) 22 ♖he1 ♗xg4 23 ♔xd3, followed by ♖ac1 and e5, White again sets up his pawn-chain.

21   g3

Keeping his pawn-structure intact.

21   ...   ♗xg4

21...d3 22 ♘c3 ♗xg4 23 ♔xd3 ♗f3 24 ♖he1 does not solve Black's problems.

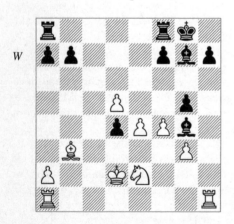

22   e5

White takes another step towards establishing a pawn-chain that runs from g3 to d6. At the same time, he shuts Black's dark-squared bishop out of play.

22   ...   ♗xe2

Black takes the knight and so preserves his d-pawn, but this pawn is incapable of influencing the outcome of the game. After 22...♗f3 23 ♖hf1 g4 24 d6 Black's d-pawn falls.

23   ♔xe2   ♖fc8

Intending to strike at g3 by ...♖c3.

24   ♖ad1!

24 ♔d3? is a serious error, as after 24...♖c3+ 25 ♔xd4 ♖xg3 White's pawn-chain crumbles.

24   ...   ♖c3

25   ♖d3

White shields the g3-pawn. For the past few moves, Black has been able to keep White busy with threats, but now he has come to the end of that particular road.

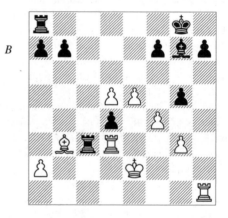

25   ...   ♖ac8?!

This makes life easy for White because the rook turns out to be tactically vulnerable on c8. Other moves:

1) 25...♖d8 26 d6 makes no real difference, e.g. 26...♔f8 27 ♖xh7 and 27...f6 is impossible because of 28 exf6 ♗xf6 29 ♖f7+.

2) 25...b5 is probably the best chance. Black intends ...a5-a4 to dislodge the bishop from b3, when he will have better chances of tackling White's menacing pawns. Nevertheless, with careful play White should still win in the end: 26 d6 a5 27 ♖xc3 (27 ♔d2 ♖d8 is less clear) 27...dxc3 28 ♔d3 b4 29 ♗a4! (best, as Black's pawns are blockaded and White's king is free to advance; Black's bishop is completely blocked in by White's pawn-chain and is as effective as a dried pea rattling around in a tin can) 29...♖d8 30 ♔e4 gxf4 (30...♗f8 loses to 31 ♔d5 f6 32 ♔c6) 31 gxf4 ♗f8 32 ♔d5 h6 33 ♖g1+ ♔h8 34

♔c6 h5 35 ♔c7 ♖a8 36 ♗c6 ♖a6 37 ♔b7 and White wins.

26 d6

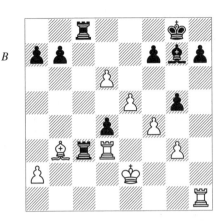

B

The culmination of White's strategy. The passed pawn on d6 dominates the position.

26 ... b5

This allows a quick finish, but Black is lost in any case, e.g.:

1) 26...♖xd3 27 ♔xd3 ♖c3+ 28 ♔xd4 ♖xg3 is not possible as White promotes his d-pawn by 29 d7.

2) 26...♖d8 27 ♖xc3 dxc3 28 ♖c1 (threatening ♖xc3 followed by ♖c7) 28...h5 (28...gxf4 loses to 29 gxf4 ♗h6 30 ♔f3) 29 ♖xc3 h4 30 ♖c7 hxg3 31 ♖xf7 ♔h8 32 e6 and White wins.

3) 26...♔f8 27 ♖xh7 ♖d8 28 ♖h5! f6 (or 28...gxf4 29 gxf4, followed by ♖f5) 29 ♖h7 fxe5 30 fxe5 ♗xe5 31 ♖f7+ ♔e8 32 ♖e7+ picks up the bishop.

4) 26...♖e8 27 ♖xc3 dxc3 28 ♔d3 and White wins much as in note '2' to Black's 25th move.

27 ♖xc3 dxc3

After 27...♖xc3 28 d7 the pawn will promote.

28 e6!

Now White acquires two far-advanced connected passed pawns. The game is decided.

28 ... ♔f8

The alternatives are grim:

1) 28...♖b8 loses to 29 e7 ♗f6 30 fxg5 ♗xg5 31 ♖f1.

2) 28...♗f6 29 fxg5 ♗xg5 30 ♖h5 ♗f6 31 e7 ♖b8 32 ♖f5 ♔g7 33 d7 is the end.

3) 28...♗f8 is the only way to play on, but after 29 e7 ♗xe7 30 dxe7 ♖e8 31 ♔d3 gxf4 32 gxf4 ♖xe7 33 ♔xc3 White will win in the end.

29 e7+

The pawns run through.

29 ... ♔e8

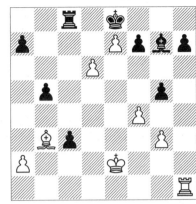

W

30 ♗xf7+! 1-0

Since 30...♔d7 (30...♔xf7 31 d7 is an attractive picture – for White!) 31 ♖xh7 c2 32 e8♕+ ♖xe8+ 33 ♗xe8+ ♔xe8 34 ♔d2 finishes Black off.

The Grünfeld is a popular and double-edged opening; White is allowed to gain control of the centre temporarily, but Black hopes to undermine this control later. In this game, Svidler chose an unusual manoeuvre at move 10, but Kramnik responded energetically, seizing more space in the centre. Black's 15th move, although natural, turned out to be a mistake. Faced with the prospect of grovelling back with his knight, Svidler tried to make use of its position at g4. However, Kramnik seized the advantage with the powerful blow 19 h3!, guaranteeing him a powerful passed d-pawn. After this Black was always struggling, and Kramnik finished nicely with a piece sacrifice to obtain two connected passed pawns on the seventh rank. An impressive game by Kramnik.

The lessons here are:

1) In the Grünfeld Defence, the burden is on Black to disrupt White's centre. If White can keep it intact, then he can expect an advantage.

2) A well-supported passed pawn is a useful asset.

3) Passed pawns become more valuable as the endgame approaches.

4) Two far-advanced connected passed pawns are usually worth at least a piece.

Rook on the Seventh

In the initial position, all the pawns are lined up on the second rank. This simple fact is the main basis for the power of a rook on the seventh rank in the endgame. Although some of the pawns (especially the central pawns) will have moved by the endgame, there will almost always be a number left on the second rank. When an enemy rook arrives on this rank, it attacks pawns to the left and right; even if one moves out of the rook's way, there will probably be another vulnerable one behind.

The normal pattern for gaining and exploiting the advantage of a rook on the seventh runs: gain control of an open file; exchange off sufficient pieces for a rook to settle on the seventh rank, tying pieces down to the defence of the vulnerable pawns; exploit the resulting advantage by undertaking activity somewhere else on the board.

In the following game, Black is prepared to sacrifice a pawn to put this plan into effect.

Game 30
E. Handoko – Xu Jun
Asian Team Championship, Singapore 1995
Sicilian, 2 c3

1   e4   c5

For comments on the moves up to here, see Game 8.

2   c3

White continued 2 ♘f3 in all the previous games in this book with the Sicilian Defence. The idea of ♘f3 is to play a quick d4, when White's lead in development compensates for Black's advantage of having an extra central pawn. The move 2 c3, however, aims to play d4 in a position where White can recapture on d4 with a pawn, thereby gaining control of the centre without making any concession. Of course, life is never so easy and Black has various ways to counter White's plan. This is a fairly popular method of meeting the Sicilian, perhaps because it can be played with less theoretical knowledge than 2 ♘f3.

2   ...   ♘f6

This is one of two main systems Black can employ against 2 c3. The other is 2...d5 3 exd5 ♕xd5, which only apparently exposes the black queen to attack; actually it is not easy for White to gain time on the queen because the move c3 has taken away the natural square from his queen's knight.

The text-move is based on a different idea. Black wants to lure White's e-pawn forward to e5, so as to be able to attack it by ...d6, thereby

removing White's main outpost in the centre. Both systems are popular and both are believed to give Black a more or less equal game if followed up accurately. It is worth mentioning that 2...e5, 2...d6 and 2...e6 are all perfectly playable systems, but have never achieved the same popularity as 2...d5 and 2...♘f6.

3   e5

The only dangerous move.

3   ...   ♘d5

Rather as in the Alekhine Defence (see Game 4), Black's knight hops around, luring White's pawns forward.

4   d4

White has achieved his ambition of playing d4, but his central pawns are no longer line abreast and Black can easily strike at the protruding e-pawn with ...d6.

4   ...   cxd4

Black should exchange immediately, or else White might play c4 followed by d5, or possibly dxc5.

5   ♘f3

This is the main continuation. White makes use of the pin along the d-file to keep Black in the dark about how he is going to recapture on d4. 5 cxd4 d6 makes life fairly easy for Black, while 5 ♕xd4 e6 is also relatively harmless – White has gained time by attacking the black knight, but this is balanced by the fact that he has made no use of the move c3.

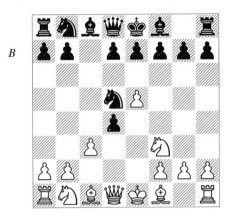

5 ... ♘c6

Black continues with a flexible developing move. It is also perfectly reasonable to play 5...e6 6 cxd4 (now that d5 is defended, White has to recapture on d4) 6...d6 (6...b6 is another popular line), undermining the e5-pawn.

6 ♗c4

The sharpest line, in which White offers a pawn, although it is not often taken. The alternative, 6 cxd4 d6 7 ♗c4 ♘b6 8 ♗b5 dxe5 9 ♘xe5 ♗d7, offers White little since it leads to piece exchanges which only serve to remove much of the tension from the position.

6 ... ♘b6

Just as on the previous move, Black can play safe with 6...e6 7 cxd4 d6, which is less challenging but probably also equal.

7 ♗b3

The bishop stays on the diagonal leading to the sensitive square f7.

7 ... g6!?

The usual line is 7...d6 8 exd6 ♕xd6, when White continues with 9 ♘a3 or 9 0-0, again offering a pawn in return for a lead in development. The resulting variations are very sharp and the text continuation, although rather unusual, offers an interesting alternative to 7...d6. The idea is still to challenge White's central pawn by ...d6, but only after Black has made some progress towards castling.

Very few players have dared to accept the pawn sacrifice by 7...dxc3 8 ♘xc3. White has a substantial lead in development for the pawn, even though there is certainly no immediate

knockout. After 8...g6 (8...e6 9 ♘e4 ♗b4+ 10 ♗d2 0-0 11 ♗xb4 ♘xb4 12 ♘d6 makes Black's development very difficult) 9 0-0 ♗g7 10 ♕e2 0-0 11 ♖d1 White has strong pressure. Black can hardly free himself without returning the pawn, but then White's more active pieces tend to give him the advantage.

8 ♘g5

A critical moment for White. He must decide whether to continue positionally by 8 cxd4, or to go for the disruptive text-move, which strikes at the traditional weak spot, f7. After 8 cxd4 ♗g7 9 0-0 0-0 10 ♘c3 d6 the position is roughly level. Black is already exerting strong pressure against e5, which he can step up by ...♗g4. If White cannot maintain his e5-pawn, then he is unlikely to gain any worthwhile advantage. The text-move is very committal. If it does not lead to any concrete concession by Black, then sooner or later the knight will have to retreat from g5, with considerable loss of time. White is therefore obliged to keep up his disruptive tactics, so that the knight move does not go to waste.

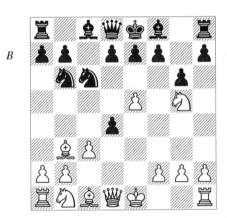

8 ... d5

8...e6 9 ♘e4, threatening both ♘f6+ and ♗g5, is very awkward for Black, while 8...♘xe5 9 ♗f4! (9 ♕xd4 d5 10 ♕xe5 f6 11 ♕e2 fxg5 12 ♗xg5 also favours White) 9...♘ec4 10 ♗xc4 ♘xc4 11 ♕xd4 f6 12 ♕xc4 fxg5 13 ♗e5 is excellent for White, so the text-move is forced.

9 exd6

White is committed to this since 9 cxd4 f6 10 ♘f3 just loses time with the knight – after 10...♗g7 Black is at least equal.

9 ... e6

Black's plan is quite simple. He aims to continue his development by ...♗g7, ...0-0 and ...♛xd6. White will probably have to retreat his knight from g5 at some stage, when he will have little to show for his early attack on f7.

10   ♛f3

10 ♘e4 ♗g7 looks fine for Black, since White cannot maintain his pawn on d6 for ever. Black also has no problems after 10 cxd4 ♛xd6, as White must attend to the threat against his d4-pawn.

10   ...   f5!?

This is a provocative and somewhat risky move. Black definitely prevents White's attack on f7, but at the cost of jettisoning the e6-pawn, which is a key defender of his king position. Moreover, in the main line Black is virtually committed to sacrificing a pawn. The only reason this move is not suicidal is that White's development is not good enough to support a really dangerous attack. He has not yet castled, and his queenside pieces are all at home, so Black has time to defend his king before White can create any serious threats. The alternatives are:

1) 10...♘e5 11 ♛g3 ♗g7 12 0-0 0-0 is unclear. Black has countered the attack on f7, but at the cost of losing time with his knight, which will soon have to move again.

2) 10...f6!? and now:

2a) 11 ♗xe6 ♗xd6 12 ♗f7+ (12 ♘f7 ♛e7 13 ♘xd6+ ♛xd6 14 ♗xc8 ♛e7+ is fine for Black) 12...♔d7 13 ♛g4+ ♔c7 14 ♘e6+ ♗xe6 15 ♛xe6 ♛f8 is a good example of how an early attack with insufficient support can backfire. White is faced with the threat of ...♘d8 and after 16 ♘a3 (16 ♛b3 ♘e5 17 ♗d5 ♘d3+ 18 ♔d2 ♘c5 wins for Black) 16...a6 17 ♘c4 ♖e8! Black wins two pieces for a rook.

2b) 11 ♘xe6 ♗xe6 12 ♗xe6 ♗xd6 13 ♛h3 (13 0-0 ♗xh2+ 14 ♔xh2 ♛d6+ is at least equal for Black) 13...f5 14 0-0 ♛f6 15 ♖e1 is slightly better for White.

11   ♗xe6

The critical move. 11 ♘xe6 ♗xe6 12 ♗xe6 ♗xd6 is satisfactory for Black, since 13...♛e7 is a threat, and after 13 0-0 ♗xh2+ 14 ♔xh2 ♛d6+ 15 ♗f4 ♛xe6 16 ♘d2 0-0 White does not have enough compensation for the pawn. Another idea is 11 0-0 ♗xd6 12 ♘xe6 ♗xe6 13 ♛e2, trying to take on e6 with the queen (which

would indeed be very dangerous). However, after 13...♗xh2+! 14 ♔xh2 ♛d6+ 15 ♔g1 ♔f7 White again doesn't have enough for the pawn.

11   ...   ♗xe6

11...♗xd6 isn't possible here, as White can simply play 12 0-0 with a dangerous attack (the knight on g5 is not hanging as it was in the analogous line after 10...f6).

12   ♘xe6   ♛xd6
13   ♘xd4

This is the natural choice. After 13 ♘xf8 ♖xf8 14 0-0 0-0-0 Black stands rather well. All his pieces are in play, while White's queenside is still at home.

13   ...   ♘xd4
14   cxd4

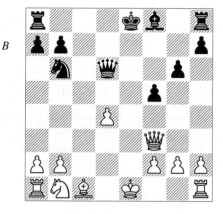

A critical position for the assessment of the line with 7...g6 has arisen. White's early attack has burned itself out, and indeed Black can even claim a slight lead in development – he has two pieces in play against one for White, and it is his turn to move. Moreover, the d4-pawn is weak. Against this, White has an extra pawn and the attack on b7 compensates for the fact that d4 is hanging. On balance, I suspect that Black's advantages do not quite compensate for the extra pawn. Even if Black can sometimes regain the pawn on d4, the time it takes can allow White to seize the initiative. If Black refuses to take the pawn to concentrate instead on rapid development, then he may forfeit permanently the chance to regain the pawn. One plus-point for Black is that even if White manages to hang on to his d-pawn, the win may prove elusive. Winning a position in which all White's pieces are tied to defending the d4-pawn will not be easy. It follows that Black will be happy to reach a draw from the diagram position, since most of the danger lies on his side.

14   ...   ♕d5

Black cannot afford to give up the b7-pawn, since the exchange of this healthy pawn for White's weak d4-pawn would undoubtedly favour White. 14...♗g7 15 0-0 0-0 16 ♕xb7, for example, is very good for White. Regaining the pawn by 14...♕xd4 is too risky; after 15 0-0 (not 15 ♕xb7? ♗b4+ 16 ♗d2 0-0, when White's king is fatally trapped in the centre) 15...0-0-0 (hanging on to the b7-pawn, but Black's king is too exposed on c8) 16 ♗g5 ♖d7 17 ♘c3 (suddenly White is ahead in development) 17...♔b8 18 ♖fd1 ♕g7 19 ♗f4+ ♔a8 20 ♘b5 White has a decisive attack.

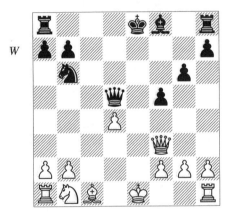

15   ♕xd5?

This move shows a misunderstanding of the position and gives up any chance to gain the advantage. In an ending, Black's pieces can quickly take up ideal positions: knight on d5, bishop on g7 attacking d4, and rooks on c8 and e8. It turns out that White cannot play ♘c3 to challenge the d5-knight, so Black's blockade is virtually unbreakable. If White wants to gain the advantage, he must try keeping the queens on. This has two advantages: he has to chance to disturb Black's king, and he might gain a tempo with ♘c3 later. The two main alternatives are:

1) 15 ♕e2+ ♔f7 16 0-0 (not 16 ♘c3? ♕xg2) 16...♖e8 17 ♕d3 ♕c4!? (the best move; after 17...♗g7 18 ♗e3 ♕c4 19 ♕a3 White is attacking a7, and will gain time by attacking Black's queen) 18 ♕f3 ♕d5 (18...♕xd4 19 ♕xb7+ ♖e7

20 ♕f3 ♕d5 21 ♕h3 doesn't give Black enough for the pawn) 19 ♕xd5+ (now this is much more dangerous, as White can at once challenge the d5-knight; if the white queen moves away to another square, such as g3 or h3, then Black plays ...♗g7 and quickly regains the d4-pawn) 19...♘xd5 20 ♘c3 and now:

1a) 20...♘b4 21 ♖b1 ♗g7 22 a3 looks good for White.

1b) 20...♖d8 21 ♗g5 ♖d7 22 ♖fe1 h6 23 ♗e3 ♗g7 24 ♘xd5 ♖xd5 25 ♖ac1 ♖hd8 26 ♖c7+ ♖8d7 27 ♖xd7+ ♖xd7 28 ♔f1 h5 29 ♔e2 offers White some winning chances.

1c) 20...♘xc3 21 bxc3 ♗d6 (21...♖c8 22 ♖b1 b6 23 ♗d2 ♖c4 is another reasonable line that offers good drawing chances) looks like Black's best line. It is hard for White to win when he is handicapped by the backward c-pawn. The continuation might be 22 ♖b1 b6 23 ♖b2 ♖c8 24 ♗d2 ♖he8, when Black has fair compensation for the pawn. It is hard to see how White can activate his pieces, but Black has the possibility of moving his king to a more active position by playing ...♔e6-d5. The conclusion is that with accurate play Black has good drawing chances against 15 ♕e2+.

2) 15 ♕e3+ ♔f7 16 0-0 ♖e8 17 ♘c3 (this is the tactical point behind White's choice of e3 for the queen; 17 ♕d3 transposes to line '1') 17...♖xe3 18 ♘xd5 ♖d3 19 ♘xb6 axb6 20 ♗f4 ♗g7 and once again Black's pressure on the d-pawn and generally more active pieces offer reasonable compensation for the pawn. Nevertheless, Black is playing only for the draw and accurate play is required to achieve this aim: 21 ♖ac1 (21 ♗e5 ♗xe5 22 dxe5 f4 cuts off any pawn support for the e5-pawn; Black draws easily by ...♔e6 and ...♖hd8) 21...♖e8 22 ♖c7+ ♖e7 23 ♖xe7+ ♔xe7 24 ♖e1+ ♔d7 25 ♗e5 ♗xe5 26 dxe5 reaches a critical position. Can White make his extra pawn count? Black can try:

2a) 26...♖d2 is probably enough for a draw; for example, 27 g3 ♖xb2 28 ♖d1+ ♔e8 29 ♖d6 b5 30 ♖b6 ♖xa2 31 ♖xb7 ♖a5 32 ♖xh7 b4 33 ♖b7 ♖xe5 34 ♖xb4 ♔f7 and Black is saved as the ending with ♖+3♙ vs ♖+2♙ and all the pawns on the same side is a draw. It is particularly easy when, as here, the defending side has f+g pawns rather than g+h pawns.

2b) 26...f4! (probably even safer) 27 ♔f1 ♖d2 28 ♖e4 ♖xb2 29 ♖xf4 ♔e6 30 a3 ♖b1+ 31

&e2 &b2+ 32 &e1 &b1+ 33 &d2 &a1 34 &f6+
&xe5 35 &xb6 &a2+ 36 &e1 &a1+ 37 &e2
&a2+ and Black draws, as White cannot hope
for an advantage if he allows his a3-pawn to fall
with check. The conclusion is that in this line
too Black can, with accurate defence, keep the
position within the bounds of a draw.

| | 15 | ... | &xd5 |
| | 16 | 0-0 | |

Now 16 &c3 causes Black no problems at all
in view of 16...&b4 17 0-0 &c2 18 &b1 &xd4
19 &e1+ &f7 20 &f4 &g7 with total equality.

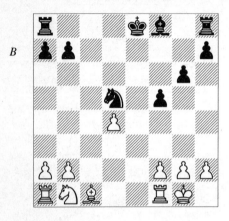

B

| | 16 | ... | &c8! |

This is the key move. Black prevents &c3 (as
here this would involve immediately returning
the pawn) and seizes control of an open file.
Now White faces the unwelcome prospect of a
black rook arriving on his second rank. The famous 'rook on the seventh' is an important factor in a wide range of endgames with rooks.
Even in the endgame, there are still likely to be
several pawns on the second rank. When an enemy rook arrives there, these pawns will come
under fire. Even if one pawn advances to escape
the attack, the problems are not over. The pawn
move may expose another pawn to attack, or the
rook may switch behind the pawn that has just
moved. Even if the rook on the seventh doesn't
win a pawn straight away, it will tie down enemy pieces to the defence of the vulnerable
pawns. Sometimes the rook can be expelled, but
a rook on the seventh that cannot be driven off
represents a significant advantage, and in many
cases is enough to decide the game by itself.

A rook established on the seventh in the
middlegame can be just as strong, but of course

this situation is less likely to arise, since there
are usually minor pieces available to drive the
rook away.

16...&g7 is inferior as White can play 17
&c3! &xc3 (17...&b4 18 &e3 is also slightly
better for White, while 17...&d8 18 &g5 &d7
19 &xd5 &xd5 20 &fe1+ &f8 21 &ac1 &d7 22
b3 &f7 23 d5 gives White a clear advantage) 18
bxc3 with a slight advantage (Black's bishop
would be better on d6, as in the analysis of 15
&e2+).

| | 17 | &d2 |

Now the knight has to be developed in more
cumbersome fashion, leaving Black's steed unchallenged on d5.

| | 17 | ... | &g7 |

Exerting pressure on the d-pawn.

| | 18 | &e1+ | &d7 |

Now that the queens are off, it is actually an
asset for Black's king to be in the centre of the
board. Thanks to the white pawn on d4, there is
no danger of Black's knight or king being ha-
rassed by the white rooks.

| | 19 | &f3 | &he8 |

A good move. The rook on e1 is White's most
active piece. Black aims to exchange it, leaving
White with only passively placed pieces.

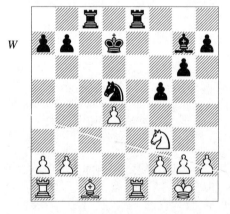

W

| | 20 | &e5+? |

A second misjudgement. Before this move,
the situation was more or less balanced, with
Black's positional advantages compensating for
the extra pawn. However, this move tips the balance in Black's favour. The combination of a
dominant rook on the seventh and White's bad
bishop outweighs White's not very useful extra
pawn. White should have contented himself

with a draw, which he could have achieved by 20 罩xe8! 含xe8 21 含f1 罩c2 22 ②e1 (22 b3 含d7) 22...罩c6 23 ②f3 repeating moves. 20 ②d2 is less clear-cut; after 20...罩xe1+ (20...罩e4 21 罩ad1 is similar) 21 罩xe1 罩c2 22 ②c1 Black need not force a draw by 22...②b4 23 ②g5 (23 a3?? ②d3) 23...②d5 24 ②c1 but can continue 22...a5 and gradually gain space, while White has few constructive moves.

20   ...   ②xe5

White's most active pieces are being exchanged off, leaving him with only the dead rook and bishop on the queenside.

21   dxe5

Relatively the best chance. As we shall see, White's chances are even worse when one pair of rooks is exchanged; for example, after 21 罩xe5 罩xe5 22 dxe5 f4! (locking in the bishop and preventing White from supporting the e5-pawn with f4) 23 b3 (23 g3 f3 24 ②f4 含e6 is also very good for Black) 23...含e6 24 ②a3 罩c2 25 ②d6 ②c3 26 a4 罩b2 White loses a queenside pawn, without solving any of his positional problems.

21   ...   罩c2

Black's rook arrives on the seventh rank, where it will stay until the end of the game. White's development is further delayed by the attack on the b2-pawn.

22   b3

Freeing the bishop. Other moves are also unsatisfactory:

1) 22 g3 含e6 23 b3 罩ec8 24 ②h6 (24 ②a3 ②c3 favours Black) 24...罩8c3 25 罩ec1 罩b2 and it won't be long before one of White's queenside pawns falls.

2) 22 f4 (this secures the e5-pawn, but it blocks in the bishop and opens up a greater range of activity for the c2-rook) 22...含e6 23 b3 罩ec8 24 g3 (otherwise White cannot develop his bishop to a3, but this move further weakens the second rank; 24 ②e3 is strongly met by 24...罩8c3) 24...a5 (intending to seal White's bishop in on the queenside as well) 25 ②a3 b5 26 罩ec1 (26 ②d6 attempts to get the bishop out before the door closes with ...b4, but after 26...②c3 27 a4 b4 28 罩f1 ②e4 29 罩ad1 罩8c3 White will lose one pawn after another) 26...b4 27 ②b2 g5! (a nice breakthrough leading to a decisive attack) 28 fxg5 f4 29 gxf4 ②xf4 30 含h1 ②e2 31 罩xc2 罩xc2 32 罩b1 ②c3

33 ②xc3 bxc3, followed by ...罩d2 and ...c2, and the c-pawn runs through.

22   ...   f4!

Black takes the opportunity to prevent White from developing the bishop along the c1-h6 diagonal. 22...含e6 23 ②h6 罩ec8 24 罩ed1 offers White better defensive chances, since from h6 the bishop controls the useful squares d2 and c1. For example, 24...罩e2 25 罩d4 (25 罩d3 罩c3 26 罩xc3 ②xc3 favours Black) 25...罩cc2 26 罩ad1 offers White considerable counterplay – giving up the knight by 26...罩xf2 27 罩xd5 罩xg2+ 28 含f1 is only a draw.

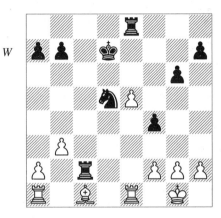

23   罩d1

Or 23 ②a3 含e6 24 含f1 g5 25 罩e2 (25 罩ec1 罩ec8 26 罩xc2 罩xc2 is very good for Black) 25...罩ec8 26 罩ae1 f3! 27 gxf3 ②f4 28 罩xc2 罩xc2 29 ②d6 罩xa2 and although White is still a pawn up, he is almost certainly lost. His poor king position means that his rook cannot leave the first rank, while the b3- and f2-pawns are both very vulnerable. In addition, Black has a useful queenside majority.

23   ...   含e6

Black's advantages are substantial, since in addition to the rook on the seventh, he dominates the open c-file, his king blockades the e5-pawn and his knight is well placed, blocking the d-file. His plan is to exchange one pair of rooks and then win one of the queenside pawns using his remaining rook and knight.

24   ②a3

Now Black cannot move the knight without allowing 罩d6+. In any case, White threatens to double rooks on the d-file and thereby force the knight to move.

24   ...   ♖ec8

White cannot afford to mark time as Black can make progress in various ways. The simplest is to play ...b5, threatening to push White's bishop back to c1. To avoid this White must play ♗d6, but then Black can double rooks on the seventh rank. Moreover, now that the threat of a check on d6 is ruled out, he can move his knight.

25   ♖d3

The following variation illustrates how Black wins if he can exchange a pair of rooks: 25 ♖ac1 (25 ♗d6 ♘c3 26 ♖d3 ♖xa2 doesn't help White) 25...b5 26 ♗b2 b4 27 ♔f1 ♖8c7 (threatening to take the bishop) 28 ♖xc2 ♖xc2 29 ♗d4 ♘c3 (this is stronger than 29...a5 30 ♖a1 ♘c3 31 ♗b6 a4 32 bxa4 ♘xa2 33 ♗d4, when matters are not entirely clear, and 29...♖xa2 30 ♖c1, when White can activate his rook) 30 ♗xc3 (30 ♖a1 ♘b5 31 ♖d1 ♖xa2 32 ♗c5 a5 is hopeless for White since his counterplay is frustrated by the excellent position of the black knight) 30...bxc3 31 ♖d3 ♔xe5 32 f3 and now:

1) 32...♖c1+ (this is too early) 33 ♔e2 (33 ♔f2? c2 34 ♖c3 ♔d4 35 ♖c7 ♔d3 promotes the pawn) 33...♖g1 34 ♖xc3 ♖xg2+ 35 ♔d3 ♖xa2 36 ♖c5+ ♔f6 37 h4 and it is not clear if Black can exploit his extra pawn.

2) 32...g5! (this is much stronger; Black advances his kingside pawns and only then heads for the liquidation with ...♖c1+ and ...♖g1) 33 a4 (there isn't much White can do other than advance on the queenside) 33...h5 34 b4 (after 34 g3 fxg3 35 hxg3 h4 36 gxh4 gxh4 the second passed pawn is decisive) 34...g4 35 b5 ♖c1+ 36 ♔e2 c2 (now this wins) 37 ♔d2 (or 37 ♖c3 ♖g1 38 ♖xc2 ♖xg2+ 39 ♔d3 ♖xc2 40 ♔xc2 g3 and Black wins) 37...♖g1 38 ♔xc2 ♖xg2+ 39 ♔c3 ♖xh2 and Black wins easily with his kingside pawns.

25   ...   ♖e2?!

Black presses ahead with the plan of doubling rooks on the seventh, but he should have spent one tempo taking the sting out of White's counterplay. 25...♖8c6! 26 ♖ad1 ♘c3 was much better, when White faces the unpleasant choice between abandoning his d-file counterplay and checking on d6, allowing an exchange of rooks:

1) 27 ♖e1 ♖xa2 28 ♗d6 ♖b2 29 b4 ♘b5 and Black has taken a pawn without releasing any of the pressure.

2) 27 ♖d6+ ♖xd6 28 ♖xd6+ ♔xe5 29 ♖d8 (29 ♖d7 loses a piece to 29...♖xa2) 29...♖xa2 30 ♗d6+ ♔e6 31 f3 ♖d2 32 ♗c7 (after 32 ♖c8 ♖xd6 33 ♖xc3 ♖c6 34 ♖d3 a5 the outside passed pawn will give Black an easy win in the rook ending) 32...♖xd8 33 ♗xd8 ♘e2+ 34 ♔f2 ♘d4 and White's b-pawn falls.

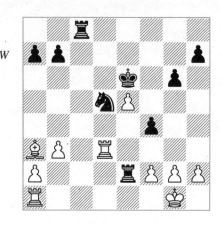

26   ♖ad1

Not 26 ♗d6 ♖xa2 27 ♖ad1 ♘c3 28 ♖e1 a5 with a decisive advantage for Black. White cannot even move the bishop so as to threaten ♖d6+.

26   ...   ♘c3

After 26...♖xe5 27 ♗b2, Black certainly has no advantage, so he is forced to move the knight and allow at least one white rook into his position.

27   ♖a1?

White misses a chance for a draw by 27 ♖d6+ ♔xe5:

1) 28 ♖a1?! ♘b5 29 ♖d7 offers drawing chances, even though Black can still obtain a slight advantage by either 29...♔f6 30 ♗d6 (30 ♗b4?! ♖xa2 31 ♖ad1 ♖c7 is clearly better for Black) 30...♖xa2 31 ♖d1 ♘xd6 32 ♖1xd6+ ♔g5 33 h4+ ♔xh4 34 ♖xh7+ ♔g5 35 ♖d5+ ♔f6 36 ♖d6+ ♔e5 37 ♖xg6 ♖c1+ 38 ♔h2 ♖aa1 or 29...♖cc2 30 ♗b4 (30 ♖e7+ ♔f6 31 ♖xe2 ♖xe2 32 ♗b4 ♖c2 is also slightly better for Black) 30...♖xf2 (30...♖xa2 31 ♖ad1 gives White fair counterplay) 31 ♖e1+ ♔f5 32 ♖d5+ ♔f6 33 ♖xb5 ♖xg2+ 34 ♔h1 ♖xh2+ 35 ♔g1 ♖hg2+ 36 ♔h1 f3 37 ♗d6.

2) 28 ♖d7! (this tactical point enables White to draw) 28...♘xd1 29 ♖e7+ ♔f5 30 ♖xe2 ♖c7 (30...♘c3 31 ♖e7 is equal) 31 f3 ♘e3 32 g4+

♔f6 33 ♔f2 and Black is unlikely to be able to make anything out of his microscopic edge.

      27   **...**   **♘e4?**

Up to here, the game has been extremely instructive as regards play on the open file and seventh rank, but the rest of the game bears all the hallmarks of serious time-trouble. Here Black should have played 27...♘b5! 28 ♗b4 ♖xa2, winning the a2-pawn while at the same time nullifying White's counterplay by covering d6, with a near-decisive advantage.

      28   **f3**   **♘g5**

After 28...♖cc2!? 29 fxe4 ♖xg2+ 30 ♔f1 ♖xh2 31 ♔g1 ♖cg2+ 32 ♔f1 ♔xe5 33 ♖e1 it is doubtful that Black has anything more than a draw.

      29   **♖d6+**   **♔f5**

Forced, as 29...♔xe5 30 ♖ad1 ♘e6 31 ♖6d2 gives White an easy draw.

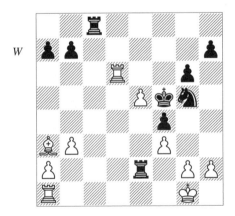

      30   **♖d5?**

White misses an admittedly surprising and unusual drawing possibility. 30 h4! is correct: 30...♘e6 31 ♖d7 ♖cc2 (there is nothing better) 32 ♖ad1 and now the threat of mate in two by 33 ♖f7+ ♔xe5 34 ♗d6# proves surprisingly hard to meet; for example, 32...♖xg2+ 33 ♔h1 ♔xe5 (33...♘c7 34 ♖f7+ ♔e6 35 ♖e7+ ♔f5 36 ♖f7+ is also a draw) 34 ♖1d5+ ♔f6 35 ♖xh7 (setting up a new mating threat by 36 ♗e7#) 35...♘g7 36 ♖d6+ ♔e5 37 ♖xg7 ♖h2+ 38 ♔g1 ♖cg2+ 39 ♔f1 ♖f2+ 40 ♔e1 ♖xa2 41 ♖e7+ ♔f5 42 ♖f7+ with perpetual check.

      30   **...**   **♘e6**

Black had a strong alternative in 30...♖cc2 31 e6+ ♔f6 32 ♗e7+ (the only chance, as 32 e7 ♖xg2+ mates in three more moves) 32...♔xe7

33 ♖xg5 ♔xe6 34 a4 ♖b2 picking up the b3-pawn while retaining considerable pressure against White's position. However, the move played should also be sufficient to win since the new blockade of the e-pawn holds White up long enough for Black to double rooks on the seventh rank.

      31   **♔h1**

31 g4+ fxg3 32 hxg3 ♖cc2 is hopeless, as the doubled rooks will make mincemeat of White's kingside pawns.

      31   **...**   **♖cc2**

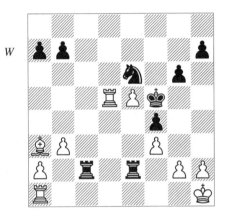

      32   **♖ad1?!**

This allows a simple win, but even after 32 ♖g1 ♖xa2 33 ♗b4 (33 ♗d6 ♘g5, threatening both 34...♘xf3 and 34...♘h3, wins after 34 e6+ ♔xe6 35 ♖xg5 ♔xd6) 33...b6 34 ♖d7 ♘g5 Black's attack is decisive. The finish might be 35 h3 (the best chance, setting a nasty trap) 35...a5! (35...♘xf3? 36 ♖f7+ ♔e6 37 ♖e7+ forces a draw as 37...♔d5 38 ♖d1+ ♔c6 39 gxf3 offers Black no more than perpetual check) 36 ♗f8 ♖ad2! 37 ♖b7 (37 ♖xd2 ♖xd2 gives Black an extra pawn and a good position) 37...♖f2! 38 ♖xb6 (38 e6 ♘xf3 39 e7 ♖xg2 mates) 38...♘xh3 39 ♗c5 ♖fe2 and Black wins material.

      32   **...**   **♖xa2**

There is nothing wrong with taking this pawn, but 32...♖xg2 wins easily: 33 ♖d7 ♖xh2+ 34 ♔g1 ♘g5.

      33   **♗b4**   **h6?**

It is hard to imagine the thinking behind this move. Perhaps Black believed that White was so helpless that he could simply play pass moves until the time-control. In any case, Black still had a simple win by 33...♖xg2 34 ♗d2 ♖f2.

34   h4?

Now was the moment for White to activate his rook by 34 ♖d7 ♖xg2 (34...♔g5 35 ♖e7 is also a draw) 35 h4 when again the mating threat with ♖f7+ secures the draw; e.g., 35...g5 36 ♖f7+ ♔g6 37 ♖f6+ ♔h5 38 ♖xe6 ♖h2+.

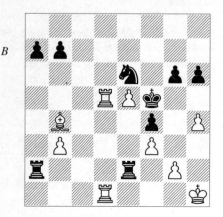

34   ...   g5!

This is a good move, which gives Black's king some air. 34...♖xg2 35 ♖d7 transposes into the draw of the previous note.

35   ♖d7

The best chance, because 35 hxg5 ♖xg2 36 gxh6 ♖h2+ 37 ♔g1 ♖ag2+ 38 ♔f1 ♖g3 gives Black a very strong attack. Neither 39 ♖d7 ♖xf3+ 40 ♔g1 ♖fh3 nor 39 ♖5d3 ♘g5 40 ♗c5 ♖h1+ 41 ♔e2 ♖g2+ 42 ♗f2 ♖hh2 43 ♖f1 ♘h3 44 ♔e1 ♘xf2 45 ♖d2 ♔xe5 46 ♖dxf2 ♖xf2 47 ♖xf2 ♖xf2 48 ♔xf2 ♔f6 offers White any hope of survival.

35   ...   gxh4

Now White cannot force an immediate draw, but he is still able to worry the black king.

36   ♖f7+   ♔g5

Avoiding 36...♔xe5?? 37 ♗d6#.

37   ♗e7+

White has to keep the momentum going, or else Black will win quickly. This applies particularly now that the h4-pawn can join in the attack; for example, 37 ♖e7? ♖xg2 38 ♖xe6 ♖h2+ 39 ♔g1 ♖ag2+ 40 ♔f1 h3 with a quick mate.

37   ...   ♔h5

38   ♖f5+   ♘g5

39   ♖xf4?

White does not make the most of his counterplay. He should have played 39 ♗xg5 hxg5 40 ♖f7 h3, and now:

1) 41 gxh3? allows Black's king to participate in the attack and so loses to 41...♔h4 42 ♖g7 ♖h2+ 43 ♔g1 ♖hg2+ 44 ♔h1 (or 44 ♔f1 ♖af2+ 45 ♔e1 ♖h2 46 e6 ♖a2) 44...♔xh3 45 ♖h7+ ♔g3 46 e6 ♖h2+ 47 ♖xh2 ♖xh2+ 48 ♔g1 ♖e2.

2) 41 ♖h7+ ♔g6 42 ♖xh3 (restoring material equality; Black's active rooks give him the better chances but the game is far from over) 42...♖a6 (the point is that 42...♖xg2 43 ♖d6+ ♔f5 44 ♖hh6 sets up an unavoidable perpetual check, so Black has nothing better than to withdraw his rooks from their active positions in order to surround the e-pawn) 43 g3! (liquidating pawns is the only hope for a draw; 43 ♖d6+ ♖xd6 44 exd6 ♖d2 is winning for Black as he is a pawn up and his pieces are far more actively placed) 43...♖xe5 44 gxf4 gxf4 with a large but not yet decisive advantage for Black.

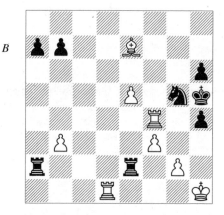

39   ...   h3?

39...♖xg2! 40 ♗xg5 hxg5 is a far simpler winning method; for example, 41 ♖g4 (41 ♖f8 ♖h2+ 42 ♔g1 h3 is also decisive) 41...♖h2+ 42 ♔g1 ♖he2 and Black will be two clear pawns up.

40   ♗xg5

40 gxh3 allows mate by 40...♖h2+ 41 ♔g1 ♘xh3+ 42 ♔f1 ♖h1#.

40   ...   hxg5

41   ♖f7

41 ♖g4 hxg2+ 42 ♔g1 ♔g6 should be a win for Black, e.g. 43 f4 ♔f5 44 ♖xg5+ ♔xf4 45 ♖g7 b6 46 e6 (or else Black takes the e-pawn and is just two pawns up) 46...♖xe6 47 ♖xg2 ♖xg2+ 48 ♔xg2 ♖e3 49 b4 ♖b3 50 ♖a1 ♖xb4 51 ♖xa7 ♖b2+ 52 ♔f1 ♔e3 and Black's king

can come in front of the pawn, leading to an inevitable Lucena position.

41 ♖a4 also fails to save the game: 41...hxg2+ 42 ♔g1 ♖xa4 43 bxa4 ♔h4 44 ♔h2 g1♕+ 45 ♔xg1 ♔g3 46 ♔f1 ♖xe5 47 ♖d7 a5 48 ♖xb7 ♔xf3 49 ♖b3+ ♔f4 wins as White's rook will be hopelessly passive after ...♖e4.

41	...	hxg2+
42	♔h2	

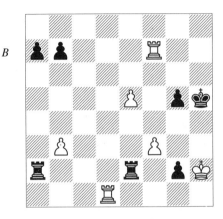

0-1

A strange moment to throw in the towel. Black should be winning, but very accurate play is still required. The best line is 42...b6! (42...g1♕++ 43 ♔xg1 ♔h4 44 f4 and 42...♖xe5 43 ♖h7+ ♔g6 44 ♖xb7 are less clear) and now:

1) 43 ♖f5 ♖ab2 44 ♖g1 (44 f4 ♔g4 45 ♖xg5+ ♔xf4 46 ♖g7 ♖xe5 47 ♖d4+ ♔f5 48 ♖xg2 ♖xb3 and Black wins) 44...a5 45 ♔h3 (White has few moves) 45...♖xb3 46 ♖xg2 ♖xg2 47 ♔xg2 ♖b2+! (certainly not 47...♖b5? 48 f4 ♔g4 49 e6!, while 47...a4 48 ♖f8 is not especially clear) 48 ♔g3 (48 ♔f1 ♖b5 49 f4 ♔g4 50 e6 ♖xf5 and 48 ♔g1 a4 49 e6 a3 50 e7 ♖e2 win for Black) 48...♖e2 49 ♖f6 (49 f4 ♖e3+ 50 ♔f2 ♔g4 51 ♖xg5+ ♔xf4 52 ♖g6 b5 53 e6 ♖e5 is winning for Black) 49...b5 50 ♖a6 a4 51 e6 ♖e5 52 ♖a5 (52 ♖c6 a3) 52...♖xe6 53 ♖xb5 ♖a6 54 ♖b2 (after 54 f4 a3 White has no

time to take the g5-pawn, so he has to retreat his rook to blockade the a-pawn) 54...a3 55 ♖a2 ♖a4 56 ♔f2 ♔g6 57 ♔e2 ♔f5 58 ♔e3 ♖a8 59 ♔e2 ♔f4 60 ♔f2 ♖a7 61 ♔g2 (after 61 ♔e2 ♖e7+ 62 ♔f2 ♖e3 Black wins the f3-pawn) 61...♔e3 62 ♔g3 ♖a4 63 ♔g2 ♔d3 and the king heads for the a-pawn.

2) 43 ♖g1 ♖xe5 44 ♖xg2 ♖xg2+ 45 ♔xg2 a5 (Black will play ...♖b5, forcing White's rook into a passive position) 46 ♖h7+ ♔g6 47 ♖d7 ♖b5 48 ♖d3 ♔f5 and Black's extra pawn and more active pieces should be enough to win. Here is a sample line: 49 ♔g3 (or 49 ♔f2 ♔f4 50 ♖e3 ♖b4 51 ♖d3 b5 52 ♔e2 a4 53 bxa4 bxa4 54 ♔f2 ♖b2+ 55 ♔g1 ♖a2) 49...♖b4 50 ♖e3 b5 51 ♖c3 ♔e5 52 ♖d3 a4 53 bxa4 bxa4 54 ♖d7 a3 55 ♖a7 ♖b3 56 ♖a4 ♔d5 57 ♔g4 ♖c3 58 ♔xg5 ♖xf3 and White's king is just too far away: 59 ♔g4 ♖c3 60 ♔f5 ♔c5 61 ♖a8 ♔b4 62 ♔e4 ♔b3 63 ♖b8+ ♔c2 64 ♔d4 ♖h3 65 ♖a8 ♔b2 and the pawn advances.

Although the latter part of this game was rather messy, the first part is a perfect demonstration of how to establish and exploit the power of a rook on the seventh. Despite White's extra pawn, the rook exerted such a paralysing influence that White was hardly able to offer any real resistance. In the end, the game tipped in Black's favour, but only after a very fluctuating struggle.

The lessons here are:

1) Liquidation to an ending isn't always the best way to exploit a material advantage.

2) A rook permanently established on the seventh rank can easily compensate for an extra pawn.

3) When your opponent is completely tied up, you can afford to take your time nullifying any potential counterplay.

4) Don't resign unless you are really sure the position is hopeless.

Index of Players

When a player's name appears in bold, that player had White; otherwise the first-named player had White. Numbers refer to pages.